PIML

535

GIVE THE ANARCHIST
A CIGARETTE

Now in his early fifties, Mick Farren
currently lives in Los Angeles. With some
twenty books to his credit, plus a number
of film and TV scripts and a wealth of
journalism, his written output remains
prodigious. He also still records and
performs, and a recent tour of Japan with
his band, the Deviants, culminated in the
live CD *Barbarian Princes*. His most recent
novel, *Jim Morrison's Adventures in the Afterlife*,
was published in the US in 2000.

GIVE THE ANARCHIST
A CIGARETTE

MICK FARREN

PIMLICO

Published by Pimlico 2002

4 6 8 10 9 7 5 3

First published in Great Britain by Jonathan Cape 2001
Pimlico edition 2002

Pimlico
Random House, 20 Vauxhall Bridge Road,
London SW1V 2SA

Random House Australia (Pty) Limited
20 Alfred Street, Milsons Point, Sydney,
New South Wales 2061, Australia

Random House New Zealand Limited
18 Poland Road, Glenfield,
Auckland 10, New Zealand

Random House (Pty) Limited
Endulini, 5A Jubilee Road, Parktown 2193, South Africa

The Random House Group Limited Reg. No. 954009
www.randomhouse.co.uk

A CIP catalogue record for this book
is available from the British Library

ISBN 0-7126-6732-6

Papers used by Random House are natural,
recyclable products made from wood grown in sustainable forests;
the manufacturing processes conform to the environmental
regulations of the country of origin

Printed and bound in Great Britain by
Cox & Wyman Ltd, Reading, Berksire

This book is dedicated to Susan Slater for seeing me through the more painful exhumations of recall, with affection, sympathy and Valium.

'Give a man a mask and he'll tell you the truth.' – Oscar Wilde

'A paranoid is someone who knows a little of what's going on.' – William S. Burroughs

Newspeak (1984) 'was designed not to extend but to distinguish the range of thought and this purpose was indirectly assisted by cutting the choice of words to a minimum . . . the expression of unorthodox opinions, except on a very low level, was well-nigh impossible.' – George Orwell

Author's Warning

I freely admit that I have left out many things that I would rather forget. I have also changed the names, or merely used the first names, of some private individuals who have committed no other offence than that they once passed through my perception. Although I have, as far as possible, checked dates and the chronological sequence of events, memory is fallible. It has also been repeatedly proved that, with the best will in the world, no two observers' impressions of the same events are going to be the same. Thus, while striving for maximum accuracy, the story you are about to hear remains highly subjective, and I suffer from a strong impulse to compact events for dramatic effect. You may also detect certain contradictions in my ideas and attitudes as time passes in this narrative. If that creates a problem, I can only refer you to Ralph Waldo Emerson: 'A foolish consistency is the hobgoblin of little minds.'

Back when the world was young
Drunk on cheap well whisky
And confused on mescaline
Walking rattlesnake curves
On sidewalks that refused to lay down
Resisting
Resisting
Resisting all the importunate invasions of reality

Back when the world was young
Searching for the gateway
To the secret garden
The maps to the labyrinth
And the silver key
With a woman in red shoes
Whose name was maybe Dolores
Dolores?
Or perhaps her name was . . . Laverne?

Back when the world was young
And fear was so perfectly academic
And the scales were so perfectly poised
That I could still pace the razor's edge
Without cutting my feet or losing any further toes
And I believed
And I believed
And I believed in every fucking drop of rain that fell

Back when the world was young
And you had but to softly ask
The crushed whisper of velvet
The sheer innocence of pure desire
And the requested favour was granted and gratified
So will somebody give?
So will somebody give?
So will somebody please
Give the anarchist a cigarette?

1996, recorded to music by Jack Lancaster
and Wayne Kramer

Contents

Prologue

Application to Become an Alien

'List all the organisations you have ever joined or of which you have ever been a member. List all publications to which you have ever contributed as a writer . . .'

He looked, I swear to God, like John Dean of Watergate fame, the boyish attorney to Richard Nixon. He was probably younger than I was and I was thirty-five. His grey suit was immaculate, his fingernails were manicured and he was shaved so closely that his cheeks were close to a baby pink. He smelled of aftershave and breath mints. By the standards of 1979, his hair was unusually short, a colourless near-blond and neatly parted. In maybe five years he would be bald. He was some kind of Under Assistant Attaché with Responsibility for Immigration, and his eyes were cold. He clearly felt part of that responsibility was to keep individuals like me from becoming Resident Aliens in the United States. On the wall was a photograph of Jimmy Carter in a light wood frame. In a year or so, it would be replaced by one of Ronald Reagan, although neither of us knew it at the time. That election had yet to come, although Britain had already made its turn to the right. Margaret Thatcher had replaced Jim Callaghan, and I was getting out of town. Unless the John Dean across the desk with the small American flag attached to the pen and pencil set found a way to stop me, I was going to live in New York City, where I would find bars with Hank Williams and Louis Jordan on the jukebox, multiple TV channels that ran all night, and a man could lawfully drink until four o'clock in the morning.

I looked at the questionnaire John Dean had pushed across the desk at me. Long and hugely detailed, it indicated I was in trouble. Most applicants for Resident Alien status and issue of the notorious Green Card do not find themselves subjected to such intense scrutiny. I was marrying a US citizen, and it should have been only marginally harder than obtaining a visa.

'Drugs?'

'No.'

'Communist?'

'No.'

'Anarchist?'

'No.'

'Syphilis?'

'No.'

'TB? Congenital insanity? Criminal record? Burden on society?'

'No, no, no and no.'

The questions asked by US immigration exactly reflect American paranoias regarding foreigners from the Ellis Island days of the 1890s to the present. The problem is that none of the US immigration restrictions are ever dumped. The old ones remain while others are simply layered on top, producing a weird bureaucratic archaeology. Once one has ploughed through this catalogue of a nation's irrational fears, the papers are sent away and are run through the big CIA fruit machine in Frankfurt, and, for the majority of applicants, that's all she wrote. Unfortunately, in my case, the big CIA fruit machine took one look and came up three lemons, and I was asked to report to John Dean. The interview took place at the embassy in Grosvenor Square, in a room very like the one in which John Vernon threatens Clint Eastwood in *Dirty Harry*, and I realised I was in trouble.

To be denied resident status at this point would be somewhere between an embarrassment and a disaster. I had just got married. My good friend Felix Dennis, then into making his first handful of millions, had thrown a lavish wedding reception, complete with inexhaustible champagne and a white Rolls-Royce. My drunken mates were all present, plus a goodly selection of what was laughingly called 'the underground', and figures from the stoned fringe of my immediate rock & roll past. Felix had rented a mansion on Embassy Row, at the western end of Kensington Gardens, for the bash. Next door was the Russian Embassy and, at the bottom of the heavily guarded, maximum-security street, stood Kensington Palace, future home of Charles and Di. At one point in the proceedings a helicopter landed in the grounds of the palace, possibly bringing Charles home for his tea. After an affair like that – not only a wedding, but a tacit farewell party – how was I going to turn round and tell Felix, 'Sorry, but I'm not going after all'? I had said my goodbyes, disposed of my stuff, given up the flat and burned my metaphorical bridges. Now this large boulder had appeared in the final stretch of the road and I had cause for cold sweat.

'All the publications to which . . .'

'. . . you have ever contributed as a writer.'

The cold eyes looked at me as though I were some kind of specimen. They reminded me of the young Roy Cohn, in old black-and-white clips of the McCarthy hearings, lurking and sinister, behind the raving senator from Wisconsin. In the Eighties I would see a lot more of them. That detached shark-gaze would be common in Manhattan, among the yuppies of Wall Street, the ones determined to be multi-millionaires by thirty. I guess my John Dean was the Washington, State Department version, but I had no time to wonder what he ultimately wanted. I was racking my brains as to what incident, action, prank or polemic the CIA, or whomever, had fixed on as a possible reason to deem me too dangerously subversive to set up housekeeping in New York City. God only knew there were enough from which to choose. In the almost sixteen years since my first night in the House of the Chinese Landlord, I had lent momentum to a good deal of mayhem.

On the possible list was disruption of a national TV talk show. I'd taken a lot of the blame, a little unreasonably I thought, for the trashing of one of the world's most ambitious rock festivals. I had also organised a very bizarre rock festival of my own. I had edited the country's largest-circulation underground newspaper for a number of years. I had been dragged into the Old Bailey to defend against major obscenity charges a comic book I'd published. But that couldn't count, could it? Hadn't I been acquitted without a stain on my character? I had founded the British White Panther Party, for reasons greatly different from those most of my critics believed. Earlier, I had been the leader of a notoriously unpleasant rock 'n' roll band, and made a number of albums. I had attended more marches, demonstrations, riots, sit-ins, pranks and pieces of street theatre than I cared to recall, and had associated with dozens of clearly undesirable – and possibly criminal – characters.

As if all that wasn't enough for them to nail me, I had also committed my ideas and dissatisfaction with authoritarian consumer capitalism to print in hundreds of thousands of words that included rants, essays, monographs and, at that point, five novels and one work of non-fiction, all dedicated to the overthrow of Western civilisation. I realised John Dean might have enough to keep me out of the USA for the rest of my days, if he so desired. As the interview continued, I found myself recounting a version of the previous sixteen years of my life and times, in a censored and highly abridged version that was nothing like the book you are about to read.

Chapter One

The House of the Chinese Landlord

Each leg of the iron bedstead stood in a small pan containing about quarter of an inch of liquid paraffin. The pans were about three inches across, perhaps the lids of Cadbury's cocoa tins. In the late winter of 1964 I had only a limited experience of West London flophouses, but I was certain these things were related to a major insect infestation. By the age of twenty I wasn't totally unaware of the lower orders of life. As a student, I'd had my share of hard-time wretchedness, particularly each term, when a government grant that was intended to last for three months was spent in three weeks on beer and Beatle boots. I'd seen cultures of alien bacteria growing in sinks of unwashed dishes that would have been the envy of germ-warfare scientists, and dirty laundry ignored so long that it threatened to glow in the dark, but that was student sleaze and came with the underlying reassurance that one day we would come to man's estate, and give up the pose of the unwashed. Except that here I was, walking into a rented room in the House of the Chinaman, not only still unwashed, but apparently hitting bottom. I was no longer a student, and this might be as close to man's estate as I was going to get. This was not a drill, but the real thing. I was unemployed and maybe unemployable. The bed in my new home seemingly had to be protected from marauding bugs, and the only reason I was able to rent even this place, low as it was on the food chain of accommodation, was that I had made a relatively modest amount of money selling clockwork jumping dogs on Oxford Street and Regent Street in the weeks prior to Christmas. Now that Christmas had jingled its bells and gone, Oxford and Regent Streets were a hard place to sell anything. Perhaps even your body.

Aside from the smell of paraffin, a presence existed in the room.

Not quite a stench, more of an emanation, old and malevolent, deep-seated and ingrained in the very walls. Had it been more aggressive, H.P. Lovecraft might have given it an unpronounceable name, but this entity was content merely to hang in its own unventilated air, because it knew it already had me low-down and terrified. Individually, no one of its parts was all that threatening. Jeyes Fluid, cooked cabbage and elderly grease, ten-year-old Woodbines, rising damp, mildew and bug powder were all fairly innocuous when taken singly. This cocktail of misery was, however, rendered more daunting when coupled with the legend of the Chinese landlord, who lived in hermit-like isolation in the ground-floor front, sharing his room, in an almost Norman Bates intimacy, with the body of his dead father, while he sought to raise the money to ship it back to China and some ancestral place of burial. It was more than enough to convince me that I had finally sunk to my true level in the world, a bottom feeder returning to the primal slime.

In retrospect, I seriously doubt there was a word of truth in the story about the landlord and his late lamented father. That dreary twilight house of strange smells and forty-watt lightbulbs had lots of rooms and every one of them was occupied. The landlord must have been raking in the cash, and how much could it cost to ship the body of a wizened and possibly mummified old man, even all the way to China? I now suspect the tall tale had its roots in both innate racism and the need of the building's other denizens for some threadbare romance. A year or so earlier Bob Dylan had played a bit-part in a BBC TV play, *Madhouse on Castle Street*, about a house not altogether dissimilar to the one I was in. The video version, however, had been chock-full of quirky, eccentric characters, and Bob himself sat on the stairs singing and strumming his guitar. No such frolics in the House of the Chinaman. Even if the father's body was a figment, the place still had the atmosphere of a mausoleum.

The other tenants were solitary, male and Irish to a man. Labourers who had taken the Dublin ferry in search of a better hourly rate working on the post-war reconstruction of Greater London. The men in the Chinaman's house weren't the wild boys who drank and sang and fought in the local pubs on a Friday and Saturday night. These were lonely sub-social individuals, far from family and friends, focused on little but the wage packet, sending it home or saving for something better, or maybe just plain lost.

One corner of a strip of wallpaper, an equilateral triangle some eighteen inches on each side, was held up by a drawing pin. Whatever paste had originally kept it in place had long since decomposed and turned to dust. The wallpaper might once have been an institutional shade of dull pink, but now, like everything else in my room that didn't actually have a thin coat of grease or grime, it had faded to an approximation of the colour of dust. In mitigation the room was relatively large, with a high ceiling still showing the paint-eroded ruins of a plaster rose. It had probably been the rear area of the drawing room, when originally a middle-class, Victorian, one-family home. It was also almost devoid of furniture. A straight-backed chair, a small table, a wardrobe that I would destroy directly I consolidated my position as the one aberrant tenant. If nothing else, I had space to pace and bemoan my lot.

My new home may have been inversely gothic in its drab squalor, but drab and squalid were pretty much the way of West London in those distant days. Outside was the Colin MacInnes world of uneasy coexistence between the white working class and newly arrived West Indians; a lot less colourful than those who never saw it would have us believe. The lights may have been on Piccadilly and the West End undergoing its Swinging London facelift, but, just a few tube stations out, the city was the monochrome of an Ealing comedy, brown on grey, highlighted in sepia, with maybe the odd yellow-painted front door, and of course convoys of red double-decker buses, but mainly dented dustbins and black, upright taxis. Even the garbage was dull, the oily black and white of newspaper-wrapped fish and chips. The garish styrofoam professionalism of American fast food had yet to arrive, and all that remained was the hardly exotic frontage of the odd Wimpy Bar or Golden Egg. About the only real indication that the times might actually be a'changing was the new look in Sunday-supplement advertising: billboards of David Bailey Beefeaters urging one to Drinka Pinta Milka Day, and photo-noir reminders by a guy who looked like Frank Sinatra that you were never alone with a Strand.

Sunday-supplement advertising, or, at least, Sunday-supplement graphic design, had been my masterplan maybe eighteen months earlier. At least it was the aim I dutifully recited when asked. Yes, I was going to rise to the affluent paradise of pink shirts, black knitted ties, suits from the younger, more dashing end of Savile Row, a black Volvo sports and a James Bond apartment. David Ogilvy, Hugh Hefner and Ian Fleming had all contributed to a deception, an illusion and eventually a lie that I'd maintained throughout my four years of art school. Except that, with each succeeding year, it had become harder and harder to remain convinced. A part of that fantasy had been chipped away in Dealey Plaza when they'd caught Jack Kennedy in triangulated sniper fire. (And please don't irritate me with any lone gunman crap. We know by now pretty much what went down, don't we? All that's lacking are a few of the lesser details and the necessary public admission.) JFK had been the apex of that specific daydream. The handsome young president, with the beautiful wife and the beautiful children, *our* president, who had faced Nikita Khrushchev across the unthinkable abyss and then stepped back from the brink of nuclear holocaust at the eleventh hour, just when us kids were close to accepting we all had only a day or so to live before being flash-fried to a thermonuclear crisp. The old men had ordered him cut down in his prime and, ever after, faith in the yellow brick road to material success had been much less easy.

Despite this, for a long time I continued to pay lip service to a conventional ambition. Even when I grew my hair, cleaved to the bohemian and began to dress in a manner that one life-drawing instructor referred to as 'a sociopathic Fidel Castro', I still fostered the illusion that the corporate straight and narrow was my goal. It kept the grown-ups quiet. A phase, they told themselves, and I let them believe it. The truth was that I'd only ever had two true ambitions in life. One was to be the first man on the moon, but that died around the time that *Sputnik* went into bleeping orbit around the Earth, and I realised that I was born too late. Immediately after that I switched my desires to Elvis Presley. Many years later, in New York City, a psychiatrist would ask me, 'So you wanted to have sex with Elvis Presley?'

A disillusionment with psychiatry was already setting in, but this was idiocy. 'No (you damned fool), I wanted to *be* Elvis Presley.'

That ambition would be maintained until 1977, when the big, bloated Elvis croaked on the Graceland toilet, irrefutably proving that not even Elvis could be Elvis. Does a pattern start to emerge? A tangible need to make a mark, to be adored? To beat death and become immortal? Hardly a target orientation congruent with a career in advertising, where all is sublimated to the product. I didn't realise until years later, but *I* was the only product I wanted to promote.

In the House of the Chinese Landlord I moved to the window. The landlord had long ago decided curtains were too good for tenants, and my isolation was protected from the eyes of overlooking buildings only by a sheet of greaseproof paper, turned with age to the colour and consistency of parchment. Clearly the landlord considered we had no need to see out. I scraped the paper experimentally with the nail of my right index finger. It flaked like the wrapping of a pharaoh's cadaver, so I picked a hole about the size of a postcard and peered out into a dank, semi-drizzle of a London winter evening. Lighted windows, vertical rectangles, the yellow of electric bulbs and the electric blue-grey of black-and-white TV sets; outside was not only Colin MacInnes' Ladbroke Grove, but also, in a wider sense, and to paraphrase Bono, outside was England. In 1963/4 we were about a year and some months into the fall of the thirteen-year Conservative government, courtesy of John Profumo, Stephen Ward, Mandy Rice-Davies and Christine Keeler. The venerable and aloof Harold Macmillan, of the Fifties economic, you've-never-had-it-so-good boom, had resigned, and the stage was set for the ascension to Prime Minister of Harold Wilson in his Gannex raincoat.

The Profumo scandal had also blown the lid off a particular stratum of London prostitutes operating exactly in this neighbourhood. The *News of the World* enjoyed a lip-licking field day with night-shadow women like Ronna Ricardo, and black hustlers like Lucky Gordon. Notting Hill was portrayed as a sink of commercial perversion. With singular irony, the self-same Conservative government had commissioned the Wolfenden Report on national sexual morality. While recommending the legalisation of homosexual acts between consenting adults, the report had also created the Street Offences Act, which effectively drove the whores from the pavements of Soho and Bayswater and into damp Victorian basements, gas-fire emporia of equally Victorian accessorised sex, where naked accountants and insurance salesmen knelt before corsets and boots, canes and riding crops. Instead of soliciting passing males, the hookers of London remained out of sight, if not out of mind, advertising their services on discreetly euphemistic postcards in the windows of local newsagents. 'French Lessons', 'Large Chest for Sale', 'Stocks and Bonds', 'Remedial Discipline by Stern Governess' – the oblique side of obvious, with a local phone number.

Only a complete inability to come up with a substitute for the old morality allowed an exhausted hypocrisy to maintain its grip. How could a young man like myself aspire to any status quo when the status quo was fragmenting into disfunctionality? Paradox abounded. An elderly gent wrote to *Penthouse* bemoaning that, in the wake of Courrèges, Mary Quant and *The Avengers*, young women now boldly walked abroad in a style of costume that he had formerly paid professionals to model for him while he guiltily masturbated. His illicit thrill was no longer thrilling in the free light of day, and his former sex life was shot to shit in the face of now and happening fashion.

The fall of governments and the crash of ethics were producing a myriad of reverberations. Somewhere beyond the window the Beatles existed, as did the Rolling Stones. A band called the High Numbers were thinking of changing their name to the Who. Two albums worth of Bob Dylan had made their way across the Atlantic, and John Coltrane had revolutionised bebop by recording *Giant Steps*. Joe Orton and Tom Stoppard were changing the course of the London theatre, Rudolph Nureyev was making ballet hip, and even the iconography of advertising, my route of least resistance and career choice of last resort, had adopted a wholly different form. The new pop art of Jasper Johns and Andy Warhol used the Campbell's soup can, and Marilyn Monroe, in a context that – to me and my art-school mates – was, at the very least, non-specifically subversive. This was the carnival with which I wanted to run away, but so far I had failed even to find the fairground.

If I claimed that only external events, trends and even fundamental changes caused my disillusionment with the fine rewards of Sixties capitalism, I'd be lying through my teeth. A nightmare childhood and an eleven-plus, grammar-school education, in a day-release penal colony, with a headmaster who knew instinctively that Eddie Cochran's big Gretsch guitar was the instrument of Lucifer, had left me with a lorry-load of baggage that made the straight-and-narrow tricky to navigate. I have resolved, in this book, not to delve into my childhood except where absolutely necessary. In recent years I've seen too many inadequates on *Oprah* looking for excuses and absolution in a lack of nurture, and attempting to blame their psychosis, stupidity or criminal self-obsession on parental deprivation or abuse. I can't comfortably cop a plea. That I had free-fallen out of higher learning, and finished up in this first-floor slum bedsit, was no one's fault but my own. This is not to ignore the fact, however, that I spent a good deal of my life being exceedingly angry.

Suffice to say that I was angry from the get go. Too angry for a life selling Sure deodorant and Smith's crisps. Maybe too angry even to be saved by full sensory deprivation and back-up drugs. Maybe too angry to do anything but strap dynamite all over my body and detonate out of this mortal coil in a crowded theatre or tube-train carriage, taking with me as many of the sons-of-bitches as I could. Alternatively, I could climb to the top of a tall building with a high-powered rifle and start randomly sniping. This anger also came with its own insoluble chicken-and-egg equation. I had been angry for as long as, if not longer than, I could remember. I had no recollection of a time when I wasn't angry. No single event could in any way qualify as the Great Primal Piss-Off. From the age of three to the age of fifteen I had engaged in violent conflict with my wicked stepfather, but I seemed to recall I'd been angry even before that combat commenced. Okay, so delving deeper, the Nazis had blown my father out of the sky over Cologne and had even, according to legend, attempted to drop bombs on Baby Me. I was convinced, however, that neither of these represented the true roots of my rage. I was certain the fury came first, and then went looking for acceptable targets, rather than the more normal process of objects, individuals, ideas and situations arousing my fury. I was constantly looking for trouble and hoping I'd come to the right place.

Perhaps that was why I had wound up in the House of the Chinese Landlord, a setting in which self-destructive rage might fester. Even back then, I was aware that self-destruction could go hand-in-hand with unwarranted self-aggrandisement, the last resort of the previously unnoticed. Here I am! Look at *me*, the *most* wretched of the Earth! Notice me or I'll do something grandiosely violent. Even striving to be last among the worst was just another way of begging for attention. The only factor stopping me becoming a human bomb, a serial killer or curling into a Kafkaesque foetal ball and hoping that I'd wake up a cockroach was that I didn't seem to be alone.

In the new culture that had been gaining momentum since the mid-Fifties, symptoms abounded of a common and similar rage. The blood, gore and hilariously twisted plot lines of EC horror comics came from roots I instantly recognised. Why else had Dr Frederick Wertham and the US Congress driven them out of business? Likewise, in the cinema, James Dean and Marlon Brando glowered with a similar, self-righteously fuck-you attitude. 'What are you rebelling against, Johnny?' 'Whaddaya got?' Jack Kerouac wrote with a familiar frenetic compulsion and, at the other end of the rainbow, *Mad* magazine's 'humour in a jugular vein' tilted at exactly the same windmills at which I longed to lunge a lance.

The mother-lode of rage, though, seemed to have firmly lodged itself in rock & roll. The pre-army Elvis wasn't only handsome, overtly sexual and blessed with the Voice of God, he was also sneeringly mad as hell and unwilling to take it. Through the duration of 'Be Bop A Lula' and a dozen other deceptively innocuous tunes, Gene Vincent positively vibrated with malcontent frustration. Even the Beatles, no matter how moptop lovable the *Daily Mirror* might pretend they were, included the baleful myopic stare of the angry young Lennon.

The only problem was that all of those on my list of supposed kindred spirits not only had skills and access to a medium through which they could channel their anger, but were finding fame and fortune into the bargain. My own attempts at an angry creativity had been notably low-yield. I had yet to try writing like Kerouac, but I had furiously slashed and splashed paint on canvas, but then sensed that to achieve any success in painting one eventually had to play the gallery game, and that seemed scarcely possible in my current mindset. Without the social/commercial skills of a Peter Blake or a David Hockney, who was currently swanning around in a gold lamé jacket proclaiming his genius, the path of painting could lead only to Vincent Van Gogh and penniless death, certifiably insane with only one ear. I had sung with my first garage bands, succeeding in frightening not only any potential audience, but also some of my band mates. The general consensus seemed to be that I 'couldn't fucking sing', but I wouldn't let that deter me. The signs were marginally in my favour. If Bob Dylan could grab the world's attention with his bizarre and grating imitation of Woody Guthrie, surely I could continue to hope?

Thus far, my only really successful channelling of anger had been in a relentless guerrilla warfare against any authority figure that presented itself. Teachers, police constables, bus inspectors, park attendants – all received the bad vibes of this baby Bolshevik and, in this, I came back full circle to the problem of self-destruction. Short of becoming a professional criminal, which I didn't see happening – lacking as I did any flair for the covert and the necessary material motivation – I knew that the automatic challenging of authority was essentially a no-win situation. As Bobby Fuller would point out a couple of years later, when you fought the law, the law inevitably won.

I moved to the bed and gingerly sat down, relieved to find that no phalanx of insects immediately rushed me. I took a Rothmans from a packet of ten and lit one. I'd smoked king-size Rothmans since I was thirteen. As the smoke drifted up into the silent air of the Chinese Landlord's room, I realised that I was making my first mark and maybe my first modification. Like a cat marking its territory, the smell of my fresh cigarette smoke was invading the room. As I dragged on the fag, I realised it was hardly the time to dwell on the wretched pass to which life had brought me. If I didn't find a distraction, the odds were on the room forcing me into a state of severe depression, and that was a victory I couldn't concede so early in the game. I stood up. With no television, no radio and my blue-and-white Philips record player still needing to be picked up from someone else's flat, plus a total disinclination to unpack my stuff or otherwise make myself any more at home, the logical course appeared to be to go down the pub. Maybe the House of the Chinese Landlord would look different with three or four pints inside me.

The Sphere of Alex Stowell

After approximately a week and a half in the House of the Chinese Landlord, I came to the conclusion that a human being could ultimately adjust to just about anything. An optimistic social worker might have said I was accepting the situation for what it was, as a prelude to turning my life around. Needless to say, I didn't see it like that. As far as I was concerned, I was questing into an indefinable unknown, without a road map and maybe without a paddle. It was also possible that the room was starting to adapt to me. The sinister presence had fallen back as I consolidated my beachhead, progressively invading its evil ambience with my own occupational smells, possessions and influence. In the matter of the bugs, I had thrown caution to the winds and courageously removed the tins of paraffin from under the legs of the bed. The presence of these makeshift devices was simply too depressing to live with. Strangely, nothing happened. No Mongol horde of six-legged bloodsuckers descended like wolves on the fold and, indeed, from that moment on the room never played host to any more insects than might tolerably be expected. In an attempt to make home a little more homely, I had obtained for myself a length of dark-blue fabric and fashioned it into a curtain after scraping away all of the dried and deceased greaseproof paper on the window. Magazines, newspapers and books had started to gather. The cover of William Burroughs' *The Naked Lunch* singlehandedly helped to put a new perspective on my abode. Although I was hardly living the life of Burroughs' fictional alter ego William Lee, I could perceive certain points of commonality. Through halfclosed eyes and stretching my imagination, I could convince myself that the room might exist somewhere in the labyrinths of Interzone, which gave me some solid fantasy cover into which I could retreat when the need arose. All my life, I had sought refuge in the sanctum of fantasy when stress or boredom grew too oppressive. At a very early age I had perfected the trick of becoming Dan Dare, Pilot of the Future, or Paladin from the TV show *Have Gun, Will Travel* whenever reality became insupportable, and I made such daydream sanctuary the frequent saviour of my mental health.

After some procrastination I had finally collected my blue-and-white Rexine record player. The delay had mainly been the result of its being in the custody of a woman I now wanted to avoid. Reclamation achieved, though, the room took on a whole new perspective. Buddy Holly and Gene Vincent, Elvis and Miles Davis, the crucial Bob Dylan, Nancy Wilson and Cannonball Adderley came in as the second wave of invasion, and after that the ominous presence didn't have a prayer and was confined to the lathe and plaster of the walls.

The rules in the House of the Chinese Landlord were no music and no women, but I played my records anyway. When I dropped the stylus onto the first disc, I half-expected threats of eviction, but, surprisingly, nothing happened. Now I'd broken the first of the rules, the obvious next mission was to start working on the second, although even with my modest improvements, the room was in no way the eligible bachelor pad as promoted in *Playboy* and *Man about Town*. I could hardly imagine many women relishing the ambience, except maybe those with very bad self-images. Try as I might, the place could still be mistaken for the lair of a serial murderer, more Ed Gein than Ted Bundy. A new variation on Groucho Marx's paradox: where Groucho wouldn't want to join any club that would have him as a member, I wouldn't want to be with any woman who'd be willing to come back to this place. Callow as I was, I had yet to realise that it is a much better idea for the single male to let the woman invite him to her domestic quarters, with possible creature comforts like food, warmth, planned decor and even a television set. I'd yet to find the confidence that women might actually do the inviting.

Rather than repeat the tired cliché that rules are made to be broken, I should explain my theory of exemption, as I applied it to the playing of records in the House of the Chinese Landlord. I figured that if I simply went ahead and put on 'Rave On' by Buddy Holly with enough confidence and panache, as if it were the most natural thing in the world, the landlord would also accept it was the most natural thing in the world and would say nothing about it. I didn't so much break rules as simply decide they didn't apply to me. Sound tenuous? Maybe, but over the years it has worked far more times than the law of averages would logically dictate. As in all things, success was not guaranteed, and I have found myself in serious trouble because some son-of-a-bitch didn't recognise my exemption, or perhaps said son-of-a-bitch actually recognised it all too well. I nevertheless continue to be amazed at how many people will accept my bullshit.

As far as I can figure it, self-exemption from the rules is a product of three factors: accent, attitude and a total willingness to appear less than sane. The accent part I learned at a very tender age. Up to the age of five, my mother had raised me to have a near-perfect Oxbridge accent and generally to behave like a little gentleman. It seemed to amuse the majority of her Martini-drinking women friends, and I was complimented and adored for it. Then, at five, on the playground of the local mixed infants school in which I'd been unenthusiastically enrolled, I discovered to my horror that good manners and enunciation didn't cut it. I had to talk common and act like a surly lout within a fast twenty-four hours; if I didn't assume the protective covering, I was going to have class war – in the form of a six-year-old accredited school bully, Tony Attfield – break out all over my sorry, Bertie Wooster, talking-through-my-nose, la-de-dah arse. Fortunately, I had enough native intelligence not to completely eighty-six the Oxbridge, but to keep it in my back pocket to be pulled out at times of threat or dire emergency.

In my subsequent war with authority, which fundamentally commenced at West Tarring Mixed Infants, threat and dire emergency tended to dog my footsteps, but I quickly discovered (in dealings with low-echelon authority figures like policemen, stage-door security and gamekeepers in rural estates when one is committing criminal trespass) that whipping out the accent and giving them a shot of their master's voice could work miracles. Of course, this technique only really works in England, or its comparatively recent former colonies, where a nuance of accent can pin your socio-economic status for the last three generations. In the United States, you can only pull it off with a particular class of East Coast snob, and some middle-aged women who are still in love with Mick Jagger. In America, the criterion is money, and given my cavalier attitude to money, that aspect of the USA has proved something of a challenge. The only people I see being given the same kinetic exemption are celebrities and beautiful women. Over and over again I have seen beautiful women circumvent regulations and surmount obstacles by a simple, impatient Elizabeth Taylor gesture: 'No, it's *okay*, I'm *supposed* to be here.'

It would be a mistake to assume at this stage of the game that I was living in hermit-like isolation, pondering the intricate vulnerabilities of the class system, but my life had become a trifle strange. For a start, the major constituents of my diet were two foods of which I didn't know the names. During times of low self-esteem life support can tend to err on the minimal side, and my routine hunting and gathering amounted to little more than a quick trip to the Jamaican general store. I had developed a liking for a sweet, circular West Indian bread and a kind of salami-like dried sausage. To this day I have no idea what either of them is called, but it hardly mattered because all I had to do was take them off the shelf, put them on the counter and pay for them. They exactly complemented my stranger-in-a-strange-land state of mind. These two unnamed items were my diet, supplemented by beer, Coca-Cola, milk, plain chocolate digestive biscuits and a cheese roll at the pub.

Eating oddly, perhaps, but I certainly wasn't a hermit. Alex Stowell, his girlfriend Hilary and her eccentric and academically distracted parents lived about two minutes' walk away in Ledbury Road. At least, Hilary lived in Ledbury Road and Alex, although he didn't officially live there, spent most of his time in Hilary's basement, which had been converted into what amounted to a self-contained studio. I had known Alex when I was a student at St Martin's, and we had spent long hours in the canteen discussing and defining the parameters of bullshit. Hilary was still attending the school. Alex did have a home somewhere in the East End, but it was also frequented by his two psychotic brothers, which I surmise was another reason (aside from the obvious one) why Alex – who was a dead-ringer for the drummer Ginger Baker – was always down in the basement, under the radar of the academically distracted.

Alex Stowell was very good at nosing out parties. His other attributes included the ability to fashion art out of whatever was at hand, and a precognition regarding the psychedelic lightshow, but we'll get to those a little later. These were the days when the post-teen party was the social salvation of those without money. A dimly lit flat would become filled with a crowd of one's peers, smoke, talk, bluebeat, Chuck Berry, early Motown, cheap Australian wine and flat Watney's Red Barrel in seven-pint canisters. These makeshift, create-your-own-nightclub bashes were leftovers from art school. I was out of the college loop, but Alex had kept his connections, dropping into the St Martin's canteen for a cheap hot meal when he happened to be in the West End. Alex fancied himself as a West End dude. In the era of Dexter Gordon and the legendary all-nighters, he'd gophered at Ronnie Scott's, the crucial British home of modern jazz, at the same time as the pre-Rolling Stones Andrew Loog Oldham. Unfortunately, Alex (unlike Oldham) never lucked into being the manager of a pre-eminent rock & roll band. His creative time was reserved for stranger schemes.

These weekend parties happened in all parts of the city, and they often concluded with long, communal walks back from the other side of town. London was a highly parental town in those days, obsessive about tucking its inhabitants into bed well before the wee hours. With the tube stations closing between midnight and one, lacking the price of a cab and with night buses so rare an occurrence that they constituted an urban legend, a half-dozen or so of us would commence a leisurely trek of maybe a couple of hours in the general direction of Notting Hill. With a few bottles surplus to, or stolen from, the party, and enough cigarettes to see us to Queensway, we hoped to run into nothing more threatening than the odd copper on the beat, or a team of zipping mods who yelled abuse from their Lambrettas.

'Poxy fucking ravers! Get your fucking hair cut!'

It was something of an insult to be called a raver. Ravers were a species of middle-class moron, vicarious quasi-bohemians who wore bowler hats and baggy black sweaters and danced to bad dixieland jazz with a peculiar skipping motion. If for no other reason than the fact they kept Mr Acker Bilk and his Paramount Jazz Band in business, they were totally beneath our contempt. We, on the other hand, were the real deal. We were the rebel intelligentsia, new Pre-Raphaelites for the second half of the twentieth century. To demonstrate this to ourselves and each other, we'd sing, we'd recite and we'd talk. Oh God, how we'd talk.

We may not have known it, but we were cultivating our subterranean education. On these drunken hikes I first learned about Hangar 18, the Men in Black and the rudiments of UFO paranoia. ('They drive ten-year-old Cadillacs, but the interiors smell of brand new leather.') I debated Jack Ruby's connections with the mob and

Lee Oswald's ties to the CIA and the FBI. ('Hoover had to know all about it. He had to.') I learned how an immortality treatment had been developed, but had been buried deep under the Pentagon and only handed out to the Anonymous Men Who Really Run the Planet. Having read my Burroughs, both William S. and Edgar Rice, I gave as good as I got, lecturing the crew on the Insect Trust, the Global Police State and the Hollow Earth. Freemasonry, Nostradamus, the Great Pyramid and the Knights Templar were all grist to our youthful mill as we passed along the paranoid rumour and cosmic gossip.

Significantly, the one thing that almost certainly preoccupied all of us – the future and what it might bring – was hardly discussed at all. Maybe the global future, but rarely our own personal futures. In this we resembled the punks of a dozen years later, more than these punks ever realised. No fucking future, Sidney, know what I mean? We were militantly living in the moment, part of the youth obsession that Pete Townshend would articulate in 'My Generation'. 'I hope I die before I get old.' And maybe we would. The nuclear stockpile continued to grow, and, on a more personal level, a few of us were already demonstrating an affinity with booze, pills, reefer and cigarettes.

I knew some were pressing on regardless, still clinging to the career concepts of working in the pay of glossy magazines, high-powered ad agencies or TV franchises, but most were as confused as I was, running from the rat race, but with little idea of an alternative, short of blindly manoeuvring ourselves into the spotlight of fame, like the Beatles or the Rolling Stones. Since the gods of fame appeared to operate in such a random manner, Beatlehood (or maybe Beatletude) couldn't be planned for, and all that remained was a frustrated sense of lurking potential, an instinct that something was waiting to reveal itself, some place a flower waited to bloom, or a flag was ready to unfurl, but feeling wrenchingly unhappy at not knowing where.

Another subject no one discussed was that of potential nuclear holocaust – in itself another future scenario. A few years earlier it had been all anyone talked about. After the Cuban Missile Crisis the kids I hung around with had fallen ominously silent. We knew an H-bomb air burst over Central London would vaporise everything as far south as Horsham and well north of Watford. We had looked into the face of the beast and did not want to look there again. My own CND badge had long been left in some drawer as, in the wake of Kubrick's _Dr Strangelove_, I had learned to stop worrying and love the bomb.

Before parting for our separate homes, a regular stopping-off point was the Automat on Westbourne Grove. The Automat was a bizarre piece of low-tech, near-Orwellian science fiction run by a family of Indian brothers, one of the few places that remained open all night and within our all but non-existent price range. In Newspeak, it would have been called Prole Food Dispenser No. 947. To obtain said food you walked up to a fake display wall that was covered in tiny glass and stainless-steel doors, only slightly larger than a letterbox. After depositing the required coins – exact change, please – the designated door would unlock and you could remove the food sitting behind the glass. In theory it was a good, if soulless, idea, but in practice it proved a continuing logistical disaster, London at its most third-world.

At four in the morning the Indian brothers were unwilling to put too much food on display. Trade was slow, and a hot sausage roll or beefburger could quite easily turn, if not actually toxic, then at least highly unappetising, well before a potential buyer might happen by. Thus, when you dropped the coins into the slot – exact change, please – a brother would hurry behind the hidden side of the glass and pass you what you wanted, through the slot, with a spookily disembodied hand. Hot and cold also proved a problem. The little doors were sectioned into hot, frozen and room-temperature, but the thermodynamics of the system were so lamentably designed that the hot got cold, while the frozen melted and oozed. Only the room-temperature remained pretty much as it was.

The shortcomings of the Automat were further compounded by the change machine. Designed to convert bank notes into coin of the realm, it was almost always out of order. This forced the purchase sequence to operate as follows. First you went to a small aperture in the wall behind which lurked the brother on duty. He would give you exact change, please, and then you'd move to the wall of little doors and make your selection. As you dropped the coins into the slot, the man who'd just handed them to you would rush around behind the wall and pass you the aforementioned hot sausage roll or beefburger. Eventually the brothers grasped the Monty Python absurdity in this routine and admitted defeat. With technology vanquished, you simply asked for what you wanted and they gave it to you. After a few months of sad disuse, the wall of little doors was torn out, although the place still called itself the Automat.

One of its main attractions was the hot chocolate. This was a boot-polish-coloured, machine brew made of ersatz cocoa, cheap non-dairy creamer and sand. To those of us who had just been walking for an hour or more, and were coming down from too much Watney's Red Barrel and cheap Australian wine, it had a perverse appeal. It also came in semi-transparent plastic cups and these gave Alex Stowell one of his more spectacular creative ideas. He was going to build a Buckminster Fuller-type sphere out of the plastic Automat cups. In its finished form it would have flashing lights inside it and resemble the set for an episode of *Dr Who*. The first move was to start collecting the cups, and we were all enlisted in the effort. We gladly handed over our own cups, but when Alex started rooting through the garbage, we balked. The Indian brother on duty went one better. He came irately out from behind his aperture. 'Excuse me, you there, what do you think you're bloody doing?'

Alex looked at him calmly. 'I'm collecting cups.'

'You can't just come round here collecting bloody cups.'

'I'm creating a sphere.'

'What do you mean, a bloody sphere?'

'A kinetic art structure.'

The brother had no answer for this. Alex pushed home his point. 'You didn't have any use for them, did you?'

The brother realised that Alex Stowell was not like other men and was obviously demented. 'Just hurry up then, and don't make a bloody mess.'

Alex also subscribed to the theory of exemption, although he played the don't-bother-me-I'm-stone-mad card more frequently and aggressively than I did. A typical example occurred one night when, motoring in South London, he urgently needed to relieve his bladder. We turned into a side-street and pulled up in front of a row of small terraced houses. Alex ducked into one of the minuscule front gardens, but no sooner had he commenced urinating than the front door opened and a male figure in a dressing gown started violently berating him. Alex held his ground even in the face of this primal and territorial wrath. 'Fuck . . . I'm sorry, mate, I wouldn't have pissed here if I'd known it was *your* front garden.' This twisted logic deflated the irate householder's fury. Only half-awake, he entered the surreality and came back with a gem of his own. 'Well, I suppose it's all right if it's an emergency, but don't make a habit of it.'

He waited until the Stowell fly was buttoned – Stowell was very particular about his button-fly Levis – and then went back inside, slamming the door.

Where exemption was concerned, Alex was always on the money, but some of his other theories were a lot less sound. The sphere of plastic cups definitely lacked a fundamental grounding in basic mathematics. He was working on the simple assumption that, since the cups were narrower at the base than at the lip, imaginary extensions of their sides would connect at a single central point, like the radii of a circle. He had concluded that if he merely stapled the cups together, side by side, like facets in an insect's compound eye, they would come together as a perfect sphere. He now made frequent trips to the Automat, each time hauling back a plastic bag of used cups to Hilary's basement, washing them out and then painstakingly adding them to the growing structure. The Indian brothers had now totally accepted the project, and treated Alex like the Holy Fool, secretly pleased to have become patrons of the local arts.

It didn't take long to discover that major flaws existed in the plan. We had all imagined the sphere might be some five feet across, and even that was going to be impossible to get through the door of Hilary's room. As it grew, though, the original estimates had to be revised. The finished thing was going to be double that size. Alex was unperturbed. Absorbed in the construction, he seemingly paid no attention to his creation's subsequent exhibition, lodging or welfare. After some questioning by Hilary, he conceded that he could put it together in three sections and then take it outside for the final assembly. What he'd do then wasn't specified, but he would take it out and that, for Hilary, was progress. Unfortunately, even before the first segment was complete, another and potentially fatal problem became depressingly evident. The sphere was torquing out of shape. As far as Alex could figure it, the rims of the cups were the problem. The thicker curved lip was throwing everything out of whack, and the sphere was evolving a shape like a deformed strawberry. Alex considered disassembling the entire thing, cutting the rims off the cups and starting again. Hilary and I shook our heads. Even if he went to all the time and effort of cutting off the rims, some new obstacle could easily arise. The project was going to have to be abandoned. Alex was depressed for a few days, but then his spirits started to snap back. They might not have revived so swiftly if he'd known that the failure of his sphere, and even the reasons for that failure, would serve as an analogue for many of the adventures that were to take place over the next four or five years.

After a reasonable period of mourning, he went back to a previous and longer-running fixation. He had somewhere acquired a junk-store epidiascope, and he would spend long hours projecting images onto Hilary's wall, distorting, flashing and strobing them in time to albums like Charles Mingus' *Mingus Oh Yeah* and Jimmy Guiffre's *Train and the River*. Although no such term yet existed, Alex was actually attempting to invent the psychedelic lightshow. In this, of course, he was not unique. Later we'd discover that other people in other parts of the city – indeed, in other parts of the planet – were doing the self-same thing. Such thinking-in-common duplication was uncannily prevalent around that time, and was certainly the priming for the hell that broke loose when we all became aware of each other's existence. The kind of multimedia environment for which Alex and all the others were instinctively heading would ideally need psychotropic drugs to complete the equation, but, having smoked marijuana for the previous couple of years, this wasn't a problem. If anything, it merely increased the sense that something was out there, just out of reach; something we couldn't exactly define, but something that absolutely must not be missed.

The Safari Tent, the Rio and Finches

It can only be self-evident why marijuana was and is illegal – back then, right now and continues to remain so. For me, the first puff was enough, and all subsequent and repeated indulgence never failed to recapture that first careless rapture. I inhaled to the deepest, and immediately experienced a drastic revision of my perspectives. As

[23]

Valentine Michael Smith might have put it, before he was eaten by his devoted followers, I groked the fullness of my role in the cosmos and didn't like what I discovered. One of the very first revelations was why those in power wanted to keep this herb well away from the likes of me. The truth, as I saw it, was that they feared the resulting shift in perspective. The habitual dope smoker ruthlessly imposes the rules of fundamental logic on those who seek to control him or her. Marijuana prompts repeated asking of the question 'Why?'

As small children we learn that 'Why?' is the one response guaranteed to drive parents and guardians rapidly apeshit. Why? Because it's the question that ultimately forces the answer 'Because I goddamned well told you so', and reduces all social contracts to the base level of 'Because I'm more powerful than you, and can make you very unhappy if you don't obey me'. Those wielding power really can't stand to make that admission. In the nuclear family, it's the final fallback. In global politics, it's the fall of democracy to tyranny in drag, even if a bovine electorate did hand the sons-of-bitches power in the first place. That's why Vietnam was such a mess. The grunts got high and asked why. Some outsiders contend that dope makes you stupid. A serious misconception. It may cause a certain vagueness and short-term memory loss but, basically, those who get stupid behind reefer are invariably stupid in the first place. It just manifests itself to a greater degree.

Cannabis reduces the user to a more child-like and innocent state, and sooner or later he or she tends to get round to wanting to know why we have to fight the communists, why we need a policy of mutually assured destruction, why the pubs have to close at eleven o'clock, and ten on Sundays. At least, that was how it was in 1965. Today, of course, we have MTV, Mortal Kombat and MAC 10s. Many kids today appear mesmerised. In my youth, however, it was definitely dope that prompted the refusal to accept the reality of the Emperor's new clothes, or, for that matter, his new guided missile, his new economic policy, his new law-enforcement measures or his latest soundbite.

A study of sufferers from aphasia, conducted during the Reagan administration, showed that these individuals, as a result of a kind of brain damage akin to cortical thrombosis, place less reliance on the context of words and glean more information from the visual aspects of the speaker. They also turned out to have a very unique attitude to politicians. A number of young aphasics were placed in front of a TV, shown tapes of broadcasts by Ronald Reagan and asked to record their impressions. The almost complete consensus was that the man on the screen was shifty, manipulative, deceitful, of only moderate intelligence and had a conman's contempt for his audience. To put it crudely, stripped of the massage of a Hollywood-trained voice reading a Washington-crafted script, Reagan came across as a dreary shill. Marijuana would seem to produce a similar effect to aphasia, making it easier to penetrate the tailored doubletalk of persuasion. The brain on pot is less easily washed, so to speak.

I know there are those who will now jump all over me, accusing me of seeking to imply that dope creates a kind of brain damage. Maybe it does, maybe it doesn't, but look before you leap, pilgrim, because you will then be expected to explain to me why, when not a single cannabis-related death has been recorded (except maybe for that of an unfortunate Afghani porter who had forty pounds of gold-seal hashish fall on his head), it is outlawed as a social intoxicant. Similar benevolent claims can hardly be made for the two judicially sanctioned highs of nicotine and alcohol. Anyway, it's my book and I'll be the one to twist the facts to suit my arguments.

About the only drawbacks to marijuana I've ever noticed, aside from going to the fridge and then forgetting whether you wanted beer or a cheese sandwich, are that it makes you a little paranoid and has to be obtained by extra-legal means. Obviously this must beg the question whether the former is merely a result of the latter, and are we talking current environment instead of an intrinsic property of the high? At the time under discussion it was possible to do six months or more in an overcrowded nineteenth-century prison for a single joint. About the only consolation was that everyone and their uncle wasn't smoking the stuff, and law enforcement wasn't as obsessively clued up to stop-and-search as a means of social control. Of course, us proto-hippies had to totally negate this safety in anonymity by growing our hair down to our feet and wearing our most freakish costumes, which was about as intelligent as carrying a sign on our backs that read 'Search Me, I'm Holding'.

The rule in the early Sixties was that white dealers had hash and black dealers had grass. The twain rarely met and, when they did, it wasn't always amicable. Since, drugwise, Ladbroke Grove in the mid-Sixties was solidly entrenched black turf, my first couple of years as a novice hophead were devoted solely to the herb. Even the places where black and white interacted were fairly few and far between and not without a certain tension. Although West Indian hustlers came and went freely and were welcomed in white hipster territory, in the reverse situation the white boy had to move with circumspection. To hang out in any of the Jamaican shebeens – the illegal drinking joints that dotted Lancaster, Golborne and All Saints Roads back then – you pretty much had to have a specific invitation. Common ground existed in the West End r&b clubs, like the Flamingo in Wardour Street, but one had to be out of one's mind to score in the Flamingo. The big Friday Allniter featured in its frenetic, ashtray interior not only Georgie Fame and the Blue Flames and the coolest dancers in town, but a whole rainbow of footpads, cut-purses, plausible thieves, serial rapists and knife-wielding rip-off artists – both gangsters and gangstas, to make a fine crosstime distinction.

One place that did specialise in facilitating cultural mix-and-match was a Caribbean restaurant called the Safari Tent on Westbourne Park Road. The owner was a West Indian with a Harry Belafonte lilt called Johnny Millington, who affected a white tux and lived in a James Bond island fantasy. With an ingratiating charm, he made reasonably sure his customers all got along, and his place scored big as a protected no man's land where Swedish au pairs could meet rude boys and get into trouble, and where the likes of Alex, Hilary and I could eat chicken and bananas and wonder if we might be able to cop a quid deal of grass off one of the sinister characters in pork-pie hats and Ray Charles shades staring impassively as we white youth aspired to cool. Johnny Millington took a definite shine to me, and his food probably saved me from serious malnutrition, living as I was on bread, salami, chocolate and beer. He was also extremely tolerant of 'characters'. He seemed to accept me as some kind of up-and-coming 'character', which I didn't believe back in those formative days, but maybe he knew something I had yet to learn.

Another 'character' of whom Johnny was overtly tolerant was a woman called Bobbie. Somewhere in her mid-twenties, Bobbie was the daughter of a sergeant in the US Air Force stationed at the base at

Ruislip. She had dropped out, allegedly to have an affair with Miles Davis. On good days she was vivacious, flirtatious, dressed to the nines and looked like Diana Ross the day after she got rid of the other Supremes. On a bad night she would be doing a weak imitation of Billie Holiday's corpse. That I would sit and talk to her in either condition resulted in us becoming firm friends, and I valued her greatly.

It was Bobbie who eventually took me to the Rio. The Rio was further west on Westbourne Park Road and considerably more heavy-duty than the Safari Tent. Its vibe was not improved by it being known to a coterie of idiot teenage mods, who only went there to score, and usually committed at least six faux pas per visit, generally fouling the atmosphere. Just to make matters worse, the joint had been the hangout of Lucky Gordon of Profumo scandal fame, and was well known to the West London Drug Squad. Here the Ray Charles shades were hostile rather than impassive, and the Swedish girls had long since enlisted in the Legion of the Lost.

For hash, as opposed to grass, we had to go out of the neighbourhood. Sometimes, when private contacts failed, the required trip was to Goodge Street, in the north-eastern wastes of the West End, which, after gentrification, they called Fitzrovia. Our destination was one of the pubs in the Finches chain. Finches attempted to give all its pubs an individual name, but no one bothered to remember them. Finches was always Finches, differentiated only by the name of the street on which it might stand – Finches on Portobello, Finches in Holborn, Finches on Notting Hill Gate, and so on. Finches in Goodge Street was the pub frequented by lank-haired, transient young men with scrubby beards, bedrolls and names like Gyp, Dosser or Junkie Paul. It was a stop in the metropolis on the rather drab, hitchhike trail of the home-grown English beatnik. (A grey and fatigue-green creature of sullen countenance, more beat as in beaten than in what Allen Ginsberg called beatitude.) Donovan attempted to immortalise the place in the song 'Sunny Goodge Street', although I can't recall a sunny day on Goodge Street until Felix Dennis moved Bunch Books there. Up until then I had only visited after dark or when it was raining. Bert Jansch, the only real contender for the title of 'Britain's Bob Dylan', had also created his first album under the Goodge Street ethos. (That's the one called *Bert Jansch*, with the songs 'Needle of Death' and 'Running from Home' on it.)

Finches in Goodge Street was frankly depressing. Its gloomy, almost cave-like interior smelled of wet wool, unwashed humans and morning-after beer, and many of its patrons – the first youthful heroin addicts I ever encountered – looked to be really hoping to die before they got old, although, of course, being the dreariest of folk fascists, you would never catch them listening to, let alone quoting, the Who.

Akin to the Rio, Finches was also well known to the drug task force out of Tottenham Court Road nick. Unakin to the Rio, where too many heavy manners on the part of the constabulary could spark screams of '*rassclat*' and run the risk of a violent incident, the cops thought they had the Finches' clientele sufficiently cowed that they could safely prowl through, two or three times a night, a squad of both uniformed plods and narcs in trenchcoats, like Jack Hawkins in *Gideon of the Yard*, flashing electric torches and radiating overt intimidation. The only whimper of protest came when some fool with a guitar, with 'this machine kills something or the other' stencilled on the body, started into the Liverpool folk song 'Johnny Todd', which also happened to be the theme tune from the BBC cop show *Z Cars*. Finches' only marginally redeeming feature was that one could usually score a quid deal of tinfoil-wrapped hash, Oxo or dried-up boot polish, depending on the condition of the market and the honesty of the traders.

A secondary consideration was that it was a magnet to runaway young women who had hitched from God knows where seeking bright lights, big city and some kind of English Jack Kerouac. All Junkie Pete had to offer was a night of nodding out in some shed with a broken lock by a railway yard. We Grove boys actually had homes, and even the House of the Chinese Landlord could look good from that perspective. Unfortunately these would-be beatnik maidens were prone to depart suddenly, stealing everything they could get their grubby hands on.

I hope the picture of these formative days doesn't seem overly idyllic, implausibly without practical worry or financial challenge. We were young, and times were relatively good. Rents had yet to go through the roof, but if you think we were worthless parasites living off the legendary post-war welfare state, forget it. Never having a legitimate job, I didn't qualify for the dole, and what was then called National Assistance came with far too many strings and inspections by social workers. The need for money nagged constantly: money to survive, money as mobility and money to turn fantasy into reality. At times we became like the Bash Street Kids in our obsession to get some fucking money. In one desperate period I went so far as to try casual labour at the Caby Hall, the Joe Lyons food factory at Hammersmith. After two days of tying up bundles of flattened cardboard boxes with hairy string and dropping them into a chute – I presume for some kind of recycling, although no one ever saw fit to tell me where the chute went – I decided factory work was definitely an enemy of the human psyche and resolved never to do it again.

This also marked my philosophical divorce from the thinking of the traditional Left. I saw no innate virtue, and certainly no vestige of dignity, in mind-numbing labour. I quickly observed that the majority of industrial jobs were given to humans only because the moves involved were too complicated for an economically viable machine. We had the technology for a leisure society, goddamn it. All we lacked was a system of exchange and distribution. So why destroy ourselves in the satanic mills when the New Jerusalem was so obviously there for the building? Unfortunately the only writings on the subject were archaic utopian fancies like Oscar Wilde's *The Soul of Man under Socialism*. Given the Old Left's condition of homophobia and cultural benightedness, these were not articles to wave around at a meeting of the Socialist Workers' Party as if they were Chairman Mao's *Little Red Book*.

In our bouts with factory work, and the telling of it later, Alex Stowell had me beaten hands down for pure absurdity. Maybe I had bundled boxes, but he had managed to snag this supposedly brilliant gig painting Father Christmas-shaped cakes of soap at a novelty firm called Chiswick Products. Unfortunately, his artistic bent caused him to take the entire afternoon to paint one soap, when the expected piecework target was perhaps fifty or so. To the hilarity of the women who made up the rest of the workforce, he was let go after the first day, and thus his career as an industrial worker actually came to an end twice as fast as mine.

I tended to fare better in the service industries, and experienced a couple of bouts of retail larceny. I also worked for a good part of one summer in the catering department of the London Zoo, during which time I became a reasonably proficient short-order cook. I quite enjoyed this stint of cooking hamburgers in the zoo. It meant constant interface with other humans, and, on my breaks, I could go and watch the different species of animal cope with the madness of permanent incarceration and inflict what payback they could on their captors. The chimpanzees were especially ingenious in the way they exacted their revenge on gawking humanity. Their best trick was masturbating openly in front of the visitors, and laughing as said visitors then freaked out and covered the eyes of their offspring. The chimps had a highly tuned and instinctive grasp of the level of sexual repression in the mid-twentieth century.

At other times I did the typography on a radical Hindu newspaper – bizarre, since I couldn't understand a word of the text or headlines – and I also worked for a theatrical designer gluing huge fake gems onto a set for *King Lear*. (See, Mum, the art-school training didn't go to waste.) For two ill-conceived weeks I actually acted in some Greek director's faux-Godard movie with a script so dire it mercifully never saw the light of day and which, I hope, was long ago destroyed by fire or celluloid decomposition. Periods also went by, though, when I merely drifted. During one of these bouts of shiftless depression I was adopted by an Australian lesbian couple who invited me over for meals and countless drinks, and tended to treat me as a pet, but then the younger and prettier of the two crossed over and had an affair with the editor of the Hindu newspaper, who was married anyway, and I decided it was time to exit that can of worms before the meltdown. If all else failed and the time of the year was right, I would drift back to selling shoddy novelties on the tourist streets of the West End, maintaining as I did my contacts among the street-trading fraternity.

I've always been a believer in the unexpected breakthrough just when progress has started to prove hopeless. As odd jobs and drifting took on an unhealthy routine, and the revelation for which I looked seemed determined not to reveal itself, I was becoming highly despondent. Then, walking along Westbourne Park Road one day, I discovered a record store where no record store had previously been. And not only a record store, but one with a stock close to revolutionary. No records by Cliff Richard or Cilla Black, no Beatles, not even any by Dylan, the Stones, the Yardbirds or the Animals. All this store appeared to carry was the cutting edge in jazz – John Coltrane, Ornette Coleman, Gil Evans, Eric Dolphy, McCoy Tyner – and spoken-word albums by Malcolm X, Melvin Van Peebles and Lenny Bruce. Just to make matters more bizarre, the store was closed, even though it was three o'clock on a Wednesday afternoon, clearly indicating that whoever ran or owned the place had little regard for conventional business hours.

I told Alex about it and we scouted the place three more times before we finally discovered it open for business. On that first visit Alex, who must have been in funds, bought Gil Evans' *Into the Hot*. I merely chatted with the guys behind the counter. Subsequent visits and chats finally revealed that the strange store was the result of a collaboration between two characters called Michael de Freitas and Alexander Trocchi. I had heard about both of these men previously, and how the two of them might have teamed up in this odd business venture presented a mystery that was unfortunately doomed never to be solved. Trocchi was a Glaswegian writer, with something of a reputation as the Scottish outpost of the beat generation. A couple of years earlier I had read his best-known novel *Cain's Book*, and then his earlier work, *Young Adam*. At the time I was somewhat in awe of Alex Trocchi, he being the first fully fledged avant-garde author I had ever met. For added cachet, he was also a fully fledged heroin addict and dope-fiend buddy of William Burroughs. This was nothing, however, compared to the different kind of awe in which I held Michael de Freitas.

By all accounts, de Freitas was a bad man. The local grapevine identified him as an associate of the slum-lord Peter Rachman, who owned some of the most loathsome, overpriced real estate in Ladbroke Grove and administered his holdings with an iron fist in an iron glove. Rachman had featured in the general media backwash of the Profumo scandal as another of the varied lovers of Mandy Rice-Davies. Michael was reputed to have provided the thumb and maybe a couple of the fingers of Rachman's iron glove. The eviction service that he ran for Rachman went about its business armed with night sticks and attack dogs. Over the years Michael would change his name from Michael de Freitas to Michael X, and finally to Michael Abdul Malik. He would make a number of power-plays for leadership of London's black militants, would found the Black House, would be the first individual jailed under the 1966 Race Relations Act and in the end would be hanged for murder in Trinidad. Michael would duck in and out of my life, and in and out of the London counterculture for the next six or seven years, and many of my closest friends (whom I have absolutely no reason to disbelieve) confronted him in situations where he plainly demonstrated that he had an evil streak as wide as Park Lane.

In all fairness, however, I have to say that I never personally encountered Michael as anything but soft-spoken and charming. It's always possible, of course, that he saw some gleam of potential in me and that I was being worked for some supposed advantage I never knew about. Certainly Michael was a master of working individuals to get what he wanted, and this may have been the story behind his partnership with Trocchi in the record store. The other adventures with him will have to be related when the time comes, but in these initial meetings he seemed nothing but respectful and courteous.

Trocchi never spoke about how the partnership with Michael came about, although he did talk about just about everything else. Trocchi was a tall Scotsman who bore a passing resemblance to Laurence Olivier and had made a name for himself in Paris in the early Fifties when he edited the literary magazine *Merlin*. He moved in a circle that included Henry Miller, Samuel Beckett, Robert Creeley, Eugène Ionesco and Pablo Neruda. By the time I met him, talking was, sadly, pretty much all he did. I have massive reservations as regards examining what might have been, but Alex Trocchi could well have been a great and significant writer, had he not resigned himself to heroin use as a substitute for creativity. By then he was already reduced to bolstering his self-respect by pontificating to young neophytes like myself. That was the difference between him and Burroughs. Where Bill was a writer who was addicted to heroin, Trocchi became an addict who, after an initial flash, never truly got round to writing with any power again. The distinction is a crucial, if cruel, one, and needs to be remembered as the characters in this narrative become increasingly drug-soaked and even start defining themselves by their stimulant of choice.

One of the things Trocchi talked most about was a scheme that he called Project Sigma. The dozens of pages of the Sigma proposal, complete with charts and diagrams, represented the design for an entire new social structure that was highly pluralistic, with legalised drugs, infinite tolerance, open education and everyone minding their own business instead of other people's – even the abolition of money and brand-new means of exchange. I fell for it hook, line and sinker when, in the initial manifesto, he likened contemporary society to a 'parasitic organism ultimately suffocating the host it was intended to nurture'. Many of the ideas that Trocchi incorporated into Sigma were identical to the ingredients of the psychedelic philosophical sundae soon to become known as the counterculture.

Trocchi was also a little sensitive about Sigma having been mauled and ridiculed, when he'd first revealed it, by fellow poets and artists like Jeff Nuttall, Spike Hawkins and Michael Horowitz, the ones I tended to think of as the CND Fifties old guard, lovers of jazz and loathers of rock & roll. The British have a tendency to ridicule anyone who actually has a plan. I guess it's a reflex that protects us against the greater political excesses of the French, but it was also why the nineteenth-century revolution didn't happen in England as Karl Marx expected. Maybe I was naive, but I went for it, if for no other reason than that someone – anyone – actually *had* a plan beyond the Victorian economic critiques of Marx and Engels, with a little more fun and prankster flamboyance. Cuba was fun until the hard-scrabble Marxism set in and Che Guevara left town. Sure, Sigma was impossibly romantic, wildly utopian and fundamentally unworkable. Sure, if Trocchi's Invisible Insurrection had been attained and put into practice, we would all have died of either starvation or cholera in the first eighteen months. Okay, so it was the pipedream of an opiate-dependent poet. Back in those days of golden haze, though, it was also exactly what many of us wanted, and within a year or so a great many of us would be playing variations on Trocchi's initial themes and embracing them as our own.

The Artesian Well

What I'd just done on the stage had shocked them, and they hated me for it. They really hated me, and although I pretended otherwise, I didn't like it. I really didn't need to wait around for another twelve years until John Rotten and Joe Strummer came along and validated what I was doing. The one who hated me most was, of course, the landlord himself. While the Irish drunks in the pub called the Artesian Well, on the corner of Talbot and Chepstow Roads, were prepared to tolerate me with six to eight pints of Guinness inside them, the landlord of this drab boozer was instinctively aware that my musical cronies and I were up to something in which he definitely wanted no part.

Of course, what went down at the Artesian Well wasn't my first foray into guerrilla performance. Back in the early days at art school there had been a band that changed its name every Tuesday and Thursday, and which only really played in the protected environs of school events and endless garage rehearsals. I had started out as the bass player, but with only a borrowed bass and no talent for the instrument, I kept lobbying to become the singer and front man. This immediately caused a head-on conflict with the guitarist, who resembled a short-sighted and tubby Brian Jones. His dream was an instrumental band wearing matching grey mohair suits and ruffle shirts, playing Shadows and Ventures tunes, in which he was the front man. I, on the other hand, envisioned an outlaw ensemble drawing on the Eddie Cochran, Buddy Holly and Gene Vincent catalogues, and I'd be clinging to a mike stand in a bike jacket and one black glove. The guitarist had attempted to ace me out, he being a rich kid with a rich mum, by getting said mum to agree to shell out for the matching grey suits the first time we got a proper paying gig. This did actually come to pass, at the Rex Ballroom in Bognor Regis, but only after I was well out of the band. It still amazes me how young men's egos are only too willing to clash and do battle over practically nothing. If we'd only known it, the band was doomed from the outset.

After that, a number of years had passed without my doing anything truly musical, except for a less than outstanding attempt to master the blues/folk acoustic guitar. Although I did manage to get my fingers around some immature twelve bars, a couple of Hank Williams songs and Woody Guthrie's 'Hard Travelling', I was hard pressed to fool myself that this was where my future lay. John Renbourne I wasn't. What I really needed was a couple of like-minded stalwarts who would follow me anywhere, if only out of a sense of morbid curiosity. Pete Munro and Ralph Hodgson could not accurately be described as 'men who would follow me anywhere', but they did share the necessary level of lunacy to go along with whatever half-baked and unformed goal I might be attempting to locate, if only to see what might transpire and maybe laugh heartily at the results.

I had met Ralph and Pete somewhere around the pubs of Ladbroke Grove. Ralph Hodgson was a Geordie from the Alan Price school, who played pretty fair keyboards, and Pete Munro was from Canada, on a post-educational wander around Europe. Along the way he had taken up the full-size stand-up bass, a less than mobile instrument that had rather anchored him in the ghettos of West London. Once we'd decided that we wanted to get together and make some kind of noise, we began by annoying Ralph's neighbours in his bedsit on Chepstow Road. He'd hammer away on an upright piano, I'd strum guitar and sing, and Pete would plunk away on the bull fiddle. To describe exactly what we were doing was not easy. Most of it was Bob Dylan's fault. Dylan was so much on a roll that he should have been topped with lettuce and tomato and covered in Branston Pickle. He had made the great step from 'Be Bop A Lula' to 'The Gates of Eden', achieving fully formed what Eddie Cochran had only hinted at. Before Dylan, the highest form of rock & roll lyric had been Chuck Berry's canon of praise to American consumerism and under-age girls. Bob had changed not only the rules of the game, but also the shape, slope and dimensions of the playing field. He had hosted the great shotgun wedding between legitimate poetry and true rama-lama. He had destroyed all limits, and the world itself was now the rocker's oyster. From love to politics, from philosophy to surrealist nightmare, Dylan had actually made it possible to say just about anything through the medium of rock & roll.

At every turn, he had been there and gone again, like Long Lost John. If I was smoking reefer, he was dropping speed. If I was dropping speed, he was shooting dope. The will-o'-the-wisp was always ahead of me. While I was merely reading *Junkie* and *Naked Lunch, Howl* and *Kaddish*, he was pillaging Burroughs and Ginsberg for style and imagery. John Lennon was in his thrall. The writing partnership of Jagger and Richards was being challenged as to content. Pete Townshend accepted Dylan's verbal distortion, if only within a strict, power popsong context, an exercise in rock & roll discipline that would initially culminate in the stammering rallying cry of 'My Generation'. As Allen Ginsberg noted around the time in question, 'Dylan has sold out to God. It was an artistic challenge to see if great art could be done on a jukebox. And he proved it can.'

The London music business was even casting around for some poor schmuck who could be marketed as Britain's Bob Dylan, just as, in the previous decade, Cliff Richard and Billy Fury had been hyped as the anglo-Elvis. The front runner was the aforementioned Donovan Leitch, a Glaswegian cat with a strangely configured jawbone in whom I had little trust. I had spotted him walking up and down Charing Cross Road, a guitar slung round his neck carrying the gauche message 'This Machine Kills', as though instructed by his manager to absorb added street credibility. Since those days I have wondered now and again what would have happened if I'd been offered the gig they gave to Donovan. Would I have had the courage to turn it down and go my own way? At the time I probably would have answered, 'Yes, of course', with the certitude of one who would never be put to the test. Who would have needed to be Donovan? You only have to watch his brutal humiliation in D. A. Pennebaker's *cinema vérité* documentary *Don't Look Back*. While paying his respects to Dylan during the 1965 tour, he is made to look a total idiot, playing 'To Sing for You' while Dylan radiates contempt like a demonic Mozart confronted by a gauche Salieri. Certainly Donovan paid the price for 'Season of the Witch', the one good song that is his legacy, and I sure as hell would like more of a legacy than that. But, I fear, had I been offered the gig in reality, I would have jumped at it – maybe even killed for it.

Of course, the music that Pete, Ralph and I were playing lacked even the commercial appeal of Donovan. To be blunt, we were raucous and horrible, and even our nearest and dearest saw no future in the acoustic cacophony and hinted that we should jack it in. It would be some months before we happened across an import copy of the Fugs' first album and discovered we were not alone. Across the ocean, in the depths of New York's Lower East Side, a trio of out-of-tune poets, also triggered by Dylan, were one step ahead of us, concocting their own maniac lyrics and setting them to backings as rudimentary as the din that Pete, Ralph and I were making. More importantly they were getting away with it, recording albums (albeit on some of the world's smallest record labels) and even managing to recruit such luminaries as Allen Ginsberg to join in their raucous hoedowns.

On first hearing the Fugs, I experienced another bad case of why the hell didn't I think of that? More like-minded parallel thinking. The real difference between us and the Fugs was that they'd grasped the nettle of writing original songs and we hadn't. We still contented ourselves with a grab-bag of other people's material, although we did cast our net pretty wide in the swamp water of common musical experience, having a shot at everything from the obvious Dylan and Woody Guthrie tunes to vintage blues like Jesse Fuller, Bukka White and the Memphis Jug Band; we even made forays into blackshirt rockabilly with select cuts from Buddy Holly and Jerry Lee Lewis, and even Elvis' 'Baby, I Don't Care'. Except for Ralph, we weren't any too good, but we sure had a full measure of enthusiasm and gall, and actually started discussing how we might take what we were doing out into the world and inflict it on the public at large.

The first target was the Artesian Well, named for the Victorian wells from which London derived much of its water – wells unique in that, as the handy encyclopaedia defines, 'the water rises under hydrostatic pressure above the level of the aquifer in which it has been confined by overlying impervious strata'. In this instance, the famous London clay. Why anyone should name a pub after this device is a mystery, unless it had some whimsical connection with the quenching of thirst. The Artesian's main advantage was that it lay close at hand, less than fifty yards from Ralph and Pete's place, and only about four streets from the House of the Chinese Landlord. Travel is complicated by a stand-up bass. The Artesian also had a music licence and a side-room with a small stage, and that's what interested us. On weekends, entertainment was provided by this old geezer that I began to refer to as Mr Showbusiness, a Grade Z variety performer and obnoxious professional cockney, who played ukulele-banjo, plus a harmonica slung on a rig like Dylan's, although that was where any resemblance ended. Not a million miles from Archie Rice in John Osborne's *The Entertainer*, his deep and enduring hatred of humanity, and his bitterness over all the accolades and showbiz fame and fortune out of which he clearly thought he'd been cheated, was concealed beneath a smutty bonhomie, and a capacity for gin that rivalled any I've ever seen. His musical repertoire ran to fast knees-ups of the 'Any Old Iron', 'Lambeth Walk' variety, and banal music-hall pieces of maudlin slime like 'My Old Dutch' and 'If You Were the Only Girl in the World'. Since the pub's clientele included a high percentage of Irish building labourers, he also threw in sing-alongs like 'I'll Take You Home Again, Kathleen' and 'When Irish Eyes Are Smiling', and less nationally specific ones like 'Goodnight Irene' and 'You Are My Sunshine'.

All in all, the act was hideous in the extreme, but we observed that Mr Showbusiness had a weakness. As the evening drew on and the gin flowed freely, he started to flag. He'd invite up 'amateur talent' (for this, read drunks who are too far gone to know any better), primarily so that he could verbally humiliate them afterwards, using them as a mark for his tired shtick. One of his favourites was a tall angular Irishman with a face like Gabriel Byrne's battered brother who, when sufficiently intoxicated, would insist on giving an impassioned a cappella rendition of the Four Seasons' 'Walk Like a Man', attempting all the parts simultaneously. We figured that we could slip under the wire during this ad hoc talent segment and bend matters to our will.

Ralph, being able to play traditional pub piano, acted as a fifth column. He would wander onto the stage when Mr Showbusiness decided it was time to take a break, seat himself at the piano, pushing his limp, dark brown hair out of his eyes and eyeing the assembled lushes with a slight but impish smile. He would then launch into spirited generic barrelhouse, guaranteed never to fail anywhere alcohol is consumed in quantity. Having won a superficial general approval, he'd wave Pete up to join him on bass and continue in a similar vein. I'd join in, initially on my limited guitar, which mercifully could hardly be heard over the piano, and then I'd actually start singing some acceptably classic bits of ten-year-old rock 'n' roll, like Buddy Holly's 'Rave On' or Jerry Lee's 'Down the Line'. We also had another trick up our sleeves. Between us, Ralph and I knew a few Irish rebel songs – 'Kevin Barry', 'The Rising of the Moon, 'The Bold Fenian Men' – enough to get the Irish section singing along with a fervour so close to sacred that neither Mr Showbusiness nor the landlord could bring the impromptu set to a finish and return things to business as usual.

At first we didn't push our luck, and we were reasonably careful not to completely antagonise Mr Showbusiness or give the landlord tangible reason to bar us from drinking there. As time passed, though, and as always happens in these endeavours, circumspection gave way to confidence, and confidence grew and escalated to a point where we just had to test the envelope's bursting point. The rupture came after our guerrilla appearances at the Artesian Well had been going for five or six weeks. We had started making our own small mark. A limited word had got out that something highly untogether, but definitely out of the ordinary, was going down in this hitherto dreary pub. More long-haired malcontents had started to show up, guys in old army coats and CND badges and girls in black Marks & Spencer rollneck sweaters and lots of Boots mascara, presumably to see what nonsense we were up to. An art student called Rob, who played very good blues guitar, had begun to come by, and Alex Stowell joined us on harmonica when appropriate, and frequently when not. A guy called Mel Isaacs, a friend from student parties, brought a five-string banjo and some obscure but hilarious cockney radical songs, such as 'Greedy Landlord' and 'The Man Who Waters the Workers' Beer'.

Although we weren't getting paid anything – all fiscal returns going to ukulele-strumming Mr Showbusiness – we were being bought enough drinks to put us in the drunkenly arrogant frame of mind that we could get away with anything. In this instance, what we tried to get away with was Jerry Lee Lewis' 'High School Confidential', a song that's harder than it looks when you are drunk, because Jerry Lee wrote the stop-time sections like a minefield, and the words come so fast that, if you miss one, the whole vocal collapses like a line of dominoes, as indeed it did. After this débâcle I took it into my head to do 'The Ballad of Hollis Brown', Dylan's monstrously depressing dirge about the South Dakota badlands farmer who goes broke to the point of starvation, and then shoots his wife, his five children and himself using seven shotgun shells that he'd bought with his last dollar. It was delivered with artery-throbbing Johnny Walker Red passion, in the early form of what an eminent rock critic would, years later, describe as my 'hallmark monotone'. I compounded the crime by playing my own dreadful guitar.

When I was through all eleven verses, the place was silent. They weren't booing, they weren't pissed off; the audience was stunned by what had come to pass. No, they hadn't liked it, and they didn't like me, but for a while I'd absolutely meant it. Idiot-savant method acting had kept the crowd sufficiently off-balance to stop the boos and catcalls, or even someone dragging me bodily away. Too shocked to be elated, but realising that I'd certainly had an effect, I walked off. Mr Showbusiness quickly walked on and, without acknowledgement of what had just happened, launched into 'Does Your Chewing Gum Lose Its Flavour on the Bedpost Overnight'.

Almost immediately the landlord cornered me. Pub landlords tend to come in two sizes, the wide and expansive, and the narrow and suspicious. He was one of the latter, with eyes too close together, a greasy comb-over and a damp Woodbine perpetually in the corner of his mouth. He removed the cigarette, indicating that what he had to say was a matter of some gravity. 'I think this has gone far enough, old son.'

'Far enough?'

'You know what I mean.'

'So what are you telling me?'

'I can't have anything like that again.'

'Anything like what?'

'You know what I mean.'

The phrase 'you know what I mean' was his counter to every probe to make him explain himself, or define precisely what was upsetting him. I shrugged. 'So, you're banning me?'

Narrow eyes peered at me distrustfully. 'No need to go that far.'

Now he was trying to hedge his bets. He wanted me out of the place, but the unholy crew of which I was a strong cohesive factor had actually brought him a whole new crop of drinking punters, maybe more than Mr Showbusiness attracted. He was trying to have it both ways, and I knew I had him.

'So what are you saying to me? I can drink here, but I'm not allowed on the stage?' I nodded in the direction of Ralph, Pete, Alex and the others. 'You think they're going to go for that?'

'Listen, I'm not an unreasonable man . . .'

The truth was that he was a totally unreasonable man.

'I'm not unreasonable, but there's got to be limits.'

There have?

'We'll just see how it goes, okay?'

Again I shrugged and handed him back his authority. 'Whatever you say. You're the governor.'

He leaned close, now that his position was restored. 'That's right, I am, and I'll be keeping an eye on you.'

For the rest of the night I was thoughtful. What I didn't realise was that a scene had just been played out that would be repeated over and over again for the rest of my life. Someone who believed he was the ultimate authority loathed, or felt threatened by, what I was doing. The silence that had greeted me after losing myself in the song wasn't conventional approval, but I'd had an effect. If what you had to say for yourself didn't meet with instant mass approval, was that any reason to give up? The hell it was. I wanted more than anything to perform, again and again, until they either got the message or finally killed me, but it would have to be totally on my own terms. It wasn't even a matter of principle. Compromise simply wouldn't work.

After the envelope burst, we went on going to the Artesian Well, but it wasn't quite the same. I lay low for a while, gradually easing my way back onto the stage and then being warned off yet again by the landlord when I went too far. It rapidly ceased to be fun, however, reduced to the level of a predictable and pointless game. It was time to move on. Again I was getting frustrated. I now had a good idea of what I wanted to do, but how to go about it was a mystery that remained to be solved.

I Do Like to be Beside the Seaside

'We are the mods! We are the mods! We are, we are, we are the mods!'
'We are the mods! We are the mods! We are, we are, we are the mods!'
'We are the mods! We are the mods! We are, we are, we are the mods!'
'We are the mods! We are the mods! We are, we are, we are the mods!'

Paul, Beryl and I sat on a bank-holiday weekend on the balustrade on Brighton sea front, with the grey-green English Channel at our back, facing the Metropole Hotel, the pubs and souvenir shops, and watched as they streamed past, all parkas, anoraks, neat hair and wild amphetamine eyes. Paul and Beryl both lived in Brighton, and I was down from London visiting. We weren't the mods, and we hadn't been rockers since at least 1961. We were something else entirely. But what? As three scruffy non-participants in boots, old army shirts, tight dirty jeans and long unkempt hair, we defied categorisation, but we were asked to define ourselves a hell of lot that day. A group of rockers lumbered up to us with beleaguered hostility, and brown ale on their breath, tougher and more massive than the mods, heavily outnumbered, sideburned dinosaurs, but more than ready to beat us bloody if we proffered the wrong response. 'Are you geezers fucking mods?'

We shook our heads. 'No, mate. We're beatniks.'

'You mean like Bob Die-lan?'

'That's right.'

'All right then.'

They moved off in search of more culturally reprehensible targets. A while later a swarm of mods rushed up, tense behind Smith, Kline and French Drynamyl (once Purple Hearts, but by then French Blues), nervous tics and slight flecks of dried foam at the corners of their mouths. 'Are you geezers fucking rockers?'

We shook our heads. 'No, mate. We're beatniks.'

'You mean like Bob Die-lan?'

'That's right.'

'All right then.'

They too moved off. Although we had to perform the same crude catechism a number of times that day, it seemed to have been clearly established in the minds of both sides that we 'beatniks like Bob Die-lan' had a protected, neutral status in the tribal combat. Certainly no one beat us up, and although repeatedly questioned, we were allowed to remain unmolested on our bit of wall. When the police arrived and the street fighting turned from internecine to anti-authoritarian, Paul, Beryl and I slunk off to some bohemian refuge like the Lorelei Coffee House, the El Sombrero or the dank dungeon cellar under the Whiskey-a-Go-Go. Paul and I, in theory, had nothing against mixing it up with the constabulary, but one invariably ended up in jail, and we had better things to do with our time that bank holiday. This was the mods' and rockers' fight, not ours, and we felt justified in leaving it entirely to them. We were also well aware that the Brighton plods were less culturally discriminating than any of the mods or rockers we encountered and would fail to recognise that we 'beatniks like Bob Die-lan' were not a part of the general mayhem.

Over the years literally millions of words have been written about the politics, metaphysics and symbolism of the mod/rocker clashes of the early Sixties. I wrote a few of them myself, and I see no reason not to quote some directly right here. The following are from the book *Watch Out, Kids*, published in 1972. Although the style may be ponderously countercultural, I still pretty much stand by the sentiments.

Alienation between the two behaviour patterns was obvious from the beginning. The conservatism and casual brutality of the rockers, and the mods' sharp, aggressive, pilled-out hostility and flash, made each side an amalgam of all that was worst by the other side's standards.

It seemed as though youth culture had turned in on itself. It was impossible for the two facets of the culture to exist side by side without conflict. Youth, forced to draw on society for its examples, had inherited the age-old weakness of any oppressed people. It had given vent to its frustration in a display of internal violence and demonstrated that, no matter what degree of expertise in the production of artefacts it may obtain, a culture without an ethic or a philosophy cannot survive intact.

Youth, through rock and roll, had discovered its bodies and developed a lifestyle based on sensuality and the pursuit of pleasure. The rockers had gone no further than bogging down in a narrow conservatism, while the mods had devalued and impeded further discoveries through becoming entangled in complicated consumer rituals and sense-dulling drugs. If there was to be no further experimentation, the culture had to stagnate and the generation would just perpetuate the social insanity it had rebelled against.

The basic thesis of *Watch Out, Kids* was that the function of the yet-to-arrive hippies was to furnish youth culture with an ethic or philosophy. Whether they did or not is, of course, the subject of continuing debate. What isn't in debate is that the hippies did appear in the wake of the mods and rockers to provide a third subdivision of Sixties youth culture. Oddly, it was only when writing this account that it occurred to me how those mods and rockers back in Brighton seemed instinctively to recognise Paul, Beryl and me as this third tribe even before we knew it ourselves.

Look at His Legs

The women might have screamed as they had screamed at Elvis, Mick Jagger or the Beatles, but they were too overawed. Control was now expected of them. They were supposed to have grown out of pre-teen hysteria, even though Bob Dylan clearly had the charisma to invoke such a response. He stood alone in the spotlight on the stage of the Royal Albert Hall, backed only by a tall wooden stool holding a glass of water and an assortment of harmonicas, looking business-like, urgent, concentrated, in his own way as controlled as the crowd, snapping his knee and leaning forward slightly between the verses of the songs as he strummed the acoustic Gibson, moving the instrument closer to the second-guitar mike. May 1965, and I was seeing Dylan for the first time and wishing more than ever that I was him.

Although Dylan hadn't brought out the rock & roll band that had featured so iconoclastically on *Bringing It All Back Home*, and hadn't given the folk traditionalists anything overt at which to become upset, this was definitely not Woody Guthrie. The ghosts of electric rock 'n' roll circled the Albert Hall's high domed ceiling. With the first indication of the big hair still to come, a leather sport coat and tailored jeans with just enough flair to hang correctly over his Beatle boots, the man on the stage, although solitary and solo, was nothing short of a full flying rock star. He didn't gyrate and hardly even gestured, but if confirmation of his status were needed, beyond that the Beatles themselves were installed in the royal box, Jane (my love of the moment) provided it by leaning close enough so that I could smell her hair and her perfume. 'Look at his legs. He's got such fabulous legs.'

Much has been made of the tour one year later when Dylan 'went electric'. The reception accorded to the Band, the cry of 'Judas!' and the disgruntled mass walkouts have all become the stuff of both rock 'n' roll history and rock 'n' roll legend, but even though the entire English tour was chronicled in *Don't Look Back*, few critics or historians seem really to have noticed the writing that was on the wall as early as 1965. Dylan started the show with 'The Times They Are a-Changin'', but it seemed rushed and perfunctory. As a retroactive single, released after being out on album for eighteen months, it had become a UK hit, but Dylan seemed to be playing the song out of commercial obligation rather than conviction. Sure, the times were changing, no question, but Dylan was changing right along with them, if not ahead of them. The signals had already been clearly transmitted that he himself was no longer a 'beatnik like Bob Dielan'.

On landing at Heathrow, Dylan had conducted a press conference while holding a large industrial lightbulb as a Dadaist prop. The message – 'keep a clear head and carry a lightbulb' – had left the pop correspondents of the national dailies confused and hostile. They might have been ready for some young and earnest left-liberal folk singer, a callow and tousled Pete Seeger, but nothing had prepared them for an obliquely surrealist Elvis from inside the Gates of Eden, protecting himself with everything from mocking humour to the relentless savagery he exhibited in his one-on-one interviews with Horace Judson of *Time*, and with Laurie Henshaw for *Disc and Music Echo*. What also confused the media was that Dylan had developed a full-scale teenybopper following. Anxious young women lurked outside his hotel and waved frantically if he so much as appeared at a window. To a media already stung by Dylan's repeated bouts of hostility, this provided more ammunition with which to denigrate his work. A snotty Maureen Cleave demanded, 'Do your fans understand a word you sing?' Only British snobbery could have accused an artist of having fans too stupid to understand him and make it sound as though it was all his fault.

Other indications that Dylan was definitely no longer casting himself as Woody Guthrie came not from the media but from the general London rock & roll grapevine. Stories circulated about how he was holding court at the Savoy for the Beatles and the Rolling Stones, particularly John Lennon and Brian Jones; how Alan Price of the Animals was his constant companion when the circus travelled up north; and how Dylan had arranged a recording session with John Mayall's Blues Breakers, one of the hottest club bands at the time, but it had broken down in a drunken shambles. We also heard tales of how, although he had Joan Baez stashed at the hotel, he was also putting the moves on Marianne Faithfull and the famous breasts of Dana Gillespie. Still only in his mid-twenties, Dylan was being lauded by the hipsters of the world like the Second Coming of Jesus Christ on a Harley. He had the contemporary rock elite at his feet and was running around with some of the most admired women in the world. As Ian Dury would remark years later, 'There aren't half some clever bastards.' Even when it became clear that the trip was driving Dylan to dope and dementia, it still seemed like one hell of a desirable ride.

Hearing Dylan on record had obviously given me an approximate idea of the power of his voice, but to hear it live yielded a few surprises. The first was how much it varied in intensity, volume and emphasis from one line to the next, rising from a reflective whisper to a near-shout when making his point, and negotiating an emotional range that stretched from a contagious sadness to a furious braying venom. It may sound a little overblown to call his delivery Shakespearian, but Dylan had a command of one-man drama that enabled him to hold the capacity audience of some 7,000 in the palm of his hand. The given intelligence was that Bob Dylan couldn't technically sing. Certainly, by the dictates of bel canto, his voice was abrasive, of limited range and he had a whole bag of tricks to avoid exactly pitching a note, but, in context, one could screw bel canto and the ice-cream truck it rode in on. Seeing him for the first time made one thing absolutely clear. Dylan was among the chosen few whose voices were capable of profoundly moving those who heard them. Conforming to no accepted standards, it was innately compelling, a jolt of voltage to the nervous system that sent thrills down the spine.

After the show I joined the crowds milling out of the Albert Hall and along Kensington Gore towards the nearest pub, with my head spinning. The folkies had it totally wrong, and everything that I'd theorised while listening to the records had been confirmed. If they hadn't been so limited in their perspectives, the folk of the Left would have known what the kid was up to and been saved from their own bitter fury when he double-crossed them a year later by strapping on his Fender and doing it with the Hawks, later to be known as the Band. The implication was that by turning on so-called folk music, Dylan had turned his back on the people. As far as I was concerned, rock & roll *was* the music of the people. No question.

When Dylan abandoned his simple social protest – what he referred to as 'fingerpointing songs' – for lyrics that were more complex and oblique, he wasn't copping out, simply attacking us all closer to where we lived. He was going for the jugular of the imagination. Maybe it was real and maybe it was a calculated put-on, but we began to think in more esoteric and symbolic terms. He was speaking to us in what Jim Morrison would later call secret alphabets, and we at least pretended to know what he meant. A few months later we heard 'Like a Rolling Stone' and of the character 'Napoleon in rags', and every malcontent loser knew in his golden vanity that it was him, and what we were calling for – and would not be refused – was an even more powerful rock & roll cocktail that included not only the sound, fury, anger and dirty passion of the wild Fifties rock gods, but also the electromagnetic howl and psychotropic mind expansion that would be the key to the Sixties. The medicine Dylan mixed up tasted of stormed bastilles; it defied conventions and the change in the mode of the music that would shake the proverbial walls of the city.

Can you mix me one of those violent cocktails, bartender? Can you whip up that dangerous sucker in your shaker and stick a paper umbrella in it? And, if you can, what will it bring us? Utopia? Or maybe only an epic thousand-day global drunk? And, on reflection, what would be so wrong with that epic thousand-day global drunk? We might all learn something.

Chapter Two

The Mysterious East

I had finally left the House of the Chinese Landlord and, as if that wasn't enough, Ralph, Pete and I decided to get serious about this band business. To say I'd caught the rock-star disease from drinking at the Artesian Well would be misleading. The contagion had been on me since I'd seen Elvis in *Lovin' You*, but the rowdy débâcles in the Irish boozer had certainly woken it from its dormant state. Visions of a rock & roll glory road were opening in front of me despite the overwhelming mass of factual evidence that logically indicated I didn't have a prayer or a road map. Why exactly Ralph and Pete went with the idea to make the ad hoc band real was a mystery I never thought to solve. The madman-who-would-be-king doesn't question the motivation of his followers, any more than he questions his own. That I could motivate anyone to accompany me on such an implausible journey was enough of a miracle, and further enquiry would surely cast a jinx. We lacked expertise, a guitar player and any coherent definition beyond that of a ragged, slap-back boho band; a bit of a joke, but we had found a resolve and that was a powerful asset.

Our first move to turn resolve into reality was to relocate ourselves in the historical heart of London's legendary East End, home of Jack the Ripper, the Elephant Man and Ronnie and Reggie Kray. Artists inspired this migration east; Alex Stowell had scouted it and then led us there. With the first of a never-ending series of property booms under way, West London bedsits were being subdivided with ugly plasterboard and cheap emulsion paint, until there was no room in the average bijou flatlet to swing a cat (even if cats were permitted), let alone stretch a canvas or chip bits out of a block of marble. Art students and practising artists cast speculative eyes over Whitechapel,

Spitalfields and Mile End, which were unfashionable, unmodernised, unreconstructed and, in parts, quite dangerous, but might just offer the necessary space to operate.

Although grim high-rise estates were being built further down the Thames, in mysterious places like Wapping and the Isle of Dogs, the areas immediately to the east of the City had remained untouched – except by the bombs of the Luftwaffe – since Victoria was Queen, and Shanghai opium dens flourished in Limehouse as haunts for the real Lord Alfred Douglas and the fictional Dorian Gray. Narrow streets were still lined with two- and three-storey houses that had been slums when World War I broke out. A scattering of open-fronted shops still remained, just as they'd been when the Ripper stalked prostitutes there. On Old Montague Street an actual soda fountain had survived complete with an elephant-head soda spigot, and the bombsites of the Blitz remained like the cavities of rotted teeth filled with rats, rubble, garbage, urban briars and bits of old prams and bicycles.

Down the centuries these areas had offered sanctuary to a spectrum of refugees, Spanish Jews fleeing Ferdinand and Isabella's Inquisition and Huguenot weavers escaping the persecution of Protestants in France. The late nineteenth century saw a vast influx of Eastern European Jews driven out of Russia, Poland and Hungary by pogroms and Cossacks, and, of course, the cockneys had been there for ever, providing London with its unique and permanent under-class. The majority of immigrants had made only transitory settlement, close to the docks and the ships that had brought them. Some had enjoyed material success and moved on to Golders Green and Wembley. Others had decided to travel further, and headed out to America, Canada or Australia, making way for the next wave. For more than a hundred years the same areas had also been targets for politicians on the make, who would rail that the East End of London was a hotbed of socialists, anarchists, republicans, nihilists and revolutionists, plus thieves, cut-purses, white slavers, whores and drug traffickers, and needed cleaning out. This kind of rhetoric had regularly given the nod to local extremists to head east for violent bouts of home-grown ethnic, religious or cultural persecution.

In the 1890s the Ripper murders, committed in the exact neighbourhood to which we were moving, had all but caused lynchings and riots. In 1936 Sir Oswald Mosley had attempted to lead his British Union of Fascists on a huge anti-Jewish march through Whitechapel, but had been stopped by an implacable coalition of communists, and the rank and file of the various transport and dockworkers' unions, armed with pickaxe handles and potatoes spiked with razor blades. In the Fifties, when Mosley enjoyed a brief renaissance, his blackshirts had again attempted to ferment the same kind of race riots in the East End that had blighted Notting Hill. Later, the National Front would try more of the same. The Nazis always knew their way to Whitechapel, and pro-and-con graffiti, the swastika, the hammer and sickle and the Star of David remained daubed on the walls, only gradually fading over the years, as graphic ghosts of hate gone by. On a less vicious level, an abandoned shopfront still carried a sign, white on industrial green, 'Christian Mission to the Jews', and many of the stores and businesses were open on Sunday but closed on Saturday.

The influx of a few visual artists, and the freaks like us who followed, hardly constituted a mass migration. I doubt our numbers could have topped a hundred even at the peak of the trend, but in a small way we added our own measure of spice to the exotic stew. The big arrival taking place when we got there was from India and Pakistan, the one that added the smell of vindaloo to the hot bread and bagels, and the perpetual yeast stench that came from behind the high, sooty walls of the huge Whitbread brewery at the top end of Brick Lane.

We might never have known about the potential of the East End at all, had Alex Stowell not kept up his art-school contacts. His entrée to the East End was via a painter called Martin, a character definitely ahead of his time. As a dyed blond skinhead with a taste in button-fly Levis, bomber jackets, boxing boots and Mary Quant girlfriends, he would have fitted perfectly anywhere in time between 1977 and the end of the millennium. In 1966, however, he was a visitor from the future. Fresh from the Royal College of Art, he painted soft-focus rectilinear abstracts in various shades of grey and was highly scathing of all that was representational. He had rented half of a building on Princelet Street, off Brick Lane, as both a home and studio, and then, to assist with the rent, sublet a room to Alex. Martin's living quarters had been wallpapered in aluminium cooking foil. It was a Warhol effect, in tune with Andy's Mylar balloons, but you didn't mention that to Martin. His opinion of Warhol was as low as might be expected from one who painted grey rectangles. The place was decorated with partially inflated vinyl toys – a Fireball XL5, a jet fighter, a cartoon submarine with portholes and a fat drooping periscope, and a Donald Duck – all sprawled limply on flat surfaces or sagging from the edges of shelves, like small Claes Oldenbergs. Flop art, Martin proudly called them.

In addition to the visual arts, Martin was also in a band. He had even sculpted his own electric guitar. Square in overall configuration, a little like one of Bo Diddley's custom instruments, except for the long spikes extending fore and aft from the body like the fins on a comic-book rocketship, it not only played very well, but was a work of art in its own right. The name of the band was the Brothers Grim, and they were fronted by a strange angular singer, whose name I forget. As tall and uncoordinated as Joey Ramone, sallow and with short greasy hair, he affected a voluminous tweed overcoat, ideal for shoplifting, and jumped up and down on the spot in a horrid prophetic vision of the pogo. Like Martin himself, the Brothers Grim were also nearly a dozen years ahead of their time and could easily have appeared on the same bill with X-Ray Spex or Wreckless Eric. The song that sticks in my memory was called 'Crash My Party', about a guy so obnoxious that his guests ejected him from his own party and he was now beating on the door trying to get back in. When, some months later, both the Brothers Grim and the Deviants were trying to get a gig at the UFO Club, we both met the same contemptuous resistance from Joe Boyd, who booked the talent, which gave us a certain outcast kinship, but that's a slightly later story.

At the time in question the Deviants were only a gleam in my eye. The immediate task in front of us was to get a band – any band – together and functioning. Flushed from our mayhem at the Artesian Well, we had actually gone so far as to enter into a dubious hire-purchase agreement for a Vox Continental Organ for Ralph, a Japanese bass guitar for Pete and a couple of second-hand amps, with the amiable and fatherly Mr Traie who ran the musical instrument store on Portobello Road and, on occasion, cannibalised bits of broken guitars for Pete Townshend. Now we had our first bits of gear, we needed both a place to store them and somewhere to rehearse on a regular basis. When Alex first came round singing the praises of the near east, the thing he most strongly emphasised was the availability of space and tolerance. It was an overwhelming attraction, but the lure of elbow room wasn't all that beckoned us to pastures new. Ralph and Pete were already having trouble with their landlord and needed to move anyway, and I had taken up with a woman named Joy Hebditch, and the circumstances of this romance began to shed new light on the House of the Chinese Landlord.

Although I can now write about it as romantic and adventurous, the festering and impacted squalor of the building was something that only a delusional and solitary young man could willingly tolerate. I realise in retrospect that Joy was coming at me with a definite nesting urge, and even a fresh coat of paint and some pictures on the wall didn't give my sordid living quarters much nest potential. I had met Joy at a Saturday-night party in Blackheath held at the huge apartment she shared with three other girls, all students at Goldsmiths College in New Cross. We concluded the party in bed together, and having absolutely nothing to drag me away, I stayed until the following Tuesday, when I finally returned to the Grove and found my own home a lot less funky and quaint.

As Joy was perfectly happy to go on seeing me after our four-day orgiastic duet, I started spending more and more time in Blackheath, lured by the prospect of frequent and unpredictable sex, cooked meals and a television, which may sound exploitative but was a great temptation to any marginal young man. Blackheath was in the depths of South London, though, and an hour or more bus ride from the Grove, and thus I also saw less and less of my own so-called home. Very soon the subject came up that we were unnecessarily paying double rent, and, since we were all but living together, we should make some more economically viable plans.

Joy was from Carlisle, as far north as it's possible to get and still remain in England. It always struck me as a place of grey winter, Roman ruins, intersecting railways and monotonous light industry, and had, as Joy freely admitted, offered very little for an adventurous young woman except the grubby delights of hanging out with the musicians who passed through the town on the northern beat-group circuit, where bands like Derry and the Seniors, Rory Storm and the Hurricanes and the Big Three ruled the road. Joy came at me with a decidedly superior erotic expertise. At the time I met her she had short, white blonde hair and the look of a working-class Edie Sedgwick. In fact, Joy was very taken with the Warhol Factory and the mode of the Chelsea girls, and accordingly wore her mini-dresses very short and her mascara almost as thick as Dusty Springfield's. She was of medium height with full breasts and hips, and a narrow waist, the kind of shape someone once described as the ideal figure for a stripper, but Joy would never have stooped to such crass display. She had an extensive occult library and fancied herself as a neo-pagan before whom the boys should abase themselves to beg entry to a world of ruined purple sheets, lace suspender belts and black stockings, and the sure and certain knowledge that he who compliantly relaxes, and doesn't ask too many questions, can be transported to any variety of streetlight fancies.

One spring afternoon, when the sun was bright but the air chill and clear after earlier showers, Joy and I lay side by side on the unmade bed, still in the House of the Chinese Landlord, sweat cooling on our bodies. I, at least, was silent, reflecting on the elaborate innovation we'd just achieved. Joy pushed herself up on one elbow and looked at me thoughtfully. 'Sometimes I think I'm corrupting you.'

I looked at her, at a loss for words. I suppose if I'd been clever I would have made some remark like, 'Corrupt away, darling, I'm loving every minute of it.' But I wasn't clever. It never occurred to me that I could be corrupted. Wasn't I a wretch among the wretched, if only in my dreams? Didn't I dream dreams to outstrip the Marquis de Sade and his libertine mates? All I could think of was to lean over and kiss her, and from the way that she then took hold of me, I knew it was exactly the response she wanted. I suppose I was symbolically putting myself in her hands, giving her tactile control. Down the years we would marry, divorce and remain for some time quite literally partners in crime, even after we'd gone our separate ways. She saw me through some bad times and precipitated a number of others, but we'd stay friends until she ultimately took herself off to a strata of the drug culture that I was absolutely unwilling to accept even as a nice place to visit.

As I look back, I guess I was probably being seduced in those first weeks we were together. The clincher would seem to be Joy's very early pressure that we ought to move in together. For my part, I would have been more than happy to give notice to the Chinese landlord, gather up my stuff, such as it was, and trundle it down to Blackheath, but me moving to Blackheath didn't seem to be part of Joy's masterplan. She may have wanted me, but at the same time, and much more importantly, she wanted a mate. I don't think Joy considered the large communal apartment at all suitable for the projected *ménage à deux*. Too much craziness with four women living together. Jealousies, rivalries, conspiracies, constant partying, boys coming and going and, I believe, discreetly being handed round, although the girls – or the boys – in question might not have expressed it exactly that way. I think Joy saw too much danger in the environment that *deux* might escalate to *trois* or even *quatre*.

When we heard from Alex that there was another empty house for rent, across the street from him and Martin, at 10 Princelet Street, we decided to go over and take a look. As it turned out, the house had the space we craved in spades. Three whole floors, plus a dank but intriguing basement, and an industrial area out the back, which wasn't strictly ours but was eminently usable until someone else rented it. Unfortunately space was about all it had. In all other respects the structure was hardly fit for human habitation and might well have been condemned, had any LCC inspector bothered to take a look. The Edwardian wiring would support nothing more than a forty-watt bulb in each room; it lacked a bath; and we had to find our own furniture. All in all, we were homesteading from the ground up and might have been daunted if we hadn't been so energised by the possibilities.

The landlords were two orthodox Hasidics with the full kit of hats, sidelocks, Z.Z. Top beards and long black coats, a father-and-son act, one in his forties and the other apparently in his early hundreds, who discussed us in Yiddish while we looked on uncomprehendingly. They struck us as almost unacceptably strange, and I firmly believe the reverse was true. Fortunately strangeness clinched the deal. We looked just strange enough voluntarily to elevate their property to a habitable state. The first phase was that we'd move in rent-free and they'd pay for the materials, if we'd supply the expertise and labour to fix the electrical wiring. This would, of course, have been completely impossible had not Ralph (God only knew where) trained as an electrician; he was therefore not only able to install ring mains on each floor, but also to bribe the London Electricity Board inspectors to overlook any deficiencies in the work. Pete and I also had a few manual skills, and Joy made it clear she could do her part, so, not without a certain recklessness of spirit, we made a deal with the minimum of formalities and became de facto Eastenders.

Although it was hardly *Little House on the Prairie*, we went to work with a pioneer spirit. I wouldn't say we exactly whistled as we worked, but we hammered, sawed and pushed paint rollers to the sound of either Radio Caroline or (wonderful) Radio London, two of the loudest pirate stations breaking the BBC monopoly by broadcasting illegally from ships moored in the North Sea, and playing the hardest of contemporary rock & roll. To a background of the Who, the Yardbirds, the Pretty Things, the Four Tops, Otis Redding, and the Righteous Brothers, we started to elevate 10 Princelet Street from a hollow shell to a habitable slum.

We quickly discovered that the East End was highly conducive to our brand of homesteading. The local markets, small wholesalers and discount stores yielded cheap paint and fabric remnants suitable for curtains and cushion covers. Weird stalls sold mismatched speakers and lengths of plastic tubing. Odd pieces of furniture could be found in the street and on bombsites, absolutely usable if you didn't speculate as to why they'd been dumped. Building sites could be looted for bricks, breeze blocks and timber for building bookshelves. Food of all kinds was plentiful and cheap, and, once we'd developed a taste for the real-deal cuisine at the local curry joints, which proved a far cry from the mild and anglicised dishes served on Queensway or Westbourne Grove, it got even cheaper.

We also lived next door to a family of low-echelon Kray Brothers' associates who could be discovered, as we returned from a party in the early dawn, or, later, coming home from gigs in the band's filthy Ford Transit, busily respraying a stolen Jaguar right there in the street. They seemed to take a liking to us, probably because we were white, unconventional and knew how to keep our mouths shut. Regularly we'd be slipped some item that had 'fallen off the back of lorry' – sweaters, shirts, sunglasses, kitchenware, a couple of bottles of Scotch – with the instruction to forget where we got it. Finally, in full exploitation of the neighbourhood, Pete even got himself a job for a while at the Whitbread brewery, but finished each day so mindlessly drunk that he quit after a month fearing complete alcoholism.

We also learned that we weren't as alone as we initially imagined. In addition to Martin and Alex, the performance artists Gilbert and George – who, as 'human statues', painted themselves gold and went on display, moving in slow robotic unison – lived in a house on Fournier Street amid a clutter of Victoriana and weirdness. A few old Gully Jimson types could be spotted shopping in the markets, or scavenging for interestingly shaped debris on the bombsites, but they were generally irascible and hard to befriend. More outgoing was the scattering of art students from St Martin's, Goldsmiths and the Royal College, easily recognisable by the self-conscious paint on their jeans.

Not everything in the East End was quite so wonderful, however, and some of the drawbacks took some getting used to. Not least of these was the lack of a bathroom, and the need for regular visits to the public bathhouse, a few streets away. This was an echoing institution of Orwellian zinc and industrial piping, where bathers would hammer on the metal partition and yell, 'More hot water in number seven, guv.' It was too prole-like to sustain its novelty, but we could do nothing about it. Ralph might have been ingenious but, even with our assorted lengths of plastic pipe, he couldn't plumb in an entire bathroom from scratch. On a more general level, the area had a large population of incredibly poor and fucked-up people. From the winos who made their home on the small and dirty tract of grass next to Spitalfields Church known as Itchy Park, and the dully desperate hookers who took their lives in their hands turning grim and disconnected street tricks, to the struggling families whom the new affluence had failed to touch, a lot of folks were hurting. The daily contact could grow deeply depressing unless you took a firm grip and didn't go near the idea that there, but for the grace of God, went you.

Of course, one of the most efficient and expedient ways of avoiding the grace of God is to get high on a fairly regular basis. In the Grove, we'd been spoiled for drugs. Beatniks with hash, West Indians with grass and mods with pills; dodge the coppers and the world was your oyster. In this respect, the East End was an unknown quantity. Did they have these things here, or would we have to take the Central Line to the other side of town? To our great relief we discovered that all things were possible in or near a pub just a short stroll down Brick Lane.

Holes in the Albert Hall

The greatest danger in homesteading was that we'd become insular. Much as we might defend our adopted manor, most of what was happening was occurring to the west, and we weren't there. For months we had to manage without a phone, having to conduct business with a pile of pennies in the phone box across the street. In those days, when British Telecom was still the impossible dream of Tory privatisers, it could take Post Office Telephones months to install a new phone line in a twilight zone like Brick Lane. They seemed to take the attitude that we were damned lucky to get letters and packages delivered. Looking back from an environment of email and cell phones, it seems almost impossible that we could have achieved anything with such primitive communications, but we worked it out.

The business of the band consumed a great deal of loose change. We seemed unable to keep either guitar players or drummers. No matter how many ads we put in the *Melody Maker*, drummers and guitarists came and went. The guitarists all aspired to be God, or at the very least Eric Clapton, and the drummers all seemed to want to be rich and famous, like Dave Dee, Dozy, Beaky, Mick and Titch, and on *Top of the Pops* by a week on Thursday. Many wanted to play like Keith Moon, and since no one but Keith Moon could play like Keith Moon, what generally suffered was their ability to keep time. In other words, the cats we wanted weren't emerging. From the drummers' and guitarists' point of view, my own strange and mostly nebulous ideas were what turned them off. I knew the end product would be offensive to a great many people, and simple commercial logic dictated that if you set out to offend large numbers of people, it was unlikely they'd go out and buy your records in sufficient numbers to put you in the top forty.

A few of the musicians with whom we attempted to work tagged me and my singing as the band's primary problem. One guitarist even told Ralph how, if they got rid of me, the band might have a chance as a commercial blues band. When I heard this I wasn't sure whether to be mortally hurt or fiendishly pleased. I disliked that plank-whacker from the start, but that didn't prevent me from wanting him to like me. That seemed to be the conundrum in a nutshell. How could you scream abuse in the face of society and expect to be universally loved? When Duncan Sanderson eventually became the Deviants' permanent bass player, he would waffle a lot when stoned about the innate duality of what we were doing. Right then, the innate duality – what one might call the primal duality – was akin to attempting to set up a side-show attraction with the barker out front screaming, 'Roll up! Roll up! Step inside and take your extremely nasty medicine and have a violent and unpleasant experience!'

How the hell could one expect to attract a crowd with a pitch like that, and a show that was everything it promised? Who in their right minds would be lured in? Was it maybe possible to base a career on performing for people who weren't in their right minds? Hardly logical, Captain. I had yet to make the connection that the next best thing to an audience not in its right mind was an audience heavily drugged, and I freely admit that I was pretty damned confused. Not so confused, though, to exclude the possibility that I might be right and everyone else wrong.

My strong sense of impending change was about the only thing that didn't confuse me. It was a distant – but not too distant – scent on the wind. This proved a very good defence against insularity. Keep your eyes open, boy. Something's coming. Don't miss this bus. Signs of possible change were now citywide, and some of the most significant seemed to centre on a series of benchmark events at, of all places, the Royal Albert Hall. One was the Dylan concert, but also in the summer of 1965, on 11 June to be precise, an event entitled Wholly Communion took place, which both contemporary com-mentators and current Sixties historians cite as the genesis of the counterculture in England. Wholly Communion was promoted as an 'international gathering of poets', but in reality it turned out to be a magnificent shambles. And I, of course, didn't bloody go.

Originally instigated by New York filmmaker Barbara Rubin, the billed luminaries included Allen Ginsberg, Lawrence Ferlinghetti and Gregory Corso, all of whom conveniently happened to be in Paris at the time, plus Bill Burroughs, who was already in London but ultimately didn't appear. Among the domestic attractions were Christopher Logue, Mike Horovitz, Harry Fainlight, Adrian Mitchell and George MacBeth. Pablo Fernandez represented Cuba, and Simon Vinkenoog came in from Amsterdam. Alex Stowell had tried to persuade me that I had to be there, but I decided to sulk and blow it off. I'd already seen Ginsberg, along with Corso and Ferlinghetti, at a reading at the ICA, and had also attended a reading by Burroughs somewhere in Bloomsbury, at which his movie *Towers Open Fire* had been screened along with a demonstration of his flashing, rotating strobe-light 'Burroughs tubes'. When Alex didn't feel this was a good enough excuse, I angrily retorted that I never wanted to hear ever again Adrian Mitchell bore the shit out of me with his long and lousy poem 'Tell Me Lies about Vietnam'.

The real reason I didn't want to go was actually because Alex, and anyone he brought with him, would be there under the auspices of Jeff Nuttall, and I had a problem with Jeff. The plan was that we were to be part of some Nuttall-staged event involving being effectively naked and painted blue. I've never had any enthusiasm for being nude in public, and the fate of Shirley Eaton in *Goldfinger* had more than alerted me to the danger of allowing one's flesh to be covered in an impermeable coat of paint: 007 had warned me about dermal asphyxiation. As things turned out, I probably did well not to make it. With their pores effectively sealed, Nuttall and his crew began to feel decidedly ill, and Jeff himself was forced to lie in a bath in Sir Malcolm Sargent's dressing room.

I really can't recall where the enmity with Jeff Nuttall started. The irony was that I pretty much agreed in principle with everything he said. Later, as the author of *Bomb Culture*, the book that defined the emergent ethos in terms of the ever-present threat of nuclear annihilation, he made a staggering contribution to the currency of ideas in the Sixties, and my only serious dispute with him was over his stance on psychotropic drugs. Jeff didn't trust the stoned, and, as one of the stoned, I thought that sucked and distrusted him right back. We had a conflict of style. Nuttall and his ilk seemed to be promoting a woolly, slapdash and amateurishly English confrontation. While I adored Elvis' gold suits, and the fins on the pink Cadillac, Nuttall seemed to be taken with dirty-neck trad jazz and the Ford Prefect. I liked slick and he cleaved to the gangrenous. He liked Tony

Hancock and I liked Frank Zappa. (This is not to say that I didn't like Tony Hancock; quite the reverse, I worshipped him, and still to this day find myself adopting his helplessly outraged speech patterns in times of stress.) With Nuttall, though, it always seemed to become an either/or situation. I assumed the verbal broadsides that were fired when our ships passed in the early days of *International Times* were just another example of the Young Turks versus the old guard. Just as the punks slagged off us old hippies in the late Seventies, so ten years earlier we set about our CND elders. I must admit, though, I had supposed that a certain level of respect existed between us until I read his remarks in Jonathon Green's oral history of London in the Sixties, *Days in the Life*.

> Mick Farren was a bad man – I thought he was a bad man, anyway. I somehow thought he was a person who was a frustrated rock star who wasn't going to get there. He had all the attributes of a rock star except the talent. His appetites for fame were infinitely greater than his comparatively right-minded politics.

Until that point I didn't really suspect quite how much the man loathed me.

I'll leave the first-hand accounts of Wholly Communion – Harry Fainlight freaking out behind too much speed, Alex Trocchi attempting to host the show from behind a miasmic heroin fog, and all the other anecdotes – to those who were there. To me, and probably to most of those more directly involved in the event, the greatest excitement was generated by the 7,000-plus people who showed up. Prior to the event, the organisers feared that they wouldn't attract the 450 paying customers they needed to break even. It wasn't the commercial success, though, that signified; it was the graphic demonstration that so many were even interested in cutting-edge poetry and inspired weirdness. The head count was what counted, and much the same could be said the next year when Bob Dylan played his second Albert Hall gig, this time with the Hawks behind him.

We've already dwelled at some length on Dylan, the measure of his achievements, his possible motivations and his effect on the culture. The two concerts at the Albert Hall have been pawed over and picked apart for the last three and a half decades by everyone with a computer and a leaning to rock-crit. Recordings of the concerts were extensively bootlegged – except, with a uniquely Sixties irony, that we all later discovered that the various bootlegs we'd listened to had, in fact, been recorded in Manchester a few days earlier – and were finally legitimately released by CBS in 1999. Again, like Wholly Communion, the most fascinating parts of the show, in hindsight, were the audience and its subdivisions, their reactions to Dylan and his interaction with them. From the start, it was clear that the shows were going to be an extremely big deal. Even the folkies who were now openly crying 'traitor' wanted to do it to the man's face, and two hours after the tickets went on sale they were sold out. How did I secure mine? Don't ask.

Going into the venue, the atmosphere was decidedly strange. The tension and anticipation were neither pleasant nor healthy, like a weight pressing down on the staid auditorium, more akin to a sporting grudge match than a concert. The schism was instantly evident. The folkies were out in force, but also a high percentage of what I could only categorise as freaks, people with whom I could empathise and identify. Arrayed in thrift-shop capes, spray-painted wellington boots, Edwardian dresses and Victorian military jackets, they presented a DIY version of what, in twelve months, would be hawked on Carnaby Street and the King's Road as flower power. Even before the show started, it struck me that this was the welcoming committee for the electric Dylan. If not, I was going to be severely disappointed.

As Dylan walked out for the first half of the show with his solo guitar, the tension crackled in a way I've not experienced before or since, and far from defusing it, he seemed bent on pushing it for all it was worth. Even his appearance was calculated to antagonise the folk conservatives: an outrageous, black-on-brown, hounds tooth suit, a polkadot rocker shirt – and his hair. Well, his damned hair was just like mine, and believe me, there was very little of that style about back then.

The agonisingly drawn-out reading of 'Visions of Johanna' told it all. He seemed to have either smoked an awful lot of dope or been doing heroin, but far from slurring his words, he was enunciating with slow and unnatural care. In a rambling set-up, he had mockingly explained how he'd never written 'a drug song – it would be vulgar to think so'. We freaks didn't believe a word of it, while the folkies' restlessness was palpable. A message was being delivered. Folksinging Bob was shutting up shop and going out of the hobo business for all time. The freight-train masquerade was over, his pseudo grapes of wrath were being trampled into a new and intoxicating wine. The traditionalists would probably have started walking out right there and then, but they'd learned how to protest in their CND days and were aware that the art lay in the timing. If they erupted before he strapped on his Fender, they'd blow their impact and diminish the point they were trying to make.

Throughout the interval everyone marked time. Hurry to the bar for a gin and tonic, and wonder what would happen next. Then back to our seats for the moment Dylan brought out the Hawks, and the shitstorm became history. No one screamed 'Judas' – that was in Manchester – but the bellowed sentiments were similar. What history doesn't record is that a lot of the noise was the result of arguments breaking out within the audience, and freaks yelling at the folkies to sit down and shut the fuck up. A good percentage of the duffel coats walked, but enough stayed to keep up their barracking all the way through to the interminable introduction to 'Ballad of a Thin Man'. It was a pity they all didn't go and leave Dylan to us, his new electric audience. Now and then I wonder what became of the anti-Dylan folkies. I've never met anyone who admitted to being among their number, but I can't believe they spent the rest of their lives abhorring electric music, and I suspect they went on to apply the same purist intolerance to blues guitar players, prog rock or real ale.

This time I left the Albert Hall after Bob Dylan thinking simply, 'Jesus, there really are a lot of us. Where do we go from here?' I'd only previously seen this new breed of freaks in brief and scattered sightings, down the road, across the street, from the top of a bus. We'd maybe smiled or nodded, but these near-encounters had offered no idea of the real numbers involved. As Dylan had just told us once again – and we had no reason to doubt him – something was actually happening, but did any of us have a clear idea of what it was? Could all these people be brought back together on other pretexts? Could any kind of further cohesion be achieved, or was Dylan the sole uniting force? When his rebel-stoned electric circus moved on, would we all return to our separate and isolated ways? Was it beyond the realm of possibility that we might find other common ground beyond the appreciation of a single artist and his work? To think that my own untogether efforts could be a part of it seemed far too ambitious, but if some common ground could be achieved, it might provide a forum for my ideas. The obvious and crucial factor in creating that common ground had to be a means of communication, a network for contacts and interaction. Although I didn't know it at the time, I wasn't the only one thinking along those lines.

The last of these four significant shows at the Albert Hall took place in September 1966, and although no one ever talks about it in the context of Wholly Communion or the Dylan concerts – perhaps because it was an ending rather than a beginning – it had a similar impact on me. The Rolling Stones, with Ike and Tina Turner opening for them, began their UK tour in the autumn of that year with two Albert Hall concerts. If Wholly Communion was one sort of shambles, these Stones shows were a mess of a different kind. Although the Stones' music had grown in both ambition and sophistication, and they were playing their new, more complex songs like 'Get Off My Cloud' and '19th Nervous Breakdown', a section of their audience had failed to grow with them.

Where Dylan had symbolically liquidated his folk business, the Stones were faced with the inescapable fact that the era of the screaming teenybopper was ending because the howling pandemonium of the old-style pop show had become dangerously redundant. The music couldn't be heard over the mass hysteria – hysteria that was becoming life-threatening to the performers. During the Albert Hall shows, as documented in Peter Whitehead's short film *Have You Seen Your Mother, Baby?*, both Mick Jagger and Brian Jones repeatedly came close to being dragged into the audience by the crazed fans who swarmed the stage. Pop stars were faced with a choice of either retreating into the protection of the recording and television studio or finding a whole new way of putting on a live show.

It had ceased to matter whether the performers were ready or not, or whether they liked it or not. A massively expanding audience, totally revised logistics and a musical technology advancing by leaps and bounds were forcing the mode of the music to change, and the walls of the city had better watch out.

The Making of the Man

One day during the Seventies punk era, the then *enfant terrible*, Julie Burchill – all tight black denim and surly mascara – strolled into the office at the *New Musical Express* that I shared with writer Charles Shaar Murray and declared, with that tone of dramatic accusation that would become such a part of her style, 'Nobody would remember Che Guevara if he hadn't been handsome.'

I probably looked up at her and blinked. Right at that moment nothing could have been further from my mind than the legendary Cuban revolutionary. 'Huh?'

'Nobody would remember Che Guevara if he hadn't been handsome.'

I thought about this for a moment and then nodded. 'You're absolutely right.'

She wandered off, a little deflated by my instant agreement, looking to provoke elsewhere. The old-timers were supposed to rise to the bait and entertain her with an argument, but, against all the tenets of the conventional Left, I freely admitted she was right. Few have read Che on economic theory, land reform or guerrilla warfare, but millions have hung his image on their walls, or worn his face on a T-shirt. I agreed so readily because, over the years, I thought a lot about it. Eddie Izzard's formula cannot be escaped. Impression rules, 70 per cent how you look, 20 per cent how you sound and only 10 per cent content. Physical appearance can make better agitprop than the most elegantly crafted theory.

I have never fully understood why revolution is expected to be so drab. The dictatorship of the proletariat has so often been interpreted as the dictatorship of the ugly and shapeless that it begs the question why glamour is anathema to so many advocates of social upheaval? In all of recent revolutionary history the only truly glamorous revolutionaries I can remember – Che notwithstanding, who was handsome but also a scruffy bastard – were the drag queens of Stonewall in Greenwich Village, who went toe-to-toe against the homophobia of the NYPD in 1969 and scored a major victory for gay rights and the crucial liberty of sartorial self-expression. Ever since, I have been with them all the way, a true believer in the legitimacy of fighting the good fight in high heels.

Prior to Joy and I living together, I too was pretty much a scruffy bastard. The care I took over my appearance consisted of selecting a look that I considered would enhance my romantic self-image and external impact, but then going for the lowest level of maintenance. At various times I borrowed from Gene Vincent, Miles Davis, Fidel Castro, Doc Holliday, Johnny Cash, or any combination of the five, but if the costume couldn't be dropped on the floor at night, and put on again in the morning with little or no trouble, it was discarded. An ensemble should also be blessed with the dual function of being equally effective when it's both crisp and funky. The white suit is a perfect example. Straight from the cleaners, you can look as dapper as Tom Wolfe, but when the suit is wilted and less than pristine, you can then pretend you're Robert Mitchum playing Max Cady in the original *Cape Fear*.

No sooner had I moved in with Joy than she decided that this approach to dressing up left a lot to be desired. A protracted make-over commenced. Anticipating the winds of fashion by careful observation of the Rolling Stones, Joy eased me into my transvestite gunfighter period. I wore no actual dresses, but considerably more satins and velvets, jewellery and even eyeshadow on special occasions, although some of these occasions were more private than public. We discovered that we could exchange clothing. One of her dresses could double up on me as a medieval tunic or an Errol Flynn pirate shirt. Rumour had it that Brian Jones and Anita Pallenberg were doing exactly the same thing, so it was all perfectly acceptable. Further delight came from shopping for shoes in the women's section. Having fairly small feet, I could fit into the larger women's sizes of Victorian-style, lace-up, pointed-toed, Cuban-heeled boots, which were much cooler than anything sold for men at the time. This is not to say that I didn't spend the working day in jeans and a T-shirt, but going out was also a form of coming out, and Joy instructed me in the cutting of a swathe. Even when I wouldn't be parted from my black leather jacket, scarves, silk shirts and decoratively studded ethnic belts were added to the mix.

Although I never quite became the afro-haired Mick Jagger that she had in mind, Joy presented me with many more possibilities than I'd previously entertained. It was one more facet of the education process we were all going through, and, from Joy to Anita Pallenberg, the women taught the class. Revised history now paints us male Sixties radicals as sexist exploiters, keeping the women in the kitchen making tea and cooking dinner while we swilled beer and fantasised about world domination, but I have to wonder where customising your old man might stand in the light of liberation? Perhaps the balance of power and oppression may not have been so clearly defined as many imagine. This psychedelic cavalier flourish also didn't come without problems, the worst being that any deviation from the drab could invoke instant belligerence among the conditioned mob. The scream of 'Poof!' and the sudden onslaught of violent rage taught straight boys like me indelible lessons about lumpen hatred of the suspected effeminate. Suddenly we were all Quentin Crisp, and, if nothing else, we learned how to leg it in silly shoes. Being threatened by lorry drivers and Millwall supporters became rock & roll, on-the-road routine as one slouched into a motorway service area in one's finery for a 3 a.m. sausage, egg and chips.

Hostility, however, wasn't limited to the resentful proles. Many traditional leftists refused to believe that anyone who came on like some neo-fop could be politically trustworthy. Jimi Hendrix could play revolutionary guitar in satin, velvet and trailing scarves, but God help you if you met with a crew of Trotskyites looking like that. My attitude was that I'd look like a bloody rock star, or as though I'd come straight from the pig-iron smelter, depending on my mood, hangover or the state of my laundry, and the idea of deliberately putting on the old army coat on which the cat slept for a meeting with the Claimants' Union seemed just as patently dishonest as cutting my hair and assuming a suit and tie for a court appearance.

I've never been sure why to be dowdy is also to be politically correct. Perhaps because our only successful armed revolt was led by Oliver Cromwell and his militant puritans. The Roundheads considered silks, satins and falls of lace anathema in the sight of God, and what they would have made of vinyl or latex is anybody's guess. Puritanism was conducted in monochrome and without frills, and almost all insurgents since have inherited that attitude. Another possible reason for the dourness of Eng-Soc is that its stereotypes were formed either during the Russian Revolution or the Great Depression, and neither was noted as a fest of glad rags.

A third explanation might be that the majority of the up-the-workers Left whom I encountered in the Sixties were really nothing more than renegade children of the middle class, who cleaved to the idea of the flat cap, muffler and overalls as a reaction against their semi-detached consumer heritage. They seemed totally unaware of the great tradition of the English working-class dandy. The wideboys of the Forties, like Pinkie in Graham Greene's *Brighton Rock*, the teds of the Fifties and the mods of the Sixties were all progressive versions of what George Orwell described as 'young men trying to brighten their lives by looking like film stars' and George Melly later called 'revolt into style'. The workers never wanted to look like the proles of *Metropolis*, but they were too wretchedly paid and brutally overworked to do otherwise. Only their criminal cousins were able to cut the desired dash. One of the great attractions of the Blackshirts, the Nazis and other fascist movements was that they offered unemployed louts snappy uniforms. The lone Red of my acquaintance who had both an awareness of power through style and the flash that came with it was a self-proclaimed Stalinist who rode a Triumph Bonneville and favoured Jim Morrison-style leathers and a sawn-off Levi jacket, with a hammer and sickle in place of the motorcycle club patch. More than once he told me, 'I'd join the Hell's Angels, but it's the bastards you have to ride with. They don't have a clue. I mean, how many could I discuss Frantz Fanon and *The Wretched of the Earth* with?'

During a political phase in the very early Seventies, when I was ramrodding the publication of *IT*, I was intimidated into going for the denim and boots end of radical chic, the basic biker-Yippie street-fighting drag of jeans, workshirt and an old Air Force jacket. I tried to maintain a certain snap by sticking to basic blue, and avoiding khaki and fatigue green, but, God, was it dull, and after maybe nine months I rebelled against the Marxist-Leninist dress code. Gussy up, and start dressing again. David Bowie was, after all, now waiting in the wings. Mac McDonnell, one of the Deviants' ex-bass players, had given me a rather beautiful white jacket for my birthday, and I began building a new look around it. It must have worked, because the second time I strolled down Portobello so arrayed, I ran into Stacia, Hawkwind's towering and statuesque dancer. We exchanged flirtatious pleasantries, as was our practice, and then, as we turned into the pub, she grinned at me. 'I'm so glad you've started dressing rock & roll again.'

I laughed and nodded. It was always good to receive compliments from a very tall woman with massive breasts. 'Yeah, so am I.'

Devoting time and space to the clothes we wore may seem shallow and facile, and all the care and planning that went into how we presented ourselves nothing more than self-indulgent narcissism. My only response is 'Think again, pilgrim'. The use of dress for self-definition is the most instant and obvious means of protest available to an individual. The doubter only has to look on the other side of the fence. A marine bootcamp takes equal pains to break the will and destroy the individuality of its conscripts with uniform olive drab and identical shaved skulls. The violent reaction to the first wave of hippie freaks indicated, as far as those in authority were concerned, that you were absolutely what you wore. Police body-search harassment of the long-haired and outlandish, under the pretext of drug enforcement, became such a matter of routine in 1966 and 1967 that, by June 1967, Home Secretary Roy Jenkins was forced to issue a directive that race, personal appearance or hairstyle was not enough on its own to constitute reasonable grounds to stop and search an individual on the street. Naturally the beat cops largely ignored the directive, but at least the statement had been forced out of the Home Office.

Historically a political revolt without a similar revolution in style was a conspicuously rare creature outside of England. The bare-breasted women and the red, white and blue sashes of the Jacobins in the French Revolution, the *charro* look of the followers of Pancho Villa and Emiliano Zapata, the ghost shirts of the last Native American guerrillas, the red and black bandannas and red and white *santeria* necklaces of the Cuban *Fidelistas* – all of these were costume used as a personal banner of insurrection. The Black Panthers in their berets, leather jackets and sunglasses scared the shit out of Middle America even before they took to carrying guns.

If further proof were needed that costume operates as a potent psychological weapon, one has only to examine how the outrage of style escalated through the Sixties and Seventies, deliberately pushing the collective buttons of society at large. The unkemptness of the beatniks offended the short-back-and-sides public sense of order. The hippies, flaunting a colourful hedonism, set off the jangling alarms of accepted decency, the androgyny of the glit-glam attacked the barriers of strict gender division, while the punks launched a visual assault on society's Freudian id by dragging all its best-kept psycho-sexual fetishes out from under its Jungian collective mattress.

Although the punks cultivated a scathing contempt for us old hippies, and their style owed more to Joseph Goebbels and Morticia Addams than Shiva and William Morris, their attitudes and objectives differed only by a nuance. Malcolm McLaren certainly borrowed heavily from the Situationists of the Sixties, and may even have cast his net much closer to what I consider home. John (Rotten) Lydon effectively gave the game away when he came up to me during my very first visit to the Roxy, the prototype punk club staged in what had been a venerable drag-queen bar in Covent Garden. To show the old-guard flag at the Roxy, I had dressed to a fairly carefully drawn line between old fartism and compromise with fickle trend. I had done my best neither to conform nor antagonise in my old black leather jeans, and a splendidly flowing black coat with a medieval eagle on the back that the brilliant Phoebe Cresswell-Evans had designed for me. The jeans did however have a slight flair, just enough to make them hang correctly over my cowboy boots. Rotten said nothing, but just stooped down and measured the offending flair with his thumb and forefinger, then looked up at me and slowly shook his head. The flair might have been minimal, but it was still unacceptable to the new generation. A man's loyalties, antecedents and social pedigree will ever be judged by the cuff and cut of his pants.

And, of course, it still continues today. In the USA in 1999 the CNN-watching world saw the phenomena of the Trenchcoat Mafia, the cult of disconnected white kids borrowing the long, sinister black coat from movies like *The Crow* and *The Matrix*, the gangsta accessory tip of carrying automatic weapons under said coats, and the philosophy of nihilist homicide from the disgruntled employee. They not only instilled fear in the squares by their look, but also punched their message home by conducting bloody high-school massacres. In comparison, the excesses of the Woodstock Nation seem positively benign.

Oh yes, we hippies of the Sixties paid far too much attention to style and almost none to political theory (or automatic weapons, for that matter). It was part of both our charm and our downfall, but what could you expect from the first generation of television babies, who believed that all the problems of the planet could be solved simply by doing it in the street and scaring the horses?

A Shed in Chalk Farm

'What's that?'

'It's the IT girl.'

'Wasn't Clara Bow the IT girl?'

'That's right.'

'Well, that's Theda Bara.'

Primary fuck-up.

It was always a great source of comfort and amusement that the logo of *IT* – the *International Times*, England's first and most successful underground newspaper – carried the picture of the wrong movie star. Instead of Clara Bow, the real IT girl, it bore the intense and sensual stare of Theda Bara, whose name was an anagram for 'Arab Death'. I wasn't around at the very start, so cannot be held responsible. According to legend, it was some friend of Jim Haynes who actually perpetrated the error, but I've always kept the primary fuck-up dear to my heart, as something to remember when we of the 'underground media' started taking ourselves too seriously. *Oz* magazine had a similar primary fuck-up. While Richard Neville and his crew were putting the third or fourth issue to bed, word came that Che Guevara had been murdered in Bolivia by the Rangers and the CIA. With no time to do a full obituary, Neville decided the smartest move would be to bind in a centre-spread memorial poster. The poster was quickly designed, no one bothered to proof it and the magazine went from the layout table to the printers and hit the street with Guevara wrongly spelled. We may have stormed the twin bastilles of censorship and disinformation, but we couldn't spell, and we confused our movie stars.

As I already said, I wasn't in on the planning and launching of *IT* as anything except an interested reader, and I only came to it because of a young woman called Zoe Harris. Zoe was very young, vibrantly attractive but highly insecure, and moved at about a million miles an hour. When she told me, in October of 1966, that I should go to a party at the Roundhouse celebrating the launching of *IT*, I paid attention and asked pertinent questions.

'What's *IT*?'

'It's a new fortnightly newspaper that some friends of mine are putting out.'

'And what's the Roundhouse?'

'It's an old locomotive shed in Chalk Farm Road.'

'Okay.' Strange but intriguing, and I decided I would make it my business to attend. Joy took some persuading, but when I threatened to go on my own she acquiesced.

As the cab pulled up outside the odd Victorian building, just down from Chalk Farm tube station, I realised that I'd seen the place before, but never taken the time to wonder exactly what it might be. I'd assumed it was something to do with the main-line railway tracks that led down to Euston Station, but that was about as far as the theorising had gone. From the outside, the entrance, distinguished only by a small cardboard sign, appeared to lead to nothing more than a derelict building, more the venue for a gangland murder than a party.

'Is this a joke?' Joy, in a short satin dress and spindly heels, was hardly dressed for cavorting amid ruins, and she had a natural female suspicion for information originating from an ex-girlfriend. Inside the door, a rickety and very narrow set of stairs, little more than a ladder, ascended into semi-darkness, but we could hear music, which is the standard encouraging sign when looking for a party. At the head of the stairs a young man was checking tickets, and three equally young women in silver dresses were handing out sugar cubes. The legend was that one in twenty had been dosed with a trip. Mine hadn't, and, since no one else ever claimed to have scored a live one, I think I had just encountered my first psychedelic myth. Once inside, we stood and stared.

'Wow!'

Wow, indeed. The place was definitely a ruin, but I recognised that I'd lucked into something exciting, new and maybe magical. In an environment of dirt, damp and debris, the same breed of freaks I'd seen at the Dylan concert at the Albert Hall were moving in the gloom, but instead of sitting in their seats absorbing Bob, they were interacting, mingling, dancing. Holy moley, Batman, what do we have here? The reek of old decaying plaster, rusting cast iron and dark satanic mildew was tempered by incense and – yes – the covert whiff of marijuana. I love the smell of marijuana in the evening. It was the smell of . . . well, maybe not victory, but perhaps some devil-may-care anarchy.

The Roundhouse was little more than a huge circular shell, with a floor of cracked brickwork, littered with chunks of masonry, empty cable drums and broken components of Victorian machinery. A rotting deathtrap of a gallery ran around the entire circumference, some thirty feet up. Later I would climb up to investigate, and discover its missing boards and multitude of holes, each one potentially lethal to the unwary. I had assumed the building had originally housed a locomotive turntable, but Miles quite recently informed me that hadn't been the case at all. It had in fact accommodated winding gear that, in Victorian times, had hauled trains up the hill from Euston. It was owned by an organisation known as Centre 42, which had acquired it from British Rail in some art-for-the-masses deal fronted by the playwright Arnold Wesker, and it had been rented to *IT* for forty quid for the single night. The Wesker plan was to create a workers' fun palace and a mecca for the socialist arts, but Centre 42 had estimated that they would need a half million pounds to start and had only managed to hold a few meetings and put up a sign proclaiming how much money they wanted in donations. The *IT* crew had scored the rental by playing on Wesker's guilt that, under his stewardship, the place was lying useless and empty.

A rickety scaffolding stage had been erected, and slide and movie projectors threw film clips and abstract images on plastic sheets hanging on clothes lines. Today it would all seem tattily pathetic, but right then, it was the stuff of dreams. When Joy and I first walked in a steel band was playing on the stage. I have never been fond of steel bands. I'll stick to ska and blue beat, if we're going that totally tropical route. Fortunately, there was plenty more to occupy my attention. To one side of the stage, someone had attempted to create a six-foot jelly. The assumption had been that it would stand up on its own, but when turned out of the cauldron-like container that had been used as its mould, it proved how a giant jelly cannot maintain the same integrity of form as the smaller, household dessert jelly. It lay in a multi-gallon glutinous blob-mass on the uneven floor, like the remains of a dead alien in a horror movie, and the more extrovert partygoers were already sliding about in it.

The first person I recognised was a young mod from around the clubs, a frequenter of places like Tiles, the mega-dance club on Oxford Street. I had no idea how he'd got there, but he seemed highly excited by all that was going on and rushed up to me, with a closed fist discreetly extended, as though he wanted to slip me something illegal. 'Here, have a bit of fun on me.'

I found myself holding four yellow pills. Dexedrine. I took two and Joy took two, and things geared up a notch. The next person I encountered was Zoe, with her new boyfriend, who looked like a Mossad agent. With boyfriend in tow, she introduced me to John Hopkins – Hoppy – for the first time. Simultaneously frenetic and stoned, hyperactive and endowed with a boundless enthusiasm, he was one of the organisers of the event and one of the group that was launching *IT*, which, with a Bill Burroughs ring, called themselves the Editorial Board. As, over time, Hoppy's background unfolded, I discovered that, after reading physics and maths at Cambridge, he had worked as a reactor physicist for the Atomic Energy Commission at Harwell, mainly to avoid national service, but had then fallen into CND, the beat generation, playing in a jazz band, dope and dealing, and had become a professional photographer. He'd already had a number of adventures in embryonic underground publishing, and had even formed early white-boy contacts with some of the first Notting Hill Rastafarians. I told him that I thought it was a fantastic thing that he was doing, with the Roundhouse party and *IT*, but after that there didn't seem much to say. Rather than degenerate to small talk, I moved on, unaware of the pivotal role Hoppy would play in my life, and in the lives of a lot of other people, over the next few months.

By this point the steel band had given up the stage to a band called the Soft Machine. Loosely jazz-based, and with an amazing drummer, they were a quantum leap beyond anything I'd heard in rock & roll. Partway through the set a motorcycle cranked up and, as it spewed exhaust fumes into the already loaded air, the noise of its engine was amplified by the PA. Hey, an electric BSA. Towards the end of their set the band went into an extended chant, an early version of their live classic 'I Did It Again'. With the speed providing the energetic basis for a fine high of multiple abuse, I augmented it with a number of hits from a communal bottle of scotch, some wine, a few beers and many lungfuls of smoke from the joints that were in free circulation. Although, stylistically, the Soft Machine had absolutely nothing to do with any musical endeavour I might have in mind, their breaking from the current norms, and open-ended innovation, gave me hope. If they could amplify a motorcycle, surely my weird-ass atonal singing could find its place.

Although equally out there, the next band up, obliquely named Pink Floyd, were located more in what I recognised as the current forms of rock 'n' roll. Back then, they had yet to lay the bricks in their wall, or develop a taste for gloomy pomp and circumstance. They sounded like one continuous Pete Townshend guitar solo, but without the physical flamboyance. Their one advantage over the Soft Machine was an extensive use of reverb and repeat echo, which was greatly enhanced by the monster-movie acoustics of the cavernous building. They had also brought their own lights, which gave them a definite visual edge as the shape of things to come. This event, however, wasn't about the bands. Although it's now a cliché, the party was solidly and unashamedly about the people. Some media-familiar faces and household pop-names moved through the crowd. Paul McCartney, in full Lawrence of Arabia burnoose and heavy sunglasses, seemed concerned that he might be recognised. And, of course, he was recognised immediately, but no one particularly cared. No shrieking Beatlemania, just a smile and a nod, 'Oh look, darling, there's Paul McCartney.'

While I was sharing a joint with a circle of complete strangers, a sheet of corrugated iron crashed down behind us, and I turned to see Mick Jagger and Marianne Faithfull creating their own private entrance. Again no fanatical reaction, although one of the group I was with turned angrily. 'Fuck you, mate, you scared the shit out of me. I thought you were the coppers. We're being a bit illegal here, if you know what I mean.'

Some claim that a camel was at the party, but I didn't see it – and a camel at a party, even in a place the size of the Roundhouse, is hard to miss. Logic would seem to dictate that it would have been wholly impossible for a camel to climb the stairs by which we entered the building. What you might call the eye-of-the-needle syndrome. On the other hand, I suppose it could have come in through the same hole in the wall as Mick Jagger. I do know that an Italian movie crew was present, filming topless young women smearing themselves with pink paint. As I gave Joy the slip and stumbled forward to take a closer look, an aggressive production assistant pushed me back, as though it was his exclusive movie set, instead of a free-form psychedelic party. The combination of speed, booze, marijuana and my natural aversion to authority caused me to snap back at him with old-fashioned rocker belligerence, 'What's your fucking problem?'

'We're trying to make a movie here?'

'So?'

'So fuck off, you're spoiling the spontaneity.'

The idea that spontaneity could be spoiled really touched an inebriated nerve, and I think I might have taken things further, had not Joy and Zoe spotted me and diverted my attention away from the escalating confrontation. For the next year or so Italian or French movie crews seemed to be present at every psychedelic event, filming forgettable starlets against a backdrop of freaks. The end product was usually a hippy-trippy sequence in some sub-Bond spaghetti spy epic. To be fair, in many instances, the Italian or French movie crews, and the facility fee they paid, could be crucial in staging the event. Their contribution to the up-front financing could make all the difference.

A little while later (all time being relative) I again slipped away from the women, looking for fresh mischief. I was still fascinated by the holes in the wall, and the possibility that they might be admitting hallucinations. Lurching around the outer circumference, I discovered that quite a few fissures gaped jaggedly in the nineteenth-century brickwork, probably knocked through in anticipation of some future construction. Some were covered by bits of corrugated iron, like the one Jagger had apparently come through, while others were draped only with a builder's tarpaulin. The obvious next move was to see what lay beyond. I ducked through and found myself facing the broad expanse of train tracks that led ultimately to Birmingham, Manchester and all points to north to Glasgow. Cheerfully courting death by misadventure, I skipped blithely across rails and sleepers, aware that some of the rails might have been electrified, but too bent on adventure to care. When I was at a sufficient distance, I turned and looked back to take in the Roundhouse as a whole. All around me railway traffic signals, and the lights of the trains themselves, were reflected to infinity in the wheel-polished steel of the rails, like a Brian Haresnape painting. Rolling stock moved in the distance, but, luckily, no trains came near me. Beyond it all squatted the rotund bulk of the building I'd just left, with its odd conical roof; a dumpy fortress where some kind of tentative banner seemed to have been unfurled. Was it a place where a new-found culture could be defended? I returned more carefully. Now I was thoughtful rather than elated. I wanted to come back to this place and the people gathered inside. It was as though I had finally found my tribe. The question asked by my insecurity was: would they want to accept me?

Chapter Three

Show Me Your Money

The hippie pointed disapprovingly at my T-shirt. 'Oh wow, man, that's ... like ... so aggressive.'

The slogan on the T-shirt read HERE COMES THE INCREDIBLE HULK, and above it was a full-colour image of the Marvel comics character. Muscular, angry, green and naked but for ragged purple trousers, this product of unchecked gamma radiation strode from the front of the garment brandishing a knotted rope. The back of the shirt had a gag payoff. It showed the rear view; the Hulk striding away. The threatening knotted rope was, in fact, attached to a small wooden toy rabbit on wheels, indicating that the monster was really quite lovable. THERE GOES THE INCREDIBLE HULK. Of course, the silly bloody hippie couldn't see the back, and like so many of his kind, his verdict was rendered by what met the eye, without feeling any need to probe further. So fuck him. 'Just get inside, okay?'

When I ran the door at UFO, that was one of my two stock responses to everything. 'Just get inside, okay?'

Keep the line moving, don't impede the flow or cause a log-jam. The policy of UFO was the diametric opposite of Studio 54 and all the 'exclusive' Seventies discos. Back in the Sixties, we wanted them inside the club. A rabble of freaks jamming the pavement was an instant provocation to the police, and the bottleneck was tight enough at the best of times, without plugging it by engaging in some pointless psychedelic discussion. The other stock reply was 'How much money have you got?'

Working the door at the UFO Club probably taught me more about the true nature of the counterculture than any other single task. Yeah, I'd found my tribe all right and now I was in the thick of it, playing psychedelic traffic cop to a multitude of chemically incapable lemmings. I didn't know if they'd accepted me, but, by God, they had to do what I told them. Each Friday night, if the Deviants couldn't hustle together a gig of some kind (which in those days was most Friday nights), I spent three or four highly intense hours confronting a constant stream of freaks in all their manic glory. My role was that of problem-solver and troubleshooter – what Chet Helms, who ran the Avalon Ballroom in San Francisco, on which much of the style of UFO was modelled, dubbed the 'hassle guy', a post I obtained by being the only hippie mean enough to deal with the creative nonsense of our stoned clientele.

'Hey, man, you know what?'

'What?'

'If we all, like, concentrated our individual vibrations, and, you know, focused, we could turn the place into a real UFO, and actually, like, take the whole thing into space, you know?'

'Just get inside, okay?'

'No, really, man . . .'

'Just get inside and explain it to someone else.'

'Listen . . .'

'No, I don't want to hear it. Just get inside.'

The price of admission was, if I recall correctly, ten shillings. It might have been more dramatic to declare that the price of admission was your mind, but it wasn't. Ten bob. Not cheap, but hardly exorbitant. Even so, many balked or tried to weasel out. For example:

'Don't freak me out with money, man.'

'Tell that to Pink Floyd.'

'Money should be abolished, you know what I mean?'

'I absolutely agree with you, and so does Fidel Castro.'

A look of doubt would cross the anti-materialist's face. 'You do?'

'Sure, I do. How much money do you have?'

'What?'

'How much money do you have? In your pockets right now.'

(A literary echo: 'What have you got in your pocketses?' The crucial Tolkien riddle from *The Hobbit* by which Frodo wins the Ring of Power from Gollum.)

'I don't know.'

'So take a look.'

The anti-materialist would fumble in his jeans, pull out a handful of coins and take inventory. 'Uh . . . four and ninepence . . .'

'Give it to me.'

'What?'

'Just give it to me.'

Reluctantly he would hand over the four and ninepence. I'd drop it into the shoebox that passed as a cash register. 'Now, inside, okay?'

Finally realising that he'd gained admission for slightly less than half price, the anti-materialist would gather his pragmatism and scuttle on into the crowd, the noise, the smoke and the lightshow. The easiest to handle were the totally vacant. They would be put through the same routine as the anti-materialist, but without the dialogue. Their proffered coins would be taken, and they'd be pushed gently on. The real pests were the ones who wanted not only to get in, but also to make a point, like the fool taking exception to my Hulk T-shirt. 'You really need to do something about your ego, man.'

'I don't think so.'

'No, really, man. Mellow out.'

Usually I was patient, but on occasion a verbal chastisement had to be delivered, if only to retain my own sanity. 'Listen, fuckhead, try doing what I'm doing without a fucking ego.'

The hippie would recoil from the out-and-out fascist bastard. 'Oh wow, man . . .'

'Just get inside, okay?'

I didn't need any criticism of my Hulk T-shirt. I was damned proud of it. It had been hard to obtain and was a psychological weapon in the UFO door operation in which I was the sole authority figure. Once inside the club, the hippies could do pretty much what they wanted. The only two points at which a semblance of, if not order, then at least coherent form had to be imposed were moving the bands on and off the stage and getting everyone into the club, making sure that at least the majority of them paid so that the bands, the rent and all the other expenses could be met, and the venture could continue to function. The first of these tasks was performed by a redoubtably efficient stage manager called Dave Harper, who would eventually be offered a job by the Doors. I did my best to take care of the latter, feeling, most of the time, that I was attempting to stuff 300 or 400 dithering and recalcitrant white rabbits down a very narrow

Lewis Carroll rabbit hole, which endowed me with a certain reputation for aggression that I have been trying to live down ever since.

UFO was the next logical stage in counterculture public events. It attempted to re-create the ambience of the *IT* launch party, with its unique combination of experimental rock show and do-your-own-thing free-form theatre, on a regular basis. Although maybe a dozen or more individuals made decisive contributions, the prime movers behind UFO were Hoppy – yet again – who at that time seemed to be achieving velocities close to the speed of light, and a character called Joe Boyd, a very tall and somewhat aloof American expatriate whose roots were in the US East Coast folk-music scene from which Dylan had just made his last exit.

In the beginning, the partnership between Hoppy and Boyd looked like a symmetrical set of checks and balances. It was only in later times of crisis that the flaws in the equation would reveal themselves, and that the duo would come to represent the very basic conflict between hard commercial opportunism and radical shooting for the moon. The initial strength of the two lay in the fact that Hoppy understood the freaks and Boyd 'knew about music'. Hoppy had a gut understanding of the hippies' idealism, while Joe was able to bridge the gap between psychedelic mania and rock & roll booking agents. *IT*, also Hoppy's baby, was now appearing on the newsstands every fortnight, pretty much without fail, and could be used as a means of spreading the word, while Joe could organise a roster of bands that would bring in the right kind of crowd. They had even managed to come up with a venue.

The Blarney Club was located in a basement halfway up Tottenham Court Road, ironically just a few doors from the police station. It was an old Irish dance club, with a legal capacity of just over 600, a place of show bands, Guinness, a revolving mirror ball and a polished parquet dance floor. One of the first problems was the Irish drunks who wandered in on a Friday night wondering why the fuck there weren't jigs, reels and a Joseph Locke tenor singing 'Danny Boy'. The owner was Mr Gannon – I never knew his first name, he was always Mr Gannon – an old-time, West End club owner who had a good relationship with the police (he used to drop off a case of Scotch at the police station at Christmas) and generally maintained a quiet life. I didn't think he had a clue what he was letting himself in for when he cut the deal leasing Friday nights to Hoppy and Joe.

Although the Roundhouse party provided one model for how UFO should be organised, a few others were already available. In San Francisco, the organisation known as the Family Dog, headed by Chet Helms, was already staging psychedelic events at the Avalon Ballroom, and promoter Bill Graham was in the process of putting on similar shows at the Fillmore Auditorium. Both were basically more commercial and accessible versions of the 'Acid Tests' run by Ken Kesey and his Merry Pranksters. Kesey's Prankster parties had been little more than a series of planned assaults on all the social conventions of the time, funded in the main by the proceeds from his bestseller *One Flew Over the Cuckoo's Nest*. Travelling in their psychedelic bus, and deploying sound, lights and considerable quantities of acid-spiked Koolaid, the Pranksters had gone about the business of spreading the doctrine of anarchic hedonism and mind expansion via the use of LSD; in course of their campaigning, they had united such diverse groups as the Hell's Angels, the Grateful Dead and the San Francisco Mime Troupe. The Pranksters also created the first market for the legendary acid manufactured by renegade genius chemist Owsley Stanley III, whose underground lab, at its 1967 peak of production, was turning out trips in batches of one and a half million a time.

Kesey himself had first encountered acid in 1959 while acting as a paid volunteer in an experimental LSD-25 programme at the Veterans' Hospital in Menlo Park in the Bay Area. Kesey and some hundred or so others, mainly students and bohemians, were paid a hundred dollars a dose to drop the acid and then allow researchers to study their reactions. (Allen Ginsberg also took his first trip as part of a similar programme, commenting that it was like 'being hooked into Big Brother'. What neither Kesey nor Ginsberg knew at the time was that the secret sponsor of both sets of experiments was the Central Intelligence Agency's MKULTRA experimental mind-control division. It might thus be possible to claim that the CIA inadvertently initiated the 'Summer of Love'. Or perhaps not so inadvertently. The rumour has regularly been repeated by Bill Burroughs and others that the CIA actually promoted the spread of acid as a recreational street drug, in order to see what might happen. If this were the case, the experiment went disastrously wrong. The agency's alleged hope was that it would yield a docile and malleable civilian population; instead they got a plague of uncontrollable hippies.

What went down at the Avalon, the Fillmore and UFO was considerably more tame than any of the Acid Tests. It was a formulaic combination of rock bands and lightshows that could be presented week after week without the absolute need to get out of town on the magic bus after each show, but it didn't preclude a whole lot of extraneous weirdness. From Manfred selling his acid to the bizarre creativity of David Medalla's dance troupe, the Exploding Galaxy, the night trip shape-warping and weird scenes in a lot of gold mines were far from eliminated. All things were possible just as long as the organisers weren't legally liable.

What took everyone by surprise was just how fast the manifestation mushroomed. Within a matter of weeks the crowds at UFO grew from seventy or eighty to several hundred, and the patrons ranged from Eton and Oxford, King's Road groovers to ex-mods who'd been fired from the Ford plant at Dagenham for being stoned on the line. Although hardly the kind of club that needed celebrity attendance for validation, the rock & roll elite began to show up, placing more stress on the door staff by their unwillingness to stand in line and their stellar need for preferential treatment. Pete Townshend was probably the celebrity regular, showing up most weeks when he wasn't recording or on tour, and usually donating a cheque for a hundred pounds or so for the 'cause'. Keith Moon was in once, but left, deterred by the lack of alcohol. Eric Burdon made sure he was fucked-up before he arrived. Paul McCartney came down a few times, again exhibiting a nervousness about an outbreak of Beatlemania that never materialised. Jimi Hendrix always came very late, and sat in at least once on bass with Steve Howe from the band Tomorrow. And real flurry of interest occurred when, of all people, Christine Keeler appeared, in the company of some heavyweight pot dealers. She looked older and more worn than she had when the Profumo scandal was bringing down the Tory party, and also seemed to have had some kind of breast augmentation. Of all the celebs who ever hit UFO, she was the one who drew the most attention.

The sudden growth of UFO brought about my direct involvement. Entry to the club was being facilitated by a couple of inexperienced women, who found themselves completely swamped by the numbers and all the attendant hippie bullshit. I had no intention of taking over the door, but just stepped into the breach to break a potentially disastrous human traffic jam that had backed up the stairs and had the cops sending messages to 'get this scum off our pavement or we bust everybody'.

Enter the Hassle Guy like Paladin in *Have Gun, Will Travel.* 'Don't worry, ma'am, I've got it covered. I'll sort out the mess.'

In the few months since the Roundhouse party, I'd discovered that no one exactly applied for a job with the underground. If you recognised that something wasn't being done, you did it, and if you didn't immediately screw things up, everyone left you alone and within a matter of days you'd become a fixture. It was by this random osmosis that, in the spring of 1967, I not only found myself running the door at UFO, but part of the emergency crew putting out *IT* in the wake of its first bust.

Ticket to the Underground

In 1914, just before the curtain rose on the trench slaughter of World War I, Aleister Crowley and his mistress Leila Waddell hosted an event in London called the Rites of Eleusis. Over some four or five nights they presented a quasi-masonic ritual, music, poetry, dance and drama. Actors pronounced that God was dead with a ponderous Nietzschean finality, readings were given from the *Tibetan Book of the Dead* and, on the final night, the audience received, communion-style, the 'Elixir of the Gods' – in fact, red wine generously spiked with mescaline. As the punters tripped out, a chorus announced the dawning of the New Aeon based on Rabelais' Law of Thelema: 'Do what thou wilt'. Sound familiar?

Whatever Crowley's intentions may have been, the Rites of Eleusis didn't hurl the city into open revolt, and Jupiter didn't collide with Mars. Just like the UFO Club, or the dawn of the punks at the Roxy ten years later, it didn't, on its own, cause the downfall of the power structure, or the collapse of Western civilisation. Maybe all

[83]

these things were just over-hyped parties, or pieces of free-form performance art, which in itself is perfectly acceptable, unless one has pinned too many hopes on the power of the moment. I'm sure Crowley walked a fairly tortuous path before he staged the Rites of Eleusis; I know I did, before the aforementioned osmosis brought me to acting as gauleiter at the door of UFO.

The effective epicentre of osmosis proved to be Indica Books on Southampton Row, on the edge of time-honoured, politely nonconformist Bloomsbury. It sounds strange today, when small sub-genres in both music and literature have their own specialist shops, but stumbling into Indica was like a ticket to the magic kingdom. In those days everything except the run-of-the-mill had to be sought out and searched for. Better Books, on Charing Cross Road, could provide a reasonable selection of beat and contemporary poetry and novels. Dobell's Record Store, almost diagonally across the street, had jazz, blues and folk covered, Musicland on Berwick Street had the psychedelic imports, but that was about it. Even though John Peel was regularly playing Captain Beefheart on the radio, import copies of *Safe As Milk* were hard to find outside the West End of London. Most other things had to be hunted down with patience and diligence. Comic books, surf, hotrod, UFO and true-crime magazines could only be culled from the international newsagents in Old Compton Street. Even dirty bookshops did their part in that. A copy of William Burroughs' *Junkie* might be ferreted out from a pile of remaindered paperback American porn titles like *Slaves of Sin*, *Girl Love* and *I Was Backseat Dynamite*. Copies of the girly mag *Cavalier*, which carried writing by Paul Krassner and Harlan Ellison, could now and again be found, or an Olympia Press edition of *Tropic of Cancer* or *The Story of O*.

Coming out of this kind of depredation, it seemed that Indica Books had it all. City Lights poetry, a whole shelf of Burroughs, *Last Exit to Brooklyn*, Malcolm X, Tantric Yoga, Terry Southern, Timothy Leary, Mervyn Peake, the Marquis de Sade, J.G. Ballard and H.P. Lovecraft. Although Indica didn't profess to be a record store, the rack of LPs by the cash register held almost unobtainable treasures like Sun Ra, the Fugs, Eric Dolphy and the Holy Modal Rounders, as well as spoken-word performances by Burroughs, Ginsberg, Lenny

Bruce, Ezra Pound, Melvin Van Peebles and Lord Buckley. The magazine rack was another revelation. I discovered that, in the USA, underground newspapers were springing up like mushrooms in the dawn. Copies of the *San Francisco Oracle*, *Village Voice* and *East Village Other* out of New York, the *Fifth Estate* from Detroit and the *LA Free Press*, featuring Harlan Ellison's TV reviews, were displayed as one great newsprint temptation. My primary reason for going there was to pick up the latest issue of *IT*, but once inside the shop I lapsed into a kind of daze. From this wealth of communication and creativity it was almost possible to imagine that freaks had an entire media all of their own scattered about the planet.

Presiding over this wonderland was Miles, a bookishly pale and amiably academic, bespectacled Brian Jones, who handled books as though they were living entities, and who would have felt at home in a thirteenth-century monastic scriptorium, except for his profound love of women, and their reciprocal love of him. Miles was a compassionate and dignified man, simultaneously neat and fashionable, erudite and alarmingly well informed. He might have made a flamboyant Oxford don except that, like me, he was largely self-educated – in other words, he went to art school. In his case, Gloucestershire College of Art in Cheltenham, but otherwise our early back stories ran in parallel. Miles had also benefited from an art-school exposure to the twin inspirations of Marxism and bohemianism, and from these ingredients, plus jazz, poetry and rock 'n' roll, he had started building his own philosophical cocktail. He'd embraced CND more fully than I ever had. He'd taken part in the Aldermaston marches, while all I'd done was wear the badge.

In addition to the wonder of Indica itself, *IT* was being published in the basement, and, while I browsed the shelves wishing that I was independently wealthy and could buy all this stuff, odd figures would emerge from the bowels via a flight of steps to one side of the store, and I was irrationally reminded of Norman Bates keeping his mother in the root cellar. At first I simply went into the shop, looked around at some length, bought what I could afford and left. It wasn't because I was standoffish, or wanted to keep myself to myself, and it certainly wasn't because I didn't like the look of the people. A true confession that you may find hard to believe is that I am very shy. In order to deal with strangers, audiences and the public at large, I simply shut my subjective eyes and become someone else.

Therapists talk about the 'inner child', but I think what I've always employed is the 'outer son-of-a-bitch'. I've noticed in many of the accounts of these times, both contemporary and retrospective, that I'm referred to as 'fast-talking', 'a psychedelic gangster', 'a verbal wrecking ball', or words to that effect. I guess few realised that the energetic glibness and steamrollering persuasion I could bring into play when required had evolved as a façade – what cockneys call a 'front' – to protect my insecurities, inadequacies and pathological fears of rejection. Not that I had to use much front on Miles. The awkward part, as with Hoppy at the Roundhouse, was knowing how to sustain the conversation beyond the first pleasantries. 'Hey, great place you've got here.'

'Thanks.'

At that point it's hard, particularly for two Englishmen, to raise the exchange to the level of actual conversation. Fortunately, if memory serves, Miles was charitable enough to make the move for me, enquiring about my tastes and interests, and obliquely wanting to know what had brought me into his store in the first place. This was typical of Miles' gentlemanly manipulation of a situation. Nothing draws out a stranger more than letting him talk about his own enthusiasms. We discovered our parallel courses, except that Miles was far better connected. After all, he owned the damned bookshop, and I was merely a punter. But, with the ice broken, an increasingly lengthy conversation ensued, until Miles would take a break whenever I showed and we'd repair to the Kardomah Coffee House just up the street to shoot the radical shit in greater comfort.

I discovered that he had used his time after getting out of art school a good deal more profitably that I had. In addition to working on various embryonic underground press projects with Hoppy, he had cemented an alliance with Peter Asher, of the singing duo Peter and Gordon, whose sister Jane was Paul McCartney's current girlfriend, and with John Dunbar, who was then still married to Marianne Faithfull. Together they had formed Miles, Asher and Dunbar – giving themselves the acronym MAD – the holding company for Indica Books and the Indica Gallery. Both the bookstore and gallery had originally occupied the same building in Mason's Yard, off Duke

Street, St James, right next door to the ultra-trendy Scotch of St James nightspot. Later, Miles had moved the bookstore to Southampton Row, when Mason's Yard had become too crowded and chaotic.

As proprietor of the hottest hip bookstore in town, and through the contacts already established by Asher and Dunbar, Miles quickly numbered the more literate Beatles and Rolling Stones among his clients, and moved in some high hip circles, in which the first acid was making the rounds and to embrace the avant-garde was a chic necessity. He'd maintained a full and lively correspondence with both Allen Ginsberg and William Burroughs that went back to his college days, and served as a crucial link between the rock elite and the intelligentsia of Swinging London – what today might be called a facilitator of cultural interface. Even though he seemed to have a knack for opening pipelines to the rich and famous, Miles was ever the egalitarian – otherwise, what the hell was he doing taking coffee breaks with the likes of me?

Miles had given much consideration to the concepts of an alternative society, and where I was wholly obsessed with the infliction of creative damage, he was already thinking in terms of an entrepreneurial materialism, in which freaks would establish their own means of underground distribution, initially in the fields of music, art and literature, that could outmanoeuvre and outperform the less adaptable systems of overground capitalism. Despite his socialist roots, Miles was very aware that capitalism might be needed to fight capitalism. The political acceptability of making money within the revolution would be a continuous bone of contention throughout the entire period covered by this book. In the Sixties the counterculture often came close to blows on the subject of 'hip capitalism', while a decade later, when the Clash signed with CBS, it was condemned as a betrayal. Miles had been to an early Sixties youth conference in Cuba and had seen the frustration of a revolution under embargo and strapped for cash.

One reason that I never fought with Miles on the sensitive question of economic pragmatism was base self-interest. The systems he wanted to create were exactly the ones needed to make my own chosen endeavours a reality. To get my rocks off, I needed clubs to play in, magazines to write for and, later, the facilities to make and distribute records. I also admired Miles' work ethic. Something was always cooking. If it wasn't the bookstore it was *IT*, if it wasn't *IT* it was UFO, and what separated him from the dog-pack of psychedelic hustlers was that he seemed to be in for the long haul and not just the quick score. In the underground, a work ethic was what separated the sheep from the goats. Too many middle-class acid-head dropouts, instead of marching forward resolutely into the utopian dawn, became lethargic, lazy and larcenous and, when challenged, able to come up with more excuses than a pimp going to jail.

It may have been my own work ethic that caused Miles to decide I should involve myself in *IT* and suggest that I should come down into the Indica basement and meet Tom McGrath, the newspaper's then editor. McGrath was an anti-establishment old-timer who had previously edited the CND paper *Peace News*. He seemed worn, and I'd discover later that he had a not inconsiderable heroin habit. I'm sure the very last thing he needed on that autumn afternoon was a youthful maniac all fired up to explain the shortcomings of his paper. The more nervous I felt, the more impassioned I became. In a nutshell, *IT* should stop printing the interminable letters of Ezra bloody Pound, and the dumb cartoons of Jeff Nuttall, and throw all its weight behind the rock & roll youth revolt. McGrath politely heard me out and then played a Zen trick I would pocket for future use. 'Okay, kid, if you don't think this stuff's being covered, why don't you go out and cover it yourself.' In the space of an hour or so I found that I'd become *IT*'s ad hoc rock & roll revolution editor. As I walked away, I was a dog with two tails, wagging both of them. Not only had I penetrated the heart of the underground, but I'd been hired to fulfil a specific function. What I didn't know was that when a paper rarely paid its contributors or even the nominal staff, assignments and appointments were all too easy to hand out.

My first move was to write a lengthy polemic that started, 'Let's face it, we're living in something of a police state . . .' It went on to make the point that any revolution that included marijuana as one of its articles of faith was vulnerable. The authorities didn't have to mount McCarthy-style witchhunts. We could simply be arrested under the all-pervasive drug laws. Far from advocating that the would-be revolutionary should stop smoking dope, though, I counselled quasi-criminal cunning and recognition of the danger. The piece was forceful, if gauche, and people seemed to feel that I could actually write. For my part, I was overjoyed to have been published the first time out.

Down the Up Rabbit Hole

I had followed the White Rabbit – in this instance, Miles – down the rabbit hole, but I couldn't shake the feeling that everyone knew everyone else, and I didn't, and I had to find out everything there was to know as fast as I could, before anyone could figure out that I didn't really belong there after all. Once again my feelings of inadequacy were brought into play as a means of motivation. And there was plenty to learn, and many strange characters from whom to learn it, in this warren called the underground. They ranged from, at one extreme, an individual called Bart Hughes, a mad Dutchman who believed that drugs were already redundant and all one needed for full spiritual enlightenment was to drill a hole in one's skull, to Harvey Matusow, an American communist who had informed on his comrades for Senator Joe McCarthy and his FBI Red-hunters, but had then turned around and revealed all in a book entitled *I Was a Spy for the FBI*.

Both Matusow and Hughes, each in their own way, were typical of the underground before the media furore, and the commercialisation. Matusow was one of the oddities who gravitated to London in 1966–7, as if drawn by the magnet of young raw energy. Hughes, although unique in his theories, was also representative of the diversity that preceded the Peter Max, flower-power commercialisation. His promotion of the idea of trepanation, and quasi-scientific doctrine of brain-blood volume, left me totally cold. I was, and still am, much too squeamish to consider boring a small hole in my skull to allow a greater degree of oxygenation of the brain, supposedly to produce both hallucinations and enhanced mental capacity. The idea may go back all the way to the ancient Egyptians, but forget it. I'll take the drugs, thank you kindly. Hippie self-medication would cause enough trouble, and I was extremely relieved that DIY psychedelic surgery didn't catch on, although stories circulated of freaks who'd sought nirvana with a Black & Decker drill.

The disc jockey John Peel proved an important early input. His overnight slot on the pirate station Radio London, entitled the *Perfumed Garden*, came as close to magic as a radio show can, and mercifully required no brain surgery. You simply lay in bed and listened, while Peel decorated the darkness with both the new-and-emergent and the tried-and-trusted – *Between the Buttons*, *Blonde On Blonde*, all the way back to Howlin' Wolf and John Lee Hooker. It was on Peel's Radio London show that I first heard the innovative, the influential and the just plain weird: Captain Beefheart, the Butterfield Blues Band, the Standells, Moby Grape, Buffalo Springfield, the Misunderstood, Richie Havens, Sky Saxon and the Seeds, Tim Buckley, Love and, perhaps most important for me, the Mothers of Invention.

Peel had been a 'British Invasion' DJ in California, had left the USA under a mysterious cloud, but brought enough of a West Coast sensibility with him to separate the wheat from the early psychedelic chaff. He also championed home-grown talent, his most notable discovery being Marc Bolan, first as part of the band John's Children, then on his own, and finally with Steve Took in the first Tyrannosaurus Rex. Peel was also prone to complain between records of the deadly boredom of life on a pirate radio ship in the middle of the cold North Sea. He seemed to like receiving letters, so I started writing to him, commencing a correspondence which would reveal, among other things, that we both had a love for heavy-duty Fifties rock, especially Gene Vincent and Jerry Lee Lewis; a retro taste frowned upon by the trendsetters of the day as being too fundamental, but what the hell? It was our secret.

Not all the important music, however, came from the radio or from the United States. Although it would be some months before the major label-signing boom of new 'underground' bands, first flourishings were happening all over. Some of the most significant were the shows being staged at All Saints' Hall in Notting Hill, organised by Peter Jenner and Andrew King, who would shortly form Blackhill Enterprises, organise the free concerts in Hyde Park and, for their sins, become the Deviants' booking agents. The shows, almost a precursor to UFO, were fundraisers for something called the

Notting Hill Free School, which I never really understood or saw in operation.

The main attraction was Pink Floyd. At the Roundhouse the Floyd had been faceless technicians, but now I could see they had two distinct frontmen. Although drummer Nick Mason and organist Rick Wright remained in the dappled shadows of the lightshow, the other two assumed personalities simply because they were standing four-square and casting long shadows on the projection screen behind them. Roger Waters stood tall behind his long Rickenbaker bass, but the member of the band to whom the eye was most naturally drawn was guitarist Syd Barrett. In all respects Syd, with his femininity, psychosis and curls, was the embodiment of psychedelic male beauty. In a satin shirt with puff sleeves and flowing collar, he was Lord George Byron with a telecaster. If only by the perfection of his eyeshadow, Syd Barrett was clearly going to be a heart-throb superstar, unless, of course, he went mad in the process.

Impressionable hippies would tell me the Floyd were playing the sound of consciousness expanding, but I wasn't buying that one, except in so far as the Floyd did seem to tap a direct line to both the horror and sadness of the tiny human juxtapositioned against the infinite universe, which I discovered from my own neural atrocities is not always the best background abstraction against which to trip. Space isn't the place. Long before *Alien*, Dan Dare had taught me that in space no one could hear you scream. The Floyd sang about Neptune and Titan, and setting the controls for the heart of the sun, but all was not science fiction, and I often regretted that the Floyd assumed such a crucially influential role in the London version of psychedelia. They seemed so Oxbridge cold in their merciless cosmos: the Stephen Hawkings of rock & roll. They lacked the Earth-warmth of, say, the Grateful Dead, and things might have been a whole lot different if their sound hadn't permeated so many of those formative London nights.

From my own position of not inconsiderable paranoia, I can empathise with Syd reaching for a philosophic and audio impossibility, and coming unglued behind the unrewarded effort, but my instinct was that, without Pink Floyd, we might have been a little kinder to each other. Some of these feelings were confirmed by visiting Americans. Chet Helms, when confronted by the early Floyd on a visit to the UK, was less than impressed. 'I don't think anyone could play a break . . . all feedback and lights.'

If, on the other hand, you were looking for both the warmth and sexuality of the Earth between electronic journeys into space, another artist provided all that and more, and he first came to me by the unlikely medium of television.

Playing Guitar with His Teeth (I)

As its slogan said, the weekend started there. *Ready, Steady, Go!* was blasting out of the TV in the kitchen, but I was doing something in another room, one of those tasks that you can't leave before it's completed or I would have gone to look very much sooner. An electric guitar had started the intro to a song I'd never heard before, a long rolling, melodic riff, and the guitar was brilliant. My first guess might have been Jeff Beck. It had all the power and attack of Beck, but also a warmth that he never approached. A voice that I didn't recognise cut in singing. Not a great voice, not Otis Redding by any means, but a voice with a definite appeal, and one whose owner had listened a lot to Bob Dylan's phrasing. The guy seemed to be singing a song about having shot his woman and being on the lam to Mexico.

'Mick, quick. Come and look at this!' Joy from the kitchen.

'Just coming.' Irritably, I still had to disengage from whatever task was at hand.

'You've really got to see this guy.'

'I'm coming, I'm coming.'

'He's got hair like you and Bob Dylan.'

The music sounded magnificent, but the first guitar solo was starting. In those days songs were generally not too long. With the exception of 'Like a Rolling Stone' and 'McArthur Park', three minutes tops. Joy administered the *coup de grâce*. 'And he's playing the guitar with his teeth.'

'With his teeth?' I dropped what I was doing. Enough was enough. I sped to the kitchen and caught my first glimpse of Jimi Hendrix just as he was finishing 'Hey Joe'.

The Highest Percentage of Social Deviants

The band had a name. The Social Deviants. It came from an article I'd read in the *Observer* about how the London Borough of Tower Hamlets – the new cheesy County Hall name for our manor – had a higher per capita percentage of social deviants than anywhere else in the country. Almost from the moment I thought it up, I hated the name Social Deviants. I think I was excited for long enough to sell it to the boys in the band, but then realised I'd made a terrible mistake. It was just so damned hard to say. In situations where being a rock band was more than enough to earn one a beating from lorry drivers or the constabulary, it didn't improve matters to come out with some bloody silly group name that implied that one was not only a long-haired poof, but also some child-molesting, axe-murdering junkie pervert. 'Did you say Social Deviants, sunshine? You taking the piss?' Thus, over the course of time, it became shortened to the Deviants and, among the hard core, just the Devies.

Not only did we have a name, but we had a guitar player who'd actually showed up for more than three rehearsals. His name was Clive Maldoon, a South London boy who wanted to be either Pete Townshend or Roy Wood of the Move. Clive was an enthusiastic if uncouth youth, which fortunately meant that he was infinitely loyal to the worst impulses of rock & roll, which I happily indulged. We also acquired a drummer who proved bizarre even by our standards. Benny was a born-again Zionist. He wore mohair suits and bow ties, and idolised Joe Morello, the drummer with the Dave Brubeck Quartet, which meant that his idea of psychedelic percussion was constantly to shift from time signature to time signature, a demented exercise that caused Pete (also a closet modern jazzer) to do things to his bass that might have been Charlie Mingus, but were more likely sheer incompetence, while Maldoon slammed out all the feedback that his yobbo heart desired. Ralph had unfortunately returned to Newcastle for the benefit of his health, so no keyboard buffered the mania. In these modern times, which have seen the likes of Trent Reznor and Thurston Moore, this might sound like a perfectly viable recipe for success. Back in the Summer of Love, though, just about everyone hated us, and I'll freely admit that we served up plenty to hate. If the sound wasn't ugly and intrusive enough, or the raps sufficiently offensive, there was always the Social Deviants' lightshow.

It had been impossible to keep Alex Stowell out of the band. When he discovered that the Social Deviants 'didn't need a harmonica player', Alex decided he was going to be the lightshow. First in his room in Martin's house, and then in the rehearsal cellar under mine, he went to work with industrial-strength lightbulbs, strange reflectors, what looked like bits of old telephone switch-boards, sheets of plywood and a mile or more of wires of different gauge and colour, doing a passable impression of a B-movie mad scientist.

At first we were quite convinced that all Alex was going to achieve was his own electrocution, but slowly the chaos was compacted until he had the mechanism relatively portable and ready for the stage. If he had learned anything from the giant sphere of vending-machine cups, it was that his inventions should at least fit through the door. In its finished form, the Stowell lightshow consisted of a large box like an amplifier, which contained all the relays and what-have-you to run the system. Two huge boxes, some five feet by three – his version of 'speakers' – housed a dozen 500-watt lamps. Where other lightshows were projected behind the band, and sought to synthesise some mellow psychotropic experience, Alex aimed these blinding beams directly into the retinas of the audience and synthesised something akin to advanced brainwashing by the KGB. In the middle of it all stood Stowell himself, right there on stage, like a red-bearded Borg, with wires and electrical contacts attached to his hands, playing this arcing, crackling guitar-like unit of his own creation.

To everyone's amazement, this unlikely combo actually went out and played in public. Happenings at the Roundhouse, some odd experimental gigs at the Marquee and Pink Floyd's efforts at All Saints' Hall were enough to convince a few club owners and college social secretaries to take a chance with this new underground thing. It seemed vaguely fitting that we should open for the Creation, an art-mod band, third-string variation on the Who, riding high with their quasi-hit 'Painter Man', whose act featured energetic spray painting of backdrop canvases instead of smashing their instruments. The East London speed-freaks who had come along to see the Creation didn't seem to mind us too much. Maybe we weren't too good, but what the fuck? At the other extreme, whoever hired us to open for Geno Washington and the Ram Jam Band was either a moron or a bastard, because it almost resulted in us being terminated with extreme skinhead prejudice.

It was somewhere down in the hinterlands of the South London suburbs, at some old *palais de danse* that actually had functioning curtains. We probably should have had more sense than to take the gig in the first place, but a gig was a gig. Washington, although he never really made it on record, had one of the top live bands in the country, playing mainly covers of Stax and Motown, to a huge and fanatical following of skinheads who greeted their hero with their very own 'Sieg heil', near-Nazi chant.

'Gee-no!'

'Gee-no!'

'Gee-no!'

'Gee-no!'

A rabble-rousing black DJ introduced us. 'And now, a big hand for . . . *the Social Deviants!*'

The curtains opened and just one look was all it took. The skinheads saw us in our self-invented hippie outfits and didn't hesitate. Straight at the stage, at us – like one of those Chinese Red Army human waves out of the Korean War. Have you ever seen a drummer wrap his arms around his entire kit, pick it up and run? Not easy, but Benny accomplished it. As the singer, I was lucky; I may have been closest to the lynch mob, but I had no equipment to save, and even a microphone stand with which to defend myself. This was Benny's last show as a Deviant. He might have entertained fantasies of joining the Israeli army, but to be lynched by skinheads was definitely not part of his agenda.

Whether this incident was the trigger or not, Benny went and was quickly replaced by Russell Hunter, a curly-haired chemical adventurer whom I found via contacts at UFO, and who would remain more or less on the drum stool for the first full phase of the Deviants, then go on to do his time with the Pink Fairies in all of their incarnations; he would also become the bane of my life for the next three years. Initially Russell was a definite step forward. He was a more conventional rock drummer than Benny, if coming straight from the Keith Moon school could be defined as conventional. He also took an instant, if amused, dislike to Clive Maldoon, saddling him with the nickname 'Grobber'. But, most important, he seemed unfazed by the idea of joining a band who 'can't fucking play'.

The 'can't fucking play' accusation was tossed at the Social Deviants over and over again, until it became one tired bloody mantra. Of course we couldn't play, you retard sons-of-bitches, but we made one hell of a ragged and magnificent din. Who set the goddamned rules, anyway? This was the Sixties and rules were being smashed right, left and centre. Cutting-edge performance art had the Living Theater, and the legendary Rudolf Schwarzkogler, who amputated pieces of himself for the paying customers, and supposedly bled to death after hacking off his own penis; and Otto Muehl, who killed poultry and tossed teargas into his audiences. Who was taking it upon themselves to decide that the Social Deviants were somehow not deserving of a hearing? The world of rock & roll, despite its pretensions to hell raising, exposed itself as tiresomely conservative, with extremely limited criteria of what was 'good' and 'bad'.

Playing Guitar with His Teeth (II)

I knew I couldn't survive without seeing Jimi Hendrix live, and when I read in the *Melody Maker* that he was going to play at the Marquee, I knew I had to be there, come hell or high water. Hendrix had already played at the Bag O' Nails, and, according to local rock gossip, had completely freaked out Jeff Beck, motivating him to phone Pete Townshend and Eric Clapton immediately and tell his fellow guitar gods that he'd just seen the end of the world as they knew it.

Of course, Beck eventually calmed down, and Townshend and Clapton were not instantly consigned to the labour exchange, but that still didn't preclude the fact that a dramatic stranger had arrived in town, with a potential majesty to rival that of Charlie Parker, Robert Johnson or even Elvis Presley.

On the appointed night I arrived at the Marquee in what I figured was plenty of time to be assured of getting in, but already the line was halfway down Wardour Street. All the usual suspects were hustling pills to the waiting crowd, just like when the Who had played their residency, only now acid was being offered as a new and radical alternative to SKF Dexedrine and French Blues. I knew the capacity of the club, and the situation looked hopeless. The crowd on the street could fill the place twice over. So what could a poor boy do? I decided the best thing was to go into the Ship, the pub that during the day was the watering hole of the British movie industry, and which, at night, served as an annex to the Marquee. Perhaps with a pint in front of me I could rationalise this crushing disappointment in the making.

The Ship is a long, narrow pub with a bar that runs half its length and then curves around to the wall. The seats next to where the bar meets the wall have always been recognised as the best in the house. They give the occupant uninterrupted eye contact with the bartender, a clear view of who is coming in and out and an area of defensible space in which it is hard to be bothered by unwanted conversationalists. All in all, this was an ideal place for Jimi Hendrix to be sitting, should he have wanted a quiet drink before his set at the Marquee. Ideal it might have been, but it took me totally by surprise to find that the man himself was actually seated there, with the hair, the scarves, the jewellery and wearing the black Victorian hussar's jacket from the famous photographs by Gered Mankowitz, or one very much like it. He was talking to an attractive blonde, and was protected by a four-man phalanx of burly roadies and minders.

I believe our modern celebrity worship would now turn such an occurrence into a bedlam of ravening fans and paparazzi, but in those less complicated days the criterion was still one of cool. Those who had drifted in from the mêlée outside the Marquee obviously and instantly recognised Hendrix, but their only intrusion was a shouted comment, a wave or a swift thumbs up. I certainly would not have approached the man, had not one of the roadies, a stalwart known as Bazz, beckoned me over. I had met Bazz via Joy, who knew him from the days when he'd roadied on the northern club circuit. Now he worked for the Nice, but was out on loan to the Jimi Hendrix Experience. I moved to the end of the bar and Bazz introduced us. I shook hands with the new guitar virtuoso and immediately noticed that his hands were huge and pliable, like those of a star basketball player. He was soft-spoken and seemed shy and a little overwhelmed by all that was happening to him.

We grinned at each other, acknowledging our near-identical hairstyles, and then I found myself in another of those awkwardly pointless conversations. Talking to Miles for the first time had been hard enough, but what the fuck do you say to *Jimi Hendrix* that doesn't come out sounding excruciatingly lame? Yes, I told him how much I admired his playing, and he, in turn, nodded modestly. I suddenly realised he wasn't actually any better at this kind of interaction than I was.

'Are you coming to see the show tonight?'

I hesitated. That was the question I'd just been asking myself. 'That's why I came down here, but . . .'

He looked concerned. 'There's a problem?'

'Only that you seem to have sold out the place twice over.'

Hendrix glanced at Bazz, and Bazz nodded. 'Don't worry about it.'

Now you might think that, as an egalitarian and man of the people, I would turn down such preferential treatment – yeah, right. Dream on. With Bazz opening all doors, both real and metaphoric, we moved into the Marquee, and not just into the body of the club, but on into the bar, through into the dressing room with its beer stains and its legendary graffiti like 'CLAPTON *ISN'T* GOD!' and 'PETE TOWNSHEND IS A ROCKER AND A NOSE TO BOOT!' When Hendrix started his set, we advanced right onto the side of the stage, so that I was standing no more than twelve feet from him, with a completely unhampered view.

Anything one might now say about Jimi Hendrix on stage has to be essentially redundant. For more than thirty years we've listened to the recordings and watched the films and video clips, and it is almost impossible to re-create the absolute awe at not only seeing the man play, but from such a vantage point. His energy was superhuman. To say that he was driven by a demon would be trite, and misleading, since there was absolutely nothing demonic about Jimi. At the risk of sounding like some New Age ditz, the shriek of Hendrix's guitar was truly a cry of love. He loved what he was doing to such a quantum degree that it encompassed the entire audience. His blatant sexuality was, of course, supremely evident, but to interpret it as sinister you'd have to be either a monstrous prude or a pathetic racist. His dirty boogie had no mean streak, and his technique was so effortless that he was able to take time out to joke, frolic and tease.

Most critics concentrated on the flamboyant showboating, the playing behind his head, the picking with his tongue and teeth, but I was more impressed by the smaller moves, the simple hammering of the strings with his fluent right hand, the easing of the whammy bar, the actual flexing of the neck against his body to produce slight variations of tone and nuance. It might seem odd to use the word 'nuance' in the context of such wildly aggressive music played at deafening volume, but Hendrix's attention to detail amid the maelstrom was uncanny. As he moved into the more profound and introspective parts of his solos, I could almost see his mind working, and his intensity of rapt concentration as he eased through the magnetic fields of the Marshall stack, exploiting each unique fluctuation between the speaker coils and the pickups on his guitar. One of Hendrix's favourite images was that of the Merman, the quasi-human who could swim with the fishes and dance with the dolphins. Maybe that was how he saw his guitar playing, as a Merman surging through the bubblefields of an electronic sea.

Although everyone else in the room was clearly focused on the man's guitar playing, I was also listening to his vocals. Clearly afraid of his own voice, believing that it was in no way a comparable instrument to his guitar, his singing was often a throwaway punctuation to his guitar parts. And yet, limited as Hendrix might have thought it, he could be moving and evocative when he sang 'Like a Rolling Stone' with so much more sympathy than Dylan's accusatory original, or shouted with joy on 'Stone Free', or when he did his later versions of Dylan's 'All Along the Watchtower', or his amazing reading of the Beatles' 'Sergeant Pepper's Lonely Hearts Club Band'. While Hendrix admitted he didn't have the vocal power of James Brown or his old employer, Little Richard, it heartened me to see how much attention he paid to phrasing and content, and he was able to use them as part of his seduction of the audience.

Over the course of the rest of his life I would see Jimi Hendrix many more times, but never with the proximity or the real (or imagined) insight of that night at the Marquee, except one time, when the insight was of a very different kind. Later in the summer of 1967 I was booked to appear on the TV show *Late Night Lineup* and talk to the bright and attractive host Joan Bakewell (dubbed by the contemporary media 'the thinking man's crumpet') about some dumb topic like 'what we hippies really want'. While waiting to make my contribution, rather than just leaving me to drink in the green room, a production assistant took me to a control room overlooking another studio where, to my amazement, Hendrix was recording for TV. While he ran through 'Purple Haze', wringing the maximum impact from his guitar, the engineer, a forty-something timeserver with a pipe and Fair Isle sweater, who would have been happier running sound for Alma Cogan or Matt Monro, slapped on more and more limiters, muttering angrily to himself, until he'd made Hendrix's supernatural guitar sound as though it was being broadcast over a phone line.

'I don't know what this silly bastard thinks he's doing, coming in here making a racket like that.'

His attempts to get some Bert Weedon dance-band guitar sound said it all about the widening culture gap between the generations. Finally he took his hands off the board in a gesture of surrender and turned to the onlookers. 'I mean, who booked this prat? Call that a guitar? He can't even fucking play.'

Art to the Rescue

The fingers of my left hand were twisted into her long, light brown hair. More of it fell across her face and brushed against my skin and the yellow velvet of my jeans. Her head bobbed, her left hand and long orange nails dug into my thigh, and my breath came in short, sharp gasps. My right hand was on her left breast, and my imagination couldn't believe that it was finally being overtaken by reality. Her lips and tongue were so diligent and willing, and my flesh so eager and weak. Only a few feet away people were laughing, talking and arguing, a crowd of total strangers, but, because they were looking out from the light, they couldn't see us even when they glanced in our general direction. On one level this was nothing more than a cheap and naughty thrill-in-the-dark blowjob, with the added jolt from the possible danger of discovery; on another, it was oral sex of massive symbolic significance. In the black rubble of the backstage Roundhouse, I didn't know her and she didn't know me, but in the very anonymity of the encounter I was filled with a sense of all-consuming triumph and a form of physical vindication of a kind that I had never experienced before. I was losing my rock & roll virginity.

Of course, even with the nameless art-school band, girls had been there, but they were friends, acquaintances, easy action or elusive nymphs of aching desire. They knew us – and took us or rejected us – for who we were, and were little impressed with our rocker pretensions. There, in the darkness on the outer circumference of the Roundhouse, she on her knees, me on my feet, my back against the dirty brickwork, with Victorian railway soot and antique plaster marking the shoulderblades of my sweat-soaked purple shirt, the pretensions had finally worked. This woman was not giving sex to me as a human being, per se, but to the singer with the band – an otherness, a symbol, a thing of my own creating. The odds were that I'd never know her well enough to guess at her motivation, at what brought her to that heated trembling, crouching connection in the darkness – indeed, I would never know her at all. That was the kick. Maybe she was operating according to her own inadequacies. Maybe she was breaking imposed patterns of school, religion and family by engaging in anonymous and all-but-public sex. Maybe she was looking for her part of the fun and applause by sucking the cock of the boy who had just come off the stage. Or maybe she was just erotically deranged. Frankly, my dear, I didn't give a damn. That I didn't care was the whole point, and therefore, before I'm accused of cruel objectification, let me point out that any objectification was at the very least a two-way street. I was certainly an object, but an object of desire, and I was revelling in it.

Oh Jesus, yes, the climax was electric, probably more than the sum of its parts. My legs trembled, my spine stiffened and then I sagged. She rose to her feet, pressing against me, then drew back and smiled knowingly into my face. Mad or not, she fully understood the nature of the transaction, and how little-boy grateful I was. Then she kissed me hard, my come sticky on her lips and chin. Was this, when you got down to it, the taste of fame? She took hold of my hand and led me back towards the crowd and the lights and the more public part of backstage, where I knew some booze was stashed and joints passed underhand. Our momentary night-whisper world was gossamer history; we'd quickly part and I'd see her, in short minutes, talking intimately with a well-known black radical. I wasn't dumped, we had both just moved on.

To recount this story feels a little strange. It echoes like a chest-beating boast, but the sexual response is such a part of rock & roll that to ignore it would be a self-censoring deception. Every rock & roller, from Elvis to Eno, took up the profession with at least the partial motivation of gratuitous orgasm, and I was no exception. That this young woman in semi-sheer chiffon and much-too-hippie eye make-up had all but jumped on me within minutes of my leaving the spotlight seems deserving of record. Like I said, the grateful death of my rock 'n' roll virginity. As a posturing whore, I had made my first sale.

The occasion was the Dialectics of Liberation conference at the Roundhouse, and the Social Deviants had become part of the event by a circuitous route typical of the new phase of what was laughingly called our career. We had been accepted into art, and not before time, either, since we were running hard up against the indisputable awareness that, without a radical rethinking of our entire attitude and approach to music, we were too outlandish for the regular sub-Yardbirds club circuit in the London suburbs. Either we found a new arena or we'd have to concede defeat and give up the fight.

The Dialectics of Liberation conference was a perfect example of why the Sixties were not famous for their quality of rational thought or discussion. The weekend of seminars, lectures and free interaction was promoted as a very big deal, with all of the heavyweight names of the era supposedly pledged to attend – Allen Ginsberg, Emmet Grogan of the Diggers, black-power leader Stokely Carmichael, radical psychiatrist R.D. Laing, Julian Beck of the Living Theater, Michael X, Timothy Leary, even philosopher Herbert Marcuse, plus a guy named Gregory Bateson, who claimed to be an expert on the language of whales and dolphins and may actually have been their human representative on dry land. With typical Sixties pre-event grandiosity, this gathering of what were supposedly the best minds of our generation was intended to solve all the problems of the planet. In fact, it devolved into yet another fine mess.

The post-conference entertainment was being organised by

Carolee Schneeman, a New York conceptual artist and choreographer, who was part of the group centred around Robert Rauschenberg and the idea of 'happenings'. Some idiot told Carolee that the Social Deviants were the authentic music of the underground, so we were hired. I believe she was under the impression that we were some electronic wind-chime ensemble, or at least the basically acoustic cacophony of the Fugs, because when we slammed into a teeth-grinding fuzz-tone thrash, a few people actually blanched. The performance was made even more edgy by it being Russell Hunter's debut gig and the fact that we were lamentably under-rehearsed, saving our lives by coasting on fury rather than sound.

Although we didn't realise it at the time, we actually provided a fitting finale to an entire weekend that had been characterised by anger and conflict. Stokely Carmichael had delivered what appeared to be a set speech, which was received with something close to a standing ovation. He then turned the tables by announcing that he'd actually been reading a speech by Adolf Hitler and castigated the crowd as a bunch of white-motherfucker closet Nazis. Later Michael X would cause even more furore by attempting to 'out-black power' Stokely, by waxing even more abusive and, in the process, laying the groundwork for the six months he spent in jail under the Race Relations Act. More chaos ensued when Laing and his Kingsley Hall anti-psychiatry gang took up a massive chunk of conference time, demonstrating what really happened when the lunatics assumed management of the asylum. I don't think we ever got to hear anything from the whales via Gregory Bateson. The entire dog-and-pony show ended in misery and acrimony, with a highly emotional Allen Ginsberg tearfully wanting to know why we all just couldn't get along. That my most vivid memory should be of my first rock & roll blowjob is a fairly accurate summation of the Dialectics of Liberation, and I think Allen, on whatever plane he now dwells, would approve.

The Dialectics of Liberation was by no means our first embrace of art as a means to the end of finding a place to play. The Social Deviants had lucked into a number of self-consciously multimedia art events. Our entry into that world had been when Joan Littlewood had us participate in some piece of mayhem at Stratford East, a

strange combination of cockney music hall and avant-garde performance in front of a full, if baffled, house. The environment was
certainly odd, but it was fantastic to play in a real theatre – just like
the one where Abe Lincoln was shot – and we seemed to generate
enough excitement to finish up, with the connivance of Ms
Littlewood, doing an extra set outside in Angel Lane, which got us
arrested for the first time. However, I got my picture in the *Waltham
Gazette*, fist clenched beside a uniformed inspector, like Che fucking
Guevara with an afro.

A second and third shot at the art crowd happened at an
environmental art gallery in Kingly Street, tucked away in the West
End, one block east of Regent Street, just behind Liberty's. The space
was a peaceful and beautifully designed combination of fountains and
reflective surfaces, part science fiction and part Japanese modern, with
a permanent exhibition of kinetic art. Only too happy to play there,
we didn't feel it was too cool to ask questions, and I never did figure
out exactly what the story was behind 26 Kingly Street. Did it
actually make money, or was it some millionaire's elaborate tax loss?
The most I gleaned was that it had something to do with the highly
successful psychedelic design trio, Binder, Edwards and Vaughan,
who had done a lot of work for the Beatles, including John Lennon's
famous customised Rolls-Royce and Paul McCartney's flower-
power piano. Whatever the answer, the place maintained a lively
roster of events, from poetry readings to theatrical performance pieces
and, astonishingly, the Social Deviants.

Glad as we were to be there, the place was hardly the environment
for Deviant aggression, but amazingly, after we'd finished, only a few
of the chilled-Chablis, culture-consuming crowd had left, and the rest
applauded politely. It seemed to go okay, and we were invited back,
although it really made little sense. I guess what we were witnessing
was a strange variation of what I've always thought of as the art con.
While not denigrating the good and true, art has its shell game that
enables the facile and trendy – what might be called the Emperor's
latest set of clothes – to fool some of the people for a certain length of
time. With the right line of bullshit, we might even have worked the
con, and nobody would have been any the wiser. Unfortunately this
kind of quasi-creativity has always stuck in my craw. I am
temperamentally far better suited to ripping away the curtain than I

am to posing as the new wizard in the Emerald City. If I was ever to reach my uncertain goal in rock & roll, I knew I would not find it at any fashionable cocktail party – attractive though that route might seem.

What I was looking for could only be achieved by convincing at least some of my peers that what I was doing had not only honesty but some kind of merit, but before we ever got to that we had a few more of Jimmy Cliff's metaphoric rivers to cross. Unfortunately one of the major rivers in my path was that, no matter how closely associated I became with the underground in general and the Friday-night UFO club in particular, the Social Deviants found themselves blocked from playing there, and the only available bridge was guarded by a tall, slim authoritarian troll (or Horatius, depending on one's point of view) in a Mr Fish suit. Joe Boyd had publicly stated that we would only play at UFO over his dead body. This being the era of peace and love, shooting Boyd was pretty much out of the question, but he was a major obstacle in our path and something had to be done. Before we could deal with the matter of the Social Deviants at UFO, however, a crisis struck that would pretty much change everything.

Busted

Miles was definitely a whiter shade of pale. It was a blustery March day and I had wandered into *IT* to see what was doing. Bright and breezy as the weather, I suddenly felt as though I'd walked into a wake. 'You look fucking terrible. What's the matter?'

'We've just been busted.'

'Jesus Christ, for what?' I knew Miles didn't keep dope around, so what was the beef?

'They came storming in with a warrant under the Obscene Publications Act.'

I could see Miles was extremely shaken, and my immediate concern was for his welfare and state of mind, rather than the greater implications. 'Was the warrant for the bookshop or *IT*?'

Miles shook his head and seemed to be at something of a loss. 'It was for the premises. It wasn't any more specific than that.'

As far as I could glean, the cops had been on a fishing expedition, designed to scare the hell out of anyone and everyone they encountered. Ten detectives had shown up, and although they had removed some books from the shop, primarily works by Bill Burroughs, their main concentration had been on the *IT* office in the basement. From there they had taken away just about everything – copies of the paper, manuscripts, subscriber lists, halftone photographic blocks for the forthcoming issue, unbanked cheques and even the personal address books of the staff. They had also carefully tipped the contents of the ashtrays into evidence bags and sealed them for analysis.

'They've done just about everything they can to effectively close us down.'

'Did they give any indication what they might have considered obscene?'

Miles shook his head. The detectives had been totally uncommunicative, and he'd been racking his brains to figure out what specific obscenity could be used on which to hang a case. The best he could come up with was an interview with comedian and anti-war activist Dick Gregory, in which he tossed around phrases like 'white motherfuckers', but that seemed hardly enough to form the basis of a successful prosecution, after the acquittal of Penguin Books in the 1960 obscenity trial of D. H. Lawrence's *Lady Chatterley's Lover*. The word 'fuck' hadn't been grounds for seizure and prosecution for a full seven years. It was then that my naivety fell away. In East End parlance, the filth had been round to put the frighteners on us. So that was how the game was going to be played from here on in? Perhaps it was time to start thinking more like a hoodlum. Up to that point, I had assumed that marijuana prohibition would be the primary weapon of social control if the authorities wanted to suppress the new cultural underground. The removal of the contents of the ashtrays was evidence that the dope laws hadn't been forgotten, but it hadn't occurred to me that the Obscene Publications Act would also be brought into play to shut down what amounted to the counterculture's first means of mass communication.

After the fact, some observers claimed that this first *IT* bust, and the others that followed, plus the subsequent *Oz*, *Nasty Tales* and *Little Red School Book* trials, really had little to do with politics and were more the result of endemic corruption of many in the Metropolitan Police during the Sixties. The graft generated by crime families like the Krays and the Richardsons had penetrated to all levels of the Met, and nowhere was this more evident than among the officers of what was known as 'the dirty book squad'. Paid off to turn a blind eye to the porno bookshops and hole-in-the-wall 'adult' movie theatres, they needed flashy prosecutions, like those against *IT* and *Oz*, to maintain their credibility. Personally I never bought this theory as anything but a minor contributory factor. To send ten burly plainclothes scuffers storming into a respectable Bloomsbury book-store must have been done with the knowledge, and at least tacit approval, of the Director of Public Prosecutions, and possibly even the Home Secretary.

My first reaction was to become very angry. This was Britain in the late 1960s, with a supposedly enlightened Labour government. Where the hell did Harold Wilson and Roy Jenkins get off using strong-arm tactics to shut down a dissident magazine? *IT* was tame, little more than a fringe arts paper, and certainly not preaching the violent overthrow of the government. To suppress such a publication said much about those in office, and none of it was good.

My second shock was a little longer in coming. It was the awareness that the people I'd just begun to work with were frightened. Oddly, I didn't share their fear. As I said, I was just plain angry. For the first time in my adult life I actually felt protective of a group of which I was a part. Maybe that was the plus-side of the gutter-level life I'd been leading since I escaped from further education. It would be overweeningly arrogant for me to say that I'd developed an outlaw consciousness. Meetings with the genuine article had made me aware that I didn't have sufficient amoral sociopathic detachment, but next to Miles I was Billy the Kid, enough of a street cowboy to keep my head in a law-enforcement crisis. I believe I also relished the prospect of a fight, the thrill of anticipation that the adventure had become dangerous. Here was the cause that, as a rebel, I'd always needed. Far from being intimidated, I was determined that those in authority should see that they'd made the first move in creating a minor monster with their heavy-handed tactics.

Miles went off to make calls to lawyers and others, and I headed down to the *IT* basement to discover more despondency. With the exception of Miles, the Editorial Board had vanished, scattered to the metaphoric hills in the wake of the bust. Tom McGrath came in one time, wrote an editorial – 'the police seizure had done us one favour in that it separated out those who are proud to associate themselves with *IT* when the praise and publicity are flowing, but quickly disassociate themselves when the trouble begins' – and then vanished, never to be seen again, making the editorial vacuum complete. I think it was at that point that I started talking. Right then, stirring rap was about my only asset. 'Are we going to lie down and give up, or will we carry on, no matter what?' I think I asked this question in every form and from every possible persuasive angle, and never waited for an answer. I waxed pothead Churchillian. We'd fight them in the streets and on the fucking beaches. We freaks would never surrender.

Initially the *IT* vacuum was filled by just three of us – designer Mike McInnerney, a cat called Dave Howson, and me – and just about all we shared at first was a determination to pick up the pieces and keep the paper running. Beyond the rhetoric, the situation was dismal. Whatever infrastructure there might have been was smashed, printers were running from us like we had the plague and there was absolutely no money. Our only advantage was that the organisation had been so damned sloppy there wasn't really much worth rebuilding. The most daunting problem was the money, but before we could get too depressed about that, Hoppy showed up, like a whirlwind of positive energy. His response to everything was just three words. 'Far fucking out!'

'Is it possible to put out a paper?'

We thought so.

'Far fucking out!'

'Can we manage without money?'

We thought so.

'Far fucking out!'

Initially Hoppy, as a respected photojournalist, hit his Fleet Street contacts, hustling to drum up a little outrage and support, but he immediately ran into an impenetrable wall of apathy and, in some quarters, actual smug glee. Good riddance to an inky gadfly nuisance; *IT* was a little beatnik pest of a paper that should never have been launched in the first place, seemed to be the general reaction. Although he used what would later be Larry Flynt's argument – if those in power bust even the most wretched publication, all free media are at risk – no one seemed to give a rat's arse. After beating his head on indifference for a while, I believe he went away, brooded and then came back with a whole new strategy. Hoppy had decided to raise money and focus a massive spotlight on the situation by staging a huge, weekend-long event somewhere in London, with bands, side-shows and all the fun of a full-blown psychedelic fair. If anyone else had announced such a grandiose scheme, we almost certainly would have declared him insane and shuffled him up the basement stairs. Hoppy, however, was different. With his energy and track record, he was about the only one who could pull it off.

Now it was our turn to respond, 'Far fucking out!'

In reality, it was even further fucking out. What I didn't know at the time was that, on top of everything else, Hoppy had troubles of his own. He had been busted for a small amount of hash and was due to go for trial in the next few months, and his anti-establishment machinations were unlikely to endear him to a judge. Thus he was not only taking a wild cash and credibility gamble on this projected event, but one hell of a risk with his personal liberty by making himself such a high-profile irritant. I was a little surprised that some of his friends didn't attempt to talk him out of it. On the other hand, maybe they did and he ignored them. It would certainly have been in character. As it was, we worked out a division of labour. Mike McInnerney and I would keep the paper coming out as best we could, and Hoppy would organise the Great Event. Effectively, the workload involved meant that we'd be going our separate ways, but, since the event and the paper were mutually dependent, we would liaise constantly.

Through those days in the aftermath of the raid Mike proved to be a quiet tower of strength. He was a magnificent graphic artist, out of Ealing Art School, with an imaginative and decidedly psychedelic vision, and would ultimately go on to design the elaborate triptych packing for the Who's first version of *Tommy*. Without Mike, I don't think we would have made it. He not only managed to find a sympathetic printer, but one that would move *IT* out of the archaic world of letterpress, with its hot type, metal photographic plates and the look of a small-town newspaper, into the world of web offset which offered the potential for colour, flexibility of layout and lower production costs. Between us, we confirmed that our major distributor would still go on handling us, despite the police action, and then began sifting through what usable copy the cops had left us. For the first few days there were just the three of us, but we quickly discovered that although Dave Howson talked a good game, he had not even my basic art-school skills when it came to producing a newspaper and, after what might be called a frank and open discussion, Hoppy took him off to be his lieutenant on the Great Event. That left just two of us.

Fortunately we didn't remain two for long. Joy pitched in and, with Miles' then-wife Sue, worked the phones to try and rebuild the confiscated business records. A greatly increased number of street sellers turned up to hawk copies of the last issue, which hadn't been in the office at the time of the raid, throughout the West End, Chelsea and Notting Hill. Finally some very serious help turned up in the form of a tall, blond, highly capable, if somewhat mysterious individual called Max Zwemmer. Max had economic acumen and a persuasive phone manner, and he quickly fell into the role of business manager. Prior to that, I'd attempted to hustle printers and suppliers by dredging my mother's upper-class accent up from my DNA, but Max was the kind of natural-born wheeler-dealer we absolutely needed. He also freed up my time to assist McInnerney, who had his hands full actually designing and putting an issue into production. As no stranger to layout, I also prepared camera-ready pages. At the same time, I found myself answering what seemed to be an unending stream of questions from well-wishers wanting to know what was going on. I seemed to be doing ad hoc public relations.

With the actual production of an issue under way – it would miraculously come out only one week late – my next major concern was not only that the paper should survive, but that it should be seen to survive. With the overground media totally ignoring the *IT* bust, the word could only come out through the underground grapevine, and the fastest way to do that was to make use of UFO, not only as a public forum, but perhaps also as a source of much-needed cash. Some money had come in from various sources – I think, via Miles, that Paul McCartney had helped out with the print bills; Pete

Townshend, a close friend of Mike's, had weighed in with a contribution; and a handful of dope dealers had slipped Max some petty cash and some much-appreciated lumps of hash. Day-to-day running expenses were still needed, however, and, since UFO seemed to be booming, I rather naively enquired why some of the UFO proceeds couldn't be channelled to *IT* in its current state of crisis.

To my innocent surprise, I was informed that *IT* and UFO were two distinct and separate entities. *IT* was controlled by Lovebooks Ltd and UFO by UFO Clubs Ltd, and although Hoppy was a common director, they had no other relationship with each other. I could understand that. Legally, and on paper, it made absolute sense. If one went down, it was singularly dumb for the other to be dragged down with it, but that wasn't the whole story. It was quickly made clear to me that the separation went much further. UFO had *absolutely no relationship* with *IT*, except as one of the paper's regular advertisers. Word even came down from Joe Boyd that he would go so far as to risk paying for the next two ads up-front, even though doubt remained that the paper would come out.

Wait just a fucking minute!

All this was news to me, and I'd been running the goddamned door at UFO on no set salary, just what Joe or Hoppy decided to hand me at the end of the night. I'd believed I was in an all-hands-to-the-pumps situation and had acted accordingly. In my mind – and, I was quite certain, in the minds of 99 per cent of the people who read the paper and went to the club – the two were indivisible: the weekly gathering and the communication medium, the two spearheads of the underground, mutually dependent and mutually supportive, building on each other's strength and presumably helping each other in times of trouble. If the 'all for one, one for all' idea hadn't been deliberately fostered, no effort had been made to dispel that impression. And it wasn't just the dumb-ass hippies who believed this. When Pete Townshend slipped me a 'contribution to the cause', or, after the bust, kids offered to pay extra over the admission price, I'm sure they weren't intending it to swell the profits of UFO Clubs Ltd.

My first disillusionment with the underground spurred me on to a form of larceny to which, since the statute of limitations has long since run out, I can freely admit. The religious term is 'tithing', and a wiseguy would have called it 'skim'. I called it survival. *IT* had single-handedly put UFO on the map, and what I now organised was a form of reverse payola that would pay for Letraset, paperclips and all the thousand things that a newspaper was heir to, and would ensure that the men and women who were working for nothing at least ate, and had a contribution to their rent and gas bill. The only people who knew what I was doing were Miles, Sue, Joy and Max, and I even kept them sufficiently in the dark to have what the CIA call 'plausible deniability'.

The use of UFO as a public-relations springboard proved to be much less of a moral stretch and, to my relief, required absolutely no effort from me. Poet Harry Fainlight, the same skinny, emotional Harry Fainlight who had freaked out on speed the year before at Wholly Communion and had inspired Allen Ginsberg to write the poem 'Who to Be Kind to', was so incensed by the *IT* bust that he took matters into his own hands and organised a post-UFO piece of street theatre, in which Harry would be carried in a cardboard coffin, symbolising the death of *IT*. He would be borne aloft from UFO, escorted by a throng armed with drums, bells, tambourines, whistles and other noisemakers, down Tottenham Court Road, along Charing Cross Road, through Trafalgar Square and on down Whitehall to the Cenotaph. It occurred to me that the planned route was quite a hike, and it was lucky that Harry didn't weigh more than about ten stone. Even so, I refrained from volunteering as a pallbearer. In fact, although I sympathised absolutely with the sentiments, I was glad I was having nothing to do with the organisation of the procession, since I've never been overly keen on street theatre. Usually a case of too much street and not enough theatre. Ambulatory Tennessee Williams it never is, and I was content to remain a spectator.

In this instance the street began to assert itself within a couple of blocks. Even Harry's frail frame began to weigh heavy on those carrying him, and the coffin was set down, Harry climbed out and returned to the ranks of the living; the coffin was then filled with some of the flowers that the 'mourners' had been carrying. With the load lightened, everyone set off again in the grey London dawn, and by the time we all reached the Cenotaph a couple of reporters with attendant photographers had shown up, so the peculiar protest at least hadn't gone completely unnoticed. At the Cenotaph the enterprise hit another snag. Harry may have come up with the coffin concept, but he'd failed to script any scenario for the full duration of the protest. The merry band of faux-mourners now developed a bad case of what-the-fuck-do-we-do-next? The question became increasingly pressing as, in the wake of the reporters, constables began to hover, and many of us knew they wouldn't hover too long. We were in one of the highest security areas in the city, right by the Houses of Parliament, 10 Downing Street, Scotland Yard itself and only a short distance down Birdcage Walk from Buckingham Palace. Perhaps a nice place to visit, but a nicer place to get the hell out of.

Someone suggested that we go down into the tube, an idea verging on the inspired. Not only would we be off these all too historic streets, but we'd cause the plods a good deal of jurisdictional confusion. Thus the underground decanted itself into the Underground, and rode around with its coffin and noise, spreading alarm among early Saturday-morning commuters. At first we rode at random, but, with a pigeon-like hippie homing instinct, we ended up circling the Circle Line until we arrived at Notting Hill Gate, where we re-emerged into the surface world and began to wend our way north up Portobello Road, to the obvious displeasure of the market traders who had just set up for Saturday, the big business day.

The problem was that these kinds of symbolic demonstrations never know how to conclude themselves and usually drag on, with dwindling numbers, until the police finally move in and break them up. I didn't feel inclined to wait around for what would probably be the bitter end, so I peeled off to breakfast on Coca-Cola and a bacon sandwich in the Mountain Grill, the greasy landmark café right next door to where the Metropolitan Line to Hammersmith ran over the street and, in a couple of years, the Westway overpass would be constructed. As I ate and wondered if I should hang out in the Grove or face the long tube ride back to the East End, I figured the whole episode had been amusing while it lasted, but had essentially been a waste of time in terms of political practicality.

I pretty much continued in that frame of mind until the next day, when I picked up the *Sunday Mirror* and discovered a report somewhere around page seven that, in essence, described how a bunch of filthy, lice-ridden hippies had attempted to defile the shrine to the nation's glorious war dead to protest at the closure of their nasty pornographic newspaper. It was no more than I should have expected, but it pissed me off. For the very first time in my life I fired off an angry letter to a newspaper. My argument was about as simple as the *Sunday Mirror* deserved, and certainly on the kind of emotional level to which it could relate. My father, Eric Farren, had been in an RAF Bomber Command aircrew and had died on a raid on Cologne. I pointed out that he and thousands of others had gone to war against Nazi Germany, among other reasons to prevent the world from being run by a power structure that could send in the goon squad any time it wanted to close down a nonconformist publication.

I didn't expect the letter even to be published, but it must have struck a chord with someone on the features desk, if only as a potential 'War Hero's Son Defends Rights of Hippie Rag' piece of confused banality. The following Wednesday a Mirror Group car and chauffeur showed up at Princelet Street and I was whisked back to the Cenotaph for a photo opportunity. I gave a lengthy interview, enlarging on my original letter, but also plugging the band and generally aggrandising myself. I figured: what the hell? If you've actually managed to grab some media attention, go for it. And, the following Sunday, there I was on page seven, with a large and flattering picture.

By Sunday lunchtime the phone was ringing. The first comments came from Miles, who thought it was hilarious, but warned me that there'd be those who'd resent what I'd done. The rest of the band could see the percentage in the publicity, but had the usual reservations that come when one member gets the ink and they don't. Hoppy laughed like a maniac, treating it as a marvellous scam on the straight press, and my mother seemed generally to approve. It wasn't until Monday that the adverse reaction manifested itself. As Miles predicted, the word 'ego-tripping' was bandied about by the lower strata of boggies, while the CND duffel-coat poets started muttering about my 'appetite for fame'. To this I can only respond that if they wanted to see an appetite for fame, they should have spent an hour or so with Angela Bowie or Marc Bolan, and they'd discover that I was positively anorexic where my own celebrity was concerned. Of course, I didn't say anything – modesty becomes the hero of the hour, even among his detractors – but I did learn that if you stick your head out of the swamp, someone will be looking to lop it off.

This lesson came on top of an already pretty outlandish set of circumstances. Down the rabbit hole of the underground we were making our own newspaper in the barn; Hoppy intended to bring 10,000 people together at one mighty gathering; and, in some quarters, I was regarded as a highly suspect, self-publicising egomaniac. Curiouser and curiouser.

Chapter Four

Technicolor Dreamin'

I did not want to go down the helter skelter. The idea of going round and round and down and down the smooth spiral track was suddenly repugnant. What the hell did I want to do that for? I'd climbed the fairground tower because everyone else was doing it – never really a good reason for anything. When I reached the top I wanted to look around and take in the extraordinary sight from this new elevated perspective, but the pressure of other freaks behind me insisted that I take a fibre mat, sit on it and go down the slide. Through the course of the long evening I'd managed to consume hash, speed, beer, rum, Scotch and, I think, a little wine. At the top of the helter skelter I suddenly realised that I didn't want to add the rush of gravity and the spin of centrifugal force to the mixture, but by then it was too late and down I went. Too inhibited to scream like a rube at the fair, I merely felt sick. Of course, that was when 'helter skelter' just meant a simplistic fairground ride. The Beatles had yet to write the song, and Charlie Manson and his family had yet to make the two words a rallying cry to mystic-nihilist mass murder.

That a helter skelter stood in the middle of Alexandra Palace, projecting like a medieval phallus above the milling throng in the huge Victorian relic of the Great Exhibition was, to say the least, a wonderment, but 29 April 1967 was a night for wonderments. That Hoppy had managed to pull off a booking at the Alexandra Palace was a miracle in itself. Dubbed 'The 14-Hour Technicolor Dream', it had become the lavish summation of all that had gone before and had a definite feeling of an opium mirage. Everything that had been growing and developing over the previous two years had been brought together in one place. Lights, sounds, effects, costumes, a new ethos that echoed the Rabelais-via-Crowley Law of Thelema, 'Do what thou wilt'. Conceptual art, spacial structures like geodesic domes and a styrofoam igloo had all been set down in the hall, along with stalls hawking all manner of acid-trip toys, from electric yo-yos to black light posters and cheap, sparking, pressed-tin Chinese rayguns. Every dope dealer in the Home Counties and beyond had shown up to ply his more clandestine trade, and the obligatory Italian film crew shot footage.

Twin stages had been erected at either end of the huge main hall so that two groups could play simultaneously. It was the only way to work through a bill that read like a complete directory of all that was either new and hip, or tried, true and demented – the Move, Pink Floyd, the Soft Machine, the Pretty Things, the Crazy World of Arthur Brown, Tomorrow, Alex Harvey, Graham Bond, Champion Jack Dupree, and the godfather of us all, Alexis Korner. Pete Townshend appeared on the bill, but I don't remember him performing, simply grooving around in ruffle shirt and paisley jacket. Marc Bolan showed up with John's Children, who, if memory serves, appeared in diaphanous togas like a trans-gender troupe of Isadora Duncan dancers, while a band called the Flies, another set of punks a decade before their time, exhibited a certain cultural confusion by throwing flour (as opposed to flowers) over themselves and everyone else.

The Deviants had the dubious privilege of opening the show, and I believe we were pretty rank behind a combination of jitters at the size of the crowd, an acoustic nightmare of a hall and a PA still in shakedown mode. I wouldn't argue with critic Fred Dellar, who recalled in a *Mojo* magazine retrospective that we 'thrashed and trashed Chuck Berry riffs', although other more contemporary reports actually commended us. Dear Sue Miles commented, 'There was the Social Deviants with their astonishing lightshow. Micky Farren was great, cos Micky was angry. He wasn't into love and peace. He had this hair and kinda lime-yellow nylon loon pants.'

About the only advantage of going on first was that we didn't have to compete with another band at the other end of the hall, and, being on first, we were off first, which left us plenty of time to thrash and trash ourselves, and watch British psychedelic history unfold before our bloodshot eyes. A number of instant stars were created that night. Arthur Brown blew everyone away with his white-boy soul voice, his dancing and his flaming helmet, the precursor to the 'God of Hellfire' act that would eventually put him in a mental-health facility. Tomorrow made their mark primarily on the inspired showmanship of their bass player, who went by the single name 'Junior'. The Purple Gang pulled off a showstopper with their hippie anthem 'Granny Takes a Trip', and probably could have been the biggest jug-band act in British rock history, except that I never ever saw them play live again.

Pink Floyd consolidated their pre-eminent position, but their set was surrounded by a good deal of controversy. They didn't play until dawn, having flown back the same night from a gig in Holland. Syd Barrett, by all accounts, was flying so high on acid that he'd reached full orbital velocity; he mistook the first rays of morning for a fundamental transformation of the entire universe and may have decided that the sun was going nova. Daevid Allen of the Soft Machine voiced the general opinion. 'It must have one of the greatest gigs that they ever did . . . I was hearing echoes of all the music I'd ever heard with bits of Bartok and God-knows-what.' Miles, on the other hand, who was probably more together than most, recalled how 'both Peter Jenner and Syd were on acid. The probability was that they weren't that good, but in that atmosphere it hardly mattered'. Something must have mattered, though, because, although no one in the crowd knew it at the time, it would be Syd's last stand with the Floyd.

In the backstage area, the happening bands all met each other en masse for the first time. We'd been assigned one vast communal dressing room, a tiled, institutional room the size of a tennis court. We corralled ourselves in our own separate little camps, with instrument cases, bits of gear, props and stage clothes defining our defensible space. My first surprise was how the denizens of backstage – considering that they were looked up to as the prime motivators – were actually more conservative than the punters outside. Consider-ably more drinking was going on backstage, and although a few world-class druggers were among those assembled, I quickly realised two things. Most bands, even though they might have their flamboyant extremists, also had members who, despite their long hair and floral shirts, still clung to a decidedly brown-ale consciousness, and would probably never change. Too many didn't believe a word of all this counterculture malarkey, and were only embracing the trend as another avenue to rock-business success.

The rockbiz presence was more than evidenced by Tony Secunda, the Move's outrageously extreme manager, who made an entrance like an incendiary whirlwind and commenced a one-man drama to ensure that the Move received the most favourable time slot, and that no other band was playing while they were on. In fact, Secunda was more out there than all but a handful of the musicians. Following a particularly outrageous promotion for the Move, he had been sued for libel by Prime Minister Harold Wilson. A few years later we'd become firm friends and do a hell of a lot of cocaine, and even get ourselves arrested together, but right then I merely watched in awe as he taught a class in rock & roll managerial madness.

Forget the bands and the business, though. The unsung hero of the 14-Hour Technicolor Dream was Jack Henry Moore. Jack was short, rotund and as loudly and unfetteredly gay as anyone could be who grew up in small-town Oklahoma and was now happily cutting loose in the world at large. He had a sharp intelligence and an even sharper sense of humour, and a habit of whipping up his T-shirt to expose his nipples and Buddha-like stomach when confronted with overbearing pomposity.

'Oh, please! *Enough!*'

He had a bizarre fund of knowledge, including which London restaurants served the most 'aggressively cold' Coca-Cola, and was notorious around Covent Garden for projecting movies late at night on the walls of the buildings opposite, from the windows of his apartment on Long Acre. He claimed both to have studied with John Cage and to have been on the road with Little Richard. He was the most lively and outspoken of the original *IT* Editorial Board and would, with Jim Haynes, shortly found the London Arts Lab in Drury Lane, where he devised the notorious basement cinema in which, instead of seats, the patrons sprawled on a foot-thick foam-rubber floor to watch the latest Warhol or Kenneth Anger. The cinema also hosted legendary after-hours, multi-gender, multi-sexual-preference orgies, while the cutting edge of avant-garde pornography rolled grainily on the screen.

Jack literally produced the entire Technicolor Dream. The performance stages at each end of the hall were his twin babies, as was the long span of lighting gantry that traversed the area's entire width, like a rickety suspension bridge, thirty feet in the air, midway between them. At that midpoint, under the lighting gallery, the sound of the two opposing bands blended into a weird atonal cacophony that both Frank Zappa and Karlheinz Stockhausen would have totally relished. Knots of stoned freaks gathered in this narrow zone of audio fusion, grooving to the random combinations of key and time signature. I suspect this may have been Jack's own devious plan to get his personal rocks off by creating a wholly arbitrary, instant, found composition, and for all I know, he may have been secretly recording the results. When he became my new-music mentor during the making of the Deviants' first album, I found this was exactly how he thought. Sadly Jack became just too outrageous for the authorities in Britain, and around 1970 they cancelled his work permit and made it clear that he was no longer welcome in their green and pleasant land. He was forced to relocate to the more tolerant atmosphere of Amsterdam, were he continued his multi-media work and his extravagant lifestyle at the Melkweg (translated, Milky Way), one of the Dutch nightclubs where open marijuana smoking was first permitted.

I may have been hallucinating, but I swear I saw John Lennon (who was certainly present at the event) standing thoughtfully in Jack's zone of dissonance, moving first forward and then back and looking quite fascinated. The presence of Lennon at the 14-Hour Technicolor Dream also provided an odd footnote of rock & roll romantic trivia. In another part of the hall Yoko Ono was staging an event at which passersby were invited to scissor the clothing from the body of an attractive young woman, but the two of them never met that night.

By most estimates 10–11,000 showed up at the Alexandra Palace to ride the helter skelter, smoke the joints, drop the acid, take in the bands, buy the geegaws and generally wander around in a haze. (The word 'haze' is common to most accounts of the event.) That the number of consumers for this kind of thing had swelled from under a hundred to a full five figures was nothing short of amazing. What the hell was going on here? Was it merely a vast fashion aberration, or were we seeing a brand-new mass art movement, like the Pre-Raphaelites or the Aesthetes, only quantum multiplied by the vast numbers of the baby boom? The idea that seemed almost dangerous to entertain was that Miles' abstraction of an alternative society was actually coming to pass, but at a frightening and uncontrolled rate, like a viral culture growing exponentially, each cell dividing and reproducing over and over again. I had a stoned vision of the calendar. As the sun came up on the Technicolor Dream, it was just a day away from 1 May, the high holiday of communism and the ancient date of the rites of spring fertility. Was the combination a bell-wether to the wind of change?

I also feared for whatever it was. Hoppy had created a magnificent gathering at Alexandra Palace, but the underground was no longer underground. He'd placed us right in the shop window, without cover or camouflage, and I worried that far from hastily developing new and needed survival skills, we were going public with a contrived and 'groovy' innocence. I couldn't identify with this and I could never comfortably be a part of it. I had a vision of it all devolving into an absurdly naive children's crusade, such easy prey for sharks and charlatans that they'd be destroyed before they reached the end of the night, let alone came within sight of any New Jerusalem.

Even at the Technicolor Dream itself, the wolf packs were already in evidence. In the headlong rush to organise the large and complicated celebration, neither Hoppy nor anyone else had paid much attention to the matter of security. Again it was a symptom of innocence; the belief that good vibrations would conquer all. Thus far the only trouble at UFO had been limited to the odd crazy Irishman and a handful of bad trips, and, if that was the model, no real reason existed to believe it would be any different at Alexandra Palace. Unfortunately the Technicolor Dream was massively more visible than the small, fairly anonymous club in the West End. Out in the hinterlands of N22, and highly publicised in the press and on TV, it was just too tempting a target for anyone who fancied a spot of freak-bashing. The first to avail themselves of the opportunity were rabid teams of North London scooter boys and lumpen mods who crashed the party, eager to beat on unresisting flower children.

Flurries of ugliness swirled as the mods attempted to escalate verbal abuse to pushing and shoving, but before the violence became gratuitous the cavalry arrived in the most unexpected form. Hoppy's girlfriend of the time, the manic Suzy Creamcheese, and a recruited crew of hippie maidens descended on each new flashpoint and smothered the potential conflagration with promised, if not actually delivered, Xanadu visions of sex and drugs beyond any skinhead comprehension. After receiving the Creamcheese treatment, the would-be troublemakers were seen dazed and wandering, staring wide-eyed and clearly wondering if maybe there were more amusing things in life than putting the boot in.

Mystery always surrounded Suzy Creamcheese (née Zieger). Was she really the Suzy Creamcheese featured on the first few Mothers of Invention albums, or had she merely usurped the name for British consumption and her own expatriate self-aggrandisement? I didn't really care. She did have these conservative parents somewhere in California, who were so appalled by her free-form lifestyle that they kept having her committed to various expensive mental institutions, causing Hoppy to array himself in a ninja outfit to break in and spend the night with her while she was so incarcerated. She also had sufficient flamboyance of character to qualify for the same Zappa encouragement given to Captain Beefheart, Wild Man Fischer, Alice Cooper and the GTOs. Even if counterfeit, Creamcheese was outrageous enough to serve our British requirements, and I will always be grateful for her innovative peacekeeping at the Technicolor Dream.

The hallmark of a good party is supposedly that you can't remember how you got home, and I have absolutely no recollection of how I returned from the 14-Hour Technicolor Dream. I did note later that, out in the 'real' world that same week, David Bowie released a single called 'The Laughing Gnome', Tom Stoppard's *Rosencrantz and Guildenstern Are Dead* opened at the National Theatre, the Beatles were finishing up *Sgt Pepper* after 700 hours in Abbey Road studios and Muhammad Ali was stripped of his heavyweight title after refusing to be drafted and sent to Vietnam. The times were not only changing, but becoming really interesting.

The Children's Crusade

The feeling was one of being carried by the riptide, with no time to stop, take stock or plan ahead. The Technicolor Dream looked to have opened the floodgates on something unstoppable. My new-found friends and companions assured me we were on the Golden Road to Samarkand, and castigated me for being a chronic pessimist and natural-born worrier, but I still feared that we might be part of one vast Donner party that would be forced to eat each other after a wrong turn in the mountains. Even I, however, had to admit things did seem to be going our way for a change. After a wait of some two months the Director of Public Prosecutions decided that no charges were going to be brought against *IT*, and the same cops who raided Indica in the first place were forced shamefacedly to hump everything back into the basement, with the exception of the bags containing the contents of the ashtrays. This was definitely good news, not only as a moral triumph, but because, had there been a court case, we would have been in pretty dire shape. Almost all the proceeds from the Technicolor Dream had vanished. The honour system among the advance ticket sellers had completely broken down. They'd sold the tickets, but then made off with the money, and the event barely managed to break even.

On the other side of the coin, the sales of papers, T-shirts and other *IT* junk at Alexandra Palace had brought in some needed cash and established the paper as a natural adjunct of the new lifestyle that vibrated in Chelsea, Notting Hill and the West End. The hoardings around building sites were now decorated with shimmering acid-art posters for psychedelic bands and clubs, with those created for UFO by Mick English, Nigel Weymouth, Mike McInnerney and Martin Sharp taking pride of place. It became a matter of honour that this form of advertising shouldn't give up its message too easily. Assorted hippies could be spotted peering intently at the posters attempting to glean information from among the curlicues.

At the crass end of the rainbow, Carnaby Street had turned floral overnight. The trendy boutique chain Take 6 was now selling knock-offs of clothing designs from Granny Takes a Trip – the pioneer King's Road boutique. You could hear opportunist idiot bands like the Flower Pot Men, or the saccharine Scott McKenzie singing 'If

You're Going to San Francisco' (be sure to wear some flowers in your hair). Everywhere one looked, money was being generated. Even before it was fully formed, the philosophy had become a fad, and the fad's economy was inflating so fast it made one's head spin. A plethora of hustlers oozed from the woodwork promoting every imaginable fly-by-night scheme involving hippy-trippy, peace 'n' love garbage. As a craps player since my art-school days, I recognised this commercial largesse as a temporary roll rather than a way of life, and wondered what would happen when flower power stopped shooting natural sevens and came up snake eyes. I knew that beads, bells and bad copies of Peter Max were no sustainable foundation. Hairline cracks were already starting to show in the Day-Glo magic castle.

Some of the most serious and most quickly widening schisms were the ones beginning to divide what could already be called the old guard. The Editorial Board had moved back into *IT* now that the legal threat had abated, and conflict immediately broke out as to the future direction and emphasis of the paper. The board seemed to feel that the crew who'd kept things running during the emergency was leaning too far in the direction of the prevailing hippie boom, and serious course adjustments were required. Needless to say, this hardly sat well with Mike and me. While we hardly wanted to turn *IT* into a flower-power comic, we were less than happy about policy being dictated to us from on high. Having saved the bloody paper against all the odds, we considered that we should be free to have some fun, or what the hell were we doing there?

One of the first fights was over design. Mike was fascinated by the graphic innovations being made by the US underground press, particularly the *San Francisco Oracle*, which was pushing the offset print process to its limit, with multiple colours and rainbow underlays. Of course this often made the text unreadable, but that was hardly a concern of any magazine designer in the late Sixties who was rolling in front of the curve. The board, on the other hand, thought we should return to a more conservative and readable style, and the dispute would ultimately lead to Mike's departure. For my part, I was still pushing the same rock 'n' roll iconoclasm as before, but with the added momentum of using it as an antidote to the dippier excesses.

While it was finally recognised that rock & roll had its place, plans were mooted to relegate my ideas to a ghettoised 'music section'.

To add even more insult, the board began hiring staff and actually offering them money. After living off theft and beggary for so long, I looked a bit askance at this, especially as the first hiring was of a brand-new editor. He turned out to be a cat by the name of Bill Levy. Bill was East Coast, campus Jewish, with a goatee, a Fifties' *Mad*-magazine, bohemian haircut and a tendency to snigger at shit I didn't even find particularly amusing. He seemed to fancy himself as some sort of renegade literatus, and I knew we had problems when I discovered that his idea of a major scoop was to publish correspondence between Anaïs Nin (whom I always imagined self-obsessed and a lousy fuck) and Antonin Artaud (whose Theatre of Cruelty had its points, but had, after all, died in 1948). I also knew that confronting him would have to wait. Whatever grief Bill Levy might potentially create was eclipsed by more pressing problems that were threatening to engulf UFO.

Joe Boyd had decided to make UFO commercial. With Hoppy's time taken up by Alexandra Palace, and then his own drug bust, the original checks and balances were history. Over two Fridays, Boyd had decided to make his mark as a club promoter by booking Pink Floyd and the Move, and he was rubbing his hands over the truckload of money that was going to be made. The Move had a single in the charts and the Floyd were now massive. Unfortunately, Joe had neglected to discuss the matter with any of us humble minions who would have to cope with the crowds generated by his megalomaniac promotion. UFO was filled to near-capacity each week with the likes of Arthur Brown and Tomorrow, and we simply didn't have the logistical resources to handle the numbers Joe anticipated.

In addition to the increasing headache of crowd control, and moving people into the club fast enough to keep the police happy, two other problems had reared from the slime. The same moddy scooter boys who had attempted to cause grief at the 14-Hour Technicolor Dream had discovered UFO and had been attempting, in small groups, to muscle their way in. I didn't think we could rely on the sensual Zen psychology of Creamcheese's Angels on any permanent basis, but at the same time the idea of hiring conventional bouncers stuck in my craw The first time I attempted to turn away one of these skinhead scouting parties, the confrontation started to turn ugly, but, with the uncanny luck that seemed to manifest itself in those days, help came from another unexpected quarter. A strange American who answered to the name of Norman, and looked fresh out of some Vietnam rice paddy, had been coming by the club for a few weeks. I have to admit that I'd been keeping an eye on him, wondering, if he was a vet, just how tightly wrapped he might be.

As the mods looked set to run right over me, Norman appeared out of nowhere, sprang onto the table at which the money was collected and landed in a ferocious martial-arts stance, making noises like a Shaolin priest about to crack boulders with his bare hands. The mods couldn't have been more shocked if I'd conjured up Beelzebub from the hellish pit. For a moment they stood rooted and then turned away, muttering 'Fuck this' and attempting to save face with a retreating attitude of 'We didn't want to go into your fucking hippie club anyway'. Needless to say, Norman was immediately put on the payroll with a roving brief to keep an eye out for any trouble that might be brewing, either at the door or inside the club.

Other staunch allies in combating the mod/skinhead problem were a motley bunch of Jewish East Londoners known as the Firm. The Firm were ex-mods themselves, but of the earlier, stylish variety whose twin dedications were music – primarily the blues – and creating mayhem and chaos wherever they went. Led by the dire duo of Peter Shertser and Ian Sippen, the Firm had taken a bunch of acid, but managed to retain a highly mutated version of the traditional mod obsession with making and spending money. They'd grown their hair and now dressed in sharp, custom-tailored suits of the most outrageous fabrics they could find. These bespoke monsters were made by an elderly tailor in the East End to whom they would present lengths of William Morris curtain material and demand that he sew it according to the same pattern as a three-button Tonik. At UFO, the Firm's capacity for confusion and disorder reached inspired peaks. They spiked a number of people, including the hapless John Peel, attacked the more disorientated hippies with water pistols and, on one memorable night, let off an assortment of fireworks right on the dance floor. After that, the choice was either to ban them or co-opt them, and since they would only treat a ban as a challenge to return by hook or by crook, I suggested that they became our resident mod neutralisation squad.

The second problem that I sensed bearing down on us was that of media attention. For a while rumours had been circulating that one of the downmarket Sunday newspapers was gathering material for a major exposé of the hippie drug menace. Digging up tales of hippie horror was childishly simple. In the cowslip field of public relations, flower children were their own worst enemies. Far from being discreet or circumspect, most refused to shut up when confronted by an investigative muckraker. Even the most muddled and benighted reporter could manage to find some freak who'd spout a line of quasi-mystic, acid-head nonsense that could be twisted into a damning admission of narcotic degeneracy. On its own, a bad press wasn't too worrying. The movement seemed to thrive on abuse. The real danger lay in the fact that a bad press was almost inevitably followed by some kind of police action, as the authorities sought to demonstrate they were doing something about the evil that the media had brought to the public's attention. One set of hippie/drug exposés in the *News of the World* early in 1967 had resulted in the arrest of Mick Jagger, Keith Richards and Robert Fraser at Redlands, Keith's country house near Chichester. It was anybody's bet what kind of round-up a second set of shock-horror revelations might produce, but UFO, as Hippie Central, was favourite for being busted.

Despite my vocal opposition to courting a potential shitstorm by pushing the club to the limits of its capacity and maybe beyond, the big nights of Pink Floyd and the Move went ahead. As expected, they were sweaty, uncomfortable and claustrophobic. The police complained a number of times about the overspill on the pavement, skinheads attempted to maraud and were repelled, and both staff and audience finished these nights irritable to pissed-off.

I don't really mean to single out Joe Boyd as the embodiment of the unacceptable face of hip capitalism. We had managed to resolve the problem of the Social Deviants playing UFO. Joe claims it was just a reward for loyal service, while I still maintain that he had to cave in when faced with the fact that the Deviants not playing UFO was plainly absurd. At first we were lumbered with the 5 a.m.

graveyard slot, playing to the demented or sleeping, but after a while folks discovered that, although we might be inept, it was an entertaining ineptitude, and we were elevated to the kind of earlier spots allotted to Arthur Brown and his flaming head.

As hustlers went, Joe was actually one of the more scrupulous but, in the wake of the Technicolor Dream, lines were quickly being drawn between the believers in some kind of cultural or political revolution and the rock & roll entrepreneurs wheeling and dealing in the new and the groovy. It was just unfortunate that Boyd and I should find ourselves facing each other across that line. I am not averse to making money when need be. While we continue to exist under capitalism, the rent has to be paid, as do the phone bill and the bar tab. I suppose I am cursed, though, by a form of puritanism that demands the profit motive should be declared up-front. What I couldn't stand was enterprising avarice concealed behind some spurious revolutionary smokescreen – the kind of thing that came to a head in 1969 when CBS Records began running a bizarre advertising campaign with the slogan 'The Man Can't Bust Our Music'.

I remember on a number of occasions meeting with some record-company house hippie, who would slip me that knowing wink that, although we might be talking the anti-establishment talk, when it came to walking the walk, we were all secretly in it for what we could get. At that point he'd see my own eyes harden, would suddenly realise that I wasn't going to enter his neat little conspiracy of profit and deception and would manoeuvre me out of their office as swiftly as if I had leprosy.

Breaking the Butterflies

Mid-afternoon, 30 June 1967, and, like all good adventures, it started with the phone ringing. I can't now remember who was calling. A number of people around the *IT* periphery had gone down to the Crown Court in Chichester, where the charges stemming from the raid at Redlands were being heard. The voice on the other end was agitated. 'That fucking bastard Block has given Mick, Keith and Fraser jail time.'

'Oh, shit. How long?'

Midsummer and the judicial chickens were coming home to roost. Hoppy was already in Brixton for nine months for simple possession, and now it seemed that two of the Rolling Stones would be seeing out the rest of the year behind bars.

'Mick got three months, Fraser got six months and Keith a year.'

'You're fucking kidding?'

'I wish I was.'

'Shit.' I felt unexpectedly angry and sick, as though it had happened to a close friend, and later I wondered why. When Judge Block handed down time to Mick Jagger and Keith Richards, a genuine personal response was completely illogical. These weren't friends, they were symbols, and the only explanation I can offer is the potent might of symbolism. In reality, any number of poor bastards went to jail every day and were even less deserving of incarceration than Jagger and Richards, so why make a fuss about a couple of rock stars? The answer was that they were being shafted as an example to the rest of us, and the rest of us therefore took it personally.

The tale of the jailing of Mick Jagger and Keith Richards has been recounted a hundred times in a hundred different contexts. Set up by the *News of the World*, busted by the West Sussex County Constabulary and sentenced by Judge Block, they would provide the first salutary opening salvo lesson, before those in power went on to get the Beatles and put a stop to this drug nonsense once and for all. Fortunately, even as Jagger and Richards were being removed from the court in very visible handcuffs, the potheads of the nation cried out in a loud and metaphoric voice.

'Fuck this shit! Just hold up a minute!'

Fuck this shit was the prevailing sentiment, but beneath the anger, hand on heart, I have to admit to a certain degree of calculation. When Hoppy had gone down, he had not been of sufficient national stature to mount any significant protest, even though it was plain he was being jailed for pranks like the Technicolor Dream as much as for the hash they'd found in his Queensway flat. Judge Gordon Friend had substantiated this during sentencing: 'You are a pest to society.' The best we could do in Hoppy's case was put out a special poster edition of *IT* – 'Summer Sadness for John Hopkins'. Mick 'n' Keef, on the other hand, presented an unparalleled opportunity to cause a fuss.

Within half an hour of receiving the news of the sentences the *IT* offices began to fill with people, asking questions and bearing tales. Weeping teenyboppers were gathering outside Jagger's and Richards' London homes. Psychedelic socialite Nicky Kramer had apparently leaped off a bus in the King's Road screaming 'The revolution starts here!' and doubtless scaring the tourists. A group of designers was already working on a poster with the slogan 'Let Him Who Is Without Sin Jail the First Stone'. A couple of UFO groupies swept in, trailing patchouli and radical chiffon, demanding that we should all go to Paul McCartney's house because 'Paul will know what to do', but were completely ignored. Miles had been on the phone to his contacts. In the corridors of Westminster it was being pointed out to the Home Secretary that maybe Judge Block had gone too far. Miles also reported that the Beatles had left town. (So much for going to Paul's house.) Brian Jones had been busted the night before, doubtless to provide a side-bar to the news reports of his bandmates going to jail, and fears of a mass round-up abounded.

I was adamant we shouldn't go quietly. We must use our resources to get as many people as possible on the streets. If they were going to drag away the hopheads, let the hopheads be visible. No night and fog; if we went, we'd go kicking and screaming. I think it was Sue Miles who suggested the phone tree. It was an idea I really liked. Call one person and get them to call five more. In theory, one could raise a huge number of people in a matter of a couple of hours. It was a telephonic pyramid scheme I'd never had a chance to use, and I was academically curious to see it work.

If a demonstration was to be mounted, the first question was: where? Obviously everyone had to be concentrated in one place, or the exercise was pointless. It was then that inspiration struck.

'Fleet Street.'

'What?'

'In front of the *News of the World* building. At ten o'clock this evening.'

As had to be expected at any gathering of freaks, counter-suggestions were immediately made – from Hyde Park (that was impractical) to Stonehenge (that was implausible). Another time-wasting discussion threatened to kill all momentum, but I'd brook no argument. Sue Miles, who could be mightily forceful when she wanted, backed me up. 'It makes absolute sense. They were the bastards who started all this.'

After working the phones for about three hours, the die was cast. The word was out and beyond recall. Nothing remained but to go to the pub and wait. Many of my more Gandhian friends disagree, but I've always found it's better to go to a demonstration a couple of parts drunk. I've always preferred my courage a little Dutch. Which was just as well, because in the cab to Fleet Street I experienced a bad bout of revolutionary first-night nerves. Suppose no one showed? The sight of fifty or sixty people already there came as a mighty relief, and more were arriving in a substantial flow. Some, like me, came in cabs; others got off buses. Cars and vans disgorged more protesters and then drove off to find places to park. Others simply wandered up on foot, while a few, with elegant forethought, emerged from Fleet Street pubs where they'd been hanging out until the appointed time. By ten-thirty we were a few hundred people strong and more kept coming. 'Satisfaction' and 'Time Is on My Side' were blasting from speakers hidden in the back of a van. It had all worked. Reporters flocked out of monolithic newspaper offices to ask us what we were doing, and were informed in no uncertain terms.

'Freeing the fucking Stones, and closing down the fucking *News of the World*!'

By far the greatest coup was that we'd taken the police completely by surprise. A single car showed up first, took one look and drove off again. About ten minutes later a couple of police vans parked, but at first nothing happened. Finally an inspector and four constables got out and walked slowly to where the demonstrators were most densely congregated. The inspector asked the perennial policeman question: 'Who's in charge here?'

We immediately employed the hippie version of 'I'm Spartacus'. Everyone pointed to someone else.

'He is.'

'She is.'

'He is.'

'We are.'

'They are.'

'We don't follow leaders, man.'

With a look of contempt, the deputation withdrew. I don't know exactly how the signal was given, but suddenly half a dozen old-fashioned Black Marias raced up from Ludgate Circus and screamed to a halt, spilling cops and dogs onto Fleet Street. Instant chaos, with the dogs creating their own kind of panic. Scuffles broke out and I saw the first arrests. Lorry drivers and print workers were now massed in the loading bays of the nearest newspaper offices and looked as though they would be only too happy to wade in on the side of the cops. It was clearly time to withdraw before real violence started and the police staged a riot of their own. In almost the same instant a means of retreat presented itself that was as unorthodox as the rest of the protest.

'Just get on a bus!'

The cops had failed to close off Fleet Street and the late-evening traffic was still flowing, albeit somewhat slowly, which was completely to our advantage. About a dozen of us quickly piled onto a number-seven bus coming from Liverpool Street Station. Others jumped onto other buses going in both directions. A protest at the imprisonment of the Rolling Stones was ending in escape via London Transport.

The next day was one of post-mortems and, as usual, I took flack from some quarters. In this case it was from our avowed pacifists. The Fleet Street action had been 'irresponsible' – 'people could have been hurt'. In fact, a number had been hurt and six arrested. Having not twisted anyone's arms, I had little patience with this after-the-fact carping. 'What was I supposed to do? Write to *The Times*?'

It was a flippant remark and hardly thought out. I was ignoring the profound effect that the day's editorial in *The Times* would have on the case. Editor William Rees-Mogg had written a leader condemning the sentences imposed on Jagger and Richards. Under a quote from Alexander Pope, 'WHO BREAKS A BUTTERFLY ON A WHEEL?', he concluded:

Young people are searching for values and for sincere human relationships, individual and social, as never before and their destructiveness is directed only at the falsities and hypocrisies of the older generation.

Rees-Mogg had, from where we sat, come down squarely on the side of the good guys. Later the same day Mick and Keith were released on bail, pending appeal, but poor Robert Fraser was left to serve out his time. Jagger was immediately flown by helicopter to tape an edition of *World in Action*, in which he was questioned about his philosophy by Rees-Mogg, a Jesuit priest and the vicar of Woolwich. At the time Rees-Mogg seems to have observed a side of Jagger that seems far more in tune with the wrinkled multi-millionaire we know today than the Jumping Jack Flash figure with which so many of us were probably deluding ourselves:

> He put forward these views which went so much against the grain of the currently fashionable left-wing ideology, I suddenly realised that Mick Jagger was in essence a right-wing libertarian. Straight John Stuart Mill!

John Stuart Mill or Karl Marx, the people for whom Friday meant UFO were still determined to use the jailing of the two Stones as an excuse for continuing to take protest against the drugs laws to the streets, even though the two protagonists were free on bail. The hippies, after their first taste of street action, apparently craved more, and one of the most voluble factions wanted to move the whole club – lock, stock and lightshow – down to Piccadilly Circus. Joe Boyd was one of the first to oppose this idea, and for once I supported him. The logistics of doing such a thing were, to say the least, problematic. The Thursday-night gathering had been a spontaneous outpouring of anger, even if it had received a little help from the coordinating telephone. Any repeat performance would have to be better publicised and better orchestrated if it were to have the desired impact. A protest not only has to be made, it has to be seen to be made. That's why it's called a demonstration, and I didn't think a few freaks wandering around Eros were going to have the authorities shaking in their boots.

The real target that deserved to be hurt where it mattered still had to be the *News of the World*. The paper had conducted a deliberate campaign of vitriolic disinformation, calculated to provoke unpleasantness, violence and worse. If the skinheads who tried to crash into UFO and the Roundhouse, or the lorry drivers who wanted to beat up musicians in the car park of the Blue Boar, needed any justification, then the *News of the World* amply provided it by suggesting that we were little short of a diseased, subhuman evil. With the *News of the World* only coming out on Sundays, Saturday was the paper's big night. If we could again stage a large enough gathering in Fleet Street – this time around midnight – we could disrupt the production and dispatch of the paper's early editions.

Again the pacifists accused me of promoting violence and, in the light of subsequent events, I suppose I was, but they were in a minority. Too many had tasted the catharsis of confrontation and wanted to do it all over again. The first thing we learned was that, just as we'd had an extra day to prepare, so had the police. In fact, they were more than ready for us. This was the City of London force, the ones with the extra Graeco-Roman ridge on their helmets, like firemen or gladiators. The minimum height requirement of their recruits was two inches more than that of the rest of the Met, and they'd always had a reputation for being hard cases. Their objective on that particular night seemed to be one of providing ample verification of this reputation.

They moved in before the demonstration was fully assembled, using batons, boots and dogs, and arresting anyone who so much as looked sideways at them. One of the first to go was Suzy Creamcheese, carried bodily to a paddy wagon by three burly coppers while she cursed like a drunken stoker. I was surprised I wasn't grabbed at the same time, but the police seemed to have something more up close and personal in mind for me. I don't know if they had me tagged as a ringleader, or whether it was just my attitude and bloody afro. The coppers grabbed me, but instead of hustling me off to one of the waiting wagons, they dragged me to a dark doorway and began working me over with short jabs to the body, in that unique law-enforcement manner that causes the most pain with the fewest visible marks. Battered and decidedly bowed, I was left with a final admonition.

'Now, you little cunt, maybe you'll think twice about coming down our manor and causing aggravation.'

Saturday Night Fevour

At various points on its journey to enlightenment a band needs a friend and, despite the Social Deviants' mean and filthy demeanour, we actually locked into more of our fair share of boosters. Some much-needed early support came from Jack Braceland who, along with Mark Boyle, had created the first lightshows for Pink Floyd back at All Saints' Hall. By some process that scarcely bears looking into, Jack had converted a former stripclub and shebeen at 44 Gerrard Street in darkest Soho into a psychedelic club, and had named it Happening 44. During the time that Joe Boyd wasn't having us at UFO, Jack offered us a residency on Saturday nights, which continued even after Joe had finally relented.

Happening 44 was one of the weirdest hippie dungeons anywhere. Although Jack had taken it to the max with the lighting and ambience, it could never quite shed its previous image. The back room was filled with cans of ancient porn loops and bits of bondage hardware, which were now and again dragged out to be part of the show. Serious gangsters from the Richardson family would shoulder their way down the stairs thinking the gaff was still a late-night drinker, and become totally bemused by the lights and the Deviants doing some impromptu fucked-up shaman ritual on the stage. Fortunately a bottle was always at hand to keep them happy. The rockers who came by usually brought their own bottles. I recall splitting one of Johnny Walker Red with a very drunk Eric Burdon, who mumbled on that the Deviants were the shape of things to come, but probably forgot all about it in the morning. Another time John Mayall inexplicably stopped by to show off his hand-carved Laurel Canyon guitar. Of all who stumbled into Happening 44 by mistake, we were most pleased to see the chemically confused strippers from the other clubs on the block, who'd sometimes shake it with the band in stockings and G-strings like their equivalent of sitting in, and maybe later treat us to weird Sunday-morning naked breakfasts.

The Deviants had entered a new phase of perversity, and we also began to locate the perverse among the audience. Although they were in an intense and colourful environment of black light and blob-show, the crowd was nonetheless rubbing shoulders with a small but significant scattering of hoods, whores, strippers, deep Soho lurkers and, this being on the edge of Chinatown, a few token junkies. The clientele at Happening 44 was amazingly tolerant of what went down in the way of entertainment, and the percentage of oddities also meant that the kind of hippie naivety flourishing at UFO simply couldn't be maintained. Night-blooming flower power took on a hint of Berlin cabaret and an edge of danger and decadence. Chock full o' amphetamines, we could blast all night, but at other times I remember sitting on the edge of the stage, glaring balefully at the audience with Alex's light boxes close up on either side of me, so that I seemed to be in a blinding prison of light, like a Klingon military execution, droning some doomed Martian-gothic stream of coming-down consciousness. And they bought it.

Happening 44 also ran like a cabaret. Bands, of course, predominated, and I well remember a night with Fairport Convention when the Deviants challenged Richard Thompson to stretch 'Reno Nevada' to a full twenty minutes. A lot of other weird eclectic stuff, however, also graced the stage. Hippie sirens Mimi and Mouse, and their gay friend Alan, went under the collective title of Shiva's Children; the women performed a kind of yab-yum ballet, while Alan played percussion and intoned. He rather charmingly tried to seduce me one night, but it wasn't to be. The Sam Gopal Dream also had a Hindu theme, as Sam warrior-pounded the tablas behind an electric raga, first provided by Andy Clarke and Mick Hutchinson and later by Lemmy.

A protracted residency can really edge a combo towards the twilight zone. The longer the run, the deeper the twilight, and it seemed like we played at Happening 44 to infinity and back. Experimentation sets in as familiarity breeds confidence, and a breakthrough comes with the realisation that risks aren't really risks if the audience is with you. An ill-gotten copy of a demo tape by a New York band called the Velvet Underground helped open us up to wider potentials with songs about sado-masochism, copping heroin and terminal narcissism, and artistically we robbed them blind. We had their classic 'I'm Waiting for the Man' down well before their famous 'banana' debut album came out and every half-arsed, pre-punk, three-chord band – including David Bowie – started playing it.

Most important, we were sorting out our audience, and finding our friends. The perverse gravitated to the perverse, and the sordid cleaved to the sordid. Unless I hallucinated the whole thing, Miles dropped in briefly one night with William Burroughs after dining in some Peking-duck emporium nearby, or drinking in the French Pub on Dean Street. Bill looked slowly around and nodded, acknowledging it as the fledgling mugwump sanctuary it was. Then he left, having seen it all before and not being particularly taken with close-proximity rock 'n' roll.

Avoiding the Light

A lot of nonsense is talked these days about the degeneracy of the Sixties, but the early hippies readily embraced an eccentric but nonetheless tiresome moralism. Hippies didn't drink, hippies avoided junk food, hippies sought enlightenment rather than oblivion, and hippies didn't wear handcuffs to bed. In fact, the hippies were bloody puritan about what Camille Paglia called 'expanding the scope of erotic response' and frowned on many passionate rituals that were close to my tainted heart. A relentless mood of sunshine is downright oppressive, and I was passing up almost all chances to attend events that took place out of doors and in broad daylight. I never went to the post-UFO bouts of euphoria on Primrose Hill, I missed Mike and Kate McInnerney's wedding, all sunshine and bells and white clothing in Kensington Gardens. I failed to see Allen Ginsberg at the Legalise Pot rally in Hyde Park. I had always been a devoted night person, but now I really cleaved to the darkness. I didn't want to watch the flower children play, finding myself completely out of place amid such bliss.

All I could hear in Hobbit Heaven was the voice of Mordor. The busts, the jailings, the gunships over Vietnam on TV every night, the US cities that, from 1966 onwards, burned every summer intruded on the Maxfield Parrish paradise. Germaine Greer called me a 'wheezing Jeremiah', but I simply couldn't shake the feeling that nothing was being stored up for both the real and metaphoric winter. The Ant and the bloody Grasshopper was being written in psychedelic script, and could anything survive the winds of November? Commercial flower power had bloomed fast and would die fast. Fashion is the fertiliser of entropy, and when rock manager Tony Secunda announced that he was pulling the Move out of 'the flower-power racket', I braced myself for the fall.

The only personal consolation was that, even though flower power might lose its petals by autumn, I was getting out of the bloody East End. Red-romantic as it might have been, a life lived both literally and figuratively between skid row and the waterfront tended to become tired. The rebels craved a few of the creature comforts, an escape from Brick Lane and society's bottom feeders. And no sooner had the desire been admitted than temptation was offered, just as if we'd said the magic word to Groucho Marx and the duck had dropped. In the summer of 1967, we – that is to say, Joy and I – were offered the chance of an apartment in the West End.

Prior to their wedding Mike and Kate McInnerney had lived in a flat on the top floor of the building that was part of the same structure as the Shaftesbury Theatre, and when they moved the place came under offer. It stood at the intersection of Shaftesbury Avenue, Endell Street and High Holborn, a junction that is actually called Prince's Circus, although few know that and even fewer care. That anyone I knew had a lease on a flat in a building which not only had a lift, but where the rest of the tenants appeared to be either psychiatrists or the kind of banker who shuttled between the City of London and the gnome caverns of Zurich, was a miracle on the level of the loaves and fishes. This rental conjuration had in fact been wrought by a wealthy globe-trotting American called Simon, who had no visible means of support, but would babble endlessly about schemes to involve the Kelloggs breakfast-cereal empire in the marketing of psychedelic posters via adverts on the back of Sugar Frosted Flakes.

After Simon abruptly left town we finally discovered that his *invisible* means of support was, in fact, cocaine. I imagine, in the Seventies, we would have sussed him out instantly (I mean . . . Kelloggs as part of the revolution?), but at the apogee of the love generation we were actually a little naive regarding powdered intoxicants, and the penny only really dropped when some dark and dangerous men showed up in search of Simon, and intimated that if they weren't fully assured that their quarry had done a runner, someone might have to die. Fortunately his departure was plainly demonstrable, and his flatmates Chris and Sandy – after Mike and

Kate left, even Simon had to have some help with the astronomical rent – remained shaken but alive, and holding the tenancy. Although expensive, the flat, with its size and location, was too good to let go. Three bedrooms (one a circular turret), a living room, kitchen and bath, plus french windows and a sixth-floor balcony, plumb-centre in the happening city; Brian Jones didn't have it this good.

Chris Rowley and Duncan Sanderson had been at public school together, and seemed to have fallen into UFO and the underground at approximately the same time. Chris was short, curly-haired and intensely bright, a definite seeker after answers and enlightenment. Sandy was tall, reed-thin, devastatingly handsome and a magnet to women. When I first met them, they were getting by on odd gigs in and around UFO and other psychedelic enterprises. Chris sold *IT* and posters at the club, and both would work for Yoko Ono rigging the gallery show at which she first met John Lennon. Sandy would shortly join the Deviants on bass and commence a career that would include playing with the Pink Fairies, the Lightning Raiders and a number of other bands, while Chris would go on to become a well-respected science-fiction and fantasy writer, and we would remain close friends for the next three decades.

Mercifully the landlords at 212 Shaftesbury Avenue were not able to employ the same methods as the cocaine wholesalers who came looking for Simon. They couldn't simply send round a trio of heavies to demand that everyone split. Simon had made a legal transfer of the cast-iron lease, and as long as Chris and Sandy continued to come up with the rent each month, there was very little they could do about any of us, no matter how much we might offend the bankers and psychiatrists when they encountered us in the lift. Joy and I followed Mike and Kate into the big room that opened onto the balcony. Sandy, who did a lot of entertaining, had the turret room and Chris was cloistered bookishly in the smaller bedroom at the far end of the rather odd triangular living room in which we all smoked dope and watched television.

When offered a share in a pad that was already the stuff of local hippie legend, Joy and I naturally jumped at the chance. Not only because it was an obvious improvement on our current living conditions, but because the disorganised kibbutz in the East End was clearly moving into the final phase of entropy. Ralph had gone and

Pete was becoming more and more uncomfortable both with his role in the band and his protracted stay in London when, in theory, he was supposed to be on his way round the world. The options were either to reorganise or to bale out and we accepted the paisley parachute, totally ignoring the fact that the situation between Joy and me was far from solidly bonded. The marriage had grown progressively more shaky with both of us straying sexually, but leaving the all-but-unconcealed infidelities unchallenged and unmentioned.

Although they were both too polite to say so, I'm sure Chris and Sandy often rued the day they'd taken us in. Joy had a fixation for adopting stray cats, both feline and human. The former culminated in the cat population growing to an uncontrolled complement of six, and the latter in a Canadian called Jamie Mandelkau, who had more gall than most living males and would ultimately steal my wife and wreck my band, while he constantly declared himself my best buddy and I wondered if I should go loudly and flamboyantly insane.

Boo Radley's Porch

The consensual opinion of a number of my friends was that all my troubles really stemmed from my not dropping acid. I tended to agree with them, but still I didn't take the acid. The reasons were multiple. I was nervous. I didn't doubt that LSD-25 was the ultimate mind-wrencher and had trepidations as to how much wrenching my mind would stand. I also rebelled against the mystic trappings with which the ingesting of psychedelic drugs had been invested by the Tim Leary propaganda machine. Many of my peers treated LSD as a spiritual rite of passage with distinctly macho overtones, and even though they sequestered themselves in their room with their pure water, brown rice and copy of *Blonde on Blonde*, a definite vibe could be felt that you weren't a real man until you'd taken your righteous trip.

Taking acid had strong connotations of the kids in *To Kill a Mockingbird* scaring themselves stupid by sneaking onto Boo Radley's porch. It all rather reminded me of how, at about twelve or thirteen, a big deal had been created around bluffing your way into your first

X-certificate horror film. In my case it had been *Blood of the Vampire*, starring veteran Shakespearian actor Sir Donald Woolfit – probably fallen on hard times despite a knighthood – and Hammer scream-queen Barbara Shelley. The film was totally unremarkable, not even a true vampire movie in that Woolfit, the director of a lunatic asylum, was in fact a regular mortal who just needed blood transfusions to go on living in the days before blood-banks. It proved far from the expected test of nerve. The true ordeal, as in most things, was the anticipation. How bad would it be? Although I laughed and joked with my friends, and pretended that the hardest part would be gaining admission despite being under-age, in private I wondered if I'd be able to handle it.

And so it was with lysergic acid diethylamide 25. Ken Kesey calling his mobile freakshow and drug party the 'Acid Test' was no empty pun. The belief in the mid-Sixties was that acid would not only bring enlightenment and a profound change in human attitudes, but would separate the sheep from the metaphysical goats. It wasn't exactly that any philosophical argument one might make was invalidated by not having dropped acid, but it was certainly diminished by the fact that one hadn't passed the test and was thus still not the recipient of the chemical revelation.

Fortunately, even as an acid virgin, I was too forceful to be ignored, but I was very aware that a number of friends, associates and cronies, who knew that my dropping acid was totally inevitable, simply wished I'd get it over with so that they'd see what kind of Farren came out the other side. Maybe he'd stop being such a bloody pessimist and constantly bleating on about the sorry state of the revolution. I believe a couple of attempts were made to spike me, but I unwittingly outwitted these, and when the moment finally came I would confound the Learyists by dropping my first trip in one of the most public and self-destructive ways possible. To my relief, I didn't emerge as the kind of blissed-out clod who, when railing against the dangerous shape of things to come, simply smiled and assured myself that 'It'll be groovy'. I would still be in sufficiently belligerent shape to snap back, 'Of course it won't be fucking groovy. The world is a mind-bogglingly complex place and no one is going to walk away who refuses to acknowledge that.'

One of the great psychedelic dilemmas centred on leadership and a coherent philosophy. In that they had neither, the hippies found both their strength and their weakness. The easy out for any liberation movement is to band together behind the first charismatic, half-decent orator who comes along, embrace said orator's narrow ideology and then march boldly into the future to found some Reich or Comintern intended to last a thousand years. This was the course taken by both the radical Right and the revolutionary Left, and had given us Adolf Hitler, Joe Stalin and, currently, Chairman Mao and the Red Guard. Early on Bob Dylan had been offered the crown, but he'd deftly side-stepped with the instruction to 'watch the parking meters'. Tim Leary was side-lining himself by insisting on the sacrament of LSD before anyone so much as blew their nose. Mick Jagger avoided the gig by the combination of vapidity and small-time Satanism that was ultimately unmasked at Altamont, and Jimi Hendrix talked exclusively through the guitar. Rumours from Havana had it that Che had split with Fidel over very similar questions.

The twin problems were agenda and direction. The Dialectics of Liberation had attempted to formulate both and had blown itself up in total dissent by the time the Deviants howled it to a close. To all appearances, the counterculture could only move by collective consent of a kind that had only previously been observed in lemmings. Obviously it would have been so much tidier if a few directives could have been issued from some central committee. Fighting inertia with agitprop could be exhausting and time-consuming. Fortunately, though, at around that time London was treated to a prime example of what happened to movements with leaders, hierarchy and an iron-bound ideology that also espoused LSD as a means of control. It came dressed up like a hybrid of Count Dracula and Prince Valiant, and made a nuisance of itself for a year or so around the London psychedelic scene.

The Process Church of the Final Judgement was first established in London's upmarket Mayfair area in 1967. Its members, with their long Christ-like, centre-parted hair and uniform of black and purple capes, quickly became a familiar sight at psychedelic clubs and hippie gatherings. They seemed very keen on recruiting bikers and hippies to their movement, particularly wealthy hippies and – best of all – wealthy hippie rock stars. In this they were less than successful.

According to legend, they had a stoned Marianne Faithfull in their clutches for a few days, but she was ultimately rescued by some burly Rolling Stones roadies and bodyguards. The Stones might have been in the throes of generating their own Satanic majesty, but they certainly didn't want some other group of power-fascinated freaks muscling in on their act, and they especially didn't want them carrying off their women. The Process philosophy that good and evil – symbolised by Jesus and Lucifer – were simply the two sides of the same yin/yang coin had its appeal and conjured loud echoes of Aleister Crowley's 'Do what you will is the only law'. Their logo, however, was a little too like a Nazi swastika redrawn by a slick Swiss typographer.

I was tempted to go and take a look at one of the open-house meetings they held at their palatial joint in Mayfair, but I kept putting it off. It wasn't that the Process frightened me, but I knew a visit would culminate in conflict and I asked myself if I really needed the aggravation. What would I really learn from the experience? Also I was warned off by a number of my friends. Chris Rowley dismissed the Process out of hand as 'Nazi psychiatry' and assured me that, although a good slanging match might be fun, it was also a total waste of my time. Steve Abrams, the amiable expatriate American academic who was one of the driving forces behind the marijuana legalisation movement and had conceived the full-page advert in *The Times*, also thought the group had definite Nazi leanings. Steve had actually given a lecture there. He would smile as though relishing the joke. 'It was on brainwashing. It seemed appropriate.' In the end, I never bothered to go.

It was only with the publication of Ed Sanders' 1971 gonzo account of Charlie Manson and his followers, *The Family*, that we really learned what the Process was all about, and even that was rendered sketchy by the removal of a crucial chapter of the book, after threats of a massive lawsuit by the Church of Scientology. Robert DeGrimston, a breakaway Scientologist, had founded the Process in 1963 as a money-spinning mind-control entity, but experienced some kind of dark epiphany in Xtul in the Yucatan and, after that, things swerved well out of hand – some claimed to the point where the Process and the Manson family committed a number of joint ritual murders, possibly in the name of Abraxas, the rooster-headed Gnostic god in whom darkness and light are both united and transcended. DeGrimston's wife Kathy didn't help matters by claiming to be a reincarnation of Joseph Goebbels and Hecate. By 1974 the Process had dropped off the radar.

Or so we thought.

In 1996 a Process website appeared on the internet, and the issue of the rock magazine *Alternative Press* for February 1997 ran a feature detailing both the history and return of the Process – without the DeGrimstons – and how the newly revived cult was having an influence on a number of 'alternative' rockers. The website and the *Alternative Press* article were both a little vague regarding the aims and beliefs of this resuscitated, but seemingly somewhat sanitised, Process, but both appeared to verify that the Sixties – both good and bad – are always with us.

Okay, so Dylan was right, you couldn't follow leaders, and the Process – and, a little later, Charlie Manson – offered us all the confirmation we needed. The hippie revolution would clearly remain rudderless, and I had to decide what I was going to do while it drifted to its eventual safe haven or destructive reef. Join Jim Morrison in preaching chaos, disorder and irresponsible drunkenness? It sounded pretty damned appealing, except that I had an underground newspaper to look after.

Or so I thought.

Sacked from the Revolution

We were eating oysters and drinking Guinness somewhere in Mayfair, and Nigel was augmenting his with double shots of Jameson. He clearly had something on his mind that was making him nervous. Although only in his early twenties, Nigel Samuel was already so far gone as an alcoholic that it was rare to see him eat, and even then it was usually something semi-liquid, like soup or the aforementioned oysters. It would be six or seven years before I'd learn what it was like to be in that condition.

After an awkward preamble, he came to the point. 'You know, Mick, the underground doesn't owe you a living.'

I gestured to the waiter. Now I wanted a large Jameson. 'What the hell are you talking about?'

Nigel looked even more uncomfortable and chased a swallow of whiskey with Guinness and yet another oyster. 'It's been decided that we're going to have to let you go.'

'Are you telling me I'm being fired from *IT*?'

'I'm sorry.'

'No one's ever been fired from *IT*.'

'Then it'll be a first.'

'So where's Bill Levy, shouldn't he be doing this?'

Nigel looked round helplessly. He'd obviously been handed the shitty end of the stick, and was being expected to hand it on to me. In that, I suppose we had a certain kinship. 'I think we'd both better have another drink.'

Nigel was plainly very unhappy, but I wasn't quite ready to let him off the hook. 'This is fucking unreal.'

I mean, here I was sitting in some expensive oyster bar, being told by a scared and drunk boy millionaire that I was being sacked from the revolution, and the only reason such a strange occurrence was coming to pass was because, over the last couple of months, he had bought up a large part of the existing underground.

The arrival of Nigel had taken me completely by surprise. Seemingly he'd simply walked into Indica one day, a tall, near-emaciated apparition with limp hair falling in his face and wearing a floor-length velvet coat in Robin Hood green, and enquired if he could be of any help. When it was discovered that this strange newcomer had a car, he was immediately dispatched to deliver bundles of newspapers to the newsstands we supplied directly; but when someone went out to help him unload a pile of returns, and the car turned out to be a Ferrari, a whole new interest was taken in the willing newcomer.

I think I must have been off with the Deviants at the time because all I remember is returning to find that the entire set-up at *IT* had changed. The business office still lurked below Indica. Joy was still a part of it, but Max Zwemmer had handed the running of the paper over to a guy supposedly called Dave Hall (although, to this day, I don't know if Dave Hall was his real name). Even more than Max, Dave was exactly what an underground newspaper needed as a business manager. I never asked any questions, so he never had to confirm or deny that the paper's turnover was being used to launder cash for the hashish trade and, at times, even finance the odd deal. It may sound odd that the entire business side of the paper should be handed over to a complete stranger with fairly obvious criminal contacts. It probably sounds even odder that I was ready to accept Dave because Joy vouched for him and was prepared to go with her judgement. Our marriage might be ready for the wrecking ball, but I still trusted her never to allow the newspaper to fall into the hands of a conman. Dave Hall was yet another of those taken-on-trust alliances that, by some serial miracle, succeeded more times than they failed.

I had no problem with the arrival of Dave in the Indica basement. What worried me far more was that the entire editorial staff, of which I was supposedly a part, had vanished. 'Where did everyone go?'

'Bill and his crew are working over at Nigel's.'

Both parts of this sentence failed to compute. I hadn't been aware that Bill Levy had a crew. I knew that the skeleton staff with which I'd been working was a thing of the past, but I wasn't aware that so much hiring had taken place that there was now an editorial 'crew'. It also struck me as kind of weird that suddenly business and editorial were in different locations. Okay, so the Indica basement was cramped, but I'd always figured that working cheek by jowl generated a valuable solidarity. Also, during the emergency, business worked by day, while art and editorial tended to work by night. I didn't get what was now going on, but rather than stand around speculating, I took a cab over to where Nigel maintained a luxury flat just off Sloane Square.

The first thing I discovered was that I really wasn't wanted by the new editorial team, except in so far as I might have a handle on the rock 'n' roll end of things. Not that Bill and his 'crew' – who were all new faces to me – were much interested in rock 'n' roll except for the fact that the record industry had finally started buying advertising in the underground press. We were back with the hated concept of a 'music section'. As for the direction of the remainder of the paper, Bill seemed to have a course plotted that suited his personality as thumbnailed by Dave Robins in *Days in the Life*: 'A middle-aged American, mid-thirties then a former college lecturer and Ezra Pound fanatic'. My hackles rose. More Ezra bloody Pound? This was assuredly not the publication I'd busted my hump to preserve, and conflict appeared inevitable. I suspected Bill and the others were probably dreading my return and the predictably self-righteous merry hell I was going to raise. As it turned out, they needn't have worried. It had been a long haul, and my reaction, much to their relief, was to wander off in disgust.

I don't think I visited the new editorial office more than twice more. Instead I sunk myself in a non-communicative sulk, took care of my business out of the Indica basement, turned in a few record reviews and had as little to do with Bill and his merry men as possible. My brief glimpses of their operating methods indicated that they seemed to have an exceptionally good thing going. They lounged around in this elegant, James Bond pad, while Nigel hung out and ordered booze, Chinese food or other goodies and they giggled at the kind of inside jokes I'd been well past in my second year at art school. The living was damned easy and they didn't need me becoming the voice of their collective conscience.

In the days after this first visit to Sloane Square I found out more about Nigel Samuel's history and background. His father had been the socialist property mogul Howard Samuel and, when he committed suicide, Nigel had inherited close to half of London. As Miles, who was about the closest to him, told it, 'When Nigel was about thirteen [his father] took him to Switzerland and stayed at some fancy hotel, and he was being shown how to drink wine, smoke cigars, all that stuff, and one day his father just went out and drowned himself in the lake, leaving Nigel just sitting there, utterly fucked up. Traditionally, every year, around the anniversary of his father's death in October, he always goes a bit loopy.' I'm not sure it was October right then, but as I recall it, the nights had started to draw in.

Matters were complicated by the fact that Nigel wasn't only incredibly rich, but his wealth came with a lot of Byzantine political ties. Howard Samuel had been a major financial backer of the Labour Party, and the estate was administered by no less a person than Lord Goodman, Harold Wilson's implacable personal lawyer; between the time of his father's death and Nigel's coming of age, Goodman had effectively controlled his life. Nigel developed a venomous loathing of politicians, and his involvement in the underground was almost certainly his way of using his wealth to stick it to a power elite. I always figured that, although confused in the extreme, Nigel's heart was in relatively the right place, but his judgement of character left a lot to be desired.

Although I personally rather liked the unfortunate Nigel, I had many misgivings about what his money and intervention would do to *IT*. Even a radical medium, if it's operating within a capitalist system, has to be sensitive to market pressures. It may deal in subversion, agitprop and be part of a dissenters' network, but it also has to move copies off the newsstand. With Nigel underwriting the costs, and maintaining Bill Levy and his editorial staff in splendid isolation, a potentially fatal buffer was being created between editors and readers. The editorial staff also seemed to have a marked prejudice against hippies. Dave Robins again: 'We never saw a hippie, Bill was no hippie, I wasn't a hippie.' Maybe so, but, like it or not, the hippies were everywhere and, as far as I was concerned, formed the paper's major constituency. If nothing else, it was an attitude that cut off this new crew from vital consumer feedback.

At approximately the same time another potentially damaging situation that had nothing to do with either Levy or Samuel got under way, which would make it possible for the same kind of editorial isolation to continue, even after Nigel was out of the picture. The lonely hearts classified ads began to grow by quantum leaps after *IT* decided to accept gay personal ads and, for a while, the paper would command a huge readership of gay men, maybe as many as 30,000, who bought it for the classified section. Ultimately it would result in the paper's second bust, which would, this time, go all the way to trial and conviction. At first, however, it wasn't the potential legal problems that bothered me. It was an odd economic subtlety that dogs any paper when it becomes too comfortable with one highly specific advertising section. Today, in the USA, much of the so-called alternative press is able to maintain its drearily impersonal and politically correct editorial content only because it's subsidised by ads for phone sex and prostitution.

The inclusion of gay-sex ads was laudable, innovative and courageous, but also a Faustian bargain. Any alternative publication that is financially dependent on sex ads creates for itself a readership that may have absolutely no interest in the general content of the magazine or newspaper. It may be an economic solution, but it distorts the relationship between sales and content. The publication might have an editorial policy that is in fact losing its real and intended readership, but this is disguised by the purely service buyers who pick up copies for the advertising. It's something an editor has very carefully to factor-in to all policy decisions, and Bill Levy and his successors simply weren't doing this.

All my instincts told me that *IT* was on its way to being managed into toothless irrelevance, but after my tête-à-tête with Nigel in the oyster bar it wasn't my problem any more, and I could now go to hell in my own disorganised basket – except that Nigel Samuel had yet to finish with me.

Chapter Five

Underground Impresarios

We had a whole factory going on the ground floor of the new *IT* building on Betterton Street in Covent Garden. It was March 1968. A dozen freaks were pulling freshly pressed records, in their white inner sleeves, out of the boxes in which they'd been delivered, slipping them into the printed covers and then repacking them. A couple more were rolling joints or making themselves available to go out for beer and sandwiches when needed. The Deviants had made an album, but it had been done in a way that few other bands had even considered at the time. With the exception of actually supplying the finance, we had pulled off the whole thing ourselves, all the way from conception to manufacturing and distribution. We had gone in knowing almost nothing and come out at the end of the process, maybe not experts in the ways of the record industry, but at least with our own finished product. The truly amazing part was that, just three months earlier, I had been on the verge of collapse, all enterprises appeared to be failing and the summer of flower power was collapsing into a winter of discontent worse than my direst paranoid predictions.

The hammer blows had come like a prizefighter's triple combination – one, two and then one more – that should have put me, if not on the canvas, at least sprawling on the ropes. I had been fired from *IT*, and just before that UFO had collapsed. Then the Deviants had all but broken up after a disastrous trip to a highly unlikely rock festival in Utrecht, called (with a tenuous grasp of both English and practical reality) Flight to Lowlands Paradise.

For the London hippie community, the disappearance of UFO was probably the most telling blow, since it had tended to substantiate that the underground, far from being able to mount a cultural revolution, couldn't even maintain a successful nightclub. After the cops shut us down by putting pressure on Mr Gannon at the Blarney Club, Joe Boyd had tried to save the day by moving the entire enterprise to the Roundhouse, but, although the Roundhouse could hold perhaps three times the audience, it generated ten times the grief.

The problem was essentially one of size. The club was now so big that the skinheads knew exactly where to find us, and we were also coming to the notice of the hoods who ran the protection rackets in Camden and Kentish Town. Where the mods and skins had come to the Blarney Club in their twos and threes, they began showing up at the Roundhouse mob-handed, far beyond anything that Norman, the Firm and I had the capacity to handle. Additional help was recruited from some very odd sources that included an East London karate club and a squad of Michael X's black militants. Although we managed to keep the worst of the aggro away from the perception of the audience, the door began to take on aspects of a rough day at Khe San. Since the *IT* party, Centre 42 had made a few structural improvements, including a more functional set of wide concrete stairs and an open foyer where potential troublemakers could be contained, but both the karate shoguns in their white kimonos and the X-men in Black Panther-style berets, turtle-necks and black leather tended to intimidate, and many of the hippies found this less than groovy.

The compensation was that, at its peak, the Roundhouse was a pretty damned spectacular psychedelic environment, with a full 360-degree lightshow projected on huge white plastic sheets hung from the circular gallery. For the lightshow to create its full impact, however, the place had to remain almost as dark as a cinema, which made it even more crucial that the bovver boys be turned back at the door. Once they were inside the auditorium, they were hard to see, let alone deal with, and when trouble did spill into the crowd, the crowd itself could be more of a hindrance than a help. On one memorable occasion I was forced to confront a team of seething young proles who bluffed their way past the door and then started harassing hippies. I figured I could get them out with a quartet of militants behind me. The secret is to be determined to avoid violence at all costs, but never to let your adversary know that. It's a kind of a

Gandhian confidence trick and, after eight months at UFO, I had my confidence well together.

We were starting to back the bad guys out of the room, without any punches being thrown, when a troupe of hippie maidens decided to imitate Suzy Creamcheese and smother the confrontation with peace and love. One of them embraced me, pinning my arms so that the leading boot-droog was able to smack me on the side of the head a number of times before my back-up hustled him out. Creamcheese had a certain deranged magic that enabled her to pull off those kinds of tactics, but God preserve me from those who didn't and couldn't, but still made the attempt.

We might have been managing to handle the skinheads, but other far more sinister forces began to close in. Things turned unpleasantly grim when Miles was robbed while depositing the UFO takings in a nightsafe. Although unhurt, he was understandably shaken, and the first thoughts of throwing in the towel were voiced. After the mugging incident, rumours flew that word had indirectly come down that similar nastiness would go on happening until an arrangement was made to pay for protection. At this point Joe Boyd declared enough was enough. With that kind of pressure, I couldn't blame him, but the closure came all too quickly. The staff were unexpectedly thrown out of work, and I was hardly happy to be one of them.

I couldn't argue any longer that closing UFO would deprive the London freaks of a place to go. The Middle Earth Club had opened up in Covent Garden. It was run by Dave Howson, whom Hoppy had taken into the Technicolor Dream organisation and who, as a result of the experience, considered himself a fully-fledged 'underground' rock promoter, but the story circulated that he was actually fronting for a couple of Scottish businessmen who'd seen the hippie potential. Under Howson's direction, Middle Earth offered a more commercialised version of the original UFO formula.

Not that UFO itself exactly conformed to the original UFO formula any more, especially since Joe had started booking acts like the tedious Ten Years After and Dantalion's Chariot, the flower-power brainstorm of 'prime looner' Zoot Money. He was also bringing in more established performers like Jeff Beck – although the ever unpredictable Beck took one look at the crowd, muttered 'Fuck this' into the vocal mike and split without playing a note.

On the positive side, the Deviants had played one of the UFO Roundhouse shows and had had one of their best nights so far. Some changes had occurred in the band during the summer. Clive Maldoon was gone. He'd failed to show up on a couple of occasions and proffered only the lamest of excuses. It turned out that he'd auditioned as a replacement for bass player Ace Kefford in the Move, and had been so super-confident of getting the gig that he'd convinced himself he could dump the Deviants. Unluckily, when fame and fortune with the Move fell through, and Maldoon came sheepishly home, we had already replaced him. Sid Bishop, a short, amiable musician from South London, came to us by the time-honoured route of a classified ad in *Melody Maker*. When he listed his favourite guitarists as Les Paul and Frank Zappa, we decided that he was our boy, all but sight unseen.

Sid joined us just in time to find himself in the middle of the band almost coming to grief on its first adventure in foreign parts. Flight to Lowlands Paradise was supposed to be the Dutch equivalent of the 14-Hour Technicolor Dream, but the promoter made the mistake of holding the event somewhere outside the provincial city of Utrecht. The entire show was plagued by murderous acoustics, a lack of heat, pitifully underpowered equipment, massive confusion over where we were supposed to sleep and a corps de ballet of traditional Dutch clog-dancers who invaded the communal dressing room and stayed there all night, drinking gin and making the smoking of dope very difficult. As a result we commenced drinking the moment we arrived and didn't stop until we were back on the boat train. Throughout the course of the ordeal we began to get poisonously irritated with each other, and I was forced to hide in a cinema watching John Wayne in *The Comancheros*, dubbed into Dutch with all the finesse of a Godzilla movie, while a gang of small children yelled, screamed and cheered at every outbreak of gunfire, and while rock & roll madness loomed nearby.

Although the others in the band had been mightily gung-ho for the trip to Holland during the planning stage, after forty-eight hours of fuck-up they rivalled wet and hungry spaniels with their big-eyed reproach. This was another fine mess I'd led them into. Dylan should have amended his line to 'Don't follow leaders, but always keep one around as a scapegoat'. The crunch came on the boat back to Harwich. The ferry pitched and rolled in a Channel gale, and British soldiers on leave from Germany threw up their duty-free beer all round us, leaving the deck awash with vomit. It was then that Alex and Pete announced that they couldn't see any future in what we were doing and were jacking it in. Sid, on the other hand, who'd only just joined the band and therefore had much more reason to be both daunted and appalled by the ways of the Deviants, was taking it all in his stride and expressed his willingness to stick around for whatever might come next. To my surprise, Russell – who, although our ideal drummer, was a past master at the art of complaint and recrimination – also decided that he would hang in with Sid and me if we could come up with a way to continue.

Before drafting plans or hunting for a new bass player, I felt I needed time to wallow in depression and self-pity. Confronted by my near-suicidal misery, Joy dispatched me north to Carlisle to stay with her arch-groupie friend and one-time comrade-in-arms, Carol. Carol had apparently always fancied me and would be happy to take me in for a few days of rest and recuperation, which said a great deal about the way things now stood between Joy and me. I actually suspect that the move wasn't as unconventionally and morally altruistic as it seemed. Joy may have wanted me out of the way not only because I was a pain in the arse to be around, but also because she had some extra-curricular romantic plans of her own.

Cumberland in November was hardly a resort location, but Carol and I didn't find ourselves going out very much. For the first couple of days we hardly got out of bed. Lewd and uncomplicated, and comfortably drunk most of the time, we turned her one-down, two-up, Victorian terraced house into a happily sordid love nest. I was actually able to switch off my brain, eat, sleep and fuck, sustained by a diet of vodka, cigarettes, hash and bacon sandwiches. I didn't have to answer to anyone as long as I kept Carol amused, and since she was a working-class heroine who bore a passing resemblance to the young Glenda Jackson, this was anything but a chore. Early in this interlude of welcome depravity I made the remarkable discovery that, even though she'd been running with rock bands for as long as she'd had the inclination, she had never had a man perform orally on her before, and that I would happily oblige was a welcome novelty. The admission may seem amazing – even alarming – but it does provide a gauge of the sexual benightedness of the supposedly hip English rock 'n' roll male as late as the late Sixties. In return for making up for all this lost time, she indulged my own fascination with black stockings, heels, garter belts and other traditional whorish trappings. A threesome with one of her friends was also discussed, but sadly the logistics were never finalised and this fantasy was left unrealised.

It was only after a blissful week that I had to own up that I couldn't hide in passion's cheap oblivion for ever, more's the pity, and reluctantly dragged myself back to London, where, to my surprise, two things immediately lifted my spirits. First, we encountered a seemingly competent bass player who went by the name of Cord Rees and looked absolutely like the generic hippie musician. Second, in a surprising turnaround after helping oust me from *IT*, Nigel Samuel phoned and suggested we meet. Over yet more alcohol, he stunned me with a proposition. He would put up the money for the Deviants to make an album. Not only would we make an album, but we would press it ourselves and use our own pool of artists and designers to create the packaging, and the distribution network established by the underground press, psychedelic poster makers, headshops and the rest would distribute and sell it. Obviously this wasn't the lazy rocker's dream of following Pink Floyd and signing with a major label for *beaucoup* bucks and instant fame. Here was a finite challenge.

I'd always been throwing shitfits over what I saw as concessions to the corporate capitalist music industry, and demanding to know why the cream of the underground bands were being sold off to EMI and Decca. Surely if we could get our shit together to distribute underground newspapers, psychedelic posters and comics, why the hell couldn't we do the same with bigger-ticket items like records? Nigel had called my bluff, and I had to go for it or fall on my sword. I felt it was only fair, however, to warn him that the learning process would have to go into high overdrive, since we knew nothing about what the project really entailed. Such an admission might have caused other potential backers to retreat hastily from the deal, but Nigel and I seemed to have one thing in common. Neither of us considered ignorance a reason to be daunted. Almost all the other enterprises of the underground had started with the same uninformed optimism. If you didn't know something, you could always ask; and if you didn't understand the rules, you didn't have to worry about breaking them. Nigel's name for the company fronting the deal was Underground Impresarios. Kind of pompous, but I wasn't going to argue. My own fantasies were being indulged, so let him have his. All we had to lose were Nigel's money and my dubious reputation.

PTOOFF!

The album was to be called *PTOOFF!* and, for once, no one had thought up the title. It came ready-made: the onomatopoeic lettered explosion that was part of the Marvel Comics panel that inspired the huge, three-by-two-foot foldout psychedelic-Lichtenstein cover. The cover concept had been Nigel's brainchild when he discovered that a large, foldout, single-sheet sleeve was actually cheaper than the conventional twelve-inch record cover. We could be flamboyant *and* cut costs; a fine example of underground lateral thinking. Nigel may have been alcoholic and crazy, but he wasn't stupid and could be counted on to come up with one inspired idea every couple of weeks. Unfortunately, the good ideas were more than offset by the dozens of zigs, zags and outbreaks of drunken lunacy that accompanied them.

In fact, my first education was in what a pain the very wealthy can be – especially the inherited wealthy. Not only on their own account, but also because they affect those around them. Like flames to a moth, they attract ad hoc courts and would-be courtiers wanting their attention, their confidence, their time and their patronage. Their world is seen through the distortion of the entourage. Their whims are humoured, and their tantrums are tolerated. They rarely receive objective opinions, are the last to hear the bad news and are constantly outfitted in the Emperor's new clothes. With Nigel being so young, impressionable and drunk, this went in spades with him, and every time we recruited a newcomer we had to figure out how he or she was going to react.

Imperial courts are invariably closed and poisonous snake pits, and with Nigel well on the way to forming his weird empire, his was no exception. The alternative society was not without its alternative social climbers, and outside our immediate circle there were plenty of Samuel hangers-on ready to advise on how the Deviants' album should be made, or possibly not made at all. By the time he offered to finance the record, Nigel seemed to have financial fingers in most of the enterprises in what remained of the underground. He had moved himself into a piece of penthouse property on the north side of Cavendish Square, which served as his dark tower where he could brood, drink and drop lighted cigarettes on the priceless Persian rugs. He had moved in one of the ladies of the Exploding Galaxy dance troupe to make his life somewhat more comfortable, but his demons still beset him.

In addition to a wild-child girlfriend – who I believe later became a wild-child wife – he had also bought a Lotus Elan, which was even more suicidal than the Ferrari. By far his biggest investment, however, had been in *IT*. He had provided it with a permanent home in Betterton Street, just five minutes from our flat in Shaftesbury Avenue, and, to prove that he was serious, he'd had the outside painted a garish orange with a large blow-up of the IT girl overlaid in black. Although it was the *IT* building, the paper took up only three of the floors. Nigel retained the top floor for his own use, and the basement was rented to ECAL, Miles' distribution company. In his own weird way Nigel Samuel was attempting to give the revolution a corporate structure. I fancy, had I been part of *IT*, that I would have resisted Nigel's masterplan with all the vocal volume I could muster, but Dave Hall and Bill Levy seemed to enjoy it, so I continued to dismiss it as none of my concern. I had an album to make, and I had to ensure that it wasn't masterplanned out of existence.

The first move was to start recruiting the extra people we'd need over and above the actual members of the band. Although Nigel was financing the deal, it didn't mean that we had unlimited funds to piss away. The budget was going to be tight, and it had to be made clear to all involved that this was going to be for love, fun and free dope and beer; no one was going to get rich behind *PTOOFF!* As we metaphorically rode around recruiting a team, like Yul Brynner and Steve McQueen in *The Magnificent Seven*, our first call was on Jack Henry Moore. I don't know if Jack appreciated what I was doing, loved me because I was crazy or simply liked the idea of having a well-equipped recording studio as a temporary playground, but he instantly signed up for the duration all the same.

In all respects, with Jack Moore, we'd struck gold. First blessing: Jack was totally acclimatised to Nigel and his ways. Also the Arts Lab was up and running on Drury Lane, and Jack's sound equipment was all in one place, set up and ready for psychedelic pre-production. We could also rehearse in the basement cinema that, after a few months of after-hours orgies, was starting to smell a little strange. With digital technology and sampling nothing more than a science-fiction dream, the pre-production was a matter of mix, match and make do, with Heath Robinson set-ups using tape loops and two stereo recorders set ten feet apart, rolling the same continuous tape. We repeated, we echoed, we pillaged industrial sounds and primitive percussion, and even attempted phoney phone calls decades before the Jerky Boys. By using the trick of the two machines and one tape, patched to an outside phone line, it was possible to call someone and have them talking to a delayed echo of their own voice.

We made calls to a selection of leading lights in the underground and the avant-garde, thinking that most would realise what was happening. It transpired that we'd greatly overestimated the intelligentsia. Most simply hung up on us, while others became flustered, confused and even angry. One well-known poet started screaming increasingly vitriolic abuse until he'd reach a peak of both volume and profanity, and then slammed down the phone. The only one who twigged, and turned the mystery into an impromptu performance, was Yoko Ono; when I later got on the line and explained what we were doing, Yoko – who, even then, had a formidable reputation as a hard-nosed businesswoman – was more than agreeable to us using the tape.

The second recruit to the team was Steve Sparks. Steve had a Romany gypsy background and was another ex-mod from East London, who thought that pop music had ended with Phil Spector, but still took a delight in anything that might cause trouble. He was one of the old-style mods, the 'modernists' who pre-dated – and rightly thought themselves infinitely superior to – the scooter boys who followed. The 'modernists' were essentially stylish beatniks, working-class existentialists who smoked Gitanes, drank Guinness, looked at the pictures in *Salut Les Copains* although they couldn't read a word of French and worshipped Miles Davis in his golden era of cool, copying his silk suits and perfect mannerisms. Steve had, in his glory days, been written up in *Harpers* or *Man about Town* as one of the leading trendsetters, and had engaged in an intense rivalry with Mark Feld, another early pretender to the spurious title 'King Mod', who would later grow his hair, write 'Hippie Gumbo' and change his name to Marc Bolan.

Like so many others, Steve had entered the music business as a social secretary – in his case at Barking Technical College – and by organising folk and rock shows in the East End. With a pretty unerring eye for happening talent, he booked acts as diverse as the Who (when they were still the High Numbers), all the way to Bert Jansch and Davy Graham; he even boasted having paid Cream a mere seventy quid to play an early tryout gig. I first met Steve at UFO. Like any old mod with a mouth on him, he always had some creative reason why he should get in for free, and after a while all pretence was abandoned and I simply waved him through. Usually he'd come back later and we'd chat. Unless he knew Joe from elsewhere, Steve must have made other contacts at the club, because when Boyd set up Witchseason, his production and management company, Steve was hired as the publicist. At the same time he agreed to work with the Deviants as publicist, manager and mentor.

I think Steve believed that I saw him as some kind of East End super-hustler who would make me a star, but the truth was that there was always a strong streak of parody in our relationship, a tongue-in-cheek Tom Parker to a hopelessly preposterous Elvis, although I was grateful even for that. We were so damned young that few realised, as the one walking permanent point on this mission, that I was subject to a high degree of wear and tear and needed someone to flatter my ego occasionally. As a co-conspirator, Sparks was the perfect foil. He would support anything outrageous and would even, at times, come on stage with us, to set fires and detonate explosions. He also turned out to be a damned good publicist, although there were times when I got tired of being pitched as the 'worst band in the world'. A sample of his hyperbolic style can be gleaned from a 1988 interview. No human could have survived in the myths that Steve conjured up:

The Deviants' fans were psychotic. Our groupies were the ugliest in the world and also among the most aggressive in the world. You didn't turn down a Deviants groupie else you'd get your legs broken. Really, really strange people. Take acid in a room full of Deviants fans and you'd end up screaming, jumping out of a window.

What Steve really wanted to do was produce the album, a process that involved him chainsmoking Gitanes and nodding knowingly with his eyes closed. Unfortunately Nigel had already installed an overseer/producer of his own, but, by way of a consolation title, we called Steve our A&R man – whatever the hell that was supposed to mean – and his production input became part of the process. At first we assumed that Jonathan Weber, our imposed producer, would be nothing more than Nigel's stooge, reporting back to him every time we fucked up, or lifted our noses from the grindstone, but as it turned out he was affable, knowledgeable and an invaluable help, and created a much-needed bond of confidence with Victor, the engineer, who like to be referred to as 'Sister George', but clearly considered the rest of us fascinating in our abnormality. And a great deal of confidence was needed. We were working with the same four-track technology as the Beatles had used to cut *Sgt Pepper*, but the Beatles had burned up more than 700 hundred hours on their masterwork. All the Deviants had was a worryingly incalculable timeframe that would end arbitrarily the day that Nigel looked at the meter and blew his stack.

The difficulty with four-track is that, since you have to constantly mix down the layers of recording progress, a great deal of pre-planning is needed, and irreversible decisions have to be made long before the overall picture becomes at all clear. In this, the unlikely trio of Jonathan, Jack and Steve succeeded beyond all expectations and, with no false modesty, I was also grasping the logistics very quickly, learning as I went. We made it easy for ourselves by restricting the album to three or four more or less conventional rock songs, plus three long and more involved pieces with various movements, which became the vehicles for most of Jack and my pre-production loops – although we couldn't find a context for Yoko. With cutups, blackouts, singing and spoken word, it was ambitious stuff for first-timers, even though shamelessly Zappa-influenced. The riff of one of the longer rock songs, 'I'm Coming Home', resurfaced four years later on David Bowie's 'Jean Genie'. Creative happenstance (and flattering), but ironic that a song supposedly about Iggy Pop was set to a recycled Deviants riff.

While the recording progressed, more individuals came into the fold. The Firm became involved in the distribution of the record, and would eventually take over the entire thing, persuading Nigel to sell them the rights in perpetuity – a perpetuity that Peter Shertser and I continue to fight over to this day. Miles and John Peel supported from the periphery, with Miles occasionally interceding with Nigel when matters grew too fraught. And fraught increasingly became the condition, as the working relationship with Nigel grew more tortuous and his pirouettes and wobblers more frequent. Fraught also seemed to be the name of the game being played by our new-found bass player.

Cord Rees was manoeuvring, but I was too inexperienced in the ways of rock groups to be able to spot it until it was all but too late. As the sessions proceeded, he seemed to be working very hard to be Nigel's friend. Not that there was anything wrong with that. God only knows, Nigel have could used a few friends, but Cord was so transparently playing the courtier when Nigel was around that I should have warned myself to watch my back. After he and Nigel had spent the evening together, I'd have Nigel on the phone the next day in some absurd fit of anxiety about the recording, which I could only figure came directly from Cord, or maybe Cord in concert with some of the often hostile, non-Deviant entourage.

I finally realised what was happening only when he finally tried to take me out. Cord's ploy was to wind up Nigel on the exhausted subject of how Mick couldn't sing. (Yeah, and Jackson Pollock couldn't draw, so what's the relevance?) The first I knew of this was when I was summoned around noon one day by an odd-sounding Nigel to his top-floor office in Betterton Street. I've never taken kindly to summonses, but the tone of today's dementia sounded extra-strained and so, instead of telling our boy-patron to fuck off, I dressed and ambled over. When I walked into his office Nigel had already been drinking for a while. Without preamble he launched into the most stunning piece of craziness to date. My voice wasn't up to recording an album, and the lead vocals should be done by a session singer. At long last I lost it. 'Fuck you, Nigel! I don't have to listen to this garbage.'

He took a step back. The self-destructive can be unstoppable when they no longer care. 'It's what I do and why I'm doing it, and if you've got a problem with that, you'd better find some other demented guinea pig to front your "first record to emerge solely from the underground".' Shit or bust-time, and I warmed to my rant. 'Of course I can't sing in the conventional sense, but the time to worry about that was when you made the initial offer, not halfway through the bloody sessions. You always knew what you were getting into.'

Now that the penny had finally dropped, my instincts told me that Cord was pitching to do all the vocals himself. Meanwhile, Nigel was ashen-faced. I don't think anyone had screamed at him like that in a very long time. Surrounded by courtiers, he'd forgotten what righteous fury was really like. I decided it was time to flip my hole card. 'I very much doubt if Sid, Russell, Jack and Sparks will go along with this shit, and even if they do, it's going to be a bitch for them to finish this record, because a lot of crucial information is only in my head. Ask Jonathan Weber.'

Nigel retreated behind his large antique desk, which dominated one end of the room, and flopped petulantly into his high-backed Citizen Kane mogul chair. This was always the move when he felt under pressure. 'Yes.'

That was all he said. No argument or counter-measure, just 'Yes'. Then he poured himself a Scotch from the ever-near decanter and, after a slight hesitation, poured me one. Finally he picked up the phone and started making someone else's life miserable. I assumed it consituted a kind of oblique apology and an instruction to forget the whole conversation. The matter seemed to be settled, but on the way out of the building I was dazed. Now something had to be done about Brother Cord. The son-of-a-bitch had been given an extremely fair shake in terms of the recorded limelight. He'd already sung on one tune, the gentle folk-mawk 'Child of the Sky', and had contributed an acoustic interlude dedicated to his wife, who went by the less-than-elegant pet name of 'Bun'. All his parts were done, since the bass invariably goes down first, and in theory I could fire him without any practical loss. I held off, though; I didn't want morale taking a nosedive in the last furlong.

Once again, blind luck held. Cord Rees solved all my problems by going spectacularly mad. Just two or three days after I'd been screaming at Nigel, he walked into the flat on Shaftesbury Avenue and dropped a bomb of epic proportions. Bun had died during a miscarriage. We were horribly shocked – not least Nigel, who had quite a thing about death after his father's suicide. We told him to take all the time he needed and that we'd stumble on without him. It was impossible to cancel the remaining sessions, but we'd cope.

Then, a couple of days later, Sandy spotted the allegedly deceased Bun walking down the other side of Oxford Street as large as life and twice as healthy. Sandy swiftly darted between cabs and buses to make sure he wasn't hallucinating or witnessing a paranormal phenomenon.

'Hey, Bun! Hang on!'

'Sandy . . .'

'Are you okay?'

She looked at him as though it was she who should be asking the question. 'Of course I'm okay, why shouldn't I be?'

Sandy mumbled his way out of both the impasse and his own shock, then dashed back to report to the rest of us. Cord's head was in some aberrant place that none of us felt equipped even to enter. Without further ado, we hustled him out of the band and out of our lives. Callous perhaps, but this was a rock band, not a therapy group. Anyway, we'd only known Cord a matter of weeks, and if there was any therapy going spare, it would have to be used on Nigel, who had been effectively rendered a basketcase by this psychiatric detonation.

Oddly, when mixed, *PTOOFF!* not only came out rather well, but sold in reasonable numbers for its limited and experimental distribution. By a bizarre irony, the record still enjoys a weird vogue today, both as an icon of the low-fi, techno fans and as an artefact prized by psychedelic collectors. I guess it's like John Huston, playing the infinitely corrupt patriarch Noah Cross in the movie *Chinatown*, remarked, 'Politicians, ugly buildings and whores all get respectable if they last long enough.' Conceivably the same thing applies to strange pieces of recorded music.

Road Warriors

To have our ideas, dreams and even our fears and neuroses turned into a solid physical object like a long-playing record, a plastic artefact that people were actually going into shops and buying with their hard-earned cash, can have a decidedly sobering effect. Perhaps 'sobering' is the wrong word for the Deviants, considering the band's avowed dedication to never drawing an unintoxicated breath, but we certainly faced the realisation that we had to treat seriously what we were doing. We'd taken the king's shilling and were now expected to behave like a commercial rock band and go out on the road to promote our album. On another level, however, we were also assumed to be packing the entire counterculture into the truck, and taking it round the country like some revolutionary revival show. In this, we really had very little choice, even though many moments of doubt ensued when individual band members, and sometimes even the entire band, wished it were otherwise. We were perceived as the rockers from the underground and, in the territory we occupied, perception was everything. If the sentiments and implied commitments made with the music on *PTOOFF!* were not just cynical or mindless posturing, we had to take the same rant and confusion out on the road.

The greater excesses of the counterculture had really been confined to London and a few major cities, and when we rolled into the medium-sized towns we were expected to bring a part of the excess with us; all that stuff they had read about in *IT*, or, in more garbled and lurid form, in *News of the World*. We were supposed to re-create the party they'd missed. They also wanted signposts – they wanted a taste of the alternative. Some even thought we should be handing out free acid, like Ken Kesey's Merry Pranksters. We were expected to fight a weird good fight night after night, venue after venue, town after town, with the surrealism of history continuously repeating itself and the uneasy sense that we could never fully meet all the expectations, short of strapping dynamite to our bodies and blowing ourselves up. I could see why Pink Floyd had so swiftly abdicated from the psychedelic underground and into their own art. The Deviants, however, didn't have that choice and remained the killer-clowns of the revolution.

Now my own view of the world began to distort. I was travelling all over the country. I was unquestionably in a unique position to observe as the rock 'n' drug culture spread to the provinces, and as our embryonic alternative society became increasingly politicised, but all the observations came through the context of being in a bloody rock band. The dilettante gadfly was dead, and I was looking at life through the windshield of a Ford Transit. Of course, I couldn't complain. It was the job I'd always craved. I was no longer writing for *IT*; in fact, I was hardly writing anything, except song lyrics and related poetry. This is not to say that I was solidly on the road throughout that period, but the Deviants were my focus.

By the time *PTOOFF!* was released, the band had temporarily stabilised itself. Russell continued behind the drums, Sid Bishop was on guitar, while Sandy and a newcomer, Michael MacDonnell ('Mac'), exchanged the chores of bass, second guitar and, at times, two thundering basses. The double-bass idea was all mine, and a very bad one. On full amplification, they could replicate an atonal B52 in a power dive and were far from pleasant, but, right then, I had little patience with 'pleasant'.

In addition to the musicians, we also acquired a road crew – Tony Wigens, the driver, and Dave 'Boss' Goodman, who started off as Tony's part-time helper, but would play a major part in all our lives for years to come. As time passed, and the road grew more inevitable, the personalities that made up the band started to gel and solidify. Russell worked on being the band's resident black wind of negativity. The drummer we both needed and deserved could be insightful, incredibly funny and a fund of bright ideas when he wanted. He was also willing to take just about every drug known to man, if offered. He was a double-edged sword, however, and a nettle to be constantly grasped. All too often the dark side would take control and he would turn into the bane of my life. One of his favourite depressing irritants was the knack of sleeping all the way to a date, and then, as the truck crested the proverbial hill with our destination spread out in front of us, waking scratching himself and announcing, 'This is going to be a really terrible gig.'

Fortunately Russell was better as a drummer and chemical explorer than as a soothsayer, because sometimes the gig was indeed terrible, but at other times it could be inspired. He just loved to create his personal black cloud and share it with the rest of us. Later, as times grew more convoluted and the pressure increased, his on-route wake-ups grew into full-blown dramas. He'd demand that we stop the truck, right there on the motorway, and let him out because he couldn't stand it any more. The one time that Tony called his bluff, Russell actually scrambled out of the truck and began jogging back down the M1, causing us to institute dangerous emergency driving measures in order to reel him back in. Even when supposedly hanging out peacefully at the flat, he'd climb onto the balustrade of the sixth-floor balcony and hop insanely from one foot to the other, threatening to plunge to his death on the pavement below at any ill-considered second. The natural assumption would have been that our drummer was suicidal, but then he'd grin and let it be known that the game was conducted expressly to upset me. Russell seemingly had no fear of heights, while I came close to suffering from morbid vertigo. Amazingly, Russell survived – all the way through the Deviants, all the way through the subsequent Pink Fairies – and thrives still today, amusing himself by umpiring cricket matches. Our clashes have long since been put behind us.

Far less complex than Russell, Sandy seemed to exist in a world of his own, apparently content with the natural goals of women, intoxication and rock & roll, coupled with a quiet Monty Python humour and a psychedelic philosophy that frequently made sense only to him. He had been recruited into the band mainly because he was there and willing, which seemed to be the way a lot of things happened to Sandy. He didn't create too many scenes or deliberately precipitate too many crises. One time, when the band was in funds after the deal on the third album, his request for a new bass had been passed over, so he borrowed a tactic from Russell. In a sudden display of totally uncharacteristic, violent Pete Townshend showmanship, he smashed the old bass to matchwood in the final number of a set at Sussex University. Fait accompli. The new bass had to be acquired. Sandy, like Russell, would endure throughout the Deviants and on into the Pink Fairies.

Sid Bishop would not remain. He'd go in the band's second Stalinist purge – the one before the purge that took me out. I was always pretty happy with Sid. He was an anchor of unflappability, who seemed to be able to keep his head when all around were routinely losing theirs.

Mac also wouldn't stay. He was a man of unfulfilled ambitions, who seemed to feel that the world owed him a measure of fame and was frustrated at how slowly it came. Both Mac and I had stubborn tempers and we fought constantly. The dynamics of a band's rivalries usually stem from who's getting the lion's share of the public attention, and in the claustrophobic boredom of travelling it can become almost obsessional. The stupidity is that there's no way it can be solved. A focal member of a band, in my case the singer, can't back off from the performance because of jealousy from upstage.

If we're talking band dynamics, though, the increasingly important figure was Boss Goodman. Boss was, and is, a big guy; a bluff King Hal figure, although even his solid exterior concealed a few unsuspected demons. Boss rapidly assumed the role of an emotional rock against which the rest of us could try and dash ourselves, but come to no harm. The platoon sergeant or team coach, Boss had considerable experience of dealing with the deranged. Both he and driver Tony (the Handsome Roadie) had been denizens of a notorious house at 32 Goodmayes Lane, which was known to most of the dope fiends in the Ilford area, and to the local drug squad, as 'Big Pig'. Steve Sparks describes it thus: 'You couldn't touch anything in Goodman's house or you'd trip. You'd open the fridge and there'd be bottles and bottles of acid. There'd be more acid than food and Boss likes his food.' In the straight world, he'd been the night manager of a supermarket, but had been busted for giving free meat to hippies. With the acid business starting to become too risky, a career move to roadie for the Deviants seemed an acceptable change of pace.

Surrounded by this cast of characters, I found myself attempting to inspire and entertain a youth movement that was growing increasingly political in an all too conventional sense. Where the hippies had smiled in idiot bliss, teeth were now being clenched and a Marxist bray had crept into the dialogue. In May 1968 France started to come thrillingly unglued. Students from Nanterre took over the Sorbonne, and eventually the entire Parisian Latin Quarter. Romantic images flickered from the TV as student rebels burned cars and hurled cobblestones, armoured riot police responded with CS gas, and rumour had it that wild, abandoned Gallic free love was practised between bouts of violence. One of the leaders, Jacques Tarnero, declared, 'We are not children at play but people who continuously reject their social conditions. We have shown in the streets and on the barricades that our revolt is effective. This is not a dream.'

Unfortunately this was a dream, and the revolution was not effective. Locked into factionalism and dialectical infighting, the French students dissipated their initial energy, and a frightened bourgeoisie swept de Gaulle back to power with the tacit aid of the French communist party. The student revolt fell apart, but still made enough waves to send colleges all across Europe reeling into romantic, fist-waving confusion. England was by no means exempt. Seats of higher learning fell to strikes and sit-ins like a row of dominoes – Hornsey Art School, the London School of Economics, Essex and Warwick Universities – and this set the Deviants off on an entirely new career course, creating a whole new set of problems.

We were a rock band, and we worked in the now. We had no Five-Year Plan or Ten-Point Programme. We could do very little beyond rouse the rabble and traffic in illusions. The citadel was stormed in hallucination, in flashes of dash and passion and visions of utopian possibilities. At best we could be propagandists, turning keys, opening minds. Sadly, from 1968 on, far too many minds started closing again, using the templates of Marxist-Leninism or the thoughts of Chairman Mao as an intellectual lifebelt when thinking for oneself became too hard. Much has been made of the role of the New Left, and although, throughout the late Sixties, I clenched my fist and promoted power-to-the-people with the leeriest and loudest, much of the New Left was just the Old Left in blue jeans, with the same Victorian perspectives and bickering ideological subdivisions.

We learned this the hard way playing to students during the 1968 upheaval. Colleges have always been the meal ticket of the middle-league rock band. They have a young, bored and captive audience, and they pay much better than clubs. With the colleges in turmoil, however, the meal ticket was – at least in part – cancelled, and that part was unfortunately the one that ensured our subsistence. We weren't supposed to complain. I mean, it was the revolution, wasn't it? Withering glances began to come from Russell and Sandy when I started acting too much like the Leon Trotsky of rock & roll, and the question of how the hell we were going to get paid on Friday frequently remained unanswered. Band finances were a disaster, and the question of cash created its own relentless flow of stress. Booze and amphetamines were now in the picture on a daily basis, which meant that the arguments over money could become downright bizarre. The new motto seemed to be that we didn't want to get fucked up, we wanted to get fucked up all the time. In addition to acquiring drink and drugs – that always seemed to happen, whatever shape we were in – we had to cover petrol, repairs, rehearsals, sticks and strings, and still have a tidy sum left over to meet each individual's domestic expenses, rent and the like, which meant that the wives and girlfriends also became involved and tossed in their nine cents' worth of recrimination.

In theory, the Deviants were a democratic, egalitarian unit; all for one and one for all; all the lads created equal. Unfortunately that only extended to the fun stuff. In matters of money, I was suddenly the scapegoat again. Tony and Boss may have physically picked up the cash from the promoter, social secretary or club owner, but I was the one forced into the patriarchal role of telling everyone how we couldn't have this because we had to give priority to that, and listening to the whining and complaining that ensued. And all I could really do was grit my teeth and curse a revolution that gave so little consideration to the survival of its troops.

Let's Loot the Refectory

'Did you bring any food?'

Tony Wigens looked at the students with total incomprehension. 'What?'

'Food, did you bring any food?'

'Food?'

'We don't have any food.'

'We're the fucking band. Why should we bring food, for fuck's sake?'

Boss, who was much faster on the uptake where food was concerned, was starting to glower. 'What do you mean you don't have any food?'

The students at Essex University were sitting-in. I wasn't clear what specifically they were protesting about, but in 1968 there were plenty of grudges to go round. It had started as a regular gig, booked through the students' union, but when the rebels took over, we received a call asking us if we'd come anyway as an act of solidarity. The original contract got us through the cordon of police and campus security that surrounded the place, but once in, we found that we'd entered a logistical disaster area. The survival skills of this revolutionary cadre were effectively non-existent, and they seemed to have been living on smuggled sausage rolls and jam tarts for days on end.

Boss was shaking his head, confounded that the supposed cream of British revolutionary youth could fuck up something so elementary. 'No food?'

The only good news was that beer had been infiltrated into the dressing room, as per contract rider, although I understood there had been some discussion as to whether providing the band with beer and a dressing room was counter-revolutionary pandering to bourgeois elitism. These items mollified the Deviants sufficiently that we went ahead and readied ourselves to rock and, when drunk enough, we gave them enough rousing rama-lama and Fourth International, up-against-the-wall-motherfucker rhetoric to convince the local Red Guards that we'd earned our ale and privacy. These ungrateful commissars probably didn't deserve all the energy we lavished upon them, but sitting-in was a tedious form of protest, made even worse by an involuntary hunger strike.

Needless to say, once through with the noise and foolishness, and out of our sweaty stage shirts, the band decided that it too was hungry. The Deviants could always be counted on to be difficult. If there'd been any food, we probably wouldn't have wanted it. As thoroughgoing speedfreaks, we boasted about forgoing food and sleep for days on end. But difficult is as difficult does and, faced with this localised famine, we wanted something to eat so badly that it bordered on an obsession.

'This is a fucking college. There's got to be food.'

True guerrillas forage. That's what Fidel did in the Sierra Maestra. With the diminutive but determined Sid Bishop taking the lead, we foraged like bastards and, by the simple strategy of following the signs, arrived at the refectory and its attendant kitchens, discovering that they came equipped with a large padlocked door, beyond which was clearly a store room. A rock band travels with a full set of tools, and a door isn't much of an obstacle to a heavy screwdriver and the application of Boss Goodman's famous hammer. The store contained enough food to feed the entire student body for a week or more, right down to a freezer full of ice cream. We immediately took a fancy to the ice cream and, as we served looted strawberry and vanilla to allcomers, the students scampered away clutching entire sides of bacon, huge slabs of processed cheese and industrial-sized cans of Heinz tomato soup. They had finally bridged the divide between liberation and larceny, and we couldn't have felt happier for them. With our mission accomplished, we made our getaway with our own looted cheese and found ourselves a transport café in the real world, where they'd serve us a hot fry-up. What sometimes troubles me, here in the twenty-first century, is that many of these wannabe world leaders, who couldn't organise themselves a hot meal without the help of a bunch of hungry and bad-tempered rockers, are the backbone of New Labour.

Kill, Zeppelin, Kill, Kill

They hated us. Oh yes, they really hated us. The only thing they hated worse than us was Led Zeppelin and Robert Plant – especially Robert Plant. They were a knot of fifty or sixty burly farmboys, red-faced and sweating, checked shirts, drape jackets and jeans with big turn-ups. They probably would have been an anachronism in the late Fifties; now they merely spelled trouble. They had marched in, full of rustic piss, vinegar and Watney's Red Barrel, expecting to find a Saturday-night dance, and had quickly realised that neither Led Zeppelin nor the Deviants played music for muck spreaders. The gig was in the West Country, of that there was no doubt. As the years passed some controversy has arisen over the exact location. I always believed it was at Exeter Town Hall, but Russell seemed to think that it was somewhere in Bristol, while others have put forward Yeovil and Plymouth as contenders. I suppose I could go back and check, but why destroy a perfectly good – if also totally pointless – running debate? Besides, I'm certain it was Exeter and I'm the one writing this tale. And I'm not recounting the story as a pivotal piece of rock history, but as an illustration of how even supposedly regular gigs regularly departed from what might be considered normality.

We'd opened for Led Zeppelin a few weeks earlier at the Roundhouse, with John Lee Hooker topping the bill. The Roundhouse was sufficiently spread out so that I couldn't claim we exactly hung out either with LZ or the formidable Hooker. In Exeter (or wherever), on the other hand, cowering in fear in a dressing room for a number of hours, we got to know Plant, Page, Bonham and the other one reasonably well. We'd also met Plant a number of times previously when we'd worked with his earlier group, Robert Plant's Band of Joy, and *they'd* been opening for *us*. This was the time when the entire music industry was watching to see whether LZ was actually going to take off, and promoters were hedging their bets and printing the words 'ex-Yardbirds' on the posters and press advertisements almost as large as the name of the band.

In Exeter (or wherever) the crowd was sizeable, but the place was far from packed. When we came on stage, the mood was fairly tepid, and we could either work really hard to get something going or just coast through, get the money and split. We opted to give it a shot, mainly because a knot of girls had convened at the front of the stage. They were dressed to the nines, in fair imitation of London groupies, and were checking us out. (Why is that the girls in the provinces were so much more instinctively hip than the boys?) I have to admit that both Sid and I hoped we might be on to a good thing and began seriously showing off. At this point the farmboys made their entrance, first stopping at the bar, then advancing to the foot of the stage with pint-pots clutched in their horny fists.

I confess: I was the one who set the spark that would kindle the violence. The farmboys' first ploy, aside from a few misdirected homophobic remarks, was to start coming on to the girls; demanding why they were so taken with a bunch of poofs like us, when manly farm labourers were right there for the asking. When the girls told them to fuck off, they further demonstrated their manhood by placing their drinks in a row along the front of the stage, which was about chest height for them and could easily serve as a bar. Unfortunately I was in the kind of mood to decide that no rustic clod was going to use my fucking stage as a bar, okay?

Mincing like Mick Jagger, and without missing a beat, I sashayed lightly along the edge of the apron, deftly kicking their glasses of beer onto the floor. The girls thought this was hilarious, but the yokels knew a mortal insult when they saw one. The first glass they threw went harmlessly over Russell's head, like some kind of warning shot. The second came right at me, but I managed to duck. A bottle just missed Sid and bounced off his speaker stack. This made him uncharacteristically and territorially angry. He stooped down, picked up a glass and hurled it with all the force he could muster, hitting his target and, I think, drawing blood. In the next three and a half seconds, all hell broke loose. The farmboys were coming at us in force, up and onto the stage, bent on doing actual (if not grievous) bodily harm. Sandy had his bass unplugged and was already on his way to the wings. Russell picked up his snare on its stand, plus a couple of cymbals, and followed him. Boss, who wasn't exactly averse to a brawl, got stuck in, while Tony whisked off the rest of the drums as best he could. I swung blindly with a mike stand, and also ran. Courage is not in contention when you are outnumbered ten to one by drunken farmhands.

As we all piled into the dressing room, Plant and Page cracked up, and even John Bonham, who up to that point had been drunkenly sullen, was grinning. 'You must have been fucking terrible.'

Seemingly they'd heard the commotion from inside the dressing room and had assumed we were being booed off. With everyone inside, we found that the dressing-room door had fairly substantial bolts on the inside and quickly secured them. Now Led Zeppelin stopped smiling. 'What the fuck are you doing?'

'We seem to have roused a bumpkin lynch mob.'

We had bolted the door in the nick of time. A terrible pounding and kicking commenced, which could only be the farmboys trying to break in and kill us. Just as the door was ready to cave in, the sound of the commotion suddenly changed. After a protracted scuffle punctuated with a good deal of cursing, a new pounding started; far more ordered and authoritative. 'Okay, open up in there.'

'Not a fucking chance.'

'It's the police. Open up.'

With no drugs in plain sight, Tony opened the door to reveal an inspector and two constables. They eyed us with West Country hostility. 'Are you the band?'

'We're two of the bands.'

The inspector looked us up and down. 'You must have done something to get those lads' blood up.'

'They took an instant dislike to us.'

The inspector didn't actually say he could see the farmboys' point. 'I think it's all under control out there.'

We crept out with some trepidation to check on the amps and speakers. Fortunately the mob of rustics had been too focused on tearing us limb from limb for the idea of property damage to occur to them. LZ's roadies were setting up as though there was going to be a show, although a line of uniformed coppers stood along the front of the stage, protecting them from the audience. Back in the dressing room, Led Zeppelin had reluctantly decided to go on. Doing 'Whole Lotta Love' over a line of helmets wasn't the ideal way to present a rock show, but under pressure they'd agreed.

I didn't stick around to watch, which was probably just as well. Led by Plant, they were back in the dressing room in the space of one and a half tunes. Despite the inspector's confidence, the remaining farmhands who hadn't been ejected had changed their tactics. With the line of police in place, they couldn't mount a frontal assault on the stage, so they hurled missiles – primarily beer glasses – from the back of the crowd. This was more than enough for Led Zeppelin, who beat a hasty retreat. Now it was our turn to do the laughing.

'You must have been fucking terrible.'

Being There at Grosvenor Square

Driving through the end of the night on the M1, maybe forty-five minutes out of London, with the Saturday-night/Sunday-morning pre-dawn starting to show in the eastern sky, a moment of weary impatience can envelop a travelling rock band. You're almost home: near, yet far. You want nothing but your bed, but there are still the final miles to cover. It's the last place you want to run into a police roadblock. The first signs were cones and lights narrowing the southbound highway down to a single lane, then we saw the flashing police cars. Definitely a roadblock. Our immediate reaction was that this was some kind of major War on Drugs operation. A flurry of checking pockets and stuffing pills and dope into hiding places ensued, as we joined the line of four or five vehicles awaiting inspection.

Fortunately we were on our way home, so the drug cache was largely depleted. Although a certain minimal trepidation was inevitable, it was largely displaced by a major vexation that our ETA at beds and welcome oblivion had been delayed by maybe an hour, and that in the meantime we were going to have to listen to a whole lot of heavy-handed cop mockery.

Immediately they had a clear look at the Deviants' disreputable black Ford Transit, they decided they'd hooked a live one. Tony, the driver, was directed to the side of the road and, once on the hard shoulder, we were ordered out of the van. This in no way conformed to the typical motorway dope intercept. Usually this consisted of a lot of torches flashing around the passenger seats and an investigation of pockets and gig bags. This time, while we stood around looking cold and bemused, these defenders of the realm immediately headed for the back of the van. The coppers also looked different. They had the grim weight of the heavy mob who foreshadowed the highly programmed Special Patrol Group.

A sergeant started barking orders. 'Okay, open up.'

Ever the roadside lawyer, I came back with the obvious retort. 'You got a warrant?'

'We don't need no stinking warrant.' Well, no, the sergeant didn't actually say that, but he intimated that if we didn't do so, a nice comfy cell waited at some nearby nick. Reluctantly Tony and Boss worked on the locks and bolts that had to be disengaged before the rear doors of the truck could be opened. Theft of gear from a parked bandmobile was a serious problem back in those days, and still is by all accounts. When the doors finally swung back, they revealed that the rear of the van was stacked from floor to roof with speaker cabinets, drum cases and all the hugely oversized luggage that a rock & roll band is forced to drag around with it.

'Okay. Let's have all that out of there.'

At the sergeant's urging, two constables moved forward to start pulling at the equipment. Tony quickly intervened. 'Hang on, hang on. We'll do it. We know how the stuff is packed.'

The system in the Deviants' truck was fundamentally simple.

Humans in the front, heavy equipment in the back. It ensured that we travelled in at least minimal comfort, but also pretty much guaranteed that we'd be smashed to a dead and bloody pulp by flying cargo if the van ever hit anything. Only Tony and Boss really knew the secret of this specialised arrangement and, to their obvious annoyance, it made more sense if they did the unloading rather than a pair of incompetent and uncaring PCs. Punctuating their efforts with obscenities and cursing, they pulled out enough gear to allow the cops to look inside and see that we really were what we appeared to be. As the cases and cabinets were piled up on the hard shoulder, the police took an almost obsessive interest in them. They felt around inside the speakers and peered down the barrels of mike and cymbal stands. I glanced at the others. 'Anyone would think they were looking for weapons.'

Under normal circumstances the rest of the band would have given me the well-known look that indicated my paranoia was working overtime. Fortunately for my general credibility, the circumstances were fairly abnormal. A huge anti-Vietnam demonstration was scheduled for the next day and an anticipatory hysteria had been mounting on TV and in the press. With Tariq Ali, Vanessa Redgrave and the Vietnam Solidarity Committee on one side and the Home Secretary and the Metropolitan Police on the other, the debate had moved far beyond the rights and wrongs of US policy in South-East Asia, to rhetorical questions like who owned the streets. The growing feeling in both camps was that, if the worst-case scenario actually came to pass, the following Sunday afternoon would see more than just a simple peace march from Trafalgar Square to the US Embassy in Grosvenor Square. Both fears and hopes were being cultivated that it would provide the spark to ignite a mass uprising of students, malcontents and the rest of what the media considered to be the great unwashed. Big-time overreaction, both conservative and radical, had begun to conjure up visions of a Trotskyite field day, at which massive blows would be struck against the Empire, and maybe the government would stagger, if not actually topple. Under these circumstances the roadblock, and the way in which it was being conducted, made absolute sense. The police had bought into the hubbub, and were now in the process of protecting London from terrorists attempting to infiltrate the capital via the M1.

Although to say that I was opposed to the war in Vietnam would be putting it mildly, some of my thinking was not quite in line with VSC and most of the conventional New Left. Years later it was summed up by the fictional Captain Willard in Francis Ford Coppola's *Apocalypse Now*. 'In Vietnam, the shit piled up so fast, you needed wings to stay above it.' From my perspective, the Americans, with an anti-communist mindset so blinkered that it fully qualified as criminal, had blundered blindly into a situation they absolutely didn't understand. The Vietnamese had been doing battle with foreign invaders for more than a thousand years, fighting for their land, their homes, the uniqueness of their culture and their identity as a nation. Unfortunately America was unable to comprehend anything of a thousand years' duration and interpreted Ho Chi Minh's struggle for independence against the Japanese and the French as merely another domino in the Great Communist Conspiracy to dominate the world. It reacted by sending in hundreds of thousands of young conscripted American males, armed and trained for some strange and unworkable high-tech version of World War II.

Obviously the war had to be stopped by any means at our disposal. No superpower should be allowed to dictate its ill-formed will by psychotic military might. The Soviet Union was being condemned for the shit that it was pulling in Czechoslovakia, and would soon pull in Poland. Harold Wilson might tacitly support him, but Lyndon Johnson should be made equally accountable. Down the hill from this humanitarian moral high ground, though, was a feeling that the prospects of mass anti-war protests presented the chance to get a few licks in against the establishment and the status quo, and to let off steam and settle some grudges by rumbling with the police. The Vietnam demonstrations provided an ideal excuse for a big televised gang fight; young men against young men, us on them, hair against uniforms, venting frustrations, and with everyone getting their fair share of abuse.

With mass protest against the Vietnam War firmly under the control of the conventional New Left, it came saddled with the entire weight of their beliefs and misconceptions. Of these, I think the one that sat most uneasily with me was their belief that the working class would provide the genesis of any revolution. It has always been my contention that revolution is, in reality, fermented by disaffected refugees from the middle classes – educated renegades, cultural outlaws, frequently abetted by forward-thinking professional criminals. Historically, the mass of the workers really only became involved in large numbers when social breakdown reached the point of shut-down and starvation, or the fall of the power structure was absolutely inevitable. That was how it had appeared in Cuba, and that was certainly my somewhat individualist reading of the Bolshevik takeover in Russia.

Unfortunately for the drawing-room Left, belief in the workers as agents of change was so much an article of faith that any questioning of it was looked on as a criminal renunciation of Marxist credibility. The worst heresy was to suggest that the industrial working class, as the Left knew and loved it, would largely cease to exist in twenty or thirty years – certainly by the end of the century – and would increasingly be replaced by an underclass that would either be unemployed and grimly dependent on state handouts or eking out a dreary living in minimum-wage service jobs. The radical rhetoric was of worker solidarity, but practical observation had convinced me that, by the Sixties, this was pure myth. The beatings that so many long-hairs had suffered at the hands of lorry drivers, housing-estate skinheads and drunken bricklayers on a Friday night had convinced me at least that a stratum of the working class was as culturally conservative as any High Tory, and as willing to put in the boot as any aggressive young copper.

At the usually disastrous social functions where New Left and counterculture mixed and mingled, I was always left with the distinct impression that should Tariq and Vanessa actually assume power, I would undoubtedly find myself executed in the first wave of purges. At the time, I wrote:

The effectiveness of a demonstration on anyone but an eyewitness is only in how it is presented in the media, and the media work for the system and against revolution. These first giant demonstrations have convinced me of one thing. It is both impractical and immoral to throw an unarmed, untrained mob against a symbolic objective like an embassy guarded by trained police.

To say that I woke on the Sunday of the demonstration bright and early would be a complete exaggeration. Having done a gig the night before, and then been delayed by the police on the M1, made it a fairly radical effort not to succumb to the temptation to forget the whole thing and lie in bed all day. Indeed, as it turned out, the rest of our Deviant comrades did exactly that. The plan had been that the others would either phone or simply show up at the flat in Shaftesbury Avenue, all set for the possible uprising, but no one did. Presumably they were all still snoring in their respective pits, all thought of social upheaval forgotten. Living in the same apartment, however, Sandy and I managed to motivate each other, and by two in the afternoon we found ourselves setting off on our mission to stop the war.

The day's schedule, as we understood it, was that the proceedings would start at approximately lunchtime with a rally in Trafalgar Square, at which Vanessa, Tariq *et al.* would address the assembled multitudes; after sufficient rousing speeches, a mighty march of protest would wend its way up Charing Cross Road, turn left onto Oxford Street, head along there as far as Selfridges department store and then turn south for the US Embassy in Grosvenor Square. We had left it far too late to be there for the speeches, which didn't bother either Sandy or me in the slightest.

What did worry us was that we'd emerged too late to stop at the pub for a couple of fortifying pints or gin and tonics before the possible insurrection. (England still groaned under the repressive weight of the absurdist licensing laws, which should, quite by themselves, have been cause for revolution, if we weren't so damned passive when it came to domestic oppression.) The only plan left was to take a short stroll to where Charing Cross Road intersected Oxford Street. In the instant that we hit the street, a tension was already in the air. The whole city seemed quiet and waiting. The sense of an impending storm was validated by the half-dozen police motorcyclists sitting silently on their bikes, faceless in white crash helmets, goggles in place, beneath the sooty trees on the large, roughly triangular traffic island opposite our front door. The vignette was like something out of a Costa–Gavras movie, an image from the prelude to a military coup d'état in some Central American republic. They looked at us, we looked at them. Both appeared to have seen the enemy.

Arriving at Centrepoint, we had not only unwittingly timed it so that we got there at about the same time as the first of the marchers, but one of the first people we spotted was Miles, along with Hugo, his right-hand man at Indica. Together we stood and watched as the marchers streamed past. The time-honoured red ensigns were mingled with the yellow star on red of North Vietnam, and with the banners identifying various student and political groups. They snapped and fluttered on the brisk Sunday afternoon, while placards and pictures of Uncle Ho bobbed and the marchers broke into now familiar chants.

> *Ho-Ho-Ho Chi Minh!*
> *Hey, hey, LBJ, how many kids you kill today?*

We waited on the pavement for a while, sufficiently pragmatic to be aware that hooking on to the front ranks was not a good idea. In the Napoleonic Wars the front ranks of an infantry assault were known as the 'Forlorn Hope', and if Miles, Sandy and I shared anything, it was a sense of history. Although the marchers were in a jovial, almost cocky mood, few could have seriously believed that the day wasn't going to end in confrontation. Plenty were hoping for it. Many demonstrators wore construction hard hats or motorcycle crash helmets. Others had heavy protective jackets. (Me? I was in a black leather bike jacket. Later I'd write a book about the garment.) Glasses and earrings had been removed and, boys and girls both, had tied back their hair or tucked it into hats or helmets. The demeanour of the police completed the pointers to what was to come. Although stony-faced and, for the moment, doing everything by the book, their body language betrayed the anticipation they shared with the demonstrators. I saw it in the set of their shoulders, the deliberation of their slow strides and the swing of their arms, the fact that a large percentage of them wore black gloves, although the day was far from chilly, and the way they refused to make eye contact with the marchers.

> *Ho-Ho-Ho Chi Minh!*
> *Hey, hey, LBJ, how many kids you kill today?*

I have often wondered how many of the officers that made up the immense police presence actually shared our belief that the United States should get the hell out of Vietnam and stop tearing up the real estate and killing the population. Simple probability would seem to dictate that there had to be a few, but my gut instinct told me it was a precious few. I'd often noticed, after being busted for one reason or another – either in the nick or waiting in the magistrates' court for one's case to be called – that hippies and other malcontents would try to engage young coppers in political discussion, but these conversations would be broken up by a more senior officer. It seemed that, to join the Metropolitan Police, you traded your capacity for free thought in return for the uniform, the warrant card, the authority and the pension.

> *Ho-Ho-Ho Chi Minh!*
> *Hey, hey, LBJ, how many kids you kill today?*

The appearance of a small group under a banner that read 'Merseyside Anarchists' decided us that it was time to join the crusade. The Merseyside Anarchists seemed like an outfit whose temporary identity we could assume without too many philosophical problems, and we were off to the fair. As we progressed down Oxford Street we could see that the stores had been rigged for violence. Display windows that didn't already have built-in shutters had been uniformly boarded over. These precautions definitely served to feed the mood that, despite the police all around us, we were taking the city. Even before we reached Oxford Circus the sense of spoiling for a fight bubbled over. Amazingly Miles, usually the most non-violent of individuals, was the first of our small group to give way to the impulse. A motorist – a gin-soaked Biggles in a Vauxhall – tried to force his way out of Wardour Street and through the march. While others yelled and cursed, Miles, without preamble, took a running kick at the buffoon's headlights, and then looked extremely pleased with himself as we whisked him away before some constable could grab him.

> *Ho-Ho-Ho Chi Minh!*
> *Hey, hey, LBJ, how many kids you kill today?*

By Bond Street some of the other marchers were starting to irritate me. A group of earnest and disgustingly healthy-looking Germans kept breaking into a vigorous, arm-linked power run that drove everyone in front of them like a bulldozer. They'd learned it from Japanese rioters who'd perfected the move as part of a mob-handed martial art. It was designed to intimidate the police, but their masturbatory trial runs served no purpose but to annoy the people in their own ranks, and made sure that the police knew exactly who they were and would be looking to neutralise them from there on in.

Ho-Ho-Ho Chi Minh!
Ho-Ho-Ho Chi Minh!

Neutralising began for Miles, Sandy, Hugo and me, plus maybe 50,000 others, somewhere around the top of North Audley Street, which led down into Grosvenor Square. The vanguard of the march slowed and halted. Ranks closed and a crush developed as those still in Oxford Street continued forward while the ones in front, in the approaches to the square, had nowhere to go. Without communication, rumours flew. Some claimed that the demonstration had been effectively cut in two, and that those already in the square were being decimated, with mass beatings and arrests. Certainly a lot of noise was coming from Grosvenor Square, but we found out later that stories of police violence that early on were exaggerated.

The Germans continued to make a nuisance of themselves, as we milled around, immobilised and guessing. When the march was halted, our original quartet had lost the Merseyside Anarchists, but we saw a small group under a Situationist banner. Among them was Dick Pountain, who'd later become Felix Dennis' formidable henchman. Instead of chanting about Ho Chi Minh, Dick and the Situationists were intoning a Cadbury's Chocolate commercial of the time, which made them even more our people than the boys from Merseyside.

Hot chocolate! Drinking chocolate!
Hot chocolate! Drinking chocolate!

After maybe ten or fifteen minutes a sudden lurch ran through the crowd and we began to move. Whatever dam had been holding back this potential torrent of people had given way. I have never found out whether the demonstrators had forced their way through or the police had deliberately pulled back. Either the Germans' tactics had actually worked or we were rushing eagerly into a trap. Such are the options of a leaderless mob, and there's not a damned thing anyone can do about it.

For a few moments I felt like we'd won a victory, but then everything abruptly changed. The account I wrote in the fairly immediate aftermath of the event is probably more accurate than anything I could now dredge from memory. This is not to say that it's not without embellishment or the small fictions that can tie a disjointed stream of consciousness into a logical narrative. I also know that I must have reconstructed some of the story from still photographs, the images from TV news coverage and other people's accounts of the action. The truth in a confrontation of this kind is that you actually don't know what's happened anywhere but directly in front and to either side of you, and even that may be a blur of confusion. And before you start sniggering at the blatant right-on prose style and the unselfconscious use of terms like 'pig', remember that this is an artefact, and that's how it was.

The sun was shining. 'It's like a fucking love-in,' I said to Sandy. At that moment there was an alien sound, thundering hooves, and a line of mounted pigs hit us. It was like a 19th-century battlefield. Men and horses ran through the middle of us, the pigs striking out at everyone they could reach with long batons, like wooden sabres, they carried. A young girl beside me went down with blood streaming down the back of her head. Her friends carried her away unconscious. A pig was dragged from his horse, but the snatch squad of police on foot got him away from the crowd. The cavalry wheeled at the far end of the square and charged back through the crowd, again hitting out at everything they could reach. Those of us who could took shelter under a tree, where the police couldn't wield their clubs on account of the low branches.

Ho-Ho-Ho Chi Minh!
Hot chocolate! Drinking chocolate!

Regarding the horses, I don't think I exaggerated. The completely unexpected development of being confronted by men on charging horses – the Cossacks, the Seventh Cavalry – was something one didn't exactly expect, and it remains vividly imprinted on my memory. In the quoted paragraph I'm merely telling the story. How it felt was a hell of a lot more complicated. As the ground actually seemed to shake from the pounding of hooves, my mind wrestled with the impossibility of it all. Fear was able to exist in tandem with a detached curiosity – 'So this is what it's like'. I was able to compartmentalise. Self-protection told me to move – get out of the reach of those swinging clubs – while incomprehension looked around in awe, and memory dredged up movies I'd seen and all the books I'd read, for images and ideas. Above all, it was so bright and graphic. The horses were so large, nostrils flared, and the muscles under their shining coats so well-defined. Harness leather and metal hardware gleamed. Their riders were pumped up, rushing on adrenaline, wide-eyed, teeth bared, so pink in the face, so clean-shaven and with no idea but to strike out and hurt. The faces of the demonstrators on the ground were more distorted, but, at the same time, more human, sharing shock, surprise, fear and anger, not only at the sudden onslaught but at the way we'd been transported to another time, where we didn't know the rules of engagement.

After their charge the mounted police formed a line in front of the embassy itself, supported by more coppers on foot, three or four ranks deep, with senior officers and the TV cameras behind them. For a while it became a static face-off.

A hail of missiles came from the crowd. Rocks, bottles, lumps of earth . . . Smoke billowed up, and for a moment we thought they were using gas, but it seemed more likely that it was a smoke bomb thrown from our ranks, not theirs . . . a few of the mounted section appeared to freak and rode full tilt into the crowd lashing out indiscriminately with their clubs, but these blind charges usually ended with the pig being overwhelmed by demonstrators and dragged from his horse. A snatch squad would detach itself, now and then, from the lines of the police on foot and charge into the crowd, either to rescue one of their mounted buddies who had got himself into trouble, or to grab a few demonstrators at random.

They evolved a neat technique for transporting those they had arrested. If the victim put up the slightest struggle he or she would be knocked down, then five pigs would lift him, two holding arms, two legs, while the fifth supported the victim's head and shoulders by hauling on his hair.

Of course, I was a terrible prig and hypocrite. While abhorring all the violence in print, I had relished the raw, alpha-male buzz. Even Hugo from Indica was spotted throwing wild punches, and stories circulated about Mick Jagger doing his dance in front of the horsemen, although no one got a photograph. In times to come I could boast about my confrontation with the mounted police. On the other hand, I would attend no further demonstrations, with the exception of a couple of unplanned street eruptions that had more to do with drunkenness than politics, until the hoo-ha surrounding the OZ trial. Oh, sure, it had been fun while it lasted, before we trailed off home to watch ourselves on television, but as far as I was concerned, television was the key. If it wasn't on TV, it hadn't happened. The revolution *had* to be televised and, in this show, we had been little more than extras in a lavish VSC commercial. My contemporary summation was typically simplistic: 'If we learned one thing from the anti-American demonstrations of 1968, it was that demonstrations don't mean shit.'

My thinking did, however, go a little deeper. As both a post-McLuhan baby and a terrible cultural snob, I knew I had better things to do with my time than act as cannon fodder at Tariq's and Vanessa's riots. My contribution lay in mass communication rather than merely being one of the masses. Newspapers, magazines, film and TV, rock 'n' roll records – these were going to be the weapons of change, not some ritualised gang-fight-by-prearrangement. This may sound elitist, but I considered myself part of an elite, the craft brotherhood of propagandists.

Chapter Six

Disposable

The album *Disposable* was named after a popular generic form of syringe that could be used once and thrown away. It should probably never have been made in the first place. (The album, that is, not the syringe.) By the point when we went into Morgan Studios to record this second album in the autumn of 1968, some of our number had graduated to shooting methedrine, hence the name. Fortunately I wasn't one of them. A phobia of needles has saved me from a lifelong mess of trouble. I have one silver ring in my left ear, the full extent of my body piercing.

By the time *Disposable* was being made, the band had exhausted everything pills had to offer, and bootleg amphetamine sulphate, so common in the Seventies, was still only a gleam in the eyes of the Hell's Angels. We'd discovered, however, a way to obtain ampoules of liquid methedrine, the only clinical use of which is the operating-theatre revival of the technically dead. These were scored from an old croaker straight out of a William Burroughs novel by the name of Dr Brody, who, when evicted from his seedy consulting rooms, just down the street from us in Shaftesbury Avenue, was actually reduced to sitting in Boots, the all-night chemist in Piccadilly, writing prescriptions for anyone who could pay. The band was divided into two factions: those who injected their meth, sometimes chased by a shot of vitamin B_{12} for the sake of their health, and the ones who popped the glass top off the ampoule and poured it into a Pepsi-Cola, putting a whole new slant on the Pepsi slogan 'Come Alive'.

As might be expected, the record was a summation of all that had gone down since we'd completed *PTOOFF!*, but it also attempted –

and with no great measure of success – to conform to some of what was expected from a conventional rock & roll band. That was both its meagre, if frantic, strength, but mostly its overwhelmingly fatal weakness. To put it bluntly, we'd reached a point where we knew enough to be bad. To craft a tune in the manner of, say, Lennon and McCartney brings one hard up against one's limitations, and ours were considerable. The drugs didn't help. When we knew we were going back into the studio, Sid and I sat side-by-side on the edge of my bed, him strumming his unamplified Gibson, and me with a lyric sheet in my trembling hand, and worked a new song into what I now recognise as a promising start. Unfortunately the promising starts tended to become entire pieces. Too speedfreak-pleased with myself to wonder about a bridge, a logical hook or a more plausible chorus, I simply suggested winding the thing up with some guitar bit, and then leapfrogged on to the next idea on the anxious agenda. I shortchanged myself with the excuse that to scream the warning you didn't have to be good, just very loud.

When we actually arrived in the studio – this time an eight-track, Morgan Sound in Neasden – our primary ignorance was to think that we could rush into the studio, straight from being on the road, and make an entire album without allowing ourselves any time for decompression. An even worse idea was to schedule a string of mammoth twenty-four-hour sessions because – full of methamphet-amine as we were – we imagined we could do our best work without either sleep or lucidity. I'd convinced myself that, if I could tap into the primal rage and then stick a lot of spooky echo on it, we would have a marketable product. All that could be said in favour of this process was that it made it possible to bypass both talent and expertise and reveal neither.

Not that a very genuine undercurrent of darkly urgent, violent and impending anger wasn't flowing through the band's collective subconscious. If the album had a message at all, it was that the sword of Damocles hung over us and our kind, and we were extremely pissed off about it. The world in which we lived writhed in a protracted agony. We saw it on TV, we saw it on the streets and we even saw it in each other's eyes. In such desperate days, could pretty pop songs have any moral justification, when I was convinced – to borrow a phrase from J. G. Ballard – that a deadly downhill bicycle race was under way? Bobby Kennedy and Martin Luther King had been shot down. Cities were burning all across the USA. The horror show in Vietnam had intensified despite all pleas and protests. At the Chicago Democratic Convention, Mayor Daley turned his police and National Guard loose on the Yippies, beating kids and even reporters senseless 'to preserve disorder'.

Closer to home, the first major clashes in the War on Drugs were in full swing, with law enforcement aggressively on the offensive; doors were being kicked in and judges handing down jailtime. The drugs themselves took their own toll of the reckless, careless and depressed, and friends and acquaintances began nodding out dead. In the darkness before a less than guaranteed dawn, our fledgling revolution was fragmenting into a state of extreme confusion. The problem was: how did one communicate confusion lucidly? The legend 'If you can't trip on garbage, you can't trip on nothing' was scrawled across the inner sleeve like a policy statement and, for years afterwards, I couldn't listen to the album, referring to it in interviews as the 'meth-monster'. I was certain I'd fucked up so badly that *Disposable* lived right up to its name; an unsaleable work that, worse still, was inarticulate in its rage. The only fond memory I had of the sessions was being all on my own after everyone else had flagged or dropped, and building my own sound collage for a gloomy spoken-word piece called 'Last Man'.

Friends and colleagues shared my misgivings. John Peel, who'd been sympathetic to *PTOOFF!*, loathed the record. Felix Dennis wrote a review in *OZ* in which he described the recording as inexplicable, except as a 'poke in the balls for the record buyer'. Anne Nightingale, in the *Evening Standard*, wrote nice things about the single 'You Gotta Hold On', likening it to a combination of Zappa and the Rolling Stones, but I think that may have been the result of some arm-twisting by Steve Sparks.

It was only in the early Nineties that I read the following comments by Robert Wyatt, back then still drumming with the Soft Machine:

I didn't know Mick Farren very well and don't think he particularly welcomed what we represented. But I certainly admire *him* because he was a sort of protopunk and saw elements immediately that were false. He heard sour notes being rung all round him at a time when everyone thought everything was in tune.

Also in the Nineties, punk obscurists rediscovered *Disposable*. Critic Dave Thompson lauded both band and album in *Rock 101*:

> Punk before anyone figured out how to spell it, Heavy before anyone applied the term to Metal, the Deviants remain among rock's most timeless unsung heroes. Farren once described 'Disposable' as 'a methedrine monster', a series of freak form jams which did or didn't resolve themselves into riffs seemingly at random. The sound of the Deviants had always hinted at violence, but 'Disposable' went beyond simple contemplation. If ever a record should have been charged with assault, it was 'Disposable'.

In the fanzine *Black to Comm*, Bill Shute raved: 'If the Clash had pared "Sandinista" down to one diverse LP, and had recorded it fifteen years earlier and had a sense of humour about themselves, their music and their message, they might have been as significant as the Deviants.' Well, thanks, guys, at least for one more demonstration of the Noah Cross theory that survivors will inherit the Earth, and that everything comes around if you wait long enough.

In keeping with the general air of driven disarray, Steve Sparks, after much lobbying, produced the record all by himself. Unfortunately, in the middle of the sessions, just as we were finishing up the recording phase and were about to start mixing, Steve – as if to prove that a grasshopper attention span was not an invention of the Eighties and Nineties – was made an offer he couldn't refuse and went off to nursemaid Jim Morrison around Europe. With Sparks gone, we only had the Morgan Sound engineer, Andy Johns, whose brother Glyn was over at Olympic working with the Stones, to look out for us. This might have succeeded if we hadn't deliberately undermined his critical judgement by insisting that everything be played at maximum volume, and spiked his coffee with methedrine every time he showed signs of wilt or fatigue.

'Come on, Andy, just a couple more hours, okay?'

Andy, a neophyte as far as drugs were concerned, and not

recognising that he was being both dosed and ruthlessly conned, would soldier on, becoming temporarily more deaf and totally confused. Damn, but I wish I had access to the original eight tracks. In the modern world they'd edit down to a monster creation.

The Doors of Perception

When Steve Sparks took off to work for the Doors, we could hardly blame him. Jim Morrison was having even more self-destructive fun than all of us combined. It was also not without irony that Steve should desert us for the Doors. He could have run off with Steppenwolf or Country Joe and the Fish, but oh dear, no. It had to be the Doors. Among the Deviants, the Doors were a bone of contention. Russell did not like the Doors. He didn't like their drummer, and he accused Morrison of being an inflation of pose and bombast. I, on the other hand, admired Morrison almost to the point of jealousy. The rest of the Doors I wasn't as sure about. I suspected that, without Jim, they'd be little more than a pretentious lounge trio. Jim, on the other hand, was the business. He seemed to have completed the phase through which I was still struggling. He'd mixed himself a cocktail of shaman mysticism, Freudian darkness, radical politics and horny guy in leather pants, and was willing to exhibit himself in public, loaded on the concoction. He was also unreasonably blessed by being almost as pretty as Elvis before the bloat. He was the psychedelic rebel who could make it to the cover of *Tiger Beat*.

The man certainly had his wardrobe together, although I was one of the few who realised that he copped the ensemble, the black leather and floppy white Mexican wedding shirts, direct from Gene Vincent – the all-time king of rock rebels and booze fighters. The shirts were Jim's real innovation. They looked Byronic or maybe Erroll Flynn, and they did a lot to hide an incipient beer gut. It was only later that I discovered Morrison and Vincent had struck up a bar-buddy relationship in Los Angeles, hanging out together in a joint called the Shamrock at the Silverlake end of Santa Monica Boulevard, in what would turn out to be the final years of both their lives.

Long before the idea had even been mooted that the Doors might come to town, I'd listened to the records and even seen the clip of them doing 'Light My Fire' on the *Ed Sullivan Show*, where Jim tauntingly sang the line 'girl, we couldn't get much higher' that the Sullivan censors had specifically vetoed; then, at the end of the song, he fell into a static flounce, the golden iconoclast, holding the vocal mike and its trailing cable like an electric bullwhip. From the very first album, simply entitled *The Doors*, I had been painfully aware that Jim's poetry was well in advance of mine, and that I'd need to work extremely hard to surpass what he had already achieved. Then, of course, the bastard had to drop dead, so I could never enjoy the satisfaction of pulling level. Another area in which I knew Jim was ahead of me was the creation of the self-obsessed and self-indulgent myth that genius is pain.

When word began to circulate that not only the Doors, but also Jefferson Airplane were coming to London and would be playing at the Roundhouse, a ripple of excitement ran through the hippie community. Among the Deviants and everyone we knew, the attitude was: be there or be square. Everyone was determined to see the two most important Californian practitioners of the new music. At the same time, a furious bout of ugly infighting ensued over who would promote the show. Unaware, however, of these dubious politics, and only knowing that Steve Sparks had ensured we'd be on the guest list and have access to all areas, I paid off a cab, walked up to the door of the Roundhouse and rather grandly announced, 'I'm on the Doors' guest list.'

I said this to soon-to-be writer Jenny Fabian, a well known groupie of the era, who usually commanded the Middle Earth box office, but on this night was overseeing access to the Roundhouse. I suspected Jenny wasn't overly fond of me, and indeed this was confirmed in the March 2000 issue of the rock magazine *Mojo* where she wrote, 'In the 60s I was apt to steer clear of Mick Farren and his noisy anarchic group the Deviants. For a start, I didn't like the filthy noise they made, and there was something dark and angry about Farren with his wild black frizzy hair.' Never one to suffer grandeur gladly, Ms Fabian immediately burst that bubble. 'You're on *Steve Sparks'* guest list.'

'There's a difference?'

'Not really.'

'So?'

'So get inside and stop showing off.'

Showing off, however, was the order of the evening, and a good deal of dressing up had taken place among the radical fashion-plates who packed the former railroad shed. It was not only a night to see, but also one on which to be seen; the alternative society at its most social. Among the first figures I ran into was Richard Neville, in flowing, quasi-medieval velvet and a rather fine macramé belt, accompanied by the beautiful Louise Ferrier. Moments later I spotted a character known only as Jesus, who, with his flowing blond locks and spotless white robe, looked exactly like a Pre-Raphaelite Messiah, lacking only the traditional beard. Jesus was one of those freaks who seemed to exist in no other context except mass gatherings. Where he came from, where he went to afterwards and how he survived were a total mystery. He had no visible means of support, no past and maybe no future. Usually of benign countenance and disposition, he didn't seem too happy about the Doors; something was definitely distressing him. On a bootleg album of the show, a voice can clearly be heard at one point berating Morrison for being a 'fucking carnivore'. I have always speculated that it was the voice of Jesus.

I had decided to strut my own style in black pants and shirt, and a yellow velvet gunfighter jacket I considered pretty damned cool. Unfortunately Tony and Boss, who'd made it into the Roundhouse sometime during the afternoon delivering a back-up organ that Sparks had wanted for the Doors, had, with their mission completed, both dropped a tab of acid. They decided I looked like Sooty, the irritating television glove puppet with yellow and black fur, who was huge among pre-school viewers. Cracking up at their own psychedelic wit, the two addled roadies started singing the theme from *The Sooty and Sweep Show*.

'Sooty – ever so naughty, Sooty . . .'

Heads turned, people were beginning to look.

'Get the fuck away from me, you maniacs!'

Unfortunately all evening they flatly refused to get the fuck away from me, and any time merriment flagged for my tripped-out road crew, the Sooty gag reasserted itself. I was never able to wear that damned jacket again without thinking about the wretched puppet.

The first general impression was that the Doors were theatrical and Airplane were untidy. The backdrop for the Doors was a wall of tall monoliths – cleanly matched black Acoustic amplifiers, each with a pale-blue, top-end horn mounted in the cabinets. The Airplane's gear looked like mismatched luggage, piled up for pure function rather than to impress the masses. The Doors' sense of theatre was also greatly enhanced by the fact that they were being filmed by Jo Durden-Smith of Granada TV for the early rock-u-mentary *The Doors Are Open*. Bathed in unnatural brightness by the intense television lights, and surrounded by crews recording their every move with heavy, old-fashioned outside-broadcast cameras, they appeared important. In total contrast, the Airplane played in camouflaged gloom created by the Joshua Lightshow that they'd brought with them from San Francisco.

Maybe I was prejudiced, but Jefferson Airplane came as something of a let-down. Although Russell totally disagreed with me, I found their sound thin and folky measured against their records. Grace Slick and Marty Balin's voices failed to blend the way they did in the studio, the band seemed less tight and, much as I adored Grace Slick doing 'White Rabbit' – and I still consider it one of the all-time great rock & roll tunes – the live version that night totally lacked the power of the classic single. The Doors, on the other hand, seemed louder, tighter and closer to what I'd been led to expect by their records.

Backstage, Morrison had looked tired and a little bemused, a deer caught in the headlights, burned out by all the people attempting to engage him in meaningless conversation, but when he sauntered onstage fourth in line behind the other three Doors, the impact of his charisma was immediate. His most outrageous excesses were still in front of him and, although a little overweight, he came on as boyish, brooding and arrogant, both seductive and confrontational, the consummately confident rock star in the Elvis Presley tradition. Both hands on the mike, one foot back, one forward, resting his weight on the stand. The pose had also been borrowed from Gene Vincent, and would later be adopted and mutated by Iggy, John Rotten, Patti Smith, Stiv Bators and a hundred other punk lead singers in the decades to come.

I really don't remember the songs Jim did that night or the sequence in which they were performed. I know the set included

'Light My Fire', 'Break On Through', 'Five to One', 'Back Door Man', 'When the Music's Over' and the Brecht/Weill 'Alabama Song' (Whisky Bar) that Jim had learned from the records of Lotte Lenya. I know the Doors performed 'The End', their epic of reptilian patricide and oedipal incest, but did they do 'Twentieth Century Fox' or 'Moonlight Drive'? That's lost in the winds of time. As I stood in a privileged vantage point, at one side of the stage, behind one of the PA stacks, I was as magnetised as the humblest fan. By far the majority of the audience ate out of his hand, and I was happy to see that those who balked were the same judgmental prig-hippies who were always in my face.

I will admit that some of his histrionics were overdone and gauche. The collapse on the stage at the end of 'The Unknown Soldier' was less than plausible. James Brown pulled off his heart-attack routine as a glorious put-on. Jim took himself just too damned seriously and probably needed a couple of roadies to start calling him Sooty. A petulant demand that the TV lights be turned off halfway through the first show also stretched his rebel credibility. He could hardly have been taken by surprise at the Granada crew and its massive cameras. As the finished broadcast would reveal, the same crew had been following his every public move since the Doors had landed at Heathrow, and that he now made an issue of them like some bratty little prince struck me as both unrealistic and undignified. And then there was the now-fabled shaman dancing. We who'd been raised on Mick Jagger's prancing and Pete Townshend's windmill really weren't buying it. The guy wasn't a natural mover, and like so many white rockers of his generation, Morrison appeared not to have studied what was right under his nose, or at least on his television. A crash course in Jackie Wilson, Marvin Gaye or the aforementioned Godfather of Soul would have instantly put a stop to his quasi-mystic cavorting.

Despite these reservations, I still came away from the Doors' show almost as thoughtful as when I'd left Bob Dylan, what now seemed like decades earlier. Jim Morrison wasn't a significant world-class innovator in the same league as Dylan or Hendrix, but he had advanced the marriage of music and poetry a few significant notches. He had lengthened and expanded the potential of the lyric specifically to tap a more literate heart of rock & roll darkness and give a name to the beast caged in the heart of the city. I was still learning the names, but if nothing else, Jim could goad me to try harder and, in the company I was keeping, God knows I needed that.

You Pretty Things

I'm not sure why the Pretty Things took a shine to us. Maybe they saw us as akin to what they'd been a few years earlier – or maybe they just liked the cut of our surly jib. I don't recall the exact details of how the two bands started going out together as a double bill, usually booked by some club promoter or college social secretary looking more for the promise of mayhem than music, but I'm certain that happenstance had a hand in it. The most likely genesis is that we were accidentally billed together a couple of times and decided we liked the situation and wanted to do more of it.

The Pretty Things had the double-edged reputation of having almost been the Rolling Stones, and very little that the Deviants could do could top their reputation for unfettered excess. They'd made three classic singles, 'Rosalyn', 'Don't Bring Me Down' and 'Midnight to Six', but, like Van Morrison and Them, they lacked that certain teen-appeal needed to move them into the elevated pop pantheon. Whereas the Stones cultivated a similar unkempt, Neanderthal danger, they still had Brian Jones and Mick Jagger, cute as all hell, no matter how they scowled and snarled. The Pretties, on the other hand, were much more convincing cavemen. The Stones original malchick manager, Andrew Loog Oldham, had been able to launch the massively effective 'Would you let your daughter marry a Rolling Stone?' PR campaign because, although it would undoubtedly bring shame upon the family, marriage to Mick or Brian – or maybe even the boyish and big-eared Keith Richards – could still remain a fluttering concept in a girlish heart. This was never the case with the Pretties. Their overall demeanour hinted more at assault and cannibalism than at scandalous matrimony. Even singer Phil May, handsome as any Stone, couldn't save the Pretties from the reputation that always preceded them.

We came upon the Pretty Things in their second, psychedelic incarnation, when the ensemble consisted of veterans Phil May and

Dick Taylor, plus Wally Allen on bass, John Povey on keyboards and, of course, Twink, recently defected from Tomorrow, who had replaced the original Pretties' drummer Viv Prince, who'd become too convivial to continue as a musician. On paper, a show at which the Deviants opened for the Pretties seemed a viable idea; the young pretenders setting the mood of chaos for the old atrocity hands. Abandon aesthetic judgement, and let's get to it. Unfortunately, as time passed, we began to grasp just how much we *could* get away with.

At the outset the formula was innocent enough. The Deviants, bowing to the Pretties' acknowledged pre-eminence, would kick off the show, playing tunes from our album like a proper rock band. With that duty dispatched, we would launch into our mutated version of the Velevet Underground's 'Sister Ray', which went down so well with speedfreaks, but tended to disturb or even enrage music lovers. This was the signal for the Pretties to start moving onto the stage to close the set with what would euphemistically be called a 'jam'. After a decent interval for the consumption of alcohol, the whole deal would start again. The Pretty Things would take the stage, play a number of tunes – again like a proper rock band – and would then launch into their free-form setpiece, a version of the Byrds' 'Why'. (Note that it was always someone else's composition selected for mangling.) At this point the Deviants would charge onto the stage and elevate matters to full-scale tumult.

On occasion I'd wonder why the Pretties were so taken with all this chaos. As far as I was concerned, they *were* a proper rock band. They had an album out, *S.F. Sorrow*, a rock opera pre-dating *Tommy* by a year or more and a very serious work. With an artefact like that to promote, what made them risk their obvious goal of being accepted as serious artists and not just propagators of outrage, by engaging in all this mayhem? With hindsight, I realise that we didn't work together all the time, and the Pretties played plenty of shows at which they could concentrate on the music, while the ones with us were their anarchic interludes that made it all worthwhile. These levels of chaos were great for the Deviants and their image of anarchy, so we didn't worry too much what benefit the Pretties derived from them. The self-interest of the aspiring rock 'n' roller rarely recognises boundaries.

The gig we played at Chelsea College was a prime example of just how few boundaries we did recognise, and it may well have established some benchmark in the molestation of an unsuspecting crowd. The specific boundary being challenged in Chelsea was part chemical and part culinary, and involved the thesis that eggs and LSD do not necessarily improve a rock & roll show, especially when added to the usual menu of booze, hash, a bit of speed and maybe a couple of mandies. The gig was to take place in the college refectory, canteen or whatever they called the large room where the students chowed down. It was right there on London's King's Road, a hometown show without any 200-mile drive afterwards. All we had to do was to get on and do it, and after that we could take a cab and go nightclubbing. At least, that was the plan, until the eggs and the acid came into the picture. Where the acid came from, I'm not sure. I'm not even sure which of us actually took it, except that it wasn't me. The eggs, on the other hand, were right there waiting for us. About eight dozen of them. The canteen kitchen had been made into a makeshift dressing room for both bands – not an unusual occurrence at a college gig, but often a somewhat unwise decision. An industrial-strength catering facility can invite a considerable amount of looting on the part of both musicians and roadies. Usually, when a kitchen was turned over to multiple rock bands, most of the food and other perishables were locked up, battened down or generally stashed out of harm's way. At Chelsea College, however, some cook, scullion, dishwasher or whatever had really fucked up. He or she had left out this huge mass of eggs, hundreds of the little organic spheroids in those impacted cardboard trays, a veritable monolith of poultry produce, standing unprotected on a stainless-steel counter. When Russell Hunter first saw them, he instinctively knew. 'This spells trouble.'

The potential for trouble was compounded by the fact that, at any gig within spitting distance of the metropolis, one could count on a gang of supernumeraries all ready and willing to get onstage with the more usual suspects. These agents of disorder would include the aforementioned and still grossly convivial Viv Prince, possibly with 'Legs' Larry Smith (the drummer from the legendary Bonzo Dog Doo-Dah Band and drinking companion of Keith Moon) and Steve Took, who, on rare occasions, might bring along a highly bemused

Syd Barrett. Steve Peregrin Took – as he called himself – was then in an uncomfortable partnership with Marc Bolan in the prototype model of Tyrannosaurus Rex, the duo version of what would be the hit band T-Rex. Bolan and Took tended, back then, to squat cross-legged on the stage and augment their basic guitar and bongoes formula with all manner of toy instruments. The pair had commenced their career busking for hippies in the natural echo chambers of the pedestrian subways under Marble Arch, but with the backing of John Peel, and the cuddly charisma of Bolan's newspaper smile, they had made records, found management and become highly successful among the bopping elf-lovers of hippiedom – the ones so full of happy-happy Toytown mysticism that they'd sooner die than brave an evening of the Deviants or the Pretty Things. Unfortunately Took was then in the process of kicking over the gossamer traces, and was determinedly hanging out with the bad boys. This resulted in an ultimatum from Marc and his management to cease playing with the likes of us, quit getting fucked up or be fired from the very lucrative pop venture. Took's reaction was to get fucked up even worse than usual. Accordingly Bolan fired him and went on to be a teen idol, while Took became a permanent fixture among the Ladbroke Grove degenerate elite. Ironically both men died within a couple of years of each other, Bolan in a car crash and Took from choking on a cocktail cherry while drowsing on heroin.

Back at Chelsea College, however, with Took still alive and kicking, all commenced according to the formula. Immediately 'Why' was under way, Twink got up from his drums and headed for the front and centre mike. This actually didn't make too much difference because his kit was immediately commandeered by Russell, Povey, Took, Sandy, Viv, 'Legs' Larry and maybe Phil, who then proceeded to provide a violently passable imitation of hostile natives in a Tarzan movie, pounding themselves to bloodlust frenzy. The guitarists, plus Wally on bass, isolated themselves, away from potential flying objects, and attempted to keep some measure of sound going.

Out front, while I roared some Beefheart stream of consciousness into any available mike – and, on nights like this, the consciousness could really be onstream – Twink started doing virtually anything that came into his head, which could easily include howling and climbing the scenery, all the way to stripping naked and exhibiting himself to the crowd. Took was also out front, scrambled and hopping, making noises like Baby Godzilla. After a while, particularly if Twink started stripping, I might retreat behind John Povey's vacated organ and attempt to do an electric keyboard impersonation of the Air Cavalry attacking a VC village. Basically we were in a mode that would continue until a janitor pulled the plugs, some citizen called the cops or it was all forcibly brought to a halt by some other external *deus ex machina*.

That night in Chelsea, I was a little surprised when Twink vanished for a few moments, and then returned, naked to the waist and carrying three trays of eggs. The shocked silence was, of course, an illusion. The massed bands were actually going full steam, but it seemed like the world had stopped. We could see all too clearly what the outcome was going to be.

Twink unloaded on the crowd.

Egg was everywhere. Nasty, sticky, yellow, wet, coming out of nowhere, the floor grew slick and dancers fell. I guess it shouldn't have been a surprise to us that not everyone, even in the Sixties, who gets dressed up to go out on a Friday night, to dance, drink and see a band, wants to be involved in an oozingly apocalyptic food fight. Very soon we were taking incoming shots – beer glasses, bottles and cans, the odd egg that had been caught unbroken. One group of students who really didn't see the joke was a gang of rugby jocks, who thought they were at a dance to pick up girls and swill beer, not at a warm-up for slimy psychedelic Armageddon. They didn't like getting egg on their sweaters and slacks and were clearly wondering what to do about it. Then they had it – the obvious answer.

Kill Twink!

Déjà vu all over again. I was back in Exeter Town Hall with Led Zeppelin and the farmboys. Jocks were coming at the stage and, in this instance, it was no less than we deserved. Twink had triggered the incident. No way to blame this on any kind of prejudice, except disliking being egged. We could also look for no exterior help in this mess. If anyone called the cops, the Chelsea Drugs Squad would almost certainly arrive as part of the package, and if they showed up, our jolly saucy crew were criminal toast.

Twink, determined not to die, was already making good his

escape, vanishing into the wings while the rest of us were still standing perplexed. As the instigator, he had positioned himself for instant flight. The rest of us were not so well prepared. Mercifully I wasn't tied to an instrument as death loomed near and the two bands were forced to save their miserable skins by recourse to the cunning and ever-reliable post-Gandhian tactic known as 'running-away-and-letting-the-poor-fucking-roadies-deal-with-the-mess'. Into the kitchen, grab up clothes and bag, sweaty and dressing on the run, out on the street. It was cold and, I think, raining and a knot of jocks boiled out of another entrance, but mercifully cabs were cruising, yellow lights on their roofs. We discovered that the vengeful jocks had been directed to the street by the roadies, looking out for themselves, but we were into the first cab before the jocks spotted us and we didn't stop or look back until, in the Deviants' case, we were back in the comparative security of the flat on Shaftesbury Avenue. I say comparatively because the flat itself was rapidly turning into a three-ring circus all of its own.

212 Shaftesbury Avenue

To wake with a hangover to the smell of bacon and eggs and then find that it's being served to you by the President of the San Francisco Chapter of the Hell's Angels was an event a little out of the ordinary, even for 212 Shaftesbury Avenue. Perhaps not *that* far out of the ordinary, but certainly remarkable enough for it to remain a landmark. We'd been playing the night before, and I had almost certainly drunk enough to render myself semi-insensible. The breakfast smell made me decidedly queasy, and when this large man with sandy hair and stubble pushed a plate of crispy bacon, toast and three almost-perfect fried eggs in front of me, I nearly gagged. Too much of a coward to tell 'Frisco Pete that all I really wanted was a cigarette and a Coca-Cola, maybe with a shot of Scotch in it, I manfully breached an egg yolk with the toast. I felt it was expected of me when the guy had been decent enough to bring me breakfast in bed, something that hadn't happened since I'd stayed with my grandmother as a child, unless you counted room service in the odd hotel on the road. Plus he was treating me with an almost formal deference.

'You're Mick, right?'

'Right.'

'You're the one I have to thank for the hospitality?'

I gestured to the bacon with my toast. 'I seem to be the one getting the hospitality.'

'Frisco Pete shrugged as if it was nothing. 'I'm a guest in your house. I figured you could use some breakfast.'

I nodded and chewed. 'It's great.'

'Steve Sparks said it'll be cool if I bunked in here for a couple of days.'

I nodded some more. 'Sure. Absolutely. No problem.'

So it was Sparks I had to thank for this unexpected morning. After breakfast, the presence of 'Frisco Pete was explained. He was part of a Bay Area scouting party dispatched to London by the Grateful Dead, and headed by two of their management team, Danny Rifkin and Rock Scully. The original plan was for the entire party, some seven or eight in number, all to share a house in Chelsea, but something had screwed up, the place wasn't ready and the visitors had to be distributed around a selection of temporary hosts. Sparks, who'd seemingly been one of the welcoming group, had volunteered the Deviants' home as temporary shelter for 'Frisco Pete, and had then proceeded to give the Hell's Angel a guided tour of the city – Houses of Parliament, Buckingham Palace, King's Road, the whole bit – from the back of Pete's Harley, specially shipped over for the visit. As it turned out, the accommodation situation was sorted out later the same day, and we never did have 'Frisco Pete as a protracted house guest, but his arrival would produce a number of future reverberations.

One of the great drawbacks of living in the West End – and being known to live in the West End – is that one's home tends to become a pitstop in the night-time perambulations of friends, acquaintances, total strangers and now legendary beings from other countries. In the end, the Shaftesbury Avenue flat would come close to driving me barking mad, but in the early, honeymoon stages it seemed like the fun magnet I'd always wished for as a domicile. The address even had a pop cadence to it. Sandy would sing it as a little rhymed couplet and snap his fingers, as in *77 Sunset Strip*. If our home resembled any TV show, however, it could only have been *The Addams Family*. We were situated approximately five minutes from the Arts Lab, seven minutes from the *IT* building, slightly more than ten minutes from Middle Earth and twenty from either the heart of Soho or Indica Books in Bloomsbury. Thrown out of the pubs at closing time and wondering what to do next, far too many of our freak compatriots' first suggestion was to 'go round the Deviants' gaff'.

With three bedrooms, the oddly shaped living room, kitchen and bath, a balcony and access to the roof, it meant that, on occasion, two or more parties might be going on at the same time. In one sequence of warm summer days, David Bowie and Calvin Lee, his cohort from Mercury Records, visited repeatedly, hanging out on the roof in shorts, with Sandy and Tony Ferguson (our fey, sometime-keyboard player) taking photographs of each other and acting coy and girlish, while down in the darkness of the big bedroom I'd be sleeping one off, perhaps beside one of the lost and pill-damaged strippers we regularly met in the pre-dawn at the all-night Greek Restaurant and drinking joint in the conveniently close basement under the Wimpy Bar on St Martin's Lane. One darker night, while a circle in the living room clustered around the yellow-painted TV set with the speech bubble that read 'HELP!' written in magic marker on the screen, positioned so that it was poised over the average talking head, Took, a male third-party and a dangerously under-age-looking female decided to attempt a Mandrax orgy in the circular turret room. This was fortunately broken up by Joy who, with her rock 'n' roll witch's intuition sussed that the notoriously irresponsible pair of bastards were fully intending to leave the girl with us when they'd done with her. Joy and I had long since ceased to be married in anything but legality; the relationship had corrupted down to an arrangement, but she had removed herself only as far as the small bedroom, where she kept her own company, continuing to act as den-mother to the hopeless and helpless males.

Shaftesbury Avenue was where we watched the moon landing and learned about the Manson murders and whence we forayed out to the cinema to see *Easy Rider*, *2001* and *The Wild Bunch*. It was where I first saw myself on television. It was the scene of freak-outs that all but required the summoning of ambulances, and was progressively festooned with the debris of a dozen uncompleted projects, like the bubble-top Rock-Ola jukebox that we never got working, and bits of guitars and busted speaker cabinets from our auto-destructive period. The walls were pock-marked from the times that airguns or other non-lethal projectile weapons had passed through.

The flat even became a refugee centre the night that Middle Earth was busted. That evening the band wasn't working, and I had intended to walk down to what was now the city's premier underground rock club. If I'd left according to plan, I would been there in time to be right in the middle of the bust, but something had delayed me – I think a long and totally pointless conversation with Sandy – and instead I found myself turning the corner and seeing a flashing constellation of blue lights in front of the entrance to the large basement space. The crisis we'd guarded against so obsessively at UFO had now descended on Middle Earth. Police and their vehicles were all over the street, intimidating the slow straggle of hippies emerging from the club, the ones who had been deemed clean and who offered no cause for further detention.

Most melted away into the night, but a few of the braver souls formed a growing knot on the pavement, standing grim and hostile under a street lamp, radiating bad vibes and waiting for companions still inside. Some still seemed stunned by the speed at which the police had acted. 'They were fucking fast, man. They came in, the lights went on, and they started herding everyone up against the walls. Guys against one wall and chicks against another. They must have had it all figured out in advance, because they knew exactly how the lights came on.'

'Did anyone try and resist?'

The group shook their heads, comparing notes. 'There was a bit of freaking out and yelling, but mostly everyone was taken by surprise. You know what I mean?' The speaker looked rueful. 'You think you should do something, but you can't think what, and by then it's too late.'

Someone else picked up the narrative thread. 'After they'd got everyone up against the wall, this second lot came in, sergeants, inspectors, the bastards in charge, and these coppers carrying screens and floodlights. And they set up all this stuff, and start searching everyone.'

One of the first women to be let go chimed in. 'Those policewomen are right fucking cunts. They start with the fucking assumption that every girl in the place is under-age, and if you can't prove different, they bang you up.'

By this point a couple of people I knew, mates of Boss Goodman, had come out and they stated the obvious – that I was fucking lucky not to have been there when the cops stormed in. 'We know you, man. You'd have been cursing the fuckers out and got yourself arrested straight away.'

It seemed that my reputation had preceded me. Maybe they were overstating it, but anger was already building inside me. A new category of freak was now being brought out of the club, the ones being held for possible charges, hustled by escorting officers to waiting police vans for the short ride to Bow Street. It was all so pointless and ugly. I knew I was watching nothing less than a classic round-up of undesirables. Okay, so they were long-haired druggers, and that supposedly precluded them from both toleration and public sympathy. They weren't an ethnic minority or prisoners of conscience. The media would dismiss them as drug offenders, but didn't the idea of the Metropolitan Police conducting mass raids on a Saturday night disturb anyone ever so slightly?

This was approximately the same time that Richard Nixon coined the phrase the 'War on Drugs'. As far as I was concerned, it should have been the 'War on Nonconformity'. The spectacle in this late-night street in Covent Garden was social control in the raw. A preference for the 'wrong' intoxicants was being used as an excuse to put a free-form cultural breakout back into the ordered box. As I watched more and more young men and women being led out to the vans, my anger was fanned to slow burn. I knew these kids were no danger to the social order, except in that they held different views and embraced different tastes. I could sense that everyone in the growing knot of people on the pavement shared my resentment. Some were even casting glances in my direction. My reputation really had preceded me, but what the fuck did they expect me to do? Lead some kind of hopeless, half-arsed rush, get myself beaten up, thrown in a cell and charged with assault on a police officer? Not tonight, ladies and gentlemen. You want a confrontation? So go for it, but don't look to me to light the fuse.

A few days later some gossip would come to my attention. Apparently some piqued freaks were repeating in hushed and scandalised tones that 'Mick Farren was there, watching it all, and didn't do a thing.' So what did they think I was? Fucking Batman? At times like that I had to seriously consider whether the bloody hippies were actually worth saving. I suspected it was probably the same ones who criticised my supposed inclination to violence who were now put out that I hadn't rushed straight at the coppers, bull-headed and swinging. In fact, what these malcontents were saying wasn't even true. I had done something. I'd invited a number of the people hanging round on the street back to the comfort of 212 Shaftesbury Avenue, where we sat around till after dawn, smoking dope and talking. I had always excelled at talking rather than fighting, but few seemed willing to give me credit for it.

It shouldn't come as a surprise that, while cops chased and imprisoned the counterculture, the corporate entertainment industry was more than happy to turn a profit from it. It should also come as no surprise that we found this extremely irksome. That the musical *Hair* should be playing in the theatre under our apartment brought the vexation just a little too close to home. From the building-sized billboard with the huge silhouette of a generic freak with a haircut just like mine, to the crowds of gawpers who thronged the pavements at showtime and seemed to assume that we were some kind of pre-show attraction hired by the producers, the proximity of *Hair* proved a strain on the nerves. It grew to be even more of strain when the denizens of 212 became familiar with the prevailing attitude of the theatre. When the wretched show first opened we gullibly took the advertised nudity and audience participation as an open invitation to stroll into the auditorium and maybe even play an impromptu part in the proceedings. We discovered the error of our assumptions the first time we tried it, when we were immediately and bodily ejected by burly commissionaires who hadn't been told about the dawning of the age of Aquarius.

We only learned later how we were actually causing some amusement among the cast of *Hair*, and even creating a minor polarisation between the straight actors simply *playing* freaks and the performers with ties to the rock/drug/counterculture who were doing the show for the pay cheque. While we were living upstairs, the late Alex Harvey, who'd earn notoriety with the Sensational Alex Harvey Band, was playing guitar in the pit orchestra, and Sonja Kristina – who'd go on to front the band Curved Air, cut a swathe on the Brit folk circuit as a singer songwriter and be married for a while to Stewart Copeland of the Police – was singing onstage. Sonja was the only *Hair* inmate to figure out who and where we were and, after an initial enquiry and introduction, became a regular visitor to the den of iniquity that lurked above.

Shaftesbury Avenue was also the location of one of the first UK experiments in the consumption of quasi-legal cannabis. When doctors Sam Hutt and Ian Dunbar discovered a loophole in the peculiar convolutions of the British cannabis laws, I hurried to the practice they'd established at the Holland Park end of Ladbroke Grove to become a patient. It was possible their alternative clinic wouldn't last too long, being under almost continuous fire from both the BMA and the National Health Service. Sam and Ian had discovered that to write prescriptions for cannabis paste and tincture was not specifically illegal under the statutes. The kicker was that writing a prescription for either lacked any real point, since no pharmacist in the country had the means to dispense it. Both tincture and paste had not been manufactured since the Thirties – or so everyone thought. I never learned how Sam and Ian had discovered that an eminent and long-established chemist just off Harley Street had an ancient – but still potent – stock of both tincture and paste. With my dubious mental health and bad lungs, I was a natural candidate for legal cannabis therapy. (Did I mention previously that I have chronic bronchial asthma and have been totally addicted to Albuterol inhalers since the age of thirteen? If not, it's probably because it's one of those legacies of childhood that I prefer not to dwell on, and because, after I first read William Golding's *Lord of the Flies*, I felt nothing but contempt for the asthmatic complaining fat kid and never wanted to resemble him in the slightest.)

I opted for the tincture rather than the paste and, for two or three months, before the stocks ran out and the whole adventure became history, I would pick up a prescription from Sam every Wednesday. After a chat with Sam, I'd take a cab over to the upper-crust chemist's on Wigmore Street to collect my half-pint of sinister green cannabis tincture; the same green that, in the Nineties, *The X-Files* made synonymous with invading alien nastiness. The prescription was dispensed with a perfectly straight face by one of the counter staff, and I then scuttled back to Shaftesbury Avenue, where a coterie of my closest mates, which always included the dauntless Boss Goodman, and often Twink and Took, awaited my return with some anticipation. In the living room, in front of the yellow-painted telly, I'd uncap the magical bottle with a ceremonial flourish, take the first swig and then pass it around. Like Hopi at a peyote ceremony, or maybe more like drunks on a bombsite, we swigged and passed. Since the extract of cannabis was in a solution of pure alcohol, the first effect was that we all became exceedingly drunk, fell around and babbled aimlessly. When, however, the effects of the alcohol began to wear off, we found ourselves as high as kites, higher than one could reasonably get just by smoking the stuff.

That we were never busted at 212 was nothing short of a miracle. We could only suppose that Detective Sergeant Norman Pilcher – the notorious 'Semolina Pilchard' from the Beatles' 'I Am the Walrus', the scourge of all dopefiend rockers – was too busy chasing luminaries like Brian Jones and John Lennon to bother with a band as humble as us. The Deviants seemed to pass completely under his radar, and very glad we were too, at least for that aspect of our apparent lack of fame.

A Cold Day in Hell

The heater in the truck was broken, our record label had turned out really to be owned by bluebeat gangsters and another winter of discontent was upon us. We'd been up North: Durham, Newcastle, all the way up the entire bloody country, with rain turning to sleet and the slapping of the windscreen wipers like Chinese water torture, no matter how many Motown classics we sung to raise our spirits. It wasn't that we weren't having any fun at all. Intoxicants abounded. The good gigs still counterbalanced the bad. The wild shows with the Pretty Things were always a satisfactory laugh. We were amassing a following at clubs like Middle Earth in London and Mothers in

Birmingham. We had even spent an amusing, if bizarre, evening at the Royal Festival Hall, playing a benefit to help cover the legal costs of one of the satirical magazine *Private Eye*'s innumerable libel suits.

Sharing a bill with what was accepted as the liberal/arts establishment – Peter Cook, John Wells, John Bird, George Melly and the like – we decided to make the absolute maximum effort. Exaggeratedly making ourselves up like a quartet of silent-movie vamps, years before the New York Dolls ever picked up a lipstick, I was amazed at just how fundamentally conservative these people really were. Only Melly seemed to realise that what we were doing was a theatrical put-on, although Russell seemed to be actively enjoying himself and would repeat the process at subsequent gigs, making himself look as much like Helen Shapiro as he could. The door of the dressing room kept opening, as familiar faces like Eleanor Bron and William Rushton peered in at us as though we were a collection of exotic mutants on loan from the galactic zoo.

With only ten minutes playing time allotted, we decided to do the short and snappy single from *Disposable* called 'You Gotta Hold On', and then grind into as much of 'Sister Ray' as we could get away with. At least, that was the plan. As it turned out, we were only a matter of bars into the brief set when the audience went into what can only be described as a fugue state. A representative percentage, particularly those in the fifty-quid seats, who had come along expecting to see the likes of Johnny Dankworth and Cleo Laine, and comedians being slightly risqué, seemed to forget that they were essentially supporting freedom of speech and expression and took an immediate and vocal dislike to us, yelling at us to get off the stage. This triggered a smaller, but louder, faction to attack the complainants for their intolerance. No fist fights broke out, but, from the stage, it was fascinating to watch the effect we were having on this entirely novel audience. The net result was that we played much longer than we intended and screwed up the entire schedule, because we refused to stop playing until the conflict resolved itself and didn't want to appear to be retreating under hostile pressure.

Events like the *Private Eye* benefit were high-voltage intervals, rather than the norm, and only briefly dispelled the gathering gloom. I suspect that the real problem in the band was that we'd started to count the cost of what we were doing and were becoming more aware of the wear and tear. We were working a lot, but somehow the ends never seemed to meet. The gigs were becoming increasingly routine and, without a record blazing a trail across the sky, we felt like hamsters on the wheel, running continuously but getting nowhere. We'd been hyped into believing in instant gratification, but all we faced was an endless grind. And this sets a band to the kind of bitching and whining that is only a short jump from conspiracy, mutiny and professional assassination. The madames in old-time brothels used to complain that whores with too little to do got religion. Likewise, musicians with too much repetition turn ugly and recalcitrant. Just to complicate matters, Mandrax, the easily abused hypnotic sleeping pills that Americans call Qualuudes, had also come into the picture, and some members of the band were constantly stumbling, wobbling, unconscious or suffering bleak and bad-tempered hangovers.

The scapegoat for the growing dissent among the ranks was Sid Bishop. At root it was petty. There wasn't too much wrong with his guitar playing, and the major accusation that could be levelled against him was that he wasn't of quite the same demography as the rest of us. Bear in mind, however, that the rest of us were, by this point, total degenerates, and Sid had only one foot in the slime. As Russell would admit, years later, 'We got rid of Sid because we didn't like his wife.' Sure, his wife Jill epitomised the conventional housewife and did little to hide her horror at the crew with which Sid had thrown in his musical lot, and, evil bastards, we did everything we could to divorce him from her influence. We even tried in vain to set him up with Jenny Fabian, but even that bohemian temptation couldn't break up his semi-detached, suburban domesticity.

Russell's admission was less than the entire truth, however. The root cause of the discontent with Sid was geographic. In order to maintain Jill in the style that she desired, he lived in darkest South London. Streatham or thereabouts. With Boss and Tony out in the eastern hinterlands of Goodmayes, Sandy and me in the West End and Russell in Ladbroke Grove, collecting and depositing Sid in South London at the beginning and end of trips constituted a major detour. Picking him up became a pain in the arse, but dropping him off afterwards, when we only wanted to lie down and die, became a resented last straw for a bunch of tired and spitting camels. It may sound ridiculous to the outside observer, but that's how the small inconveniences become magnified into capital transgressions, when a bunch of men have been around each other far too long and have heard all the jokes.

On the road up North I had become so heartily sick of the Edgar Allan Poe vibe permeating the truck that I asked to be dropped off in Carlisle to spend a couple of days with Carol and then return to London by train. A big error in that I'd given the band, on the apparently miserable drive back to London, far too much time to talk about me behind my back. When I got back to the capital, the first person I heard from was Steve Sparks.

'You've got big trouble.'

'I have?'

'Oh yes.'

As Steve told it, a plan had been hatched to get rid of both Sid and me, get a new guitar player and bring in Russell's girlfriend as lead singer, thus turning the Deviants into the West London Jefferson Airplane.

'You've got to be kidding.'

Steve shook his head. He wasn't kidding, although he may have been exaggerating.

'It's fucking crazy. They'll never pull that together.'

'Did anyone ever claim the Deviants were sane?'

He made sense, but I wasn't prepared to see the band come to ultimate grief on the rocks of an unworkable malcontent fantasy. For once in my life, I made a fast and highly self-serving move. Despite *Disposable* turning out to be something of a débâcle, Steve – as a way to reinstate himself after defecting to the Doors – had drummed up the chance of a recording deal with Nat Joseph at Transatlantic Records, who had taken it into his head that there might be a percentage in creating a roster of progressive and psychedelic bands. To head off the benighted ugliness that seemed to be festering among my comrades, I got Sparks to instigate a meeting with Nat and, after talking and drinking his boardroom Scotch for a couple of hours, we came out of his offices on Marylebone High Street with a three-album deal. My hole card was that only two albums would be by the Deviants and the third would be, if I so decided, a solo Mick Farren work.

The Transatlantic deal was less than ideal in many ways. The advance was far from fantastic, but that came as no surprise. Steve had warned me that Nat was parsimonious, not to say cheap, but losers can't be choosers, and I urgently needed both a stick and carrot to drive and lure the insurgents back into line. Also Nat had no real experience of selling rock 'n' roll. He was a dapper businessman whose first love was folk music. He'd given first-album shots to Bert Jansch and John Renbourne, and also held the UK rights to the Folkways catalogue, which meant he was the local connection for Woody Guthrie, Big Bill Broonzy and Blind Lemon Jefferson records. The closest he came to rock was when he discovered that he owned a couple of albums by the Fugs as part of a catalogue licensing deal. He had also released the legendary psychedelic single 'Granny Takes a Trip' by the Purple Gang, but the record's underground success was so immediate that Nat hadn't been able to press copies fast enough for it to make the charts, even though the demand was there.

I didn't, of course, relay these misgivings to the rest of the band. The fait accompli that I laid on them was that we had a shot at making another album, but I was also, down the pike, going to be doing another record on my own. This raised a few eyebrows, but they were provisionally lowered when I told them about the possible third album. If they were still set on being the bloody Ladbroke Grove Airplane, they could go right ahead and pitch the idea to Nat as the third record on the contract, and I wouldn't say a word. In calling their bluff, I had also covered my own arse. Nothing comes without a trade-off, though. A couple of days later, after brooding on it, Russell and Sandy – backed up by Boss and Tony – made it clear that, if the Deviants were going to continue and make this next album as the first of three, Sid had to go.

Enter the Canadian

Paul Rudolph was a huge lumberjack from British Columbia with hair past his shoulders and a withered right arm. He'd had polio as a kid and been given a guitar as occupational therapy. He had arrived at Heathrow with a cherry-red Gibson and a Fender Precision bass. What clothes he had were stuffed into any spare space in the two guitar cases. He had checked into the airport at Vancouver with a suitcase as well, but, when Air Canada told him that his luggage was overweight and liable for surcharge, he had dumped it in favour of the instruments. The move was typical of Rudolph. The Deviants' new guitar player had virtually no interest in anything except playing his music, smoking the best dope he could get his hands on, occasional sex and, as we'd learn later, riding state-of-the-art racing bicycles. He never went to the movies, only watched TV by default, infrequently listened to anyone's music but his own and the joke was that he'd read a book once, but hadn't liked it and hadn't tried again. His sense of style was all but non-existent, as was evidenced by the way he arrived in London in hideous elephant-cord bell bottoms and a shirt that appeared to have been stolen from a convict.

With so little in common, it was hardly surprising that Rudolph and I didn't exactly see eye-to-eye. I really dug his guitar playing, but this wasn't quite reciprocated in his attitude towards me as a poet and performer. It wasn't that we didn't get along. On the surface he was amiable, but the Freudian waters ran deep. The conspiring factors that had landed him, his guitars and his Freudian waters in our world were, to say the least, complicated. The fulcrum had been another Canadian called Jamie Mandelkau, plausible, good-looking, bespectacled, with flowing Haight Ashbury locks, who started showing up at 212 essentially at Joy's behest. I had no grounds or even much motivation to complain when the two of them started seeing each other. Joy and I were doing nothing more than sharing an apartment. I brought girls home fairly regularly and, after some vestigial awkwardness, the situation settled into a reasonably workable routine, a little out of the ordinary perhaps, but by no means outrageously unorthodox by the standards of the time. Or maybe I was both deceived and deceiving myself. Let's not forget that, after some three years in the depths of the underground, my appreciation of the orthodox was extremely atrophied.

That Jamie should actually move in was never discussed, but rather came about by increments and fait accompli. The actual transition from Jamie the gentleman caller to Jamie the resident was also camouflaged by an outbreak of high drama. As far as I could piece the story together, Jamie had been hanging out in Earls Court with a partner who went by the name of Longhaired John. John unfortunately wound up dead, apparently the victim of some bad speed that someone may or may not have given him by accident. Cloaked in a crisis that hinted at possible murder, Jamie, shocked and grieving, came seeking aid and comfort from Joy, and somehow never went away.

Okay, so he turned up with his stuff, such as it was. That was understandable. The heat was on, and it made sense that he should stay away from his old haunts in Earls Court. When some days had passed and he was still ensconced in Joy's room, it seemed churlish to ask when he might be going home, since clearly he had no home to go to. Jamie rapidly became a fact of life, part of the 212 community, and that seemed to be that. Again it might have been okay, had some boundaries been observed. Jamie was funny, friendly, easy to get along with and a consummate hustler, who actually talked his way into both the pub and the off-licence giving us credit. He was also my size and I could borrow his clothes. He contributed when he could to the domestic expenses, with money from sources that had nothing to do with the Deviants. This on its own scored him a hell of a lot of points. The problem for a band, or part of a band, living in the same place is that they stand or fall by a common fortune. If Jamie had just kept his opinions to himself, all might have been well; needless to say, he didn't, and it wasn't.

Jamie had an opinion on just about everything. Some I agreed with, and others were simply full of shit. He even had an opinion during the endless bickering about the band and what we were going to do about Sid. He started telling us how he knew this shit-hot Hendrix-style guitarist back in Vancouver, who would jump at the chance to join us. I probably should have told Jamie that, while I had no quarrel with his fucking my wife and living in the end bedroom, he really should keep his nose out of my business. The problem was that we functioned as a community round at 212 and, as a community, free speech was an absolute article of faith, so individual business rapidly became family business. To some degree, the Deviants really were everyone's business. If we didn't have a working guitar player, the phone and electricity bills didn't get paid. To compound the situation, Sandy, Russell and Boss became quite fascinated with the idea of Paul Rudolph, this guitar god on the other side of the world. In short order, avenues of communication were opened and it was decided that, if Paul wanted to give it a shot, we were willing to do the same.

When the first rehearsal was convened in a room above a pub in Islington, it turned out that Jamie, although prone to exaggeration in most things, had told it to us straight. Rudolph really was a shit-hot Hendrix-style guitar player. He also had a pleasing personality, a love of marijuana and a tendency to drop into the persona of a cartoon pirate called Black George, exclaiming catchphrases like 'avast there, you lubbers' in a bad Robert Newton/Long John Silver accent. Sid had jumped ship seconds before we were going axe him, sparing me from feeling like too base a betrayer, but we were under the gun. We'd cancelled a couple of weeks of gigs, but a promoter in Southampton kept phoning, claiming he'd sold a lot of tickets and we just had to put on a show. With only two rehearsals behind us we played our first gig with Paul, after which the promoter had the gall to burn us for half the money, claiming that we'd played a short set and didn't sound together.

In the beginning, it seemed as if Rudolph was the answer to our collective prayers. The band took on a new lease of life. The novelty of a new member in the van lowered the level of acrimony, and the music not only came back alive but quickly developed a more plausible edge. My only complaint was that the guitar solos grew longer and longer, which left me with that Roger Daltrey, onstage redundancy of hopping from one foot to the other and banging a tambourine or some other infant noise-maker while the great guitar screeched and thundered on and on.

Deviants Three and Me

When the album *Deviants III* was reissued in 1997 by Capt Trip Records in Japan, I provided the following sleeve notes.

In the time space that this album was recorded and released, Apollo 11 *landed on the moon, the Manson family went on their kill spree in Los Angeles, Jan Palach burned himself to death in Prague, protesting the Soviet occupation of his country, Lt William Calley was sent for trial for* the My Lai massacre in Vietnam, and the world population reached 3.5 billion. In the realm of the counterculture, optimism peaked at Woodstock and then crashed and burned to the sound of the Rolling Stones at Altamont. 1969 was a time of chaos and violent confusion, both in the world at large and, on a much smaller scale, within the microcosm of the Deviants.

After two albums and two years on the road – even riding in a two-tone Ford with fins, and a female driver with outrageous breasts and a taste in skimpy, comic-book costumes – the Deviants were getting kind of frayed at the emotional edges. We'd received a positive morale boost at the beginning of the year from the arrival from the wilds of British Columbia of lumberjack guitar giant Paul Rudolph (who would go on, after stints with both the Deviants and the Pink Fairies, to play with Brian Eno on Here Come the Warm Jets and replace Lemmy in Hawkwind). Rudolph, however, also brought a fresh set of problems to the band – primarily the question of whether the band was going to continue its unique creation of rock & roll anarchy or, with Rudolph's superior guitar chops, become a more conventional guitar band. That basic conflict is, good and bad, what this album is really all about.

The dispute – fuelled by amphetamine paranoia, and complicated by constant skirmishes with the forces of authority – was never resolved and it would eventually tear the Deviants apart in Vancouver, Canada, in the fall of '69, at the start of a collapsing tour of North America. Paul, Sandy and Russell would go on to form the Pink Fairies, and cut Never Never Land, while I recorded the solo album Mona. The split wouldn't prove irrevocable, though. In the years to come, the four of us would all work together many more times, both live and in the studio.

Even what seemed to be the final days of decline and fall weren't without miraculous high points. Just two weeks before we flew to disaster in Vancouver, the Deviants played a final, hometown London show in Hyde Park along with the Soft Machine and the Edgar Broughton Band. Buzzing on mild acid, and feeling like battered gods, we picked the perfect time slot and played directly into a magnificent late-summer sunset. All the pissed-off anger and confusion welded into an assault of energy that had even the Hell's Angels up and dancing and naked girls storming the stage and getting us on the TV news and the front page of the next day's tabloid News of the World.

*I guess it was the way we wanted to remember that Wild Bunch phase
of our lives and how we wanted it to be remembered.*

I really have nothing more to add except that the title *Deviants III*
should have said it all. It plainly announced that we were so creatively
tapped-out we couldn't even come up with a snappy name for the
damned record, something that I've always managed, both before and
since. To get a little more psychiatric, the title could well have been a
subconscious expression of the way I saw the situation. Three
Deviants and one rapidly disintegrating singer. No one writes totally
negative booklet notes for a CD that the company hopes will sell a
few copies, so I'd tried to remain upbeat and let the intervening thirty
years soften the bitterness. The actual truth was a great deal bloodier.
If I'd been more of a grown-up, I would have quit the band even
before we started making the third album.

My downfall had really picked up momentum during a period in
Cornwall in which we'd 'gone to the country to get it together'.
'Going to the country to get it together' was all the rage with bands at
the time. I considered it a pastoral waste of time, but the others
fancied the idea, so why should we be different? Through the sorry
duration of the entire trip about the only thing to work out was the
weather. Although an early spring chill sharpened the air, the sun
shone and everyone was able to get out and about, which was just as
well. Had it rained for the entire week, murder might have been on
the agenda. Even so, the games began to verge on a three-against-one
mind-fuck. The equipment had been set up in the local school hall,
but suddenly no one wanted to play. In the morning the conversation
would go as follows.

'Let's go rehearse.'

'Can't.'

'Why not?'

'Russell's gone to the beach with Jenny.'

In the evening there'd be another variation. 'Let's go rehearse.'

'Can't.'

'Why not?'

'Sandy's gone to look for UFOs.'

Needless to say, I played into the stupidity by assuming that
everything was deliberately and specifically directed at me, and was

designed to make me even more desperate and unhappy. I responded by making myself as totally rigid and unapproachable as I could. I'd come across Sandy and Tony, the driver, staring square-eyed and stoned at a dead seagull at high-water mark and immediately suppose that the entire encounter had been arranged to mess with my head. I drank heavily and took all the drugs I could get my hands on. I prowled the night, climbed cliffs, at risk to life and limb, and hid in every way I could, while my head threatened to cave in under a near-suicidal paranoia that screamed like the horse in *Guernica*.

Later in life I'd realise that a band is really only a floating crap game, to be organised on a project-by-project basis, recruiting the most suitable musicians one can find and, while still doing everything possible to create the most agreeable working conditions, trying not to get excessively involved at any emotional level beyond the task in hand. Unhappily, a first major band is rarely organised with such mature sanity. All too often it's a sharing of dreams and ambitions that may not be wholly healthy, a tension-fraught collective marriage. And we were still supposed to be fighting the revolution, which made quitting uncomfortably close to desertion. 'They shall not pass' doesn't easily translate into 'Take to the hills, I'm having a nervous breakdown'.

Even if quitting had been on my menu of options, two substantial carrots were being dangled in front of me. The first was that we were booked by Pete Jenner at Blackhill for the last of the year's free Hyde Park concerts, and I'd be damned if I was going to let the other three reap the benefit of the goodwill I'd cultivated, and the hard work I'd put in, to make this landmark show possible. The second carrot was that, according to Jamie, we were going to do a tour of America. At first this seemed highly implausible, but then letters and expensive phone calls were exchanged with a promoter in Vancouver and, on paper, the excursion started to make a degree of sense. Our records had been picked up for release in the USA by Seymour Stein of Sire Records (who would later launch the careers of both the Ramones and Madonna), and he'd expressed a qualified willingness to support a tour if one could be put together, although he didn't exactly specify what form that support might take.

Jamie was now playing an increasingly prominent role in the business of the band. Steve Sparks, by that point, had wafted out of the picture and found other things to keep himself amused. Jamie had earned the nickname Ace, because every day he'd hammer away on a typewriter working on a hard-boiled detective novel about a shamus called Ace Smith. I was reluctantly willing to let Ace pick up some of the administrative slack, even though he did seem to act as Rudolph's *consiglierei* most of the time. Before the park show, and before the possible American tour, we had to go back into Morgan Studios to cut the third album. It was the first one created by committee, rather than the dictatorship of my personal megalomania, and I hated the process. A committee rarely has vision, and Rudolph lacked the balls to have it all his way. About the only thing I really liked was a cut called 'Billy the Monster'.

> *Watch out, Billy, as you walk around*
> *There's ugly people living underground.*

The sessions were tense, but by restricting ourselves, as far as possible, to beer and marijuana we pretty much managed to keep our tempers in check, although Russell now claims that he can't remember anything about the recordings at all. The two things that stand out in my recall are that, even though I tried to put an enthusiastic face on it, I was convinced in my gut that the third album sucked, and, while it was being made, I commenced a brief but memorable affair with Germaine Greer.

That relationship was all John Peel's fault. I don't recall how it was that one Sunday night he invited me to ride up with him to Mothers club in Birmingham to see the Who, but I wanted to see the Who in the worst possible, and was grateful that John had thought of me. This gig at Mothers was allegedly one of their very last club dates, part of the tour that yielded the classic 'Live at Leeds'. When I arrived at Peel's mews house in St John's Wood, I discovered that another passenger would be riding up the M1 with us. She was a tall, square-jawed Australian with curly hair that almost qualified as an afro, an angular Amazon of talkative energy in a Thea Porter, A-class groupie costume. Hey, hey, I thought, who the hell is this?

To say that Germaine Greer was complicated is like describing quantum physics as a brain-teaser. Even her job description boggled the mind when I first met her. Three days a week she was the outrageous radical English professor at Warwick University. Then she hopped on a train to Granada TV in Manchester, where she hosted a teen-show called *Nice Time*. The rest of the week she was down in London, in the alternative social whirl, running with compatriots like Richard Neville, contributing to *OZ* and to Bill Levy's Amsterdam-based porno tabloid, *Suck*. She stayed in Peel's spareroom when she was in London, but would soon move into her own place in the fashionable Pheasantry on the King's Road. She had just made a deal on her first book. This was going to be *The Female Eunuch*, but, still unwritten, it meant nothing to me at the time, except that some opinion-makers considered her the up-and-coming radical girl intellectual. On the ride to Brum I went from interested to fascinated, to captivated. The woman was so damned bright, and the more attention I paid her, the more I believed I sensed a reciprocal stream of pheromones.

At Mothers, the Who were nothing short of magnificent, even though 1,000 people seemed to be jammed into a club designed for 600. All the breathable oxygen had been used up by halfway through the set, and Moonie collapsed and was revived with God knows what. Nights like that contributed greatly, I believe, to Pete and John Entwhistle now being as deaf as posts. After the show, our departure snagged on a moment of awkwardness. Peel was going to detour and drop Germaine off in Warwick, where she'd be teaching the next morning. I was dismayed. 'That's a pity, I'd hoped we'd go on talking.'

Germaine's solution was simple. 'So come to my place.'

She invited me and I went, and Peel looked a bit miffed that he'd have to make the drive back on his own. Germaine and I spent a boudoir night, of sex, conversation and red wine, that set me thinking about her for all of the next week, and even treating the band with a more amiable courtesy. I sent her a thank-you note, along with what I thought was a very sexy picture of me performing. We spent the next weekend together and so it went on. Now ensconced in her new pad at the Pheasantry, we had a lot of sex and we talked and talked and talked. God, she was bright, but of course we were frequently at odds. She considered violence unthinkable under any circumstances, and I had a long list of people who'd be improved by a bullet. Needless to say, the discussion frequently returned to gender.

Germaine, for as long as she believed such a thing was possible – and she believed it for longer than many – did not want to see the counterculture become just another revolutionary micro-patriarchy. She frequently waxed angry at what she saw as squaw hippies, relegated to rolling joints, making tea and boiling lentils. She refused to accept my contention that the role of women in the underground was not as subservient as she made out, and that much distaff power was wielded behind the scenes, as it had been by generations of matriarchs and courtesans. Her mouth would set in a determined line and she'd proceed to decimate me with her brilliance. Behind the scenes was no longer acceptable.

In her brilliance, however, I feared an oddness festered. She was sensual, but cerebral in that sensuality; she was sexy, but sex also seemed a banner for which none of us boys could provide a sufficiently strange device. I think she enjoyed her liaisons with low-lifes on an earthy level of lust – including a three-day marriage to George Lazenby, the forgotten James Bond – but I couldn't help suspect an element of Diane Fossey and her gorillas. Were we also case studies? For someone who would become a feminist icon, Germaine went to unusual pains to please her man. We took baths together, and she decorated her new apartment in the nude, pointing out the practicality. She was always getting on my arse to start writing seriously again, which I found flattering. She made breakfast, and I could count on beer always being in the house. When I invited her to the recording studio, she charmed the others, flirting with both Rudolph and Sandy, although Russell remained decidedly reserved. Did she do all this because she wanted to make me happy, or was she acting out some deliberate charade of oppression? I also found it a little strange that she flatly refused ever to visit me in 212. Did too much proximity to my world threaten her, or was she just too well aware that men are domestic pigs?

I'm hardly qualified to comment on the depths and ramifications of Germaine. Most of the time I didn't have a clue what was going on. To complicate matters we had also become something of a public couple – the rising feminist star and the crazy motherfucker. We saw the Rolling Stones in Hyde Park together, but at Blackhill's backstage garden party her social shrill began to grate, and I escaped to hunt stimulants, leaving her with Ginger Baker, a former paramour. I also flanked her when she held court in the Speakeasy on the night the early editions of the *News of the World* devoted all of page five to an exposé of her. A dirt-digging reporter had put together the triple threads of Germaine's life and turned it into a 'Do we need some rockband-fucking commie tramp hosting a show for our TV pop kids?' I think that was the end of *Nice Time*.

To this day my regret is that Germaine and I were together at a time that I wouldn't have inflicted on an enemy, let alone a warm and emotionally generous woman of whom I was very fond. When I went into my act of lunatic hiding from the world and the phone, and refused to speak even to her, she decided enough was enough and the affair was at an end. Instead of a dramatic breaking up, she wrote a scathing piece in *OZ* profiling me as a semi-brilliant emotional ruin, referring to me as 'Il Duce' and describing my life as nothing short of a 'tyrannical dance with death'. Apparently I'd never find 'fulfillment and true orgasm' until I'd faced down squads of coppers with a blazing AK-47, and my screaming paranoia was about to hurtle me straight out of the band in which I'd invested so much time. The former was fanciful, but the latter proved right on the money.

Concert at Tyburn

I had ingested something. I can't quite recall what. I'm pretty sure it wasn't acid, more likely one of those alphabet-soup fringe psychedelics, ineptly manufactured from some hell-spawned combination of nerve gas and horse tranquilliser, which either fried your mind or did nothing at all. In this case the result was to make me paranoid and jumpy, and transform visuals into the cheap colours of a Japanese monster movie. We all knew that the afternoon's show in Hyde Park was significant and so, being plainly drugged, I was already getting some looks from Rudolph and Boss. While breaking up with Germaine, I had moved into a terminal Caligula phase. I'd decided that everyone was plotting against me, and my dreams were sliding rapidly into the toilet. When I'd shut myself in my room with the phone unplugged, and refused to come out, I'd also had a selection of cast-iron industrial objects ready to hurl at anyone who attempted to enter and reason with me. When slightly recovered, I'd promised to be good for the park show, but in the car, almost there, I wasn't acting too chic. Dead band walking?

The final Hyde Park concert of 1969 had been moved, by some inexplicable official decree, away from the Cockpit beside the Serpentine, where the Rolling Stones had played, to the flat meadow that spreads out from Speakers' Corner. Originally it was supposed to have been a giant extravaganza with the Grateful Dead, Jefferson Airplane, Quicksilver Messenger Service, Crosby, Stills and Nash, and Joni Mitchell, but this was cancelled because of 'problems in America'. Now we had a more manageable domestic bill that included the Soft Machine, the Edgar Broughton Band, Al Stewart and us.

Rounding Marble Arch, I noticed the sign commemorating the fact that this had formerly been the site of Tyburn, the place of public execution up until the late eighteenth century. Obviously, with my decadent sense of history, this sent me off on a rampage of the imagination. I recalled that it was common practice for big-time highwaymen and other popular criminals to regale the waiting crowd with jokes, moral lectures, salutary speeches and even a song or two before the hangman sprang the trap. The atavistic fantasy of a performance for the multitude, culminating in glorious ritual death, was rock 'n' roll self-evident – even though Ziggy Stardust was hardly a gleam in Bowie's eye. As I began to babble out my Dick Turpin stream of consciousness, the looks graduated from dubious to exasperated. Fortunately some threadbare fragment of common sense asserted itself and I cooled it. We were almost there and I definitely wasn't going to parade my mania in public.

The first thing required for any effective swansong is an equally effective entrance. This final Hyde Park show of 1969 wasn't exactly made for grand gladiatorial arrivals. All the pomp and circumstance had been used up on the Rolling Stones a month or so earlier. A weary Pete Jenner and the Blackhill tribe had decided that this one was going to be easy on their heads, a reasonably low-key, hometown affair. A bunch of Hell's Angels was idly guarding a lackadaisically roped-off backstage. None of the bands had a rabid fan following, and the bikers found themselves with little to guard and almost no one from whom to guard it. It required the Deviants to roll in with sufficient panache to change all that. One of the best things we'd lucked into during that otherwise fraught summer was a personal driver called Vivienne Bidwell, an American hippie who had moved her tarot cards to London, and who now transported us to gigs in a magnificently, if strangely, customised two-tone Zephyr 6 that was about as close as we were going to get to Elvis' Coup de Ville. Bidwell also favoured highly revealing outfits, style precursors of the costumes for *Xena: Warrior Princess*. We liked this. It made us feel like hot stuff. Boss and Tony weren't so keen, though, as they were now relegated to the truck, with just the gear and each other.

Bidwell rose to the moment and blasted the Deviants into Hyde Park like a Chuck Berry '45. Engine gunning, tyres kicking up dust, the Ford barrelled right up to very side of the stage, and bollocks to any sensitive singer-songwriter who happened to be on the intense jingle-jangle right then. We were rock & roll with fins immaculate and even Pete Jenner, who'd seen it all, could scarce forbear to smile. Bidwell, with no urging, was out of the car and, in not a lot of leopardskin, was organising the Angels; Sheena Queen of the Jungle taking command. Before we knew it, she actually had them protecting us as we got out of the car. As I've already pointed out, there was really nothing to protect us from, but – and this may be one of the Great Secrets of Rock & Roll – the average stoned, festival-going rock fan is a strange combination of bovine and curious. He or she will be content to amble aimlessly, or sit in one spot for hours on end, until shown authority figures apparently protecting something, and then will instantly go and take a look.

As the Angels 'protected' us, we found that a crowd formed, pushing forward for a look, which in turn caused the Angels, who had been well bored up to this point, to push back. The long, narrow scrum escalated until we found ourselves moving on a cleared path, between two flanking lines of motorcyclists, straight to the artists' beer tent, with a curious mob looking on. I think I saw Robert Wyatt ruefully shaking his head. He knew what we were up to. It was the best display of backstage swashbuckling they were going to get that day.

'Ready in ten minutes, okay?'

By this point I'd been handed joints and beers, and much of the public-execution fantasy had abated. It was time for nerves and business: 70,000 people were out there, stretching all the way to the trees, but stagefright had to be put on hold while we defined our objectives. In Hyde Park the only one we had to worry about was the Edgar Broughton Band. The Soft Machine were topping the bill, and that was their righteous place. Pink Floyd might be heading for the stadia of the USA, but the Softs had more respect than you could load into a freight train. A band called Quintessence, as far as we could tell, were from Narnia, so hardly relevant. The target for the day was the Edgar Broughton Band.

The Broughton Band had an easy crowd-pleaser in 'Out Demons Out', a mantric call and response, originally conceived by Allen Ginsberg and the Fugs as a magical means of halting the war in Vietnam by raising the Pentagon ten feet in the air. (Some claim the Pentagon did rise, but so briefly and suddenly that nobody noticed.) Edgar had taken this beatnik performance piece and totally rocked it into a psychedelic soccer chant that could have every malcontent boggie in Christendom up and roaring his lungs out. Since we didn't stoop to community singing, we had to prevail by sheer raucous determination.

By the luck of the draw, Edgar had gone on first and we knew the furore level we had to top. As we climbed the thirteen steps to the scaffold (the public-execution fixation had not totally gone away) we discovered that we were benefiting from another piece of luck. The setting sun, still some way above the trees on the horizon, was directly in our faces. It was at exactly the right angle for us to cast long gunfighter shadows and generally come on hyper-dramatic, standing proud against the light that would all too soon fail. Not only were we working in a golden sun-haze, but looking pretty cool that day in assorted lace, leather and velvet, and with Russell as close to being in drag as he could get without actually wearing a dress. Suddenly the peaks were breaking in our favour.

I looked out at the crowd, thousands upon thousands of the bastards, stretching as far as the eye could see, all expecting us to do something significant, to entertain them, to pull the energy out of the air and get them going. In the first second all I could read was an inertia comparable with that of a small asteroid. How the hell was I going to get this lot on its feet and doing the dirty boogie? We had played other largish festivals, but they had been at night, when the stage was the brightly illuminated focal point and the crowd was little more than indistinct, almost abstract shapes, in the outer darkness. Here, in broad daylight, it was a bloody awesome biblical multitude, and us without a loaf or a fish. Rudolph, who very rarely spoke directly to the crowd, turned from plugging in his Fender and adjusting his boxes and leaned into the microphone.

'Now we're going to have a little fun.'

The response was a ragged cheer. They'd had rabble-rousing from the Broughtons, pastoral psychedelics from Quintessence, and the Soft Machine would be giving them class, so we were expected to bring the anarchic fun to the party. That the normally reticent Rudolph had made the move also changed the dynamics. It was no longer me – it was us. Despite all the angst, we were suddenly a unit again. I guess, with the subconscious knowledge that Hank Williams' Lost Highway was no longer stretching to infinity in front of us, it meant that we could come solidly together for a last epic stand. Boss said it was the best that line-up ever played, and I believe him.

A dark-haired young woman, bombed as Hiroshima, baring most of herself in something negligée-like, sheer and revealing, was suddenly beside me, shaking her stuff, intent on exhibiting her breasts – and more – to the assembled throng. I was happy to dance with her during a Rudolph solo, but the bikers weren't having any and hustled her away as though she had defiled the sacred stage of rock & roll, or maybe simply to have her for themselves. Later, while in post-gig carouse at the Speakeasy, the early editions of the Sunday papers arrived and she and I had our picture right there on the cover of the *News of the World*. This was really the icing on the cake. Got you, Germaine. Front page. Another fifteen minutes of bogus fame. My cup literally ranneth over, spilling Jack Daniels all over my leather jeans.

Thumbs in their belts, doing their head ducking, shoulder jerking, ritual dance, the bikers, plus a crew of radical European gay guys who had maybe taken our name a little too literally, played a crucial role that day in the park, generating the first shot of Reichian energy. As a nod to the London Angels' Billy Fury roots, we played our deformed version of Buddy Holly's 'Midnight Shift' about the girlfriend who takes up hooking. By this point the power was palpable, better than any drug I'd ever taken, moving back and out, spreading from Loser,

Gnasher and Nasty Pete in their studs and Nazi regalia to the main body of the crowd, only to be remetabolised and quantum-looped back to us, pushing us to greater efforts. We were winning, we were fucking winning! Vindicated – and it was wonderful. *This was why we did it!*

Weird Scenes on Chemical Row

I was sitting on a washed-up, sand-scoured log, on another beach, looking at another night-fog-shrouded sea. This time it was Kitsilano Beach in Vancouver, Canada, and the sea was the Pacific Ocean. I was out of the band, 7,000 miles from home, hallucinating out of my mind on acid and about as low as a man could go. The other three weasels had finally found the courage to stage their coup d'état, but they'd waited until I was far as possible from any support; even then, the miserable bastards had been scurrying around having secret meetings in laundromats for days, before they came right out and faced me. In all fairness, I was no innocent victim, but I did feel that more humane tactics could have been employed. To get me that far from home and drive me three parts mad, before hammering in the stake, still strikes me as cruel and unusual, not to say a trifle excessive. You'd think I was actually formidable.

That all in the New World was not as Jamie had advertised became apparent immediately we cleared customs after the long Air Canada flight. The old DC9 had been almost empty, and we'd behaved like flash little rock stars, hitting the booze cart and flirting with the cabin attendants. We came down to earth, however, with a unique and vengeful bump. We hadn't expected a limousine, but the stinking, beat-up van waiting to collect us could only be looked upon as a disheartening omen. And indeed it was. I was in North America, the place I'd always wanted to be, sitting on a plastic milk crate, unable to see a damned thing in the back of the closed and lurching van. The van conveyed us to the next unpleasant surprise. The contract had guaranteed us a hotel, but had not specified the quality. I've always had a taste for old and funky wino hotels, but this fleabag, hard up against the Canadian Pacific freight yards, was beneath even my tolerance of rough urban charm. Later, by way of conscious revenge,

I managed to set fire to the bed in one of the shared rooms and actually got us thrown out of this palace of derelicts, Thunderbird Wine and vomit.

Jetlagged and awake a little after dawn, I exited the flophouse and breakfasted on pancakes and sausage in a greasy spoon full of marginal Charlie Bukowski characters. This first American meal left me in no doubt that we had landed in the heart of skid row. As I poured the maple syrup, I reflected with a certain grim satisfaction that no one could hold me responsible for this fine mess. Vancouver was Jamie's and Rudolph's turf, so they could field the shit when it hit the fan. For a while things did improve. An actual car showed up to take us to a radio interview and a morning-show promo spot on a local TV station. Although a battered, fifteen-year-old Chevy, it wasn't the stinking van of the night before. On the street, in downtown Vancouver, we also found that we cut a high-profile swathe in our London lace, leather and velvet.

'Hey, are you a group?'

'Damned right we are.'

We also found that attractive young women made excuses to talk to us. In a town where most of the male hipsters dressed like Davy Crockett, we constituted an exotic diversion, and during our less than happy stay in the city we shamelessly made the most of it.

At the radio station we picked up one more disturbing titbit of information. The joint where we were booked to play, the Old Colonial Music Hall, had been closed for some years and we were to spearhead the re-opening. We were going into a place with no regular audience – in other words, a completely unknown quantity. The next stop was the venue itself, to check out the equipment and do a soundcheck/rehearsal. The place smelled of mildew, mummified rodents and other things we didn't care to identify, and looked as if it had been boarded up since the Klondike Gold Rush. I know all our hearts sank, but Russell was the first to act out our collective disappointment. As we started into the try-out song, no drumming materialised. Russell sat immobile. 'I hate this fucking tune.'

I think that was the moment I caved in. Fuck the tantrums. I wasn't going to roll this bloody adventure uphill. Of the three nights we played at the Old Colonial Music Hall, the first was sober, shaky and tentatively attended, the second uninspiring, and by the third –

which was actually quite well attended – I went into revolt and decided the audience needed setting straight. We hadn't come all this way to play any Pacific Northwest boogie in this mould-encrusted, one-time burlesque house. This was British amphetamine psychosis music and, if they didn't like it, they could fuck off and listen to their Iron Butterfly albums. An enthusiastic cheer came from one quarter. It's funny how attack can, in some situations, be the best means of gaining respect. And then I howled. Free association, non-verbal, veins in the forehead pumping, arms threatening, all the way to primal drooling, and I loved – yes, I loved – every minute of it. A total abrogation of responsibility, and the fracturing of the few rules that remained. So Russell was tired of playing this fucking song: fuck him, and fuck Rudolph and his fuzz-box expertise; and fuck the Robert Plant bel canto that everyone thought was so fucking cool. Free at last, free at last, great God Almighty, I had mastered at least partial synaptic disengagement. Admittedly I was playing to the segment who'd cheered, and they were eating it up, but they were only a minority and the rest of the spectators were looking appalled, but you can't win them all, right? The ones who knew, really knew. They were actually seeing a human being in neural disintegration, right onstage, without hesitation and shame. Now how often do you see that, neighbours?

At the party that followed, a guy handed me a pint of Canadian Club and started telling me about a dude called Alice Cooper who was playing clubs up along the US/Canadian border. Seemingly this Alice wore net stockings and corsets and bit the heads off chickens as part of his act. The guy with the Canadian Club seemed to think we should go out together as a double-bill. At least someone had the right idea. On the other hand, others were looking at me as though I might be in need of some restraint, and I believe Rudolph, Sandy and Russell were among them. When I caught them doing it, I treated them to a stare both mad-eyed and enigmatic. I didn't know at the time that their sole topic of conversation was how exactly to throw Mick out of his own band. What also didn't occur to me was that this new, mad cunning of mine might not be overly healthy. I was firmly convinced that the state of mind I'd entered was only a dramatic persona, a precursor of Aladdin Sane. It never dawned on me that I might actually be going out of my mind.

In the cold light of the next day a number of highly disturbing pieces of news reached us. Jamie had unexpectedly flown in the night before, and now he revealed the true depth of the shit. It's hard to be crazy early in the morning, so I just listened like the others, in the same stunned silence. As we had pretty much figured, the promoter was refusing to pay, claiming he hadn't sold enough tickets, blah, blah, blah. Promoters have a million ways to explain how they've fucked you, but now won't buy you dinner. Bottom line, this meant that we had no hotel, which was absolutely no loss. We also had no money, except what was in our pockets, and that was nothing short of a disaster. We were broke in Canada, which was about the worst-case scenario, but we also had no money to wire back to pay the rent owed on 212. And we discovered that Jamie had settled for some jive-arse discount return air tickets that had expired before we'd even finished sleeping off the gig and the party.

I should probably have murdered Ace on the spot, but I was down-and-zombie, mentally immobile, and in no condition to sort out this mess. Jamie could carry the weight. He could organise the only course of action left to us. He could call Seymour Stein in New York, grovel for some survival chump change and find out what we were supposed to do next. As far as taking care of business was concerned, I was out of there. Call me a cab. I was going to get drunk and stay drunk until someone told me, simply and without any long words, what I was supposed to do. From that point on Jamie would attempt to buttonhole me for conspiratorial business discussions, but all I could do was stare at him in glazed horror. I believe he did raise some pittance from the record label, and Seymour told him to sit tight for a few days. He was going to LA and then he'd fly up to Vancouver and sort us out. That much I grasped, but mainly I stared, glazed and uncomprehending, wondering when someone would finally realise that I was emotionally tapped out and had nothing more to contribute.

Or maybe, to be more precise, I had nothing more to contribute to one wretched, graceless and disobliging rock & roll band. It took me about one cab ride to find a bunch of folks who were more than happy to accept my bullshit, and even feed me booze and drugs to hear more of it. I was cashing in my underground credentials and playing the traditional role of the traveller from another land with tall tales to tell. Thank God for groupies and dopefiends, and one notorious street behind a hippie strip of bars, headshops, poster stores and wholefood emporia, known to hippies all over the city and to the RCMP narcs as Chemical Row. Chemical Row was two blocks of run-down, psychedelic-painted frame houses where freaks called to you from the front porch to join them in a bong. Hot damn, I fell for Chemical Row like an albino alligator falls for a sewer. From Chemical Row, bikers took me to bars where my money was no good and a guy who looked like Lee Marvin cut out lines of crystal meth with a buck knife. Robert Crumb blondes in short shorts and Patsy Cline boots gave me a Valium or half a 'lude, hooked me up to the water pipe and had sex with me, which in my state could take for ever and further enhanced my rep as an obliging afternoon caller. For all practical purposes, I became a bouncing-ball basketcase in black velvet and sunglasses, passed from hand to hand, and place to place, a creature lacking will or self-determination. I knew, if you attempted this as a way of life, that your welcome would quickly wear thin, but for the few days it lasted, it was better than Disneyland.

All went well as long as I stayed away from the rest of the band and they stayed away from me, although we were all denizens of the Chemical Row theme park, so avoiding them altogether was impossible. We kept crossing paths and running into each other and, in public, we had to behave like the best of mates. Even that kind of worked. I mean, I didn't hate these guys. I was just burned-out on listening to them. Then Boss delivered the word that the band was going to *do something*. What exactly *doing something* constituted was a mystery to me, and I made sure it remained so until well after it was over. Boss claims the night in question was the first time I took on a full load of acid. I tend to disagree, for I think what was going on that night had more to do with nerve gas than true psychedelics.

As far as I can figure out, we arrived at some kind of recording studio with dim lights, Moog synthesisers and other stuff I hadn't a clue how to work. Equipment had been set up, and it looked uncomfortably like we were expected to play. My memory is of swaying and blinking. 'Play for what?' It wasn't a gig and it didn't seem like a party. Just a group of affluent-looking hippies in beaded buckskin jackets, with the judgemental air of local counterculture movers and shakers. Why the hell were we playing for these people?

Was it some sort of audition? If so, what for? Or were we giving some private show for the city's elite, and what the hell were we doing anything as humiliating as that for? Were we men or performing monkeys? One guy even reminded me of Joe Boyd, and the vibe was of some kind of trial by rock & roll.

Russell got behind the drums, Rudolph and Sandy strapped on their instruments and they launched into some spineless funk-shuffle. (By this point I'm operating on totally subjective recall, so what I think was happening and what was really happening may be extremely divergent. Once again I wish I had the tape.) I remember staring at a microphone like it was a live cobra. Paralysed by fear, the monkey was unable to perform, but pretty soon I ceased to be a primate or even mammalian. I was down with the limbic reptile. I opened my scaly phaser ports and fired at will. I commenced raising Lucifer and talking in the tongues of Ancient Evil. An infernal monologue with the reverb of Cthulhu, monstrously atonal and probably unintelligible, and I knew it was reaching the desired depths because, out there, the hippie elite was looking dismayed, disgusted and, I flatter myself, maybe even frightened. The music faltered to a stop and the damned band had the utter gall to look embarrassed. Don't be embarrassed on my account, you bastards. I'm Mick fucking Farren and, like it or not, we are still the Deviants, and if I decide to do it, it has validity, no matter what a bunch of provincial dope dealers and media hustlers might think. It can be a primal fucking scream, and it's still art. Ask Yoko. I've pissed off better than them.

And that was the end of it.

The next day we convened at the place where Rudolph was staying, the home of some hostile ex-girlfriend. Ace did most of the talking. The little dears didn't want to be underground clowns any more, they wanted to be legitimate musicians. To this end they were going to press on to San Francisco without me. I think I remarked how they could have had the balls to do the deed before we found ourselves stranded in bloody Canada. Then I came unglued, weeping and shaking. Many years later Russell admitted that they might have treated me with more humanity, and I totally agree with him. Out of there, my first stop was the biker bar, where it was still early enough to drink with some peace and quiet. As the night grew later and noisier, however, I could no longer wrap shock around me like an isolating shroud, and when a short bearded guy with jailhouse tattoos offered me an orange tab of sunshine I went for it. In for a penny, in for a pound. What the hell? When and where better to take your first full-blown trip? In a biker bar at the height of rejection shock.

Safe at a Wild Bill Hickock table with my back to the wall, the first fairyland phase was quite delightful as everything became haloed in rainbow auras. For a while I think a hippie maiden sat beside me, gently warning those who sought to involve me in some bout of motorcycle rowdiness that I was tripped out of my mind. All might have gone on as it started, had not Jamie, with the timing of a demon from the pit, arrived just as things were undulating into the more serious. Acting like he was planning the Kennedy assassination, Ace insisted that I leave the table and follow him into the piss- and disinfectant-smelling corridor that led to the lavatories. As he handed me the envelope, he turned into an alien biped lizard from Draco 3. The envelope contained an airline ticket and some cash.

'You're going home.'

I took the ticket, but never asked him how he'd managed the scam. I don't think I thanked him. I'm not actually sure I had the power of speech at the time. The reality of having to organise myself onto a plane relatively early the next morning freaked me right out. I wandered the streets around Chemical Row horror-struck, at times hallucinating so intensely that I couldn't see my feet, let alone understand traffic. I sat on the beach for a while watching the fog move in until I realised I was freezing. At one point I ran into Sandy, who talked at me in Hittite psycho-babble. The only place I felt safe was the biker bar, which I think is where Boss found me, fed me chocolate milk, then took me to where my stuff was stashed and had me in a cab to the airport in a blazing psychedelic dawn – as orange as the tab I'd swallowed.

The Flying Zombie was on Air Canada to Heathrow, via Montreal. I didn't want to go home because I wasn't sure I had one, but what else could a poor boy do? I was too fucked-up to burn my visa and seek my fortune in the Americas. On the first leg of the flight, the plane was again all but empty. Some other freaks were sitting in the dark rear, with just a single reading lamp to indicate their presence. With the boldness of he who doesn't give a good goddamn, I stumbled back and made myself known to them. Two guys and a girl who looked like the Mod Squad were drinking Jack Daniels and invited the Flying Zombie to join them. 'Drinking Jack and kicking back.' They believed I was a rock star but they didn't know who, and I played along, if only for ego therapy. 'You're *that* guy, right?'

'No, man, the *other* guy.'

After about three more drinks one of the guys, with only a minimum of ceremony, pulled out a joint that he insisted on referring to as 'doobie', and we smoked it right there in the plane, with the cabin crew taking not a blind bit of notice. Eight miles high and by no means ready for touchdown, but like Mr Natural said, 'Quest into the unknown'. And I was now so far gone I would follow any pointed finger.

Chapter Seven

They Don't Call Them Decades for Nothing

Where the Sixties had the feel of a continuous rolling wave, constantly moving, sometimes with violent force, but always in the same direction, the Seventies seemed to be a succession of squalls and flurries that could come at you from any point of the compass, setting you spinning and bobbing and sometimes fighting to stay afloat. This wasn't to say that the Sixties had been without risk. Quite the reverse. You either surfed the wave or you drowned. If you kept this in mind, the early Seventies weren't as bad as many made out. Truth is, much that was credited to the Sixties didn't really come to fruition until '72 or '73.

A lot of fence-sitting, quasi-hip pundits have always made a big deal of the exact point at which the Sixties ended, and the spirit of peace and love slunk off snarling. The easy answer in America was that – woe is us – the Rolling Stones and the Hell's Angels killed it off at Altamont. Their Brit counterparts like to pin it on the violence and confusion at the Isle of Wight pop festival. Others cited the deaths of Jimi, Jim, Janis and Brian. Get the fuck out of here! Nothing died except people. Only the superficial went away, and some rethinking had to be done regarding some of the more excessive stupidity. Any gambler worth a damn knows that luck fluctuates. A down-trend doesn't mean you have to go out on the terrace and blow your brains out. You hang in. Ignore that bloody silly Don McClean song 'American Pie'. The music didn't die, Don, it simply mutated.

We certainly knew, if there had ever been a revolution, we'd lost it, and a multitude of betrayals and sell-outs would occur as the establishment that we'd so carelessly challenged looked for payback. Ironically, we would later learn from his White House tapes that, of all people, Richard Nixon took the so-called youth revolt absolutely seriously. What the future had in store was a series of holding actions and regroupings, devilish compromises and constant struggles to hold on to anything that we might deem worthwhile and actually survive. I suppose, in terms of survival, that we one-time bigshots of the underground had it easy.

Easy? You Call This Easy?

After stumbling reasonably unscathed from the clutches of customs and immigration at Heathrow, a phone box and a handful of change were my only implements to discover the immediate shape of my life and even where I'd sleep that night. What was that song? 'I just called up to see what condition my condition was in'? It took about four calls before I discovered not only my condition, but also where my estranged wife and what was left of my possessions might be after the hasty departure from Shaftesbury Avenue – 212 was history, but Joy had borrowed some money from my mother and rented a two-room k&b on Chesterton Road at the top end of Ladbroke Grove. So we were back in the Grove. Okay, life went on. I didn't know, as I walked away from the phone box, that Joy's plan wasn't intended to include any *we*. My only response was intense relief that I could now get in a cab and give the driver an address that was substantively home.

The flat on Chesterton Road was a step down from Shaftesbury Avenue, but it had a certain charm. It was the top-floor flat and therefore self-contained. The place seriously needed painting, but Joy had negotiated a deal with the landlord for a number of weeks rent-free if she did the redecorating. Some junkies had just been evicted and, as Joy told it, the landlords had been reluctant to rent the place again before they'd renovated and refurnished, but she'd managed to talk them into letting it to her as it was. All the landlords had put in were a couple of brand-new double mattresses. I guess the ones the junkies left behind were simply too disgusting for even the most flexible of tenants.

To my surprise, when I rang the bell, it wasn't Joy who answered, but Su Small. Su was short, fulsome and with long, straight dark hair and a taste for short skirts and black beatnik sweaters. She was practical, smart and vivacious, and had great legs. She had been the advertising manager of *IT* almost since Dave Hall had taken over the business, and we'd been friends for maybe eighteen months or so. In the last few days before I'd left for Canada we'd also become lovers. She had turned up one evening and stayed, happily determined to bed me, something I found both flattering and highly acceptable. Su was skilled in fun and its arts. She made me feel like the warrior hero receiving the blessing before going off to war. Now it seemed that she was there for my return, and for this I was profoundly grateful. I wasn't exactly on my shield, but damned close. She grabbed me and kissed me. 'You look shell-shocked.'

'In some kind of shock.'

Su kissed me again, a don't-worry-kid-you're-back-home-now kiss, and led me up the three flights of stairs to where Joy was waiting. On the first landing she looked back at me and grinned. 'Did you know there's stories going round that you went off into the forest to live with the bears?'

'The bears wouldn't have me.'

It was immediately clear that Joy had so recently moved in that she'd hardly begun to unpack. I dropped my bag and flopped down on one of the new mattresses. She was superficially pleased to see me, but I could sense a tension in the air. Joy went to the kitchen to make some tea, and Su began to roll a joint. 'So it was a bit rough?'

I let out a long sigh. 'Fuck . . .'

Su was the kind of person with whom I didn't feel I had to make constant conversation. It was enough just to watch her deftly roll a joint. She lit it and passed it to me. 'Get that down you, kid. You'll feel a whole lot better.'

Joy came back with the tea, but after a few minutes Su got up and started putting on her coat. I didn't get it. 'You're going?'

'Just to the shop. I need some fags.' She looked at Joy. 'Maybe I'll bring back a take-away.'

'That sounds like a great idea.'

As Su exited, even my scattered instincts told me something was up. Her departure looked too much like a discreet withdrawal so that

Joy and I could talk about something. Since I had absolutely nothing to talk about, I bided my time and waited to see what Joy had on her mind.

'Listen, Mick, there's something we have to get straight.'

I shook my head. 'I don't think I'm up to any more revelations just now.'

She ignored me and pressed on. 'I've had a talk with Jamie . . .'

Now that was news. He'd told me he didn't know what was happening back in London.

'. . . and he doesn't think he could be comfortable if you were living here.'

'Right at this moment, I don't give a fuck about Jamie Mandelkau's comfort.'

'We *are* living together.'

'You conned the money out of my mum to get this place.'

'I had to do something.'

'You told some bullshit sob-story to my family so that you could set yourself up in a cozy little love nest with fucking Mandelkau.'

'It's not like that.'

'Yes, it is.'

'We want to have a place together.'

'And what the fuck am I supposed to do? I've just been to hell and don't even know if I'm back yet.'

'I don't want it to go like this.'

'If you and Ace want the place, give me back the money my mum gave you and I'll sling my hook.'

'I can't do that.'

'Of course you can't.'

'But . . .'

I'd had enough. 'Shut up, Joy. Just shut up and listen. Since I've known him, fucking Mandelkau has shacked up with my wife, manipulated me out of my fucking band and now he wants my folks to provide him with a home, while I sleep in the street. How fucking stupid do you think I am? I'm going to set up home in the small bedroom and, if Jamie doesn't like it, he can go fuck himself.'

Right then the bell rang. 'That'll be Su coming back.'

I churlishly didn't move, so Joy went to get the door. She and Su came back up the stairs preceded by the smell of curry. I suddenly realised how hungry and tired I was. Su set down the food and looked from me to Joy and back again. 'So did you get everything settled?'

'I'm staying in the back room, pro tem.'

Su raised an eyebrow, and I got the vibe that she and Joy might already have discussed the situation and that Su hadn't approved of the neat little Joy-and-Jamie scheme. With the housing crisis at least temporarily settled, I knew the only thing left for me to do was fall over. Which I did, Su along with me, and oh lord, was I glad of the warmth and comfort. I slept on and off for about three days. It seemed to be the only cure for the immobilising combination of jetlag, hangover and total exhaustion. Throughout those seventy-two hours Su ministered to my needs, and even Joy weighed in with cups of tea and bowls of cornflakes. I think she realised I'd been pushed too far. On the third day I rose from the dead, and decided to survey the wreckage. I didn't feel my perspectives had been drastically or fundamentally transformed by all the acid I consumed in Vancouver. I certainly hadn't undergone the kind of Road-to-Damascus mental make-over to which other acidheads laid claim, but that might have been because my thought processes were pretty made-over already.

I did find myself a little reluctant to reunite with my old drinking buddies straight away. I felt a trifle too bruised to leap right back into the old routine and, besides, for the moment I had no credentials. A drunk without a band is nothing more than a drunk. I needed to assess the situation with some care. For a start, I had no money to speak of, but in the short term, this was fairly easily solved. The Deviants' PA had been purchased with part of the Transatlantic advance, was still in excellent condition, nominally mine and I was able to sell it back to the manufacturers for a sum that would keep me going for a couple of months. Next I called on the end of the music business that directly affected me, and discovered to my pleasant surprise that everyone was very pleased to see me safe, well and back where I belonged. The general opinion was that the other Deviants didn't have a clue, because I'd totally been the driving force behind the band. Nat Joseph wanted me to go into the studio as soon as I felt ready and make my solo album. I began to feel a good deal better about myself.

I also found that our Canadian disaster hadn't gone totally

unnoticed. Steve Mann, one of the pre-eminent Ladbroke Grove freaks, had been hired as a publicist at Transatlantic when Nat had decided to move into the psychedelic rock business. Jamie had apparently sent him some kind of managerial bulletin about the Deviants and I parting company, and how the other three would be going on to greater fame and glory by completing a tour of America and then returning to the UK in triumph. Steve hadn't been particularly impressed, and Ace's boasts were rather negated by word from Seymour Stein that the Deviants were of little interest to him without me. Accordingly, Steve had put out a hilarious press release that I'd gone completely mad and was missing in the Canadian forest like some kind of neo-Jeremiah Johnson. As Su had put it, 'living with the bears'. The story had run in *Melody Maker* under the headline 'Farren Deviates Away' and, if I'd planned it myself, I couldn't have imagined a better welcome home. When I saw the piece, I laughed like a drain.

Trouble at Mill

When beset by care and woe, the suggestion that life continues outside one's own sphere of misery, and that other people also have their troubles, can come as quite a surprise. In this case the surprise came almost as soon as I was ambulatory, and Su filled me in about the problems at *IT*. Since I'd been off in the world of rock & roll, a mess of change had come to pass at the underground newspaper. Bill Levy had gone, and so had Nigel Samuel. Hoppy had pulled some strange number after he'd come out of jail, which had dissolved the original Editorial Board and turned *IT* into a supposed workers' cooperative. The paper had moved out of Nigel's building and into new offices above an Italian café, just down the block in Endell Street.

Dave Hall was still there, but new editors had arrived, in the form of Peter Stansill and Graham Keen, and under their stewardship *IT* had grown fat but not half so sassy. Although many other underground ventures were hard up against a contracting economy, *IT* had two lucrative factors going for it. The corporate music industry had finally embraced the counterculture. For the alternative press, the advertising revenue was now rolling in. At the same time *IT* had stumbled across the huge growth market in gay men's lonely-hearts adverts. As I'd observed during Bill Levy's tenure, the gay ads had a weird effect on the paper. They made it money and increased its circulation, but – although the gay classifieds would provide an excuse for the first criminal charges against the paper and its editors – the money buffer they created seemed to have made it possible for the paper to turn decidedly white-bread and red-brick.

To compound the problem, this combination of comparative affluence and political domestication drew a bottom-feeder envy that was at its most tangible in the form of a crew of low-rung activists and dopefiend opportunists who called themselves the London Street Commune. I suppose you could describe Phil Cohen and the London Street Commune as the Jacobins – the *sans-culottes* – of the Sixties underground, and I've always preferred Jacobites to Jacobins. During the summer of 1969 they had come into the public and TV eye by occupying an empty building at 144 Piccadilly, right by where the Hard Rock Café now resides. I was never sure of the exact political goal of the occupation, except as another gadfly irritant to the establishment, but I assumed it was an attention-getter for squatters' rights and the city's lamentable housing situation. What the LSC did manage to achieve was an agitprop eyesore right on Hyde Park Corner, within spitting distance of both Buckingham Palace and the London Hilton. They held it for a number of weeks – the time it took the authorities to move through the cumbersome legal process that would allow the police to storm the building and evict the malcontents.

When the Piccadilly prank was forcibly concluded, the LSC turned its attention to other targets, one of which was the perceived elitism in the underground itself. In this, the street people had something of a point. The underground was elitist, and the alternative society had evolved its own social strata absolutely from the outset. At one end of this caste system, Mick Jagger and the sons and daughters of the nobility lolled in fashionable restaurants like Sloane Rangers on acid, while at the other extreme lank-haired junkies squatted in burned-out basements with the needle and the damage done. It's been the human way all through history, with only rare and minor exceptions. So what's the answer? For the LSC, it was the Dalek cry

'Exterminate! Exterminate!' and seizure of the *IT* offices. To my mind, the move was nasty, violent, destructive and nothing short of fucking ridiculous, but maybe they weren't as conflicted as I was. I'd dragged myself up from the House of the Chinese Landlord by a process of self-education and relentless determination. A part of me – the conditioned superego of Freudian capitalism, if you like – felt that I should be rewarded for these efforts and, in some ways, I had a greater right to fun and creature comforts than a lazy son-of-a-bitch who simply sits on his arse cultivating a smack habit and scowling resentment.

If I seem to be advocating an underground meritocracy, however, that's hardly my intention. On the other hand, my sympathy for those who felt some form of forcible levelling should take place was strictly limited. It's too easy an answer; and, in its most extreme form, the one used by Pol Pot and the Khmer Rouge when they declared the Year Zero, reduced everyone to the status of the most wretchedly poor and illiterate peasant and killed all who weren't overjoyed by the prospect. I have serious reservations about any revolution that seeks to render everyone equally miserable, with or without the killing fields.

I guess this is as good a time as any to make a confession. Deep down, I'm a snob. I may care passionately about the rights and freedoms of the individual, but I am also inordinately fond of much that life has to offer. I like books, music and video tapes around me, I like twelve-year-old Scotch, vintage port, ripe stilton, strawberries and clotted cream, cocktails on a sunny afternoon, the paintings of Gustav Klimt, the photographs of Helmut Newton and have a preference for the best drugs available. I'm attracted to beautiful and flamboyant women and, now and again, they are attracted to me. If I'm going to the show, it's nice to have a backstage pass. I like pedigree cats, exotic aquaria and Japanese animation. When I get really ancient, I'll probably affect a silver-topped cane in the manner of Quentin Crisp. At the same time, though, I'm certainly not obsessed with money. I'll go through penury to pursue the realisation of a completely non-commercial creative idea, but I'm not about to subsist on toast and Marmite, and sniff glue while watching black-and-white broadcast TV, just because the Commissar, Führer or Chairman says so. I also believe, down at the real nitty-gritty, that committees and collectives do not produce vibrant media art. Successful group efforts – be they magazines, rock & roll bands, motion pictures or theatrical productions – are benign dictatorships, led either by a small oligarchy or a single alpha individual, and although the voice of the collective does need to be heard, the major decisions are inevitably made by those best at thinking on their feet. This is how things are, and how they will remain, until human nature undergoes a radical change.

A perfect example of the supposed elitism in the counterculture of the Sixties and Seventies can be found in the role of street sellers in the underground press. Modelled on the freelance newsboys who ran down the streets, shouting the headlines, the years before World War I – and crucial to the circulation of what was known as the gutter press – the street sellers at *IT* and *OZ* picked up their bundles of papers and magazines, initially on credit, and then hawked them along the tourist strips and through the major hippie enclaves. Now and again a bundle of papers would be ripped off, but the system worked pretty well. The magazines enjoyed a significant local sales boost, and a handy petty-cash flow – more than once, we'd waited around for a big-volume street seller to come in and cash up, so that we could all go down the boozer – and the system provided indigent freaks with some fast change by a process better, and more legal, than panhandling.

To the external observer, the relationship between the underground papers and their street sellers would have looked like classic employer/employee inequality. Why, you might ask, in a truly egalitarian set-up, weren't the street sellers present at editorial meetings and their opinions and ideas routinely solicited? The answer is that, to some degree, they were. It just wasn't in formal committee. When I was in control of *IT*, I was obsessed with the impact of each issue's cover, and regularly quizzed the street sellers as to which ones moved and which didn't. Some were well aware that a fast-sell cover made them their money with greater ease, and would talk at length about which designs worked and which didn't, and the features that moved papers and the ones that rolled over and died. I'd have been an idiot to ignore this feedback, but it would have been equally idiotic, in the name of political principle, to give the street sellers carte blanche as contributors and veto power over policy content, except in so far as a number of them actually did join the editorial teams of the various underground papers with which they made their first contact as street sellers.

The greatest of them all was, without doubt, a legendary kid named Felix Dennis, a rock drummer on the lam from a paternity suit or shotgun wedding in the suburbs. Felix immediately demonstrated a gut genius for the sale, production and promotion of successful magazines, and within a couple of weeks Richard Neville offered him the position of business manager. Today, Felix heads Dennis Publishing and has a net worth of around £300 million, which brings us squarely back to meritocracy again, and the fraught problem of workers' control, not only of the means of production, but of the flow of information and the individual creativity of the artist.

Although on a smaller scale, the problem is the same one that John Reed discussed in *Ten Days that Shook the World*. If the original design of the revolution is to free the individual to pursue his dreams and exploit his potential, what is achieved when the revolution immediately circumscribes the dream and limits the potential? It might be incumbent upon the artist to put himself at the disposal of the struggle, but for that revolution – for the dictatorship of the proletariat, as it was called in Reed's time – to go as far as wielding total censorship over creativity, forget it. It's as Pete Townshend wrote in 'Won't Get Fooled Again' – 'here comes the new boss/just like the old boss'. If you really want to see the dictatorship of the proletariat in action, don't look to old-time Soviet paintings and statues; just observe the horror of box-office, bottom-line-driven, Hollywood movies – Adam Sandler, Bruce Willis and *Titanic*.

And so, after this loop of digression, we come back to the dilemma created by the London Street Commune. Acting like our Khmer Rouge, they trashed the *IT* offices, stole typewriters, an Addressograph machine. They ripped off bundles of back numbers, which were of little significance, but also destroyed a collection of Hoppy's photo negatives that extended back more than ten years and were totally irreplaceable. Two things personally pissed me off when Su Small told me about what had gone down. The first was that the LSC should choose to make their point with a revolutionary act that was so chicken-shit and diminutive. Even though they used a crew of bikers and petty criminal low-lifes as their heavy mob, they knew that they'd meet no effective resistance and that any kind of retribution was highly unlikely. They were well aware that even what they perceived as the underground elite wasn't going to call the cops on them.

Su had been alone in the office, catching up on some paperwork, when they made their break-in, and they'd seen fit to put their populist frighteners on her. That was the second strike against the LSC in my book. Not that Su was any shrinking violet. Even in the face of their prole bluster, she remained eminently practical. The advertising accounts are a vital driving component of any magazine and, realising that the Communards and their bike-gang cohorts were bent on removing anything that looked of value, she simply sat on the files, then sneaked them away when she had a chance to leave. For some days – as far as I can reconstruct what I didn't witness – the Street Commune maintained a kind of feet-on-the-desk occupation, and the *IT* old guard wandered in and out, having arguments and wondering what the hell to do next. Su's plan, as far as I could gather it, was for me to amble in like some impartial Man-They-Couldn't-Hang and put the fear of the absolute into all concerned. In that brief moment I was the rock star who'd just been living in the woods with the bears. Don't fuck with Dolomite, motherfucker.

When I first turned up, the fun part was that no one except myself and Su knew what side I was on. I'd already decided I was going to put whatever weight my chips carried behind the old guard. The Commune had upset Su, so that made it personal. I was also completely certain that no Street Commune was going to be able to handle the complexity of publishing and distributing a newspaper, while the old guard had the routine down. No contest. I also discovered, since I'd been off on the rock & roll trail, that a couple of new guys – Mark Williams and Edward Barker, both from Birmingham – had joined *IT*, and they seemed like the kind of cats to whom I could relate. Mark liked to ride motorcycles at absurdist speed, and his later problematic adventures would become the stuff of local legend. Edward was, to say the least, strange. Young and beautiful, like a curly-haired Brian Jones, he not only drew the most original and surreal cartoons, but at times seemed to actually live in a world where the people around him presented themselves as anthropomorphic comic-strip animals. Edward's personality was rendered even more appealing by the fact that he frequently had to drink rather a lot to keep the menagerie at bay, a practice that usually left him in a state of befuddled innocence.

In a few short days it became clear that my assessment of the LSC's expertise in the magazine business had been entirely accurate. They didn't have a clue and, after hours of face-saving and pointless discussion, they melted away, and life at *IT* coagulated back to what passed for normality. (I firmly believe the time wasted in arguing about political trivia is why revolutions are lost, or annexed by the slaughterers.) The Communards put out, I think, one issue of something called *The International Free Press*, which not only featured unreadably convoluted polemics, but was as drab and grim as a wet Sunday in Marxist Albania. I'd done absolutely nothing to solve the *IT* crisis, but seemed to be getting the gunslinger points for saving the day, so good for me. Feeling better about myself, I decided it was the time to face the alcohol. I made contact with Twink and Took again and arranged for a welcome-home night. And where do we go? Why, down the Speakeasy of course, which was about as politically incorrect as a lad can get.

Speakeasy, Drink Easy, Pull Easy

It was hard to tell whether Ginger Baker was fucked-up or just in an extremely foul temper. He sat at the end of the Speakeasy bar, right by the door, and insulted people as they entered and left. I think Baker's intention was to provoke someone into taking a swing at him, so that he could have an excuse to pound them to pulp before the bouncers dragged him off. As I exited for a piss, he started on the subject of my hair. It was the latter days of Cream, and Eric Clapton had put in the curlers to look more like Hendrix. I told Baker my fucking hair grew like that naturally, he told me I was a fucking liar, and the next move on his obvious agenda was that I should try and hit him. Fortunately I was still sufficiently on top of things to reject the provocation. I simply turned my back. He might have come off his stool after me, but I doubted it. He was a star, and he wanted the fight brought to him, but I wasn't going to oblige. I've learned never to get physical with a drummer. No matter how destructive and wasting their lifestyles, all that pounding makes them strong of arm, bull-headed and hard to stop.

From Scott Walker to Johnny Thunders, the Speakeasy was the late-night, rock & roll rendezvous. The pubs might shut at eleven, with five minutes' drinking-up time, but the Speak served booze until 3 a.m. and then allowed its patrons another hour in which to loiter while emptying their bottles and glasses. Located in an anonymous basement behind Oxford Circus, the nightclub had opened a couple of years before flower power, during the throes of the Swinging London, Bonnie & Clyde craze, and the decor was Prohibition chic with an ornate coffin just inside the entrance and lots of blown-up sepia prints of Al Capone, Frank Nitty and Pretty Boy Floyd.

The Speakeasy was not only the place for late booze. It was also where the girls were; one of the city's high temples of the groupie culture that would so fascinate the media. The lipstick killer parade of assumed boredom, platform shoes, scarlet talons, transparent chiffon, fishnets, false eyelashes, appliqué glitter, hotpants, short-short dresses and attitudes of superiority would continue for more than a decade. Much has been made of the oppression of women in rock & roll. Was the groupie a brainwashed victim craving a second-hand and illusionary contact high, or an independent woman making her own choices, fully in control of her own body and sexuality? Germaine appeared to cleave to the former in both word and deed when I knew her, but in later life I understand she has recanted her former hedonism.

My own observation was that, at least in the limited context of their rock & roll nightclub domain, the women wielded the true power. They manipulated, they inspected, they selected or rejected. They dictated the pecking order and set the rules. Some, like Bebe Buellin – whose liaisons were legendary, but is now better known as the mother of actress Liv Tyler – promoted the concept of the muse, the mistress-goddess who provides the artist's crucial motivation. I must confess I've never bought into the muse theory. I don't know about other guys, but I am absolutely sure that my allegedly creative outpourings have been the sole and exclusive product of my own warped imagination and nothing else. That does leave me open to the suggestion that I might have done a whole lot better if I'd got myself a muse, but I still don't think I'm buying it.

Jenny Fabian, on the other hand – whose *roman-à-clef*, *Groupie*, set half London substituting the real names for the pseudonyms (although they were able to stop when the full directory was published in *OZ*) – appeared to take an entirely different stance; groupie-ism was a grand and decadent game, an almost eighteenth-century merry-go-round of couplings and partners, and in that magically erotic interlude between the pill and the retro-virus who dared won. Miss Pamela Des Barres adopted a more Reichian view, seeming to believe that rock & roll was the essential energy, and that the groupie was an indispensable component in its orgonomic generation, but what would you expect from someone from southern California?

In the early days of the Speakeasy, the sexual hierarchy was simple and market-driven. The male musicians' desirability was linked directly to the top-forty performance of their singles. As the album took over as the primary medium, the situation became more idiosyncratic. The demi-god status of members of global mega-bands like the Stones and Led Zeppelin set even the hardest and most calculating hearts a-flutter, and Jimi Hendrix was the apotheosis of the unspeakably desirable voodoo child, but not all were judged simply on their record sales and tour grosses. Frank Zappa, who sold comparatively few records on the platinum standard, was continually surrounded by eager, if not always exquisite, young women; but then again, Frank was both a supporter and promoter of groupie culture, with his championing of the GTOs, the LA groupie vocal group, and the Plaster Casters of Chicago, two strange young women from Illinois who collected models of the erect penises of the loud and famous.

Perhaps I can only talk with this kind of detachment because, despite my best efforts to behave like some obnoxious little rock star, I hardly figured in the groupie pecking order; little commercial potential and, as Jenny Fabian said, too 'dark and angry'. Sandy was always the babe magnet, culminating his groupie contacts with an affair with Miss Pamela, who tells in her book, *I'm With the Band*, how she broke his heart when they split. I can't say I personally noticed any outward manifestation of this heartbreak, although Sandy drank so much it was hard to tell what he might be feeling.

Although some of the boys prowled the club with their metaphoric dicks hanging out, others of us simply got drunk, took drugs in the bathroom and made stumbling yahoo nuisances of ourselves. In my time at the Speakeasy I witnessed many world-class drunks in full cry. I recall Greg Allman in the restaurant, face-down in his soup and in danger of drowning like Grandpa in the TV show *Mary Hartman, Mary Hartman*. I will never forget the towering figure of Howlin' Wolf, drunk out of his sexagenarian mind, advancing on a table of petrified party girls, phallically waggling a Shure vocal mike clutched to his crotch, proving that the real Back Door Man was just too much for them. One especially spectacular night Keith Moon, who was pretty much the Speak's resident nuclear attack when off-duty from the Who, arrived with the notorious Oliver Reed in tow, plus Peter Sellers in a long leather coat and a Nazi helmet, which the ex-Goon referred to as his 'drinking outfit'.

Not content merely to watch, the specific coterie with which I hung out felt, by macho necessity, compelled to create our own less-celebrated mayhem, which put us in decisive opposition with the club management. The serious business of the club was overseen by a duo of Italians – Mino and Bruno – whom we all imagined were made mobsters. Mino and Bruno commanded the door, and their vision of a nightclub in no way encompassed whisky-swilling ruffians of bad character and dubious financial resources, like Twink, Took and myself. The only one of the supposed Mafia crew that seemed to like me was Luigi, who ran the restaurant. Early on, in the course of some idle conversation, he discovered my partially cultivated taste for Italian cuisine. The food in the Speakeasy was hardly fit for a dog and the menu included a cunningly dangerous Chicken Kiev that, when you stuck a fork in it, spewed super-heated butter in all directions. As I came to know him better, I asked Luigi why the food was so disgustingly awful, and he gestured resignedly to the tables of rock & roll drunks. 'Anything else would be pearls before swine.'

It was fortunate that we had some non-gangster friends inside. One of these was Tony Howard. By day, he was the unflappable cockney booking agent for Pink Floyd and the Pretty Things, and he had even handled the Deviants for a while until we moved to Blackhill; by night, he doubled as the club's 'creative director', which mainly involved hiring the talent and then sitting at his corner table in the restaurant, smiling benignly as all manner of mayhem roared around him. Tony guaranteed us easy access past the doormen, except after some especially rabid atrocity – like the night members of the Pink Fairies, the MC5 and a naked young woman finished up disporting themselves in the Regent's Park canal.

Our other ally was Howard Parker, commonly know as H. Although I first encountered H as the DJ at the Speak – indeed, he was the first person to turn me on to the Stooges – he'd already racked up quite a résumé. A stocky, muscular man with long blond hair and a face that betrayed a far higher degree of intellectual curiosity than any run-of-the-mill roadie, he'd nursemaided Jimi Hendrix and been assistant to Frank Zappa, who never suffered fools gladly. H not only had many a tale to tell, but also owned the charred and decimated Stratocaster that Jimi had burned up at the Monteray Pop Festival. For the next few years he would participate in numerous of our adventures, and was always a tower of intelligence, strength and reassurance. He was unflappable, cheerful, effortlessly efficient and unwilling to admit that anything was impossible unless it absolutely was, and even then he'd search for other ways round the problem.

H seemed to know everyone and commanded a massive reserve of goodwill and respect. He had no time for hierarchies or pecking orders, taking an unusually egalitarian attitude to even the biggest stars. H wasn't easily impressed, and H wasn't a courtier, just a straight-shooting gem in an environment where flattery, deviousness and infantile tantrums were gangrenously endemic.

On most of the occasions I worked with him I was holding down some organisational role, but when the Deviants threw a reunion bash at the Roundhouse, H was stage manager, and I discovered why so many stars competed for his services. The band had been broken up for about two years and that night could have been one of tension, corner-of-the-eye distrust and wounds only superficially healed; also Sid was included and that could have brought another dimension of negativity. H, however, made certain the positive ruled. Through the run-up to the gig and while onstage, he made me feel every inch a star, all the way to the end when he handed me a huge magnum of champagne after the second encore.

When Dingwalls Dancehall opened up in Camden Lock, H left

the Speakeasy and became the new club's creative director. He very quickly designed a venue where the hot London bar bands could find a sympathetic stage, but one that was also big enough to book visiting luminaries like Bo Diddley and Curtis Mayfield. H saw no reason why rock stars and the regular punters shouldn't enjoy the booze and the music in the same saloon-like atmosphere, without the velvet-rope discrimination of the Speak and other supposedly celebrity nightspots. He hired Boss Goodman as DJ, and made sure that all of his old Speakeasy cronies received lifelong get-in-free passes. No accusation of disloyalty or jumping ship could be levelled. H went way back with the owners of Dingwalls, and they'd given him the chance at least partially to fashion the club of his dreams.

Damn, but I wish H had stayed around. While on a well-earned holiday in the Greek islands the bloody fool bought himself a boat – a rickety, sprung-at-the-seams, piece-of-crap scow – and spent all his free time fixing it up and supposedly making the cursed thing seaworthy. At the launch for its maiden voyage, friends stood around laughing and applauding. They firmly believed it would leak so badly, even in shallow water, that H would be forced to turn back. To everyone's amazement, he sailed on like the young-man-of-the-bloody-sea, rounded a headland and was never seen again. The boat had sunk – maybe even broken up – in deep water, and H, although a powerful swimmer, had been sucked down by an Aegean undertow. His body was never recovered, and it was one of those dumb, ill-luck, purposeless fatalities. Howard Parker was loved by too many people just to vanish without a trace.

Back at the Speakeasy, had it not been for the tolerance and tacit encouragement provided by H and Tony Howard, it would have been unlikely that our particular clique would have formed what became known as the Pink Fairies Motorcycle Gang and Drinking Club. The name would ultimately be appropriated and truncated by Twink for a supposedly commercial rock band, but in its original form the PFMG&DC was dedicated to the most raucous after-hours fun we could devise. The 'fun' usually began under the guise of 'getting up to jam', which in reality meant a mass stage invasion followed by about forty minutes of shrieking cacophony until all players declared themselves exhausted and retired to the bar, leaving a debris of bottles, glasses and distressed equipment. The hard core of

Pretties and Deviants would be augmented by the usual suspects: Viv Prince, Steve Took, a harmonica player called Mox and, more occasionally, 'Legs' Larry Smith and Viv Stanshall.

These impromptu events caused massive consternation among the up-and-coming bands who had actually been booked to play. Many were conned into appearing at the Speak for no money, in the naive belief that it would provide a rock-biz showcase and they'd have a single zooming up the charts by the following Thursday. When our intervention resulted in a ravaged stage and an alienated audience, they were understandably miffed. On the nights when 'Legs' Larry was joined by Moon, miffed would turn to wide-eyed nightmare as a brand-new drum kit was reduced to kindling. Fortunately Moon had a habit of staving off the horror by instantly handing a signed cheque for the full purchase price to the stunned drummer. The worst of these confrontations took place when the entire crew, including a mute Syd Barrett, dragged along by Took, arrived in full cry and loaded for beer after finishing Twink's *Think Pink* album. We were also unnaturally flush with money. As the producer, I'd conned noteworthy drinking money out of Decca Records, by invoicing for session men – phantom string and oboe players who were in fact nothing more than the Pretty Things' keyboard ace John Povey reproducing them on a Melotron – to finance what we hoped would be a party sufficiently apocalyptic that it would have impressed Attila and his Huns. What we didn't know was that another party was also supposed to be taking place that night. The showcase, record-industry debut of a new band called King Crimson.

At that stage in their development King Crimson had a habit of playing very loud, then going into a sudden breakdown and playing very quietly. Of course, the PFMG&DC had no idea of their arrangements and cared even less. During the loud bits we could only communicate by yelling to each other, and in the quiet bits it took us a minute or so to adjust, making our conversation suddenly louder than the band. Some sections of the audience, especially the reserved tables of corporate-entertainment flunkies, assumed that we were vociferously disrespecting the musicians onstage, and even suspected some stinking underground intrigue to disrupt the show. In fact, nothing could have been further from the truth; just two celebrations running headlong into each other with the force of a train-wreck.

Record moguls started calling for our ejection, but – and here I'd played my cards rather shrewdly – on arrival I'd handed Mino some hundreds of pounds with the instructions to keep the booze coming until the cash ran out. No way was Mino going to hand back our alcohol deposit, so no way were we going to be bounced. The mayhem continued until Twink staggered up to the stage and started demanding that King Crimson play Chuck Berry's 'Nadine', because he didn't like their other songs. Even some of us thought that was going a little too far. Happily, my peace was made with Bob Fripp years later in the Grass Roots Tavern in New York City and all was water under the bridge.

Hey, Hey, Hey, Mona

Personal vindication may not be the best or most sensible reason to create art, and my wonderful solo album entitled *Mona – The Carnivorous Circus* was, in almost every respect, the product of a desperate need for vindication. After my fall from the Deviants I had a lot to prove. The hard part was my confusion as to what exactly I wanted to prove, and in the end all the recording really demonstrated was the confusion itself. For the longest possible time I thought John Lennon and Yoko Ono were the only people on the planet who liked this record. Even I couldn't stand to listen to it. The packaging was a pretty fair indication of my fucked-up motivation during the making of the conflicted gem. The front cover bore a custom logo by Allen Jones, who'd designed the cover of *A Quick One* for the Who, overlaid by the famous photograph of the long, faceless ranks of Wehrmacht soldiers, hands raised, taking their personal oath of loyalty to the Führer. The choice had been between that and one of those Fifties shots of a cinema audience all staring at the screen through 3D glasses. I was looking for a symbolic image of the cookie-cutter destruction of the individual, which alone should have been a measure of my mood. That my final selection should have been of the helmeted Nazis was an even more precise gauge of the bleakness of my hostility, there at the end of Nixon's first year in the White House.

Right from the start, the making of *Mona* was a supposedly

planned descent into a very dark labyrinth. I have friends who even now tell me that the record frightens them. By the time I got to 'Mona', I was determined to aim for the furthest extremes I could achieve. The rest of the Deviants had chickened out and become a guitar band, but I would demonstrate my superiority by walking on to the crossroads and beyond, totally alone. A Nietzschean fucking *Übermensch*, right? I would fight with monsters, and take no care lest I become one.

Of course, I still wanted to be a rock star like Elvis. (Who was a monster anyway, but I was one of the very small minority who'd noticed at that point.) Not by any conventional, or even rational route, though; I still remembered the parts of *Naked Lunch* that had put me off my toasted bacon sandwich. Could I do the same, for other up-coming, would-be bohemian sprogs, and be loved for it? In fact, a deeper and more devious cunning may have been at work. With hindsight, I suspect I might have been looking to destroy myself as an artist, and maybe even as a human being, in some personal audio twilight of the gods. Fight the monsters *in order to be one*. It is absolutely no mere whim that I solicited, and received, the seal of approval of the local Hell's Angels and displayed it proudly on the cover.

I could in part validate what I was doing by claiming, with some degree of truth, that, with *Mona*, I was attempting to destructure the rock LP as Burroughs had destructured the novel. Whether I was actually equipped to do this was another matter completely but who had tried it, except maybe John and Yoko? I didn't have any yardsticks against which I could be measured. Thus I started preparing pre-production tape loops and finding material. Even the recruitment of the band was somewhat unorthodox. I ran into an American called Steve Hammond at some record-company party and, after a few measured yards of small-talk, we got round to exchanging the information that I had an album to make, and he not only played guitar but could act as musical director and put me a band together. The musicians he seemed able to bring in certainly sounded impressive. As a bass player, he suggested Johnny Gustavson, who had played with Liverpool's legendary Big Three. Steve also claimed to be able to get Paul Buckmaster, the classical cellist who had turned to rock 'n' roll when he'd orchestrated 'Eleanor Rigby' for Paul McCartney.

Usually in these situations it's the booze that's talking, and when the pretty balloon has burst and both the party and the hangover are over, the call-me promises and plans prove a chimera. Not so with Steve Hammond. He called the very next day, confirming not only his reality, but also his togetherness, efficiency, determination and being as good as his word. Johnny Gus would do the session for only a tad over scale, and we could go and talk to Paul Buckmaster later in the week. Trying for a soft landing on a very strange planet here, Skipper, but hell, wasn't that what I wanted? It was sometime around this point, though, that I made a fairly serious mistake. Steve asked me if I had any special drummer in mind and, without thinking, I responded, 'Twink'.

The choice was a damned fool one. Aside from having a self-serving personality and a secret agenda that would only be revealed later, Twink's timing could be decidedly suspect on the wrong night. Since, courtesy of Nat Joseph, I was actually paying people, I could have had an almost free choice, but I had to fall victim to bar-room loyalty. Ah well. The meeting with Paul was considerably more inspiring and productive. When I told him that I was making the main theme of the album a protracted variation of Bo Diddley's 'Mona' interrupted by a lot of electronic cut-ups, he said one word.

'Bartók.'

'Bartók?'

Paul got up from his chair and went to a wall-sized record collection. He pulled out an album of string quartets by Béla Bartók and put it on the turntable. Partway through one of the pieces, there it was, clear and plain. Unsyncopated, maybe more percussive, but beyond any shadow of a doubt the Bo's trademark rhythm pattern. Paul elaborated: don't fear the gulf between classic and pop. It's only in the mind and radio marketing. Steve strummed the rhythm on an acoustic guitar, and Paul hummed a possible Bartók-based figure that would work as a counterpoint to the Diddley beat. For the first time in recent memory I was truly excited. I was hearing . . . well, maybe not something new, but a totally original juxtapositioning and matching of sources. Intercut with a dubbed version of Hitler's speeches, backward tam-tams, Sabre jets in a power dive, a recurrent serial-murderer character, a chant of 'who needs the egg' and a gratuitous Eddie Cochran song, it could hardly fail. Oh yes, this was assured to get me on *Top of the Pops*.

We went into Sound Techniques in Chelsea, where we'd made *PTOOFF!*, I guess looking to cook up some past magic. The sessions were efficient and the musicians came and went, and either I worked on my own with Sister George, or Took and I overdubbed the vocal whoops and chipmunk yodels he'd perfected behind Marc Bolan. We mixed the thing with the same relatively sober dedication, and what I then believed was attention to detail. And we delivered the tapes and people listened to them and started looking at me very strangely. I still claim the song 'Mona' with the cello – all ten minutes of it – has a unique and timeless quality, but I had come out with something a tad too bizarre even for those who wished me well. I reacted by turning round and going into a complete physical collapse.

As I Was Lying in My Hospital Bed

I was walking down Ladbroke Grove on a chilly afternoon when the tops of my cowboy boots felt as if they were cutting into the flesh of my legs. At home I investigated, and found to my horror that I was being attacked by an organic unpleasantness. The next day a mysterious swelling appeared under my right ear. I'm glad that AIDS had yet to be invented, otherwise I would have been convinced I was doomed. As it was, I was more than a little perturbed. I went to the doctor and fell asleep in his waiting room. The doctor took one look at me and sent me to hospital. I took a cab to Wormwood Scrubs, past Her Majesty's Prison, into Hammersmith Hospital, and had myself dropped off at Emergency. I then fell asleep again in the waiting room. At the hospital they took one look and admitted me.

They put me in a cubicle all by myself and, for an indeterminate length of time, I drifted in and out of functional awareness. People came in, looked at me and went away again. I might effectively have been abducted by aliens. I hadn't been in hospital since I'd had my adenoids removed at the age of two, and that long-distant memory in no way prepared me for hospitalisation's disorientating lack of reality.

Even the headphone radio didn't seem to get anything but Mahler on the BBC Third Programme. Hospitals possess an eerie hollowness, no matter how crowded they are. People die in those places, and it's noticeable.

A nurse informed me that I was going to be operated on, couching the information in medical baby talk – 'Just a little cut so the doctors can see what that thing under your ear is' – which caused me immediately to assume I had cancer. Naively believing that honesty was the best policy, I'd attempted to explain my unyielding lifestyle to a doctor. He'd asked what drugs I'd taken in the last year or so, and how much I drank, but before I'd even completed the list, or outlined the quantity, his eyes had glazed over. I ought to be dead a couple of times over, so how could he diagnose me? He hadn't studied mutants in medical school. I suggested that he should put me on some wide-spectrum antibiotic and see what happened, but doctors hate patients with specific suggestions. He vetoed the antibiotics and opted for the knife.

They prepped me, wheeled me in, the anaesthetist loomed over me and I had that inevitable thought that I might not wake up again, flavoured with a dash of 'That'll show the sons-of-bitches'. But I did wake up, from a dream in which all the secrets of the universe were revealed unto me; but, as I opened my eyes, I forgot the entire thing, down to the smallest detail, and burst into tears. I was wheeled back to my isolation cubicle, and then no one came near me for the next twelve hours. With unchanged dressings, and the distinct impression that I'd gone astray in some NHS-Kafkaesque bureaucracy, I started to worry that nobody knew I was there. Finally a sister discovered me, and I heard some just-out-of-earshot berating going on. My dressings were changed by an upset-looking nurse, I was fed and then put on the wide-spectrum antibiotic I'd wanted in the first place. My condition rapidly began to improve – so much so that I was beginning to wonder why all my lousy, so-called friends weren't flocking to visit me. I learned later that when they called, they'd been told that I was still post-operative and not ready for visitors. In fact, I was lost in the system, but they weren't to know that.

The evening after surgery, just as my isolation was starting to get to me, I heard a commotion somewhere beyond the confines of my patient's perception. A voice I recognised was raised and authoritative. 'I'm not interested in your rules, lady. I don't care that it's not visiting hours. I'm his manager, and he's my goddamned client, and I need to see him right now. My time's valuable and you'll find that screwing me around is very bad idea.'

Danny Halperin was a previous-generation New York beatnik, a Lenny Bruce contemporary who will be played by Sydney Pollack in the movie. Although it could be said that I was one of his clients, he definitely wasn't my manager – just doing a pretty fair impression of Allen Klein to get past the ward sister. Such were Danny's resources of bluff and bluster. He was a graphic designer with ties to Atlantic Records, who rented a studio in the back of Joe Boyd's office, and when Steve Sparks and I were hanging out there, plotting the 'Disposable' phase of the Deviants, we'd become pretty friendly, to the point that, one Friday afternoon, he'd turned me on to my first line of cocaine, a highly educational experience that made me wonder how come I'd been missing out for so long and caused me immediately to make sure that Nat Joseph gave Danny the commission for the cover of *Mona*.

Su Small was also a regular visitor at Danny's studio, picking up record-company artwork in her capacity as *IT*'s advertising director, and shooting the shit as a friend. Sometimes these 'tea party' afternoon gatherings in Danny's studio would grow to as many as five or six in number, with the addition of Anthea Joseph, an old revered folkie mate of Dylan's, and Judy Collins, whom Joe had hired as a governess for Fairport Convention. Heather Wood of the Young Tradition might show up, having slid by to see Anthea, and now and then Sandy Denny would put in an appearance. When the party reached these proportions – and Danny was a mighty teller of tales and a great raconteur with whom to waste a few hours – Joe Boyd would be forced to show his face. He essentially disapproved of hanging-out as counter-productive, and not what went on in a 'real office', but we had him so outnumbered that he was forced to smile nicely and participate and, on occasion, behave just like a human being.

When Danny had been informed, probably by Su, that I was languishing in the infirmary, he cabbed it over to the Scrubs. The end of Danny's day was well past visiting hours, hence the tussle with the ward sister. With the starched dragon vanquished, he entered bearing magazines and a Philip K. Dick novel. 'I should probably have brought you a bunch of daisies.'

'I wouldn't have appreciated it.'

'Didn't think you would. I also thought of a bottle of Scotch, but I decided it wasn't a good idea.'

'I'm on antibiotics.'

'So I was right?'

'That you were.'

'How are you?'

'I think I've decided to live.'

Danny didn't stay too long. The ward sister hovered, and both he and I knew he wasn't going to win round two. Even though brief, the visit encouraged me. To see anyone from the outside world was a massive relief. After Danny had left, the idea of lying around in a hospital bed for a few days recuperating seemed positively attractive, if people came to visit me and brought me stuff. That was not, however, how Hammersmith Hospital played it. I was informed by the dragon sister that they were throwing me out in twenty-four hours. My visions of peeled grapes were abruptly snuffed out and, instead, I was faced with the prospect of being back on the street, no longer accredited as sick, and on my own, to figure out what the hell to do next.

Ragged Company

So this was the Seventies. From my immediate perspective, I figured you could keep them. I was cold, damp, miserable and penniless. The snakeskin was wearing thin and the velvet was tatty and threadbare. After coming out of the hospital, I had grown a beard by way of compensatory displacement. It had started as long stubble when I couldn't shave around the dressings, but after a few weeks I looked like Phineas of the Furry Freak Brothers. Steve Took and I stood on the Broadwalk in Kensington Gardens in a fine drizzle, smelling, as he put it 'like old dog beds' and attempting not to face the fact that, by February 1970, we'd become too wretched for it to be funny. At that grievous, eight-o'clockish time of the morning, decent people are going to work and all hope fails for the lowdown and disconnected. Right then. Took and I were sufficiently disconnected to be walking from South Kensington to Ladbroke Grove because we didn't have the cab fare, and to take the tube in the rush hour would have been too emotionally damaging. This route march at such an ungodly hour was all Took's fault. After a perfectly reasonable night of drinking and drugging, he had gracelessly picked a fight with his girlfriend Angie and she'd thrown him out of the apartment she shared with her flatmate Chrissie. Of course being his buddy, pal and partner in crime of the moment, I had to go with him. The only possible refuge was my gaff in Chesterton Road, and we were walking because, when Took added insult to injury by asking for the cab fare, Angie had thrown a vase at him.

I still occupied the back bedroom at Chesterton Road. When Jamie returned, a repeat confrontation took place, but Ace backed down even faster than Joy. It worried me slightly that he'd caved in so fast, and then it occurred to me that, without any tangible occupation except managing the remaining rump of the Deviants, he was probably glad that I was there to help pay the rent. For a few weeks I bided my time, wondering where to move, and when; then keeling over and winding up in hospital put the brakes on any ideas of immediate relocation.

Not that my own situation was very much better than Jamie's. With my solo album being viewed as a symptom rather than a masterpiece, the entertainment industry was far from beating a path to my door. The first plan was that Twink, Took and I would put some kind of band together. Calling ourselves the Pink Fairies, we even performed something less of a gig and more of a protracted harangue to a confused and increasingly angry crowd at Manchester University. In later years some chroniclers tried to compare that act to the early and messy shows by John Lydon and Public Image Limited. I can't comment. The show was so unthought-out and unprepared that I resorted to getting blind drunk before the train even arrived in Manchester, and remember nothing of it.

Took, Twink and I supposedly went back to the drawing board, although Took and I weren't aware that, even as the three of us sat around at Chesterton Road, plotting future moves, nefarious phone calls were being exchanged setting up a completely different scenario. Twink, in cahoots with Jamie Mandelkau, was seeking his own salvation with a scheme to form a band with Rudolph, Sandy and Russell when they got back from the US, and to call it the Pink Fairies. I guess he hoped to capitalise on whatever minimal momentum and fuckhead profile the old PF drinking club might have garnered. Twink's duplicity disappointed me. Had he been upfront about what he was doing, I think I would have accepted it. I fully understand that a man must examine all his options, but he should have called Took and me to the pub and said, 'Look, lads, I'm talking to the three ex-Deviants, and we might get something together. Sorry, but that's what I see as my best shot right now.' Instead, he seemed to feel the need to choreograph an absurd fight with Took over what the music papers euphemistically called 'creative differences', and then ran off into the night claiming we were 'freaking him out with our negativity'. In a day or so, the Pink Fairies scheme was made public. Having experienced what I subjectively perceived as two back-stabbings in the space of three or four months, I began to have grave doubts about the whole rock-band business and, at about the same time, I was presented with a salutary example of the price that might have to be paid for the privilege of conducting said business.

Sweet Gene Vincent

The Blackfoot tribe have a proverb that goes 'When legends die, there are no more dreams, and when there are no more dreams, there is no more greatness.' Sometime in the aftermath of *Mona*, while re-examining my own dreams, I saw one of my personal legends for the last time. When I heard that Gene Vincent would be playing at the Country Club in Belsize Park, backed by Brit-rock revivalists the Wild Angels, I couldn't decide whether I was excited or dismayed. I already knew that he was in failing health and pretty much on the skids. John Peel, Kim Fowley and Jim Morrison had played their own parts in arranging that Gene should make what would turn out to be his last respectable studio album, but an aura of defeat seemed to cloak him like an ominous thunderhead.

For more than fifteen years, even before he had an international hit with 'Be-Bop-A-Lula', Gene had been living a regime so profoundly destructive that it was a near-miracle he even made it to the end of the Sixties, let alone was attempting yet another European tour. As those of you who know the legend will be well aware, Gene had seriously injured his leg in a motorcycle accident in the mid-Fifties while on leave from the US Navy. 'Be-Bop-A-Lula' had set him off on a treadmill of one-night stands, and the shattered bones were never given time to heal. This quickly led to a significant painkiller habit; the painkillers made him slow, so he took speed to get back in gear; the speed made him edgy and he drank to mellow out. In the morning he'd wake with a hangover and his leg would still hurt. The cycle was repeated daily, a process that gradually eroded his heath, talent and stability. By the time he was scheduled to play the Country Club, osteomyelitis had set in and amputation seemed only a matter of time.

Of course, I wanted see the man, whatever condition he might be in. Although Elvis Presley may have been my most cherished, rock & roll, teen-lifestyle influence, Gene was a close second and so much more accessible. Gene Vincent at the Brighton Essoldo in 1960 first convinced me of the awesome power of live rock pushed to its outer and ultimate limits. He manifested the menace of a Stephen King creation. Morrison would later talk about rock & roll as a demonic shamanism. Gene simply and inarticulately conjured it. He looked like a man in the grip of some dark, wrenching religious experience. The contorted figure in the black leather suit stood with one leg forward, knee bent, and the other, held rigid in its steel brace, thrust awkwardly out behind him. The stance was unnatural – all but unholy – body twisted, almost tortured. At peaks in the act, his whole frame would vibrate as he clutched the microphone stand with his gloved right hand and naked left, desperately, as though it was the only thing preventing him being borne away by rage and passion. His corpse-pale face was framed, Dracula-style, by the upturned collar of his leather jacket, and a sweat-soaked bunch of grapes had collapsed on his forehead. His eyes were raised to an imaginary point, high in the auditorium, higher even than the cheap seats in the upper balcony, as though he was staring into some unknown place, seeing both the horror and the glory.

Back in those days, us kids got around on Southern Region commuter trains without corridors. On that train back home, my hands were all over my date's body and hers were all over mine. No alternative, and damned if we wanted one. We had just been part of a dark invocation of post-Fifties teenage lust, backed by the loudest electric guitars we'd ever heard in our young lives. We had passed childhood's end, but would kick and scream bloody murder before we'd allow ourselves to be forced into what was currently being promoted as maturity. Shoot the works for rock & roll.

To see him again, at the Country Club, a joint that held maybe 400 max, and where the Deviants had played time without number, made it hard to ignore that this was the humiliating depths to which the 'rock & roll Richard III' had sunk. When Gene came on he was trying hard, holding the old pose, but his voice was painfully weak, as though he was worn out from an endless diabolic conflict. Very soon he would return to Los Angeles to die. Back in LA, he found that his wife had not only left him, but had cleaned out his bank accounts. He promptly went on an intensive drunk, finally destroying the already ulcerated lining of his stomach. Soon after stumbling into his mother's house in the LA suburb of Saugus, Gene apparently fell to his knees and began vomiting blood. He looked up at his mother and told her, 'Mama, you can phone the ambulance now.' Within an hour he was dead.

In the final distillation, legend was Gene Vincent's legacy. Without becoming unduly metaphysical, he had to be one of those totemic spirits, in the company of Robert Johnson, Johnny Ace, Jim Morrison, Keith Moon and Sid Vicious, who watch over rock 'n' roll in all its diverse forms, doing their best to ensure that an excess of mental heath and sobriety don't reduce the music to the predictable; that the sweat, tears and suicidal stupidity continue; that the bop for which they died never sinks to a mundane bloodlessness. My vanity wishes that I could take on a tiny fraction of the sacred duty, but, on the familiar stage at the Country Club, I saw the penalties that could be exacted, the price that might have to be paid.

Nevermore

Shortly I'd be hearing the voices in my head, and the fillings in my teeth would be picking up alien radio. The most intelligent way to handle an intense emotional crisis may not be to throw so many micrograms of LSD at it to precipitate a complete psychedelic meltdown. Unfortunately, so much acid happened to be around at the time. Took had decided he was going to finance his show-business comeback by dealing in the stuff, but this had proved a severe miscalculation. The overwhelming majority of our immediate community was drinking, wobbling around on Mandrax or, *in extremis*, nodding out on heroin. No one wanted to drop a tab and wrestle with God and the Devil. Took's stash of bright-pink acid tabs proved powerful and of fine quality, but largely unsaleable, and we ate them like candy out of a combination of poverty and boredom. This almost precipitated a whole mess of an afternoon when we'd run into a gang of nuns coming out of the convent at the top end of Portobello Road and had actually fallen to the pavement hysterical with laughter. On another occasion, Took happened to suggest that the hallucinations we were experiencing were not merely in our hearts and minds, but actually circling around us like a tangible external aura, fully visible to every passerby. The idea had so rattled me that I was forced to flee into Finches to down a couple of large whiskies.

It was in this context that I'd decided to drop a tab and attempt to figure out where my future might lie. Instead of delivering the blinding but interpretable revelation for which I hoped, the dose precipitated me into an arid and schizophrenic Marscape: blood-red sand and razor-sharp rocks, where I was simultaneously Captain America and the most humble mould on the Wonderloaf of the Universe. All alone in a growing hallucinatory horror, I masochistically forced myself to listen to *Mona*. I crouched in the Martian wasteland with headphones clamped to my skull, volume cranked up to the pain threshold, reliving every misguided moment, and with the realisation coming upon me that this was no work of art, but one of brutal psychosis, not entertainment, but a case-study. Now I turned the Dalek cry on myself. *Exterminate! Exterminate!* Away with the grooved and circular black abomination! I wanted to wrench the vinyl from the turntable, scratch it until it was unplayable, but, even as high as a kite, I couldn't kill my baby. All I could do was slowly turn down the volume, sunset on Mars, a fade into the darkness of ghosts, and then burst into tears. My whole rock dream had been a cruel charade. I had to tell someone. I had to confess and seek absolution, or neurons would fuse. Germaine had been right – it *was* a tyrannical dance with death and I was too exhausted to dance any more.

With every effort of my scarcely remaining will, I pulled myself back from Mars and into the reality of escape. Out of the door and down the stairs, into the street and into a cab. 'Where to, mate?' What a monumental question! I was still enough of a Martian to be without words. The driver didn't put the cab in gear, and looked back at me distrustfully. 'Are you going to give me a problem?'

'No, no.' I blurted out the address of Chrissie's and Angie's flat, as if by rote.

The night streets were like a combination of a Wally Wood *Mad* cartoon and *Taxi Driver*. Of course, *Taxi Driver* hadn't yet been made, but what's a cultural timewarp when you're being wrenched by ancient and alien ergotamine visions. The cab pulled up in front of Chrissie's and Angie's building. I thrust money at the driver and looked around wildly. The streets were rain-slick, reflective and humming with dangerously charged colours. I pressed the bell repeatedly. I probably sounded like a drug or vice raid, but I was desperate to get inside.

'Who is it?'

'It's me. Let me in.'

I was starting to sound like a Cheech and Chong record. Took met me at the top of the stairs. 'You're sweating, man.'

'Yes, I know.'

'What the fuck's wrong with you?'

'I've made a decision. A very important decision.'

'What decision, man?'

'An important decision.'

'You already said that.'

'I . . .'

'You want to release a few crucial details to the masses?'

'I . . .'

'After coming all that way, I couldn't articulate it.

I, the ineffable centre of the universe, was only able to make this single vowel sound . . .

'I . . .'

'You better come inside, man.'

I spooked like a skittish horse. 'No.'

Took reached out to take me by the arm, for concerned conversation on the stairs would carry to the neighbours. The overhead light made his face a relief map as the electricity wormed through the wires. He became a narrow-beaked reptile. A saurian vulture. No contradiction. Aren't birds and reptiles supposedly related?

'Steve . . .' It was Angie's voice from inside. I fled. Some might have come after me, but Took wasn't like that. He had a very strong sense of preserving number one. The street was humming electric again. I couldn't see a cab and began to panic. Then a wondrous and warm, orange 'For Hire' sign came into view.

'Chesterton Road, please. It's fourth on the left past Ladbroke Grove station.' At least the homing instinct still worked.

With Joy and Jamie asleep in the other room, I couldn't rampage even the limited length and breadth of the flat. I wasn't being considerate. I just didn't want them anywhere near my nightmare. Never again. My best idea was to lock myself in the bathroom. Never again. At least no one could interrupt my disintegration. For a long time, I sat cold and rigid on the edge of the tub, but then I began to shiver and sag. Never, never again. A heater was attached to the bathroom wall, but it didn't occur to me to turn it on. Never again, and the colder I got, the more that special resolve of petulant self-pity had me in its grip. I would never play rock 'n' roll again. Never. I swore. Never, never, never, never, never, never, never, never, never, never, never, never, never, never, (colder) never, never, never, never, never, never, never, never, never, never, never, never, never. I promised. I would never play rock 'n' roll again. Never, never, never, never, never, never, never, (still colder) never, never, never, never, never, never, (I'm freezing) never, never, never, never, never, never, never, never, never, never, never. A mantric vow. Never, never, never, never, never, never, never, never, never, never, never, never. I wished to hell I had a Valium. Or a half-bottle of

Scotch. The chill porcelain against my skull was far from adequate comfort. Never again.

Encounter and Reunion

Does the first door have to be closed before the second door opens, like the airlock on a spaceship? No matter how much you may drown destiny in acid during the quest for enlightenment, and no matter what grandiose hallucinations that may produce, at the end of the night, the patient comes down confused as ever. Okay, so I'd resolved never to play rock & roll again. Dandy. I wasn't playing rock & roll anyway. Since Twink had departed, Took and I had done bugger all, except half-write a couple of half-songs, but he had also introduced me to a guitar player called Larry Wallis who'd just fallen out of a band called the Entire Sioux Nation.

Larry was a hard-drinking, dope-smoking, good old boy from South London with a red Fender Stratocaster and a quick wit, and was well versed in TV and movies. Indeed, just the kind of guy I figured I could live with in a band. The first time we all met up, Larry arrived with his girlfriend Shirley. Both had fluffed-out dandelion hairstyles and, before I could stop myself, I tactlessly observed, 'My God, they match.'

For some sensitive artistes such a blurt would have been ample excuse to walk right out, but Larry just found it amusing. After some discussion he expressed a willingness to work with Took and me – if, and when, we had our ducks in a row – which as far as I could see would be sometime in the next century. Larry lived in the top-floor flat – what used to be called the attic – of a tall building above a busy row of shops in Walworth Road. To gain admittance, you rang the bell, Larry threw down a key protectively encased in a joke-shop rubber chicken, and the spectacle of the rubber chicken falling on the scurrying shoppers of SE17 added a suitably Toon Town prelude to any visit.

Larry Wallis wasn't the only important face to emerge during this period of doubt and dilemma. A very old friend appeared out of schoolboy twilight to play, in the short term, a vital role in the next phase of my life. Gez Cox was the Saturday-night henchkid with whom I'd shared my teenage-weekend wee hours getting adolescently maudlin over Frank Sinatra's 'For Only the Lonely'. I don't know if he called me or what, but somehow we arranged to meet. Years earlier, after we'd both left Worthing High School for Boys, I'd gone off to art school and he'd bummed around the world for a while, finishing up in Australia, working in an office in Sydney during the era when the bars in the business district closed at six in the evening and rail commuters threw up recycled Foster's all the way back to the suburbs. Finding it all a little much for his mind and his liver, Gez wended his way back to England by an almost Joseph Conrad route, including stops in Hong Kong, Singapore and other romantic points east.

When the appointed reunion took place, I was slightly surprised to find that an extremely attractive young woman was with him, and she rather distracted me from giving Gez what should have been my undivided attention. Ingrid von Essen was a Finnish beauty with the ever-popular Brigitte Bardot look, except that Ingrid's Bardot pout came with a more brittle Helena Bonham-Carter judgementalism.

No reason existed why Gez shouldn't have a good-looking girl with him. Although, like mine, his nose was a little over-large, he was slim, charming and urbane, and I naturally assumed that Ingrid was his girlfriend, or, at the very least, his date for the evening. They didn't act like a couple, though, with no signs of either courtship or intimacy. They had known each other for years, Ingrid having spent time in Worthing as a teenager as part of a student-exchange programme, but, if anything, Gez seemed to act as Ingrid's neutral escort. This was, in fact, revealed as the case, when, as we prepared to go our separate ways, he confided in me that Ingrid would be more than happy to spend the night with me, and that she'd actually pressurised Gez to take her to meet me in the first place.

This took me completely by surprise. I'd been too much of a gentleman even mildly to come on to what I was still thinking of as 'my mate's bird'. I was also flattered and excited, turned on by this forward and unorthodox approach – and I didn't hesitate to invite her back to Chesterton Road, where we discovered an unexpected sexual compatibility. She also revealed a highly complex personality, part of which was an admiration for me that, from today's perspective, would seem totally unhealthy, but at the time was truly marvellous. In a very short space of time, Ingrid would become my girlfriend and companion for the next nine years, and Gez would be a strong right arm in the next phase of my adventures, even though that strong right arm would often be lifting a pint of Guinness.

Phun City, Here We Come

I sat on the bonnet of the official Mercedes, one foot on the heavy steel fender and the other swinging free. A few hundred people were gathered round to hear what I had to say. And, for a few moments, I didn't say a word. After the angst, tension, waiting and worry of the previous ten days, I was now acting out at least three lifelong fantasies at once; worse than that, I was enjoying it shamelessly. I'd even dressed for the moment: jeans tucked into Victorian riding boots, a studded biker belt and one of those blue denim jackets that Parisian garbage-men wear. Ingrid had embroidered a multicoloured dragon on the shoulder of the jacket, a quasi-military, mystic insignia, and I'd pinned a de luxe scarlet-and-gold Chairman Mao badge to my lapel. I was aiming for a combo of Che, Rommel and some Sicilian bandit chief. Getting a large number of the dedicatedly undisciplined to acquiesce to one's will is far from simple. Triumphs of that kind require bluff, ingenuity, bullshit, downright lies, plus a mess of projected vanity. It's Patton and his pearl-handled revolvers. No one wants to be led into a potential disaster by a drab schlepper. They prefer to convince themselves that they're following a warrior poet, even if it's only into a three-day rock 'n' roll orgy in a damp Sussex field.

The trick of waiting before you say anything is one used by both Churchill and Marlon Brando in *The Godfather*, and, for what I was about to do, it seemed applicable. This was going to have to be a tad Churchillian. The vibe at the half-constructed Phun City was on the cusp of ugly, and I was expected to restore morale. All day Boss, Gez and Mac had bought themselves time by insisting that all would be made clear when Farren arrived from London. Mad Dog Pete Currie from Africa had gone to fetch him in the Mercedes staff car. Don't worry. He'd have all the answers. (Sons-of-bitches.) Thus, after Boss had called everyone to order, I took a moment to look out over the assembled hippies. Their expressions ranged from sullen to disgruntled, and my task was to win them over and head off any dopey ideas of yet another people's takeover. Before I'd even been driven down from London, Boss and Gez's phone bulletins told of the natives, who were arriving in larger and larger numbers and far earlier than we ever expected, growing progressively restless. They started calling him and the other organisers, and even the freaks building and installing all the rock and open-air art hardware, the 'super-hippies' in a tone that was growing more uncomplimentary by the moment. The super-hippies had retaliated by referring to these early-to-arrive nomads as the 'boggies'.

'Okay ... here's what's happening. The first thing you have to know is that it's going to be a free festival.'

I think it was Edward who coined the term boggies. It came to indicate a Neanderthal form of hippie: stoned insensible, generally uncooperative, prone to complain and likely to steal everything that wasn't watched, let alone nailed down. They looked at me suspiciously, requiring to be convinced. I was after all the *capo da tutti capo*, the autocrat of super-hippies.

'We don't intend to put up any kind of fences or try to collect any money. The stage is up, the generators are in, the water's connected, although we can't pipe it as far as the woods.'

At the bottom of the large sloping field were a gratuitous six or seven acres of densely overgrown woodland that the landowner didn't mind including as part of the rented site. The boggies had immediately taken to the woods, cleared some of the undergrowth and commenced to set up Narnia, which turned out, in fact, to be extremely magical, with highly creative treehouses and, at night, fairyland candle play (there being no generators in Narnia). Unfortunately most boggie construction and special effects had been created with pilfered materials, which were needed for stuff like the stage and the lighting rigs. Boss had been forced to lead a raid into Narnia to retrieve irreplaceable items, and hostilities had been briefly joined, followed by an uneasy truce that left the boggies to their own devices in the woods, on condition that the thieving kindly be mitigated. I could live with the deal as long as no idiot Robin Hood strode from our own little Sherwood to waste my time. We had enough slings and arrows already, thanks. Our super-hippie backs were so far up against the wall that the boggies could have made it a free festival themselves any time they wanted, and we couldn't have done a damned thing about it. Accordingly, we beat them to the punch by giving them what they could easily have taken. What needed to be impressed on them, however, was that only us super-hippies – and most specifically Gez Cox and I – were standing between them and the outside world.

'We also have a deal with the police, by which uniformed officers won't come onto the field unless they observe a disturbance.'

'What's a disturbance?'

'It's anything the cops think constitutes enough excuse to come steaming in team-handed and bust everyone.'

'You think they will?'

'Yes, but they'll wait until it looks like some major fuck-up, or they'll wait until no media are around.'

That was the truth as I saw it, but the meetings with the police had been little short of Dadaist. Me in one of my old rocker velvet suits and Gez in business pinstripe with his hair gathered in a ponytail and stuffed down the back of his shirt; we sat in an imposing wood-panelled office, attempting to convince an inspector from the West Sussex Constabulary and a couple of local Worthing councillors that what we were having was some combination of a Renaissance fair and folk-music festival, rather than a psychedelic picnic-of-the-damned. Legally, we had them by the balls. We had every break that the West Sussex upper crust had built into the local by-laws for their horse shows and point-to-point meetings. The same rules that allowed the aristocracy to rampage around the countryside, drinking themselves stupid and riding roughshod over the lower orders applied to any minor multitude of freaks who wanted to get fucked-up in field. After firmly but diplomatically pointing this out, we spent the best part of two hours hammering out an informal policing agreement, but whether it would hold remained to be seen.

'I'm not going to bullshit you. We don't have a clue as to what's going to happen next.'

The admission of total mystification went down well. Boggies like their leaders a little bemused. An excess of clarity is viewed with frowning suspicion.

'When the bands show up they're going to be presented with an ultimatum. There's no money, except to cover their expenses, but there's a good time to be had, so they can either stay and play or fuck off. That should separate the sheep from the goats.'

With some irony the only sheep were the band called Free, who heard the deal and fucked off without even getting out of the car. All the other performers had a look around and decided that, if they were looking for trouble, they'd come to the right place. Unfortunately it fell to me to explain the situation to each band in turn. It was something I obviously couldn't delegate, and it quite spoiled the first night of the festival for me, until someone noticed I'd started walking in small circles, muttering how all this bloody stress wasn't worth it and wondering if I should kill myself. This worthy interventionist insisted that I swallow an assortment of various forms of speed and tranquilliser, making me finally able to operate from a point of view of philosophy rather than embarrassment.

How I'd come to that point had started innocently enough. As far as I can recall, the decision that we should stage some kind of open-air event was taken late one night, in someone's flat around a pipe and a bottle. It might well have been at my brand-new flat in Clifton Gardens in Maida Vale, where I was now living with Ingrid and her friend Caroline McKechnie. In very short order, even by the standards of the early Seventies, I had exited the less-than-healthy situation with Joy and Jamie at Chesterton Road, and Ingrid had moved out of her minuscule bedsit in darkest Earls Court. She and Caroline had gone househunting, and had found a light, airy, first-floor flat with high ceilings, two bedrooms and french windows that opened onto a narrow wrought-iron balcony. I could almost have pretended that I was in Paris, but for the red number-six buses trundling by. The rent was a bit steeper than Ingrid and I could manage between us, so Caroline took the extra bedroom, a plan with which I readily concurred, despite everything that Shaftesbury Avenue had taught me about the hazards of flat-sharing. I was still young and self-aggrandising enough to be taken with the idea of sharing a pad with two glorious women. While Ingrid was the Nordic/Bardot blonde, Caroline had luxuriant red hair, pale freckled skin and could have modelled for Dante Gabriel Rossetti.

Aside from the aesthetics of the arrangement, I also found myself living in a state of previously unsurpassed cleanliness, and eating real food on a regular basis. I hadn't entirely cleaned up my act, however; and Ingrid enjoyed a daily routine of Valium and amphetamine, and rolled an expert joint. Ingrid and I were going through the getting-to-know-you, wonder-of-us phase of our relationship, having a great deal of sex and talking almost non-stop. I learned that she was far better read than I, coming as she did from an awesomely educated family of Swedish-speaking Finns. I think her great-aunt had dated August Strindberg or something, and she loved books to the point that she would wince in pain to hear the spine of one crack. She was also passionate about the Beatles and had a full religious devotion to Elvis Presley. She identified with Alice and all things Lewis Carroll, and with the hard-pressed and anxiously courageous rabbits in Richard Adams' *Watership Down*. She doted on the plays of Tom Stoppard, the films of Michelangelo Antonioni and the writing of Margaret Drabble. She maintained a subscription to the *New Yorker*, and had a chill meticulousness that I would find echoed decades later in overdrawn cartoon form by Jeri Ryan as Seven of Nine in the TV show *Star Trek: Voyager*.

It was while I was with Ingrid that I finally buckled down to some serious writing. I guess it was inevitable. Germaine had repeatedly urged me to get started on a book, but she'd also suggested that said book should be a study of male violence, at which I inwardly groaned. 'Yeah, right.' Before I backed into what I feared would be literary isolation, however, I still felt the need for a couple more piratical adventures, and the first of these would be Phun City.

At the gathering where the idea of an open-air festival was first mooted, after we'd resolved we'd attempt to do this thing, someone asked the first and most obvious question. 'So what, right at this moment, are our collective resources?'

A fast audit revealed that our assets totalled a half-finished bottle of vodka, an almost untouched quid deal and two and ninepence in cash.

'Is that enough to launch a rock festival?'

We all looked at each other and shrugged. No one had told us it wasn't, so what the hell? Hoppy had launched the Technicolor Dream without too much more going for him and, like Hoppy, we had a newspaper and its resources pretty much at our disposal. I'm a little hazy about who exactly was at that first meeting. I know Gez was there. He'd been a regular visitor since he'd come into my life and brought Ingrid with him, and seemed eager to get in on whatever the next scheme might be. I know Edward Barker was there, and may well have been scribbling the first sketches for the festival logo even as we talked. Edward and I had pretty much hit it off since we first met, and had become drinking partners well before we got into anything more serious. Su Small and Steve Mann were definitely present. Su and I had made the transition from friends and comrades to lovers, and back again, with none of the formally expected weeping, recrimination or gnashing of teeth. Not even a diatribe in an underground newspaper. In the best possible terms, Su was a highly progressive woman. I think the only key figure absent was Boss Goodman, off on the road with the newly formed Pink Fairies, who were attempting to take up where the Deviants had left off.

After the first crystallisation of the idea and intent, the next move was to go into *IT* and sell the idea to Dave Hall. I think by that point the name Phun City had been mooted, and Edward had created a logo, a naked dancing cartoon figure with an expression of demented gullibility that seemed to symbolise our hopes and aspirations. It had also been agreed that we would make the event an *IT* benefit, all profits going to pay the fines and legal expenses for the bust. Dave, who was nothing if not shrewd and totally versed in the devious wiles of freakhood, knew what we were up to straight away. He recognised that our most pressing desire was simply to have the biggest and most subversive party possible, somewhere in an English meadow.

'I just don't want you lot taking the paper down with you.'

'But we're going to make a profit. We can't fail.'

The blind optimism was, of course, a put-on. Both Dave and I knew that a project of this kind could end in total financial disaster, and he wanted the paper buffered from liability for any Phun City debts. I believe he also figured that letting me run Phun City out of the *IT* office in Endell Street was a handy way of having me where he could keep an eye on me. I think Dave realised that I was an ideal figure for all those who didn't like the current direction of the paper to rally behind, and if I was seriously motivated, I could take over the running of *IT* any time I wanted. Phun City was something to keep me busy, and I was happy to be busy. A novelty always gets my attention. After very little discussion, a deal was made. A separate limited-liability company, Phun City Ltd, would be formed as a fire wall, but, until I could generate my own finances, I'd be paid a modest salary out of *IT* funds, as some kind of special projects editor.

Obviously the first thing we had to do was to rent a field. Without a field to call our own, all else would be fantasy. Fortunately I had a card up my sleeve. I had spent my teenage years living down the way I was raised in the woods, but finally it was proving an asset. The woods in question were owned by an impoverished aristocrat who had inherited vast unproductive acres, and even vaster debts. The rumour in the village was he'd do pretty much anything for hard cash, and I got my field for £1,500 off the books, with funds for a fifty per cent down-payment raised from a consortium of London herbalists. With the field in hand, I realised that I was acting out a piece of psychedelic revenge for my childhood. I was depositing a rock festival little more than a mile from the village where I grew up. I would be confirming the worst expectations of the yokels who had once mocked me, the junior beatnik, wandering lonely as a cloud. Nothing like a few thousand hippies to put Dan Archer in his miserable Thomas Hardy place.

For a while, all seemed to run according to plan. We raised more money by selling the catering and other concessions. Posters and fliers began to be printed and Edward's naked dancing guy was all over the place. Getting contracts on the best of the touring bands proved to be no great difficulty. Guys with inflatable domes and other art exhibits pledged to be there. We knew we were out of the music business running for any big international acts, like the Grateful Dead, but I did want to put on one band with a chance of ensuring that the name Phun City might live in infamy. The MC5 had carved themselves a niche as the house band of the revolution with their live album *Kick Out the Jams*, and as the only band that actually played at the riots at the Chicago Democratic Convention. Their manager, John Sinclair, had been handed ten years of Michigan jailtime for a couple of joints and, all in all, they had such a rep as radical troublemakers that it was unlikely they'd ever make it to Europe, unless someone like me brought them over for something like Phun City.

A dialogue was started with Detroit that revealed the MC5 as both ready and willing to play Phun City as the centrepiece of a UK mini-tour that would cover their expenses. Back in the USA, the band was having its problems. They'd been bounced off Elektra Records, home of the Doors, for being too loud and political. Although quickly signed by Atlantic, their troubles were by no means over. They'd been blacklisted by rock impresario Bill Graham after a group called the Motherfuckers – the New York equivalent of the London Street Commune – had trashed the Fillmore East while the 5 were attempting to play a benefit for them. After a massive initial promotion, *Rolling Stone* seemed to have turned on them, and rumours of first-phase destructive drug use were spreading.

Okay, so we had the MC5 as the capstone of what was rapidly growing into the alternative (or maybe read 'parody') rock festival, but unfortunately around that time we ran out of money, and the prospects of getting any more was rendered hard – going on impossible – when the West Sussex County Council and Constabulary obtained a court order against us. All I remember was riding a shrieking telephone, but the facts are succinctly laid out in Roger Hutchinson's *High Sixties*.

On 17 July, lawyers acting for West Sussex County Council sought an injunction to prevent the festival taking place. On the following day its financial backers pulled out. On the day after that the injunction was withdrawn.

A New York City hashish dealer, with extensive contacts in pre-Soviet Afghanistan, donated enough money to keep us in a holding pattern and I went to see our last hope, Ronan O'Rahilly. The legend was that Ronan's father was *the* O'Rahilly, a hero of the battle at the Dublin Post Office in 1916. This gave Ronan a lot to live up to and, both to fill a need in the marketplace and thumb his nose at the English, he conceived Radio Caroline, the great pirate radio station of the early Sixties that broadcast from an old trawler parked in the North Sea. By the time of our Phun City discussions, the Marine Offences Act had long since killed pirate radio. Ronan was now involved in a maniacal scheme to buy an old Lockheed Constellation that would circle the sky above London, landing only to refuel and broadcasting pirate TV. I was never sure whether this was for real or just a work of magnificent blarney, but either way the concept was one of grandly abstruse madness.

The real financial hope to make Phun City all it could be was to sell the film rights. To that end, Gez and I had trolled up and down Wardour Street meeting the proprietors of horror and soft-porn sweatshops at one end and David Hemmings at the other. We even talked to the Italians and the French. A couple of live ones were about to bite the bait, but then the WSCC injunction scared them shitless and they vanished. Early in the game, Ronan had told me that, if all else failed, I should come and talk to him. After forty-eight hours of legal drama, I had to face the fact that all else had definitely failed. Thus I called Ronan and took myself off to his mews house in Mayfair, with the cherry Harley Davidson Electroglide that Marianne Faithfull had ridden in *Girl on a Motorcycle* parked outside. Ronan had produced the trash classic and was justifiably proud.

He was a master of indecision and procrastination. He hummed, he hawed, he told irrelevant anecdotes, he phoned the MC5 in Detroit and checked that all was well with them, while all the time his huge bodyguard, Big Jimmy Houlihan, lurked in the background. We went down the pub for a Guinness and came back again. I sweated. Gez, Mac and Boss were already at the site waiting to build a rock festival. A full two days of nail-biting and hanging-in passed before Ronan finally called the travel agent for the MC5's tickets and began to write cheques. As he spent money, he winked at me.

'We're flying here, boy. We're really flying.'

Ronan had one stipulation. It should be a free festival. He not only wanted to maximise the crowd, but he had spotted the fatal flaw in our figures. As Ronan read it, security would cost us a pound to collect £1.30 from the paying customers. If you protected your site with something as formidable as the Berlin Wall, the cost curve might level out at the high end, but you needed to pull in about a million people to make the mathematics happen. I suspected that was what Ricky Farr was planning to do down at the Isle of Wight later in the summer. Okay, it was a free festival, and that was better than nothing, but I was being forced to abandon the original purpose of raising money for the *IT* bust. Before setting off for Sussex I had personally to break the bad news to Dave Hall. As it turned out, it may have been honourable, but hardly necessary.

'Don't worry about it. I figured this might happen.'

Dave was hip. He wished me luck and told me he'd see me down there. We were off to Phun City to have ourselves a rock festival. On the way down, I was torn between relief and the feeling I'd personally fucked up. I'd failed with the original objective, and I also realised the festival had now taken on a life of its own. Fortunately I was able to bounce back and, halfway through the two-hour drive, I was already preparing my address to the boggies.

The chronicle of Phun City is so replete with family legends that it's hard to know which to include. Certainly the tale of Boss Goodman and how the stage was moved manually in the manner of building the Great Pyramid has been told before, but it still deserves pride of place. My greatest regret is that I wasn't there to witness it. As the large scaffolding stage was almost complete, Boss noticed an overhead high-tension cable, running between two National Grid pylons, right above the structure.

It would be fucking dumb to have a whopping great PA directly below the main electric cables, especially if it rained. The only and unavoidable answer was to move the stage. This little guy who had put the stage together couldn't believe it . . . the thought of dismantling it all. But I said, 'No, man, we'll carry it.'

'Impossible.'

'Rubbish, we'll get the hippies out of the woods and we'll go 1–2–3 and lift, and we'll carry the fucker over there.'

'Go on then, fucking do it.'

So I got my gang and we went into the woods where about 500 hippies were camped out.

'Can you do us a favour?'

'What?'

'The stage has been put in the wrong place and we've got to move it.'

'Let's go.'

'1–2–3.'

And the fucking hippies lift the stage and carry it a hundred yards across the field.

I also won't forget two chilly Hell's Angels and two Worthing coppers swapping Woodbines and tea from a thermos, at the top end of the field by the vehicle entrance, each pair keeping to their own side of the demarcation line, like guards on a Cold War frontier. Neither will I forget the Shit Squad – the crew of the strange and psychotic who had volunteered to empty the chemical toilets *for free*, provided they were equipped with wellies and yellow rubber gloves, and navy overalls emblazoned with SHIT SQUAD in yellow biker-style script across their backs.

By far the most awkward moment came on Saturday afternoon when I had to explain to the MC5 how things at the festival weren't exactly as they had first been pitched to them. Fortunately the blow had been softened, first by Ronan having (so far) taken excellent care of them, right down to hiring Howard Parker to do the hands-on babysitting. In addition we had a cat called Mitchell Rothberg – a passing-through American, a friend of John Sinclair and with the most impeccable of international radical–underground connections – to vouch for at least our good intentions. The 5 were far from stranded. They had return air tickets and other gigs were in place to pay their way, but they were silent at first; their faces a combination of disappointment and resignation. They'd seen this shit a hundred times before. A bunch of freaks sitting on a situation that hadn't come out totally as planned. Guitarist Fred Smith finally turned to guitarist Wayne Kramer. 'Let's take a look at the equipment.'

I knew I was off the hook. At Phun City the gear was perfect; Boss had seen to that. The matched HiWatt stacks came directly from a stage plan used by the Who, plus provision had been made for an extra guitar player. Absolutely nothing could be complained about.

It took until Saturday night, after sunset, for everything to start to make sense. I suddenly became aware I had nothing more to worry about. Whatever had happened had happened, and what was going to happen would run its course without any help or intervention. The bands had all done their part, although for me they tended to blur. The Pretty Things had delivered the goods. The Pink Fairies and the Edgar Broughton Band had engaged in a joust similar to the one in Hyde Park in which the Deviants had engaged a year earlier. Despite the Fairies' two drummers, Edgar gained a riotous sing-a-long edge with the perennial 'Out Demons, Out', but then said drummers trumped Edgar's ace when Twink and Russell stripped and cavorted naked and homoerotic, while Rudolph and Sandy did a fair impersonation of the solar wind on guitar and bass. If my recollection is correct, a relatively unknown and just-up-from-the-country Hawkwind first came to public attention at Phun City, but I'm afraid we old lags from London treated them with unconscionable city-slicker condescension. Phun City also saw the debut of the Blackheath Foot & Death Men, an atavistically violent, six-man team of Morris dancers, composed of three Hell's Angels, two massive sociopathic roadies and Pete Currie, our driver. Eschewing the polite ribbons and garlanded poles of conventional folk-dance troupes, they stomped their engineer boots and knocked nine bells out of each other with full-sized Friar Tuck quarter-staves, totally vindicating the ethnomusicologists who claim that Morris dancing originated as a drunken rehearsal for Saxon shield-wall combat. Later in their career the Blackheath Foot & Death Men would open for Motorhead at the Marquee.

Enough of my mission had been accomplished for me to be happy that I'd accepted it, and it hadn't self-destructed after fifteen seconds. I walked onto the stage, into the full glare of the lighting set-up. I think I was about to introduce the MC5, but was greeted with a standing ovation that I figured was merited. The MC5 were about to come on. Out there somewhere in the darkness, William Burroughs stalked the night in his FBI man's hat and raincoat, requiring hippies to talk into his portable tape machine while he baffled them with instant cut-ups. Ronan had brought an entire British Lion Outside Broadcast unit, plus a mobile home for himself, like a villa on wheels; all under the command of Tom Keylock, the Stones' old minder, and the formidable Big Jimmy Houlihan. The flare of the lights, and the big cumbersome OB cameras flanking the stage, lent an impressive – if probably spurious – media importance. The gang and I had thrown one hell of a party. Give the lads a big hand. On the light tower, the lightshow guys, not wanting to be outdone by the British Lion, plugged in everything they had and pointed their full battery of slides, loops and blob-shows at anything that would carry an image. The large inflatable dome pulsed with light from within, like a huge narcotised alien blob, while the canvas of tents became cinema screens and the field itself undulated.

The MC5 were the icing on the cake and I believe we got to them in the nick of time. We witnessed one of the very last shows that offered the original majesty, before the road and the bullshit took their toll. With Rob Tyner on his knees offering the testimonial, Wayne Kramer spitting a stream of Johnny Walker Red with great accuracy into the lens of a camera, and Fred Smith tumbling back over a bent-double Boss, as our yeoman stage manager attempted to rescue a fallen mike stand with roadie panache, what more did I want? My cup ranneth over. Then, after the 5 had climaxed, encored and exited, I was taken on a conducted tour of Narnia by night, and moved from campfire to campfire and from habitation to habitation until I was as ripped as Crazy Horse. All of this put me in such a good mood that I didn't even get irritated with Took constantly pestering me as to when his new band, Shagrat, featuring Larry Wallis on guitar, would get onstage. I simply referred him to Boss, who was much sterner in these things and took no guff from bleating artistes.

Sunday at Phun City was enough to convince me that the tradition of the damp-and-doomed English Sunday went back to pre-history, and came from deep within the mother-earth of Albion. A light drizzle and, even in a field of freaks, you can't escape an English bloody Sunday. The ground was wet and the crowd had dwindled. In Narnia many had decided to sleep late. Some snored and others had sex, only minimally disguised by the less-than-complete walls of their Ewok bivouacs. Others cooked breakfast with a fifth-century AD domesticity, while on the stage Sonja Kristina charmed everyone with gentle acoustics. Pastoral but wet.

Sunday was also the time for taking stock. Item one – the bar tent had been looted by the Hell's Angels. The bar tent was organised by the Marquee Club. By a loophole of licensing laws designed for gymkhanas, it had to be that way, and the word was that their prices had been less than humane. One of the bartenders had been left to guard the liquor through the night, but the Angels neutralised him by getting him comatose, then made off with all they could carry. When the Marquee guys came to the operations tent to complain they'd been robbed, Gez, Edward and I had difficulty keeping straight faces as we promised to conduct a full investigation, while standing up to our ankles in empty Carling Black Label cans, representing our cut of the heist.

Item two – a reporter from *The People*, who'd arrived to do a sex 'n' drugs shock exposé, had been dosed with acid and had decided to give it all up to become a nomad. Item three – the talk in Narnia was that they had a good thing going, so why not camp where they were, at least until preparations for the massive Isle of Wight Festival got under way? They were all for setting up a free state in the few acres of woodland, encouraged by the presence of a pub called The Fox less than 500 yards away. Item four – a large contingent of dope dealers had somewhat overestimated the size of the crowd and were now conducting a mass going-out-of-business sale, and a haze of hashish smoke flavoured the mist. When a squad of pathetically disguised 'undercover' drug-squad officers made their way through the haze, they were surrounded, publicly ridiculed and forced to flee. Later in the evening, after a stomping, revival-meeting set from Mungo Jerry, the entire cast of hundreds climbed on the stage to take a bow, and the stage slowly and majestically collapsed, finally succumbing to the torque it had endured while being carried a hundred yards by straining boggies. After that absolutely nothing was left to say, and I went back to our rented farmhouse to sleep for maybe twelve hours.

I was shaken awake with the information that we were under no circumstances to go back to the field. The constabulary had arrived loaded for bear and were making busts right, left and centre, while also ripping up Narnia by the roots. They had freaked out a couple of Worthing councillors who had come to inspect the squalor, but had actually been rather charmed and were just taking tea with some hobbits when the coppers crashed in.

'Don't even think about it. Just get the fuck out of town.' It was the best advice I could have been given. Any grand gestures could only result in Go-Directly-to-Jail, and I had no Get-Out-of-Jail-Free cards. I'd had another of those glimpses of how it could be if the system was subservient to us, rather than us being subservient to the system. Or, on a less grandiose scale, as Hawkwind manager Doug Smith put it, 'It was exactly what would happen if you let Boss and Mick put on a festival.'

Twilight of the Gods

All the way from London to Southhampton we had worked hard on becoming increasingly intoxicated. Rock 'n' roll class action couldn't have been further from our minds. As far as the *IT* crew was concerned, the necessary subversion had already taken place and we were on holiday. By the time we drove aboard the ferry to the Isle of Wight we were roaring, but not *so* drunk that we didn't square away the needs of narcotic security before disembarkation. This was fortunate, because almost as soon as the wheels of the truck touched dry land, the drug squad took us apart. They turned us upside down, inside out and sideways, but they never found the dope.

Our elation at having bested the law lasted all the way to the festival site, the unrecognisable Worthy Farm, but our first sight of the chaos was enough to slow us down. We arrived in gathering twilight in a place of complete confusion. People and vehicles milled about and, as the country darkness grew more total, no overall impression of the place was possible, except the tiny pinpoints of campfires that went on and on. At Phun City we'd been big on lights, but of course Phun City was less than one-twentieth of the size. This festival's night was dark shadows, and a certain thrill of fear. I've always imagined the chaos of the prelude to a battle as being similar – the night before Waterloo, Agincourt or Marathon – or perhaps that was merely my own mindset. The blanket-swathed hippies could easily have carried pikes or muskets. We were, of course, in one sense, entering the compound of the enemy, and I knew that the chaos we were driving into was some of my own doing. What I didn't know was that I'd also get the blame for chaos I hadn't instigated. For a while, certain lace-curtain hippie factions treated me like the most hated man in the counterculture.

Run a rock festival, then wreck a rock festival. Examine the phenomena from both sides and test the concept to destruction. It wasn't really like that, but to this day people still refuse to believe otherwise. I wish Carl Jung had lived long enough to take a good look at a rock festival. To put a quarter of a million or so people in an open field is a logistical nightmare, but psychologically it exceeds the boundaries of conception. The audience at a giant rockfest spends by the far the majority of its time being bored. It is expected to sit on either hard and dusty ground or in a sea of cloying mud, in various types and stages of intoxication, watching roadies break down the equipment of the band that has just played and re-rigging for the next. I'm sure Jung would have noticed that a multitude of this size develops a collective consciousness, sluggish at first, but picking up speed as it adopts a fantasy specific to the event.

At Woodstock, the fantasy had been one of striving and prevailing. 'The person next to you is your sister or your brother.' The myth was that united hippiedom could survive storm and stardom. With an almost predictable swing of the pendulum, Altamont had become the great convocation of imagined and symbolic evil under a winter sun; a visitation of angels from Hell and sympathisers for the Devil, with violence and death perceived as the only possible outcome. The previous Isle of Wight festival – which I hadn't attended – seemed to have pulled through on the lone charisma of Bob Dylan. Now the attitude was rapidly turning into a confrontation between us and them, albeit with a large degree of confusion as to who was 'us' and who was 'them'.

When I first became concerned about what might be going on down at the Isle of Wight, I was thinking economy rather than psychology or mass fantasy. At Phun City I'd clearly observed the counterculture's disposable income already reduced almost to nothing, and the average freak so distanced from the macro-economy that he or she didn't have the pot of proverb in which to piss. I could see the IoW event being close to a death blow. Acting like some giant Hoover, it would suck up every last quid, and recycle only peanuts back into the culture it purported to represent. Promoters Ricky Farr and the Foulks Brothers were staging an upheaval of money that might push the cashflow of dozens of underground enterprises clear into the toilet.

At Phun City we'd given up on the impossible cost of actually collecting the money and made it a free festival. Fiery Creations – the company through which Farr and the Foulks were running the event – was plainly on a diametrically opposed course. With a million-pound roster of talent, including the Who, the Doors, Jimi Hendrix, Joni Mitchell, Sly and the Family Stone and Jethro Tull, it was obviously going need to push the cash-collection equation to the crest of the curve. I couldn't see how it could so much as break even without the most horrendous security measures, and I couldn't come up with an image of any possible site that didn't look like a prison camp. As it turned out, even my imaginings were completely outstripped by reality.

As an *IT* journalist, Gez talked the Fiery Creations' publicists into letting a group of us take a tour of the site, about ten days before the bank-holiday weekend when the five-day fest was scheduled. We recruited Pete Currie and the Mercedes staff car yet again and headed down to see what was what. As we drove into Worthy Farm, we could plainly see that Fiery Creations were protecting their box-office with every security device short of a minefield, and appeared to be deploying the ambience of the East German frontier. Double walls of scaffolding and corrugated iron, with what looked uncomfortably like a freefire zone between them, were patrolled by security men in shabby, badgeless, ill-fitting coppers' uniforms, accompanied by equally ill-trained and tense-looking Alsatian dogs. To make matters worse, the area in front of the stage, the main viewing arena, had recently been under crop and was a mess of broken earth and hard spiky stubble, which would be turned into a swamp by even a minor shower.

'Dearie me,' thought Edward, Pete, Gez and I quite independently of each other, 'this is really not on.'

As we strolled around the festival-under-construction, it also appeared that all available capital had gone into these formidable defences, and that nothing had been allotted to peripheral diversions. Where was the helter skelter from the Technicolor Dream, the inflatable domes, the counterculture side-shows, or any of the other fun-of-the-fair stuff that could transform the event from Dachau-with-bands into a mighty gathering of the tribes? Before we'd left London Gez had done a bit of checking. The franchise fees for catering and the other sales operations were quite high enough to exclude all the small-time merchants who wanted to sell electric yo-yos, solar-powered beanie hats or bootleg Bob Dylan records. Commercial overkill was being taken to mammoth proportions.

'Something needs to be done,' we resolved. At that point we spotted the hill. As far as we could tell on first observation, the whole enclosed festival site was overlooked by the shallow side of a massive grassy escarpment with the Solent lurking behind it. Nonchalantly, and not wanting to appear overly interested, I hailed a passing guard. 'That hill, is it part of the site?'

The guard shook his head. 'No, and it's going to be a right fucking headache.'

'It is?'

'We're supposed to keep it free of gatecrashers.'

I think they call it the defining moment. I stared at the guard and his human and canine colleagues, their bits and pieces of ill-matched uniforms, and found that they suddenly and forcibly reminded me of the Black and Tans, the paramilitary bastards who had brutally stuck it to the Irish in the bloody aftermath of the 1916 uprising. Once the image had presented itself, I couldn't shake it loose. This IoW bash was going to be a black hole of decidedly negative energy, and it was time to salvage whatever we could before we were buried under overpriced hotdogs.

'This is a job for the White Panther Party.'

At the time, the British White Panther Party was a very secret society. The primary secret being that it didn't exist at all. Driving back, Edward, Gez, Pete and I agreed that we could only call it as we saw it. We'd seen the IoW under construction, and it wasn't good. We needed to put the word out, but at the same time we weren't completely and suicidally altruistic. If we were going to put the Fiery Creations' feet to their own fire, and wring some humanising concessions from them, we'd be daft to use *IT* as a spearhead. We needed some generic organisation that could appear out of nowhere and then vanish again. The organisational equivalent of Zorro, the Masked Avenger.

'This is *definitely* a job for the White Panther Party.'

Accordingly we photocopied a few thousand copies of a single-sheet leaflet and put it out on the usual underground networks. For a first attempt, I thought the Red Guard, Newspeak prose style was suitably streamlined.

WHITE PANTHER MINISTRY OF INFORMATION
BULLETIN ON THE ISLE OF WIGHT FESTIVAL
The Isle of Wight Festival is an obvious example of capitalist interests seeking to exploit the energy of the People's music.

They have erected ten-foot double corrugated-iron fences around the main arena and manned it with dogs and guards to enforce this exploitation.

The festival site has weaknesses.

A) *The fencing would not withstand a well-organised attack by the People.*

B) *The arena is overlooked by a large hill (not part of the site) from which the bands can be seen in comfort and for free.*

The Panthers, together with the Pink Fairies and other groups, will be running a free festival on land adjoining the official site. It will attempt to provide information, free music and free food.

Take part.

POWER TO THE PEOPLE

We also called Joly, the Badge Man, and distinctive white-on-purple White Panther Party badges were on Portobello and moving outward within a matter of hours. Although I didn't know it at the time, Jungian psychology was coming into play. Even before the festival started, I had seemingly kindled the sparks of a collective fantasy, anticipating a mood whose time had come, and I'd also projected it into an area devoid of too much other Jungian magic.

Not a great deal of magic is derived from the unilateral ambition to make a lot of money, for the romance of a fiscal killing is monochrome and very limited. Even the faux-flamboyance of a faux-revolution will outshine it like a rainbow every time. Of course, it wasn't just us. Anarchists in Paris, Provos in Holland, God knows what in West Berlin, and probably malcontents all the way from Stockholm to Tangier – not to mention a couple of hundred thousand domestic boggies, bikers, acid heads, university students, rock fans and pop kids, plus half the dealers in Europe – were planning to converge on what was now building to be the last of the truly enormous rock festivals. And the huge gathering would attract, both on and offstage, a great many individuals with fuses ready to blow.

Ricky Farr sussed out who was behind the White Panther Party in less than twelve hours and was on the phone to me at *IT*. At first he threatened, then he attempted to convince me that he was part of the revolution, too. He seemed most concerned that I'd revealed that one could see from the hill for free, as though a bloody great hill was something that could be kept a secret. Finally he demanded to know what we wanted. Basically all I could tell him was to let in the counterculture – provide facilities for the macrobiotic caterers, the underground service organisations, the underground press, theatre groups, street performers, and give the local street bands a stage on the camp site.

Ricky defended his participation in the community. 'Release is already putting in a bad-trips tent.'

'Release *always* puts in a bad-trips tent. I was thinking more of the proactive, rather than the reactive.'

Ricky wanted to know what he'd be getting in return if he waxed proactive. My answer was not what he wanted to hear. 'You'll be getting a very much more enjoyable and manageable festival.'

He seemed to think we were still negotiating. If he agreed to my demands, I'd essentially call off the troops? Right? That was where the philosophical chasm suddenly yawned. All I had was a few leaflets and some badges. Everything else was an illusion. No troops to call off, and no control or even influence over the crowds who were already setting up camp on the hill. No one was leading the charge, but no one could sound the retreat, either. In no way could Ricky embrace the lesson I'd learned at Phun City. *Appear to give them what they want, because if you don't, they will take it anyway.* A few concessions were made, but on the Wednesday night Fiery Creations made their fatal tactical blunder. With what must have been the tacit approval of the local police, they sent in their Black and Tans to clear the hill. They attempted to rout the hippies with dogs and batons, but the hippies weren't about to go. The Black and Tans skirmished with Brit bikers and '68 riot-hardened Parisians, plus a lot of youth who'd been pushed around just too often. The die was cast and grudges were set.

From there it went off on its own parabola of confusion, chaos, violence and disorder. French Anarchists, British Trots and Hell's Angels had a whale of a time pulling down sections of fence and mixing it up with the B&Ts, while I mediated dozens of pointless arguments between opposing factions of troublemakers, alternately calming them down and winding them up as the increasingly deranged humour took hold. I'd stumble into the FREEk press tent, which stank of sex-sweat and patchouli, and where Richard Neville was playing newsman with a Gestetner machine, and dictate hideously grandiose, Red Guard communiqués, royally pissing off Richard with Dadaist radical shtick way beyond his Australian sense of humour.

I recall the ticket-holding punters being quite upset when the rebels got in for free, and I remember walking slowly down the Desolation Row encampment, reflecting on its post-nuclear refugee squalor. Su Small earned everyone's admiration by inventing an exchange system for backstage passes, because the backstage bar was the only place one could get an acceptable cocktail. Unfortunately I had constantly to dodge Ricky Farr whenever I dropped in for a quick gin and tonic. As we foraged away from the site for whisky, cigarettes and other essentials, the locals bad-vibed us like a loathsome army of occupation as we roared around in Pete Currie's jeep. The Who were magnificent. Jim Morrison looked desperate. Sly Stone blew the roof off the sky. And Jimi was disturbing, like a man on a mission but without a map.

As the situation worsened, Charlie Murray thought it was the end of the dream and maybe the end of the world. Young Liberals took over direct negotiations with Fiery Creations. A crew of Trots running the food-refrigeration trucks threatened to shut down the freezers unless retail food prices came down. The Angels seemed to be conducting an internal purge. Things burned. Smoke markers normally used by yachtsmen were regularly being detonated, creating thick billows of multicoloured smoke. A flare hit the stage while Hendrix was playing and set fire to the canopy. I was blamed. I didn't bother to explain that any freak could buy flares and smoke markers at any of the dozens of marine chandlers on the island. The organisers appealed for peace, love and good vibes, and even sent Joni Mitchell out to do their dirty work for them, calling for docile passivity from those who were no longer either stardust or golden. I'm recorded as responding, 'Rock's becoming an opiate designed to create docile consumers.' Even Richard Neville, who, I was coming to suspect, really didn't like me at all, had to grudgingly admit that I was 'not only right-on, but right'.

My most vivid memory came sometime on Sunday afternoon when I stepped through an iron fence that was twisted into a tortured sculpture. Ricky was on the stage, barking-crazy and abusing the crowd for having thrown beer cans at the local vicar. A hotdog stand was burning and part of the stage was also charred from the flare of the previous night. Helicopters circled overhead, while at ground level blanket-wrapped figures, and others in togas of plastic sheeting, wandered around aimlessly. I was looking at a Class One Rock Apocalypse, and filing away the visuals. Mad Max had arrived a decade before they ever made the movie. And I wasn't the only one taking pleasure in all of this. As far as I could tell, everyone – each in his or her own perverse way – had a jolly good time. Wasn't it a little silly to be mourning some burst balloons? Another party was over, and yes, maybe a certain part of the Sixties was over, too. Lou Reed was starting to make a lot of sense. What costume *would* we wear for all tomorrow's parties?

Chapter Eight

Screwing Causes Clap

The moment was one of inspiration and giant Letraset. For a number of weeks the first statistical proof that cigarette-smoking causes lung cancer had been made public, as if anyone but a few self-hypnotised ad-men had entertained any doubts in the first place. A phoney media furore dragged on, while the medical profession stated the obvious and the tobacco industry blew smoke. I think Steve Abrams suggested in *The Times* that maybe marijuana should be substituted for tobacco, but was largely ignored. A parody of the whole spurious debate seemed in order, and almost like automatic spirit-writing, the huge headline stared back at me from the camera-ready art for the front page:

SCREWING CAUSES CLAP! – Official

In two-inch sans-serif type, just like the *New York Post* or the old *Brooklyn Eagle*, it stated the crudely obvious as though it was the bombing of Pearl Harbor. I had always admired the worst kind of banner tabloid, at times to the point of fetish, and it was one of the games Edward and I agreed we'd play directly I took over the running of *IT* again. I can't pretend that moving back to *IT* wasn't inevitable. At the risk of sounding coldly Darwinian, I was on the loose, I knew how to do the job, I had some things I wanted to try and the old guard were close to burned-out. I also can't pretend that my assuming control was exactly a smooth and rationally conducted transfer of power, or that it was achieved without major personality clashes and some legal sleight of hand. A couple of major rows did blow up, as Chris Rowley recounts:

> Micky went in there and fought with Dave Hall. This was serious baboon stuff. He turns up and starts yelling at Dave that Dave had to go. He just couldn't do this. This was corruption and this was the nadir of it all. They yelled and had fights and tantrums and threw things, and eventually Dave got up and left; the old buck had been pushed to one side. Now at this stage Micky was in his prime. He had a deadly rap; he'd get hold of this liberal, some hapless reporter from the *Guardian* or the *Observer*, and just start on them. Start soft and gentle and then gradually build up to this cascading crescendo of vehemence.

I guess you can't always do the right thing and come out smelling like Mary Poppins.

As both a salve to my conscience and an extra motivation, I had another and more altruistic motive for moving in on *IT*. If it hadn't been me, it might well have been Richard Neville. The grapevine had informed me that, not content with being the recognised editor and publisher of *OZ*, he was now dallying with a fantasy of carving out an underground media empire. Aside from the maxim we would learn in the Eighties — 'Beware of Australians with publishing empires' — I had always found Richard extremely contradictory. I couldn't do otherwise than admire the courage he exhibited when the *Schoolkids' OZ* bust came along. I freely admit that I would never have had either the style or the balls to show up at a court hearing in a gymslip. But even with this degree of respect, I could never figure out his real motives. The first issues of *OZ* were little more than sophomoric Kangaroo Valley versions of *Private Eye*, with a decidedly anti-freak bent. I can fully accept that Richard may have had his psychedelic road to Damascus, but after the world in which the original *OZ* apparently desired to function — that of *Private Eye* and the *New Statesman* — closed ranks against it, I always wondered if his sudden conversion to the hipster cause contained some element of following a market trend.

A part of him gave the impression that he would have been perfectly happy with a TV talk show, like a velvet and less bestial

Clive James. He affected the pose of the languid faux-Oxbridge wit, yet also worked in harness with Felix Dennis, who had all the finesse and room-devouring energy of Tasmanian Devil from the Bugs Bunny cartoons. In retrospect, I have to wonder if Felix really didn't get the credit he was due for the courage and innovation at *OZ*. As many have learned to their cost, it's a *cardinal* mistake ever to dismiss Felix Dennis as nothing more than a money-maker.

I probably wouldn't be discussing Neville if I hadn't been hearing from Australia that he's been recanting for more than a decade now, and if I hadn't been so irritated by his 1995 memoir of the Sixties, *Hippie Hippie Shake*. In his lamentable book Richard pictures me as a thug with hopeless pretensions. At the same time he exhibits a deeply bizarre fascination with my footwear. Huh? I suppose I should have had an inkling of this one night in the early Seventies when he and his girlfriend Louise Ferrier came to dinner with Ingrid and me. He lingered over shelves of books that included Che, Mao, Fanon and Debray along with Robert Heinlein, Iceberg Slim and Marshall McLuhan. 'Have you read all these?'

The question was fatuous. What was my response supposed to be? 'No, Richard, I just ran out and bought them to impress you with my radical chic.'

Hippie Hippie Shake was silly, but I'd liked Richard and I always assumed he'd at least had a degree of respect for me. After discovering otherwise, I called Chris Rowley, who knew us both equally well. 'Have you read this book of Neville's?'

Chris laughed. 'Yes.'

'What the fuck?'

'Forget about it. He resented you. You were the real thing.'

I sighed and shrugged, but after decades I was reminded of my trepidation at the idea of Richard being in control of both *IT* and *OZ*. Mercifully I also heard that Felix quickly vetoed the scheme, not only convincing Richard it would just mean more debts and hungry printers to feed, but reminding him he was a lazy son-of-a-bitch when it came down to the routine grind. *OZ* might be able to meander out when it was good and ready, but *IT* was a bi-weekly newspaper. It came out on time, and was dependent on its dateline.

At the time Edward and I went into gross tabloid mode, we were aware that Neville shared our enthusiasm for 144-point bold headlines. Australia, even more than the USA, is the spiritual home of the shrieking press. By going down that route we could not only get our graphic rocks off, but rub his nose in it at the same time. And, for the first time ever, *IT* had to survive completely on its own merits. No UFO Club or Nigel Samuel to subsidise it any more, and the laundering of herb money was a thing of the past. Without the gay ads, revenues had dropped and the circulation figures had fallen. With *Friends, Rolling Stone, Gay News* and a growing number of monthly hippie rock-mags coming onto the market, the competition for advertising was more intense than it had ever been. I'd also happily agreed that we'd drop the haphazard 'What's Happening' section, which no one liked compiling or designing, so that Tony Elliot could get his London listings-magazine *Time Out* under way. That left us without even a service function in the capital city.

We had no intention of abandoning the bedrock principles of agitation and aggression, but the fact was that we had to break even or die. We had to work according to a page budget dictated by advertising, and profile a target reader. As it turned out, the target reader was primarily male, an upmarket boggie with a disgruntled anger, a healthy dose of paranoia, a juvenile-delinquent obsession with sex, drugs, rock 'n' roll, comic books and a tolerance for up-against-the-wall-motherfucker polemics. This long-haired demographic was as much justification as Edward and I needed to conduct our first tabloid experiments.

And it wasn't just a matter of large and loud schoolboy jape headlines. We balanced the features with a great deal of short, easy-read items in a form that greatly resembled the format *USA Today* believes it pioneered. Without fail, we ran a full two-page comic section, just like in the *New York Daily News*. The old guard at *IT* had sporadically published Gilbert Shelton's *Furry Freak Brothers*, but the readers within our sights wanted the strip every week, complete with *Fat Freddy's Cat*, easily found in every issue, and no excuses. We even had the equivalent of sports pages in our recreational drug coverage. As far as features went, we flung a wide net over the popular preoccupations. We covered animal rights and alchemy, the environment and assassination theories, mysticism and Marxism, mass murder and the atrocities of the Central Intelligence Agency. Heaven knows we had enough to write about. Nixon's new drug war, Henry

Kissinger's geopolitics, the Manson family trial, the overthrow of Salvador Allende, the deteriorating situation in Iran and the heroin it brought with it, civil war in Belfast and Derry, John Lennon's Green Card, the extermination of the Black Panthers and the suicidal tendencies of the Weather Underground were all consistently reported. We sought the thoughts of Pete Townshend, Allen Ginsberg, Bobby Seale and guys doing thirty years in a Turkish jail. The perennial William Burroughs clued us in on the alien conspiracy long before the Majestic-12 documents were found and, since Monty Python was now among us, all was presented with a noticeable sense of the absurd.

Newspaper production is a tactile experience. You break open the first bundle of papers and pull out copies of a new issue; ink comes off on your hands as you flick through the pages. No matter the politics, in that moment every publisher is Charles Foster Kane. It may end up lining a rubbish bin, but a new edition of a paper is a tangible object, a new creation, words, images and ideas given physical solidity.

We had set up a new corporate structure and even moved offices to a second and third floor above a Pakistani fabric shop right in the heart of Soho's Berwick Street Market – with no fewer than five pubs in a 100-yard radius. The SCREWING CAUSES CLAP headline, which was one of our first, and maybe our finest, pieces of tabloid dumb insolence, also proved that, in a weird way, we were in the business of street theatre. On publication day that cover was visible over and over again, thousands of times, on newsstands and in paper shops, in head-shops and hippie emporia all over the country. Just to take a cab down Oxford Street was to see the headline, like an impish brandished fist, a dozen or more times.

I must also give special credit to the London news vendors for putting it on display as usual, between *Exchange & Mart* and the *Sporting Life*, and not far from the *New Musical Express* and *Melody Maker*. What's more, it moved like a motherfucker. The carriage trade just couldn't resist its sheer stupidity, and picked up a copy as a gag along with the *Evening Standard*. For the two weeks the issue was on sale I couldn't have been happier.

Compared with the hectic times preceding them, the three years in the early Seventies that I spent at *IT* settled into an intense but manageable routine. To put it bluntly, Edward and I lounged around for one week, annoying the daytime staff, making phone calls, having meetings, taking care of business, thinking a lot and frequently going down the pub. As the second week began, we girded ourselves to put a paper together and pretty much did that between the Tuesday and the Friday, with maybe one break for sleep. It took between fifty and sixty hours to put an issue of *IT* together, and amphetamines and alcohol once more came into play. Paul Lewis, the editor, would sit down on the first floor, sorting and marking up copy, while up in the second-floor art room Caroline McKechnie and Shirley Divers hammered raw print, ready for pasting, from a pair of IBM typesetting machines. (Caroline was recruited from Clifton Gardens, and Shirley Divers was Larry Wallis' girlfriend with the curly hair. In the end everyone was drafted. Joy came in as mysticism editor, den mother and office manager.) Edward and I were the conclusion of the process. Smelling of beer and Cow Gum, we actually laid out the finished artwork, while Gez shuttled from floor to floor, keeping the printer apprised of our progress and running out for sandwiches, fish and chips and Chinese take-aways.

This Ford-like production line was considerably humanised by the people who dropped in. Some, like photographers and freelance illustrators, knew they had a better chance of getting their work published if they could hand something to either Edward or me that was instantly suitable to fill a space. Cartoons and line drawings might be executed right on the spot. Each visitation provided the excuse to stop work, roll a joint and, if the visitor was a special favourite – like George Snow, who brought us his pre-computer graphics, or Joe 'Captain Snaps' Stevens, who was our virtual house-photographer when not getting himself thrown into jail while doing a *Friends* photo-essay on the Provisional IRA – we'd even stop work and head for the pub.

Not all the visitors to the *IT* offices were so benign. An underground newspaper is a magnet for all varieties of hustlers, psychos, panhandlers, seekers after truth, undercover policemen and extreme theorists who'd stopped taking the Thorazine. The panhandlers were no problem. We only handed out cash to a couple of indigenous, old-time Soho drunks. The hippie beggars could have a bunch of papers on credit and go out and sell them, but we didn't have any bread to hand out, man. Among the real malcontents, we developed quite a reputation for throwing people down the steep flight of stairs that led to Berwick Street.

Sadly, we couldn't eject all the delegations from underground special interests from whom we regularly took flack. We had to sit and hear them out, as when we ran a cartoon satire about Bob Dylan's lust for fame, and John Wilcox, the 'Father of the Underground Press', denounced us as anti-Semitic. On another occasion the Radical Feminists, a gang of angry, unshaven drag queens in clown make-up and heels, decided we were homophobic, trashed the art room and tore down our poster of a naked young woman on a Harley, a gift from Crazy Charlie of the Hell's Angels. They also stole a prized item that was known as 'The Pig Book', a collection of photographs of a Danish performance artist who copulated with pigs. Never rivalled in her field, she totally eclipsed Karen Findlay, the New York performance artist who courted fame by introducing assorted fruit and veg into various bodily orifices, and we mourned its loss. When overly distressed or beleaguered, we would threaten to flame-out in kamikaze splendour by printing a double-spread excerpt from 'The Pig Book', but now our ultimate weapon was gone.

When Edward and I unearthed a cache of early-Sixties, US trailer-trash girlie mags, and Irving Klaw-style absurdist bondage pictures, and started scattering them liberally through the paper, we innocently believed it would be treated as post-Warhol pop art. I know now that we were catching the same bus as Vivienne Westwood and Siouxsie Sioux, but we'd hopped on a couple of stops early. The full assault of the attitude squad descended on us, proclaiming us the worst counter-revolutionary, sexist thought-criminals this side of Russ Meyer. We were lectured for hours by women who'd later bond with the Angry Brigade, but, in just four years, the same images would be emblazoned on the sweaty T-shirts in the Roxy in London and CBGB's in New York.

Almost as soon as we stopped placating our enemies on the Left, we'd get hit from the other side by the police, most notably in the case of Nasty Tales. Gez, Edward and I had cooked up the idea of the comic-book Nasty Tales as a masterplan to ease our finances. Our grand money-making scheme was to put out a regular anthology of the top underground comics, both US and domestic. Nasty Tales would feature Robert Crumb, Gilbert Sheldon, Greg Irons, Spain Rodriguez and Rick Griffin, along with our own Chris Welch, Brian Boland and Edward, in the proper DC/Marvel format of a glossy colour cover and newsprint interior. It was an innocent little earner and, apart from the need to find top-flight material, should have all but run itself. It was a project that Edward and I could put together at our leisure and, like *OZ*, publish when we were good and ready. Instead, a completely unexpected criminal prosecution fell on us out of a cloudless Hiroshima sky, and the nagging possibility of jailtime became a resident mental background clutter for the next two years.

Harry Palmer with a Warrant

No one wanted to be the first to mention the eerie feeling that Sunday night. It was somehow too strong to be comfortably discussed. If no one else shared it, I might be losing my mind again, and if that was the case, I'd rather keep it quiet for as long as possible, thank you very much. That Boss was not only looking remote and preoccupied, but was quietly tidying away drugs into their hiding places and generally securing his room, caused me to break the as yet unspoken code of silence. Not wanting to alarm Ingrid, who was reading a book and seemingly unaware of any portents, I waylaid Boss on the stairs to the kitchen in the split-level flat.

'This may sound weird . . .'

'You don't have to say it.'

'Are we nuts, or what?'

At approximately six forty-five the next morning the Special Branch walked in. Neither grim and judgemental like the Obscene Publications boys, nor spivvish, like the Jack-the-Lad drug squad, these were men of the hardest aura, and visibly carried 9mm Remingtons under their Crombie overcoats. The Heavy Mob. Remember a long-gone TV show called *Callan* that starred Edward Woodward? Or Michael Caine as Harry Palmer? These guys coming through our door were cut from the same cloth, only they were the real thing. As trouble went, we'd hit the big time and it was not an occasion for humour. Just look as frightened as you actually are.

I suspect what Boss and I had credited to supernatural premonition was really a subconscious awareness that, for some days, our home in Clifton Gardens had been under surveillance. Not only by the Special Branch, but also, we discovered later, by the US Federal Bureau of Narcotics. Our friend the International Hashish Smuggler had passed through London a few days earlier and spent a couple of nights with us. What he didn't tell us was that he was riding herd on a large shipment of Afghan hash destined for New York City, and what he didn't know was that the deal was blown and Federal narcs had been following him halfway from Kabul. Throughout the previous few days law-enforcement agents from two countries had been all but tripping over each other outside the house.

The situation at Clifton Gardens had changed slightly. I think Caroline was living at Felix's place, while Boss and Paul Rudolph bunked in her room so that we could all make the rent and thrive in a modicum of style. The Special Branch hit Boss and Rudolph first and then moved on to Ingrid and me. While we sat glumly in separate rooms, they turned the place upside down with great efficiency and minimal mess, but all they came up with was Boss's Chairman Mao button, most of our drugs and reams of mildly subversive literature and documentation. Our understandable first reaction was that we were being raided for drugs, but we very quickly discovered that the warrant was for bomb-making equipment or evidence of a terrorist conspiracy. It was the period when a gang of urban guerrillas calling themselves the Angry Brigade had commenced a loony-tune terror bombing campaign by leaving an infernal device on the doorstep of Robert Carr, a Cabinet minister, and Special Branch were under the misapprehension that we might be them. Clearly disappointed with their haul of non-evidence, they served me with a second warrant for the *IT* offices. Before they took me away, I needed to piss and a detective came with me and watched. I tentatively asked what would happen next.

'About what?'

'Well . . . about the drugs, for one thing.'

'You think we're interested in drugs, son?'

'No, but . . .'

'We wouldn't give those drug-squad slags the time of day.'

With which he handed me the house collection of hash and pills.

'Flush.'

I dropped the dope into the bowl and flushed, then we went off to *IT* in an unmarked car. The production cycle had just finished and the place was a pigsty. Plainly the office was exactly what it claimed to be. A wretched hippie newspaper without a hope in hell of blowing up Cabinet ministers. Harry Palmer was again disappointed, and he and his mates sat me down.

'The Angry Brigade?'

'I honestly don't have a clue.'

It was the truth, and I think Harry Palmer realised it. My instincts told me that the group doing the bombing was very isolated and out-there, probably a political commune gone Manson family, but in a reptilian, Bader-Meinhof manner. Out on the mutant fringes of the counterculture, craziness was close to endemic. One thing I knew for sure, however, was that it had nothing to do with any of the old lags in my life. A few degrees of separation lay between us and the authors of these explosions. All we knew was that their communiqués had been left anonymously in the downstairs hallway at *IT*, just inside the street door. As Steve Mann would point out, when he was picked up a couple of days later, the likes of us were too stoned and disorganised to be blowing up the homes of Cabinet ministers. Disrupting *The David Frost Show* had been about our speed. Unfortunately Special Branch was pretty much as clueless as we were, and they had to start somewhere.

Personally I found the Angry Brigade a total pain in the arse. I suppose they had as much of an effect on the early Seventies as a marginally significant rock album, but it was an album I didn't like. I was also puzzled by their long-term strategy. Did they have a five-year plan? Would they escalate to bigger and bigger explosions, and then take to the Scottish highlands and fight a guerrilla war with the SAS? Their wildest dream could only be a five-minute workers' uprising, and – after it was ruthlessly crushed – fascism would get its three wishes, and start building the camps.

After the Brigade's first detonation, my friends and I found ourselves with the heavy-duty security services of the nation running all over our creaking little alternative society in their size thirteens, learning far more than they needed to know. We were virtually

compelled to offer the Angries a public right-on, as long as no one
was actually dead, but my private and heartfelt wish was that they'd
either blow themselves up or give themselves up. If these morons
actually did kill someone, all hell was going to break loose and
workers would be lynching hippies while onlookers cheered. How
they eventually gave themselves away and went to jail has been told
many times. I recount this segment only because, mercifully, one
didn't have Special Branch swarming over one's flat every day of the
week, even in the early Seventies.

Mists of Avalon

Two thickset, burly, roadie-like long-hairs stood beneath the
pyramid stage looking at a length of thick steel chain. One end was
wrapped around a pointed iron stake, while the other was attached to
a horizontal scaffolding pole at the very centre of the base of the
pyramid stage. One of the long-hairs was holding a formidable
sledgehammer and clearly intended to drive the spike into the
ground, like he was electrically earthing the large, complex structure.
The other seemed intent on stopping him. 'I'm telling you, man.
You disrupt the leyline, and you could split the fucking planet in
half.'

The one with the hammer shook his head. 'Not a chance.'

The stage at Glastonbury Fair was a work of grandeur; a massive
and precisely formed pyramid, constructed from scaffolding and
transparent plastic sheeting that glowed silver in the night, from
interior batteries of lights. It had been built according to the most
sophisticated architectural plans, and some hoped it could be seen
from space. I never knew if these two mystic yeomen were part of
the masterplan, or just independent theorists adding what they
supposed was an extra cosmic boost to the already energised mix.

The one without the hammer was having serious second thoughts.
'You shouldn't risk it, man. I mean . . .'

The one with the hammer was probably a Taurus. 'I've done my
calculations.'

'You're taking some fucking risk, man.'

'It'll complete a circuit connecting the power of the sounds with the power of the Earth.'

'And suppose you're wrong? Suppose you fucked up the co-sines or something?'

Hammer was exasperated. 'These are leylines, man. Not fucking long division.'

No-Hammer wasn't convinced. 'I don't know.'

Hammer hefted his sledge. 'You don't trust me?'

No-Hammer backed off a little. 'No, man, I didn't say that.'

'Well?'

'I . . . still don't know.'

Hammer positioned the stake. No-Hammer continued to look distraught, but his innate passivity prevented him from actually doing anything. The hammer swung and I must confess that for an instant I held my breath. It struck, and the head of the stake was eight inches lower. The hammer swung again and the stake went deeper into the ground. No cataclysm occurred, and both men looked extremely relieved. No-Hammer made a drawn-out deflating sound of some profundity. 'Sshiiiiiii . . .'

Hammer was a little more cocky than he really needed to be. 'You should have trusted me, man.'

No-Hammer shook his head. 'I still think you're fucking lucky.'

Hammer became at least a little defensive. 'I knew what I was doing.'

No-Hammer saw his chance to wax portentous. 'There are powers down there we can't even imagine.'

The exchange was a dumbly weird, Dada/psychedelic echo of the conversation Robert Oppenheimer reportedly had with his colleagues on the Manhattan Project. Just prior to the test of the very first atomic bomb, the fear had been expressed that the bomb might trigger a nitrogen chain reaction and entirely burn off the Earth's atmosphere. Although I don't equate the crude paranormal engineering of Hammer and No-Hammer with the technology behind the A-bomb, it was interesting to watch someone go ahead with an action even after the suggestion had been made that it might destroy the planet.

Scenes like I'd just witnessed were due in no small part to the fact that Glastonbury Fair was held on one of the most myth-steeped pieces of geography in all England. The tents, wickiups, kraals, hooches and pavilions swept down a grassy incline to the unbelievable pyramid stage, beyond which was a view of the Vale of Avalon where the sixth-century wizards of paganism made their last stand in the face of the drably determined monks of Christianity. This was Merlin's turf. The great earthwork of Glastonbury Tor reared up less than a mile away, the towering and ancient man-made pyramid with its allegedly psychotropic spiral path to the summit, and the bizarre Christian chapel perched on the top, clear indication of how the monks feared the power of that mound, be it the burial place of Arthur or a landing marker for mother-ships.

The first night of the festival, when the underground press convoy arrived in its truck and Land-Rover, Camelot was drenched by torrential rain, but by morning the skies had cleared for a full week of uninterrupted sunshine. We had churned up enough mud, however, trying to drive through the site and pitch tents in the downpour that, come the sun, everything was covered in a layer of red dust, which made it all too easy to imagine oneself in a very benign spaghetti western, or maybe one of the more relaxed and amusing bits of the Third-Crusade. The combined underground press had a large military tent with a Soviet naval flag flying above it. Our next-door neighbours were Hawkwind, in a massive tepee of psychedelic tarpaulin supported on a conical cluster of scaffolding poles.

Our crew, which included the Pink Fairies and other wastrels of the parish, drank, drugged, made music and fell where we lay. We ate custard pies from the baker's in the village. We took LSD from strangers and swilled it down with the local scrumpy which had the taste and potency of gasoline and crushed apples. I became an absolute obsessive about building fires at night. After sundown, to have the biggest and most roaring orange blaze in your section of the landscape was akin to declaring that the pub was open. Strange hippies appeared out of the darkness offering up what they had to the circle around the fire: rum, kif, magic mushrooms or an opium pipe. We might as well have been in the sixth or even the twenty-sixth century as we told tall travellers' tales of intoxication, of outwitting the law, of the lights in the sky, lost continents, the lies of governments, collective triumphs and personal moments of gross stupidity, while the music of past, present and future roared from the pyramid stage. On that same stage Hawkwind hammered out their legend, and David Bowie, in a dress and still with his Veronica Lake hairstyle, played a magical set in the dawn.

And we all got along so fucking well, the Elves and the Bladerunners, the Druids and the Gunslingers, the Earth Goddesses and the Suspected Aliens. No one to shock and nothing with which to shock them. The only flurry of authoritarianism came when an Eco-Attitude Squad descended on us, wanting to know where we were finding all our firewood. They feared we were hacking down trees and burning them. Mac, John Manly and I – the trio of Fire Panthers responsible for all this pagan flame and jollity – responded irately. Had we not driven all the way to a local sawmill in the mighty Land-Rover and filled it with a few hundredweight of off-cuts and trim? And we would probably do the same again on the morrow.

Regretfully the Glastonbury Fair constituted a last meeting of many tribes, a final potlatch before we all took our separate paths into a future few of us believed would be anything but inescapably darker. It was symbolic that we should come to this place, this land of our Once and Future King. I really hoped Hammer *had* tapped us into the power of the leys, because – whether you believed in the myths of Avalon or not – we'd soon need all the help we could get.

Our own hard times kicked in faster than I'd imagined. We were still at Glastonbury, communing with the tribes, when we learned we'd been busted. A messenger came hotfoot from the farmhouse to tell Edward, Gez and me that Joy – who had no empathy for fields and was holding the fort in London – had phoned from the *IT* office. The Metropolitan Police Obscene Publications Squad had visited with a warrant and seized all the copies of *Nasty Tales* they could find. Our first response was to break camp and hightail it to London, but Joy made clear the pointlessness of rushing back like headless chickens. It was unlikely we'd be charged with anything for at least a month, so we might as well stay and enjoy ourselves while the Director of Public Prosecutions considered our fate. We did our best, but in the time left to us in Camelot, we switched from psychedelics to the local cider and fire-water whisky purchased in the villages of men.

A Nasty Ball

Each of the Pink Fairies arrived bearing the head of a dead pig on a pole. Although we assumed they had obtained them from a pork butcher rather than mounting their own hog hunt, it set the tone. *Lord of the Flies* meets *Monster Mash*. The preparations for a legal engagement – particularly one that might cost us our freedom – took some diverse forms. To hold a series of what we called 'Nasty Balls' was one of the more obvious and enjoyable ideas. We needed to raise money, and organising a string of fairly outrageous parties took our minds off our troubles. I was reading everything I could get my hands on about obscenity, jurisprudence and erotica, and I needed a break.

We had found a down-on-its-luck disco called Bumpers in Piccadilly, on the site of what had once been a Lyons Corner House, and the owner offered us a very tempting deal for an evening's event. One factor that especially endeared itself to Edward and me was a central Plexiglas DJ booth that lit up and flashed like a flying saucer going into warp drive. 'Cool,' we muttered as the owner turned it on for a demonstration. And just to prove that wonders sometimes did never cease, the place also had a late-night liquor licence. We had finally caught ourselves a break, and it was about time. Matters had not been going well up to that point. Not only had the Director of Public Prosecutions brought charges against *Nasty Tales*, and its editors and publishers, but, in a ten-minute hearing, a magistrate rubber-stamped them and we'd been committed for trial. We were also discovering that the earlier *OZ* obscenity circus was a hard act to follow. The underground and its sympathisers were suffering from prosecution fatigue.

Felix, Jim and Richard had just about done it all; from showing up at Marylebone Magistrates Court dressed as schoolgirls, to proving themselves lucid and eloquent at their trial at the Old Bailey. They had thrown some splendid parties, and John Lennon had cut a benefit single, but, like Mick and Keith before them, they'd been found guilty and freed only after protests ranging from editorials in the 'quality papers' to a free-form demonstration that meandered around the West End, with John and Yoko in the vanguard. The same funfair and day at the races could not be repeated. About the only option open to *Nasty Tales* was to win. I was pretty damned sure that, if convicted, Edward and I at least would do some time. No editorials, no demos and definitely no deal. The primary task in front of us was to convince a jury that cartoons of anthropomorphic dogs having sex might not be to their taste, but posed no threat to society. The riff had been played over and over; from Henry Miller to Lenny Bruce, to poor Jim Morrison who might have been doing time right then, if he hadn't taken the poet's way out and fled to Paris to die. Wasn't it finally time the general public accepted that judicial censorship was a dead issue? Our tales might be nasty, but surely not a crime.

My reading of the situation told me that winning was crucial not only to keep us out of durance vile, but also because scoring ourselves a not-guilty verdict might actually put an end to this nonsense. If the DPP failed to get a conviction, that might actually act as a deterrent to future busts of the same kind, and those in power would have to use something other than the criminal law as a means to censor print.

Four of us had actually been charged: Edward, Paul Lewis, Joy and myself as the directors of the parent company; and then Edward and I were double-dipped as the actual editors of the offending publication. Our only fallback, should our fortunes turn ugly, was that Edward and I would attempt to distance ourselves from Joy and Paul and absorb the worst of the heat. If there was to be a rap, Edward and I, as gentlemen, would attempt to take it, but winning always remained the goal. To achieve this we first avoided all the usual liberal lawyers and went to a well-known criminal-law practice, defenders of the Krays and other villains, and presented them with our problem. Far from telling us to piss off and not bother them with our hippie nonsense, the senior partners were amused by the challenge. It would be a diversion for some of the younger chaps, a wit-sharpening change from routine fraud, armed robbery and GBH.

We made it clear that we wanted to win and they agreed that they did, too. When we added that we wanted to win, but we weren't going to grovel merely to stay out of jail, they stayed with us. They pointed out, though, that to use the technicalities of the law in our own defence should not be considered dishonourable, and they reserved the right to dive into any loophole that might present itself. They conceded that, in return for not ideologically tying their hands, I could conduct my own defence, enabling me to rant when I felt the need. Our barristers had defended enough gangsters to know the thin line between the law and show business. Joy, Paul and Edward had a barrister apiece, plus an extra one representing the company. That gave us four barristers and me arrayed against the prosecution. We could but hope.

Nasty Tales itself proved to be one of our greatest sources of income, and we put out new issues as fast as Edward and I could commission and gather material. To do otherwise would have been an admission of guilt, and we figured the dirty book squad wouldn't be back until the ongoing case was concluded. Bust us again and our lawyers would be screaming harassment. To our great delight, these new issues sold like hot cakes; I think to pessimistic collectors who wanted copies before they were all consigned to the incinerator. The only compromise – after issue no.2 – was the words ADULTS ONLY printed boldly on the cover. The core of the prosecution case was that comics, by definition, are for the young and thus, once again, we were sinister tot-corrupters, only one step from actual molesters.

We entered a time of hyper-activity, with that unique energy generated by fear. *IT* came out, on the deadline, and in our spare time we decided to raise some small (but, we hoped, historic) debauchery before we found ourselves carted off to the Scrubs – or, in Joy's case, Holloway. Hence the Nasty Balls at Bumpers, with the flying-saucer DJ booth ready to count down, and booze till 3 a.m.

Although this prosecution was part of the running fight that started with the first raid on *IT* in 1967, it was now being conducted against the background of a city, from its sleazy heart outward, in the throws of profound change. Something hummed – same instrument, but with a new and different note. Hardening times were bringing back decadence, if only as a shelter from the storm. Kurt Weill was chic all over again, as was a brief vogue for swing bands played at dance-mix volume. The Radical Fems were on the loose and still never found time to shave before putting on their make-up. The Ladies of the Canyons had also pretty much had it with dressing like Chairman Mao, and embraced a Rita Hayworth retro-vogue for pearlised metalflake slink, feather boas and rising platforms, the second-hand-store version of what, in modernised and mass-produced form, would appear in Kensington Market and the King's Road within about a year. David Bowie – laughing gnome that he was – would start looking like Katharine Hepburn, and where were the spiders from Mars?

The Spiders were still waiting in the wings when Iggy, Lou Reed and Bowie were conducting their pre-Ziggy gavotte, which would yield *Raw Power* and *Transformer*. Coloured girls were definitely going doop-da-doop some place not too far away. Bowie had formed an alliance with the two refugees from the Sixties underground who – in his opinion – had the best chances of survival. And I would never in a million years have disagreed with him. At that moment in time, Bowie's sense of wind direction was Darwinian in its accuracy. The early Seventies were so philosophically lean that I knew they were ready for CANNIBAL POP MESSIAH TAKES STEP DOWN THE FOOD CHAIN.

I received reports from the neo-faux-gay labyrinth that seemed to be centred on the Sombrero Club. They came mainly via my friend Gwen, late of the Exploding Galaxy psychedelic dance troupe. After doing some time in the Cook County Jail for a bit of ill-conceived hash-muling into Chicago's O'Hare Airport, Gwen – who had flaming red hair and freckles, but otherwise looked a lot like Sophia Loren on amphetamine – had become what is now known as a lipstick lesbian (a new rail on the Rita Hayworth track) and, while still dallying with the boys, had formed a fairly violent relationship with a female Swiss stormtrooper whom we nicknamed Madame Charles. She cursed like a stevedore and could be counted on to pursue Gwen publicly across town by phone and furious cab on nights when Gwen's heterosexuality reasserted itself.

As if in confirmation of Bowie's confidence, Lou and Iggy had done a killer show at the King's Cross Cinema, at which Lou had looked a little portly in his black velvet, but Iggy (never previously experienced in the UK) stripped to his narcissistic waist in silver leather jeans and did everything for which he was famous, except throwing peanut butter and walking on the crowd. I was gratified that Iggy showed up at the first Nasty Ball in the same silver jeans, proving that he was doing the ultra-degenerate Morrison trick of wearing them all the time.

This is not to say that the other old lags were lagging, hopelessly mired in flower power, or about to make their exits. Hawkwind played at the Nasty Balls, as did the MC4 – singer Rob Tyner having fallen out with his bandmates and winged it back to Motown – but, like I said earlier, the Pink Fairies showed up with pigs' heads on poles. (A pink cartoon pig with wings was the logo that Edward had assigned to the band, like their heraldic colours.) Such an act would have been unthinkable a couple of years earlier, and even then it was still fairly outrageous. Grinning and grisly, those pigs' heads were definitely a summation of the times and the attitude. 'Alternative society' had given way to a surly 'fuck you'. We'd lost this round of the cultural revolution, and losers should expect payback.

This new attitude, however, wasn't wholly negative. Aside from the triumvirate of Iggy, Bowie and Lou, Alice Cooper was among us, and very shortly the New York Dolls would come to town. They were being brought over for an incredibly implausible benefit at Wembley Pool that featured them, the Pink Fairies and the Faces. The Fairies played one of the most god-awful sets of their entire career. Paul Rudolph had left the band to play with Sparks and Brian Eno, and Russell and Sandy were discovering that new guitarist Mick Wayne was not the boy for them. The Dolls' set was interesting in so far as bass player Arthur Kane was dressed as a ballerina, but they had very obviously never played to an audience of more than 300 and were lost in front of 13,000 Faces fans in the cavernous and echoing auditorium.

The Dolls made a great deal more sense a few days later amid the elitist art deco of the Rainbow Room at the top of Biba's new department store on Kensington High Street. On this closer inspection their supposed androgyny, with the possible exception of Arthur, was revealed as a cultivated pose, but they'd learned to cultivate it from the best – Jackie Curtis, Holly Woodlawn, Candy Darling and all the other legendary denizens of Max's Kansas City. Even though the women of the Angry Brigade had, I believe, at one point plotted to blow up Biba as a gross example of counter-revolutionary consumerism, most of the old underground and the new glitterati turned out to see them. Many were dismissive, discounting the Dolls as nothing more than an absurdist parody of some of the worst aspects of the Rolling Stones, but at Biba they made me very happy. They had clearly returned to the Deviants' ethic that rock & roll should not be the exclusive preserve of virtuoso players. David Johansen told the old tale:

We were very raw, we were into confronting the audience. People who saw the Dolls said 'Hell, anyone can do this' . . . basically we were these kids from New York who would spit and fart in public. It was just so obvious what we were doing in rock 'n' roll – we were bringing it back to the street.

Backstage with the booze, I discovered the NY Dolls were less of an art-school project than either the Deviants or the Stooges. 'There wasn't a lot of intellectualising going on when we started the New York Dolls.' Dumb was also coming back. I liked that.

To say that our humble Nasty Balls played any part in this process of evolution from the old and strange to the new and strange would be an inaccurate conceit, but they were where I was able to witness it going on, from the supreme vantage point of host and momentary centre of attention. We had expected events to be a little out of the ordinary, but the reality was considerably more bizarre that we'd dared hope. We found ourselves presiding over a disco-lit, near-pagan debauch featuring leftover drag queens from the Roundhouse production of Andy Warhol's *Pork* cheek-by-jowl with the local Hell's Angels, Iggy Pop getting stoned with Wayne Kramer, and Magic Michael, an aggressively bi-sexual singer-songwriter and possible psychopath, who would perform backed by future pub-rockers Brinsley Schwarz, to the amusement of some and the consternation of many. Most of the chemically enhanced from the West End and Ladbroke Grove, not to mention points north and south, turned up both to demonstrate their solidarity and to interface with the first scattering of embryonic glitterites of the new decadence.

In *Days in the Life* Jonathon Green recalls:

Buttons [the president of the Hell's Angels] *is sitting there, legs spread, a dyed blonde head bobbing up and down over his cock. He sees me, grasps this hapless head and drags the girl off his cock. 'Hey, man, want some of this?' Great moments in underground etiquette: do I join Buttons and this not wholly appetising Mama, or do I reveal my utter wimpishness, not to mention that my girlfriend is standing ten yards away and staring? Fortunately my saviour arrives: William Bloom, the publisher, appears, says he has some cocaine and suggests we vanish into the toilets to consume it.*

Not everyone was so discreet. As the night wore on, lines were being razored out on tables with no attempt at concealment and joints were openly smoked. Dealers suddenly became magnanimous, and strange women who had spent too long maintaining the cat's cradle equilibrium of coke, vodka and mandies gave up the effort and collapsed in corners. If Edward and I did end the movie on our way to jail, at least we'd conjured up a few shining memories to sustain us.

We Fought the Law and, For Once, We Won

It was the morning of 25 January 1973, the day when, if everything went according to plan, we would hear the verdict, but the subject under discussion was the Ali/Foreman heavyweight title fight. The Jamaican mini-cab driver, Edward and I were of one uniform opinion. George Foreman was a huge pig-ignorant slugger with nothing going for him but brute brawn and a long reach. Ali would blind him with science, finesse and tactics, and that would be all she wrote. The routine was to ride to court talking about anything but the trial. This major disruption of our life, liberty and the pursuit of happiness intruded on most of the rest of our waking hours, and invaded at least my sleep as anxiety nightmares, so we used the forty minutes it took to get from Ladbroke Grove to the Old Bailey to sham apparent normality.

This particular morning it was more of a pretence than usual. That we wouldn't come home that night loomed large in our fearful imaginations. The previous evening had been a quiet horror of preparation for the worst. In the final weeks before the trial Edward and I were drinking a *lot*. The previous night, though, I'd stuck to beer and, while the telly prattled on banal and incongruous, I'd signed a whole bookful of cheques for various eventualities. I'd squared away all that could be squared. With preparations for the worst-case scenario complete, Ingrid and I tried for some sleep before the cab came to get us. I recall lying awake as the pendulum swung from anxiety to total fucking unreality that this shit was happening to *me*.

For the duration of the trial we'd travelled to court in a car from the same mini-cab firm. In a flash of inspiration, Edward had opened an account that wouldn't be presented for payment until after the trial. I found this an old-world criminal fraternity trust that could almost move me to tears when the night and the Jameson's grew late. Everyone in the mini-cab depot on All Saints Road, from the dispatcher down, knew that we were going to court every day. The mini-cab world was populated by aspiring quasi-gangsters, and its business methods leaned to the rough and ready. The penalty for non-payment could be a medium duffing over rather than any protracted legal process, and yet, here they were trusting us with credit, when gamblers' logic dictated that we might not be paying them for a couple of years or more. Asking later, when we settled up, yielded nothing. Just a wink and a grin. 'We knew you'd get off.' I still like to think the blind-eye credit with the cab company amounted to a potential gift to those who faced being banged up. 'Go in peace, lads, and be lucky. We bless you with untroubled transportation, and we'll sort it out later.'

The absolute unreality of getting out of a mini-cab in front of the Central Criminal Court at the Old Bailey every morning at nine-thirty – as if I was going to work, with my briefcase stuffed with legal papers like Horace bloody Rumpole – is actually too extreme to describe. Sartorially we'd gone for Mick-Jagger-at-a-business meeting, but we still stood out in the august building's cathedral corridors, like whores in a nunnery. It's the Old Bailey, goddamn it. It was real, and I suppose it had to be a kind of career high point. Above us was that dome we'd seen in so many movies, with its dominating golden statue of Blind Justice. Echoes of the voice of Edgar Lustgarten, and those cheap, second-feature *Scales of Justice* movies, which used a slowed-down version of the Shadows' 'Man of Mystery' as a theme tune. These were the courtrooms in which the elite of evil had met their fate – Crippen, the Kray Twins, John Christie, Neville Heath, George 'brides in the bath' Smith, Christopher Craig and Derek Bentley, Lord Haw-Haw, Ruth Ellis, Roger Casement, all the great stranglers, arsonists, poisoners, thieves and embezzlers, the anarchists and IRA men. This was the criminal equivalent of batting at Lord's, or playing the Albert Hall, except that it went on and on. Although fleetingly brief compared with modern American trials, thirteen days at the Old Bailey can seem like a way of life.

The court itself provided a perfect insight into the bifurcated nature of law and order. In the courtroom all was calm and genteel courtesy, in which, as my own counsel, I was provisionally part of the gentlemen's club. My only disappointment was that we'd drawn one of the courts in the modern extension, streamlined and Euro, and not one of the magnificent older venues that you see in Charles Laughton movies. I could interpose, or object, or, after all my reading, I could even at times offer clarification, as when no one else could remember the details of *The Crown v. Acme Chewing Gum*.

(The Acme Chewing Gum case was a bizarre Obscene Publications prosecution, in that the offending material had absolutely no sexual content. In the early Fifties Acme had marketed a line of bubble gum called (I think) Atom Horror, which included a series of fifty cards showing black-and-white photos from Hiroshima and Nagasaki after the bomb. Many were exceedingly grisly and, needless to say, were snatched up by nasty schoolboys right across the country. This was back in the days when the government was very reluctant to let the proles know just how fucking nasty a nuclear attack could be. The DPP, supposedly after the usual complaints from outraged parents, brought the Act to bear on Acme. I never did find out if the Acme bubble-gum guys were clever pacifists or just sick fucks making a buck.)

The Old Bailey also had its hidden Morlock side. Beneath the robes, the precedents, the wigs and the watchchains lay the subterranean labyrinth that was the opposite pan on Justice's scale, the grim-tiled dungeon of slops and shouting, of cops and screws, heavy intimidation and sub-standard TV dinners. We visited it every morning when we surrendered to bail, and each night when bail was continued. I was even banged up in it for two unfortunate lunchtimes while on the stand giving evidence under oath. Doing my best to mind my own business, I found myself the recipient of furtive whispers. ''Ere, John, are you going back to Brixton tonight?'

An old mod fallen on hard times was talking to me out of the corner of his mouth as we waited for something. Furtively I shook my head. 'I got bail.'

'Pity, I hoped you'd take something to this mate of mine.'

Right. I was about to smuggle mysterious somethings into the nick. Up the steps and back into the courtroom charm, but after the labyrinth you know it's only a shell, the mask of institutional brutality.

Judge King-Hamilton wasn't a bad man, merely a pillar of the establishment at its most established, with a Victorian sense of absolute patrician rectitude. He was perfectly well aware that we were vermin, something of the order of the deathwatch beetle, gnawing at the very foundations of the venerable constitutional monarchy. Within the confines of his perspective, I had absolutely to agree with him. He knew troublemakers when he saw them. The mutual recognition and dislike were instant. I'm not at all sure that art cannot serve as an instruction to depravity, and to be truthful I don't care. One person's depravity is another's freedom and, beyond the semantics, the judge was fundamentally correct: we *were* seriously seeking to deprave and corrupt everything he held dear. By the same token, everything King-Hamilton held dear was anathema to me. We were joining battle in a war of cultures.

A trial is a slow waltz on a single axis. The law specifically required the prosecution to prove that *Nasty Tales* intended to deprave and corrupt. Our basic defence was simple. Since all properly conducted scientific studies tended to prove that no graphic representation was in fact capable of depraving or corrupting a mature human, we could not be guilty. We were playing according to their terminology, but our interpretation. The prosecution's position, a considerable fallback since the *Lady Chatterley* case, and even the *OZ* trial, was to define a comic as a publication for children; thus we were not dealing with mature minds, but with the unformed and highly impressionable. We countered with the long and noble tradition of adult strip-cartoons all the way back to Hogarth and beyond. They responded that they had a seven-year-old in North London who'd purchased a copy of *Nasty Tales* no. 1 in the local newsagents and taken it home to his mom. We were not overjoyed by the prospect of mother and child giving evidence, but then, by some bureaucratic fuck-up or police malfeasance, the cops couldn't come up with either. We thought we'd won. One of our barristers attempted to bring the proceedings to a halt.

'We would submit, my Lord, that if the actual complainant, the original accuser, cannot appear, no evidence exists of a crime committed, and there can be no case to answer.' We held our breath, but King-Hamilton didn't agree and ruled that, since *Nasty Tales* was on general sale, such a scenario *could* have occurred and he would continue.

'Can he do that?'

In the pub, over Scotch and dry sherry, the professionals of the defence team shrugged. It was something to argue at appeal. I didn't want to think about an appeal, but they took the longer view. Once the barristers had taught me not to confuse logic and the law, the combined defence team was formidable. We'd all get a go at each witness, and our hammering of the lead cop on the matter of selective prosecution – and how he would have had to push his way past half the porno stores of darkest Soho, passing everything from pony bondage to Dalmatian fellatio, in order to make the raid on our offices – was a joy to behold. Although porn videos were still a few years in the future, by the early Seventies, if you could imagine it, someone in Holland or Denmark had photographed it. The theme of selective prosecution was harped on constantly, in an attempt to ease the jury into wondering why, when the world was so awash with commercial porn, the authorities were picking on a bunch of obviously weird, but well-meaning, hippies? Implications of hidden agendas, social control and plain, old-fashioned vindictiveness were laid on with a trowel.

Although lay-ignorant of the law in general, I discovered that I knew a lot more about the actual subject at hand than pretty much anyone else in the courtroom. I'd done more homework. I discovered, however, that I knew almost nothing about juries. I had castigated myself without mercy after feeling I'd completely fucked up my closing speech. I had started with the casual remark that, down in the labyrinth, a prison-officer had laughingly remarked how we should have put 'adults only' on the front of the magazine and we wouldn't have been in this mess. King-Hamilton took immediate exception. 'No, no, no, no, we can't have that. The jury will ignore that remark. Please start again, Mr Farren.'

'Yes, my Lord.' But he'd blind-sided me like a rocket from Krypton, and my mind went blank. As I understood it, for a judge to interrupt a closing speech was almost unheard of, and I stared at the jury in confusion. 'I'm sorry. Please bear with me for a moment, I have completely lost my train of thought.' I believed that I'd completely lost the jury, and essentially torpedoed my own defence.

From a faltering start, I strengthened as I went along. One of the defence lawyers had stated that 'You might think *Nasty Tales* was the least offensive magazine ever to be prosecuted.' Another had pointed out that the comic 'no more encourages drug taking than Andy Capp encourages the consumption of alcohol and wife-beating.' I could only add a counterpoint to the same refrain.

'We are all-aware that society is burdened with problems. The question is whether these problems can be solved by forbidding the discussion of them. It is my opinion, and the opinion of many of our readers, that the use of marijuana is a matter for the individual, not a matter for the law. *Nasty Tales*, I think, carries through this ideology. It makes a number of jokes about the failings and weaknesses of soft-drug users. They are similar to the kind of joke that has been made about drunkards from time immemorial. We have not presented the glamorous, attractive view of sex, so common in advertising, glamour magazines or pornography. We have presented sex warts and all. The prosecution has put forward the idea that *Nasty Tales* supports a plea for disobedience and a lack of respect for law and order. If this is grounds for prosecution, we would find ourselves still in a world where slavery and the hanging of children were common events. It is only the questioning of the current state of authority and the law that can lead to any type of reform. The jokes in *Nasty Tales* took a robust view of our society. It poked fun at some of the authority, at the hypocrisy, at the failings of many sections of our society. If you, gentlemen, feel this is contrary to the good health of our society, then I suggest you convict myself and my friends.'

It was only later, when we had a brief chance to speak to a couple of members of the jury, that I found out my initial flounder had actually won sympathy. Up to that point they'd considered me a little too slick, too well prepared, too combative and too clever by half. By stumbling, I'd actually humanised myself. We'd made a similar mistake on an earlier occasion, when, under cross-examination, Edward admitted, 'If we had discouraged drug taking, it [*Nasty Tales*] would not have been bought.' The admission had come before lunch, and in the pub across the street from the Old Bailey I raged at Edward for making such a dumb and damaging slip. I was so pissed off that my mother, who had come up from Sussex to see her son play the Central Criminal Court, took me to one side and told me that I really shouldn't be so hard on Edward. 'He wasn't raised by your stepfather.' Again, I had completely misjudged the effect on the jury. We discovered that Edward's blurted admission had actually made him seem guilelessly honest, and they'd liked that.

The two days I was on the witness stand were the closest I came to having real fun. I felt I was finally fighting them, face to face, on their own ground. If the technique was to keep the prosecution – and the judge, who seemed to act as the prosecution's relief-hitter – at bay and prevent them scoring points, I figure they were hard-pressed to lay a glove on me. In an obscenity trial where the law is far from being clear-cut, the character who defends himself has something of an advantage. You may not know the law, and are obviously inexperienced in the ways of the courtroom, but you do get to say exactly what you want. Since you cannot ask yourself questions without appearing both absurd and a little demented, you take the stand and give your evidence in the form of a statement/monologue. The only permitted interruptions are by the judge – requests for amplification or clarification on certain points – but in King-Hamilton's case these came thick and fast. I got the impression he was quite unable to keep quiet for more than five minutes at a stretch. It was his courtroom and he liked to remain centre-stage at all times.

I think I talked for maybe an hour, and then had to brace myself for a lengthy cross-examination by the prosecutor, aided and abetted by the judge, who under the guise of gratuitously assisting me with my defence sought to negate or neutralise as many of my points as he could. The best word to describe the prosecutor was dogged. He had the determination of a bull terrier with its jaw locked. He appeared baffled by the idea that, as a responsible publisher, I should keep abreast of all the scientific studies of the effects of erotica and sexual imagery, and how they confirmed that such material was harmless and maybe even socially beneficial. When one line of questioning failed to get the desired result, he would come at it all over again from another angle, forcing me to repeat my argument until the jury must have known it by heart. I could only assume he hoped I'd break down and reveal a heinous Lex Luthor masterplan of fathomless mass evil.

I think Joy had the greatest impact on the jury. The court persona she created made it abundantly clear that she was no mere office manager, or the little woman shut out from the boys' exclusive loop. She presented herself as determinedly idealistic, but at the same time uncharacteristically prim. 'I don't like the idea of group sex, but it is possible in certain circumstances.' She even managed a hint that she didn't absolutely like *Nasty Tales*, but vehemently defended our right to publish it. At one point the cross-examination turned to how selling *IT* and *Nasty Tales* on the street was a means for runaway kids to survive without turning to crime or prostitution. In a sour and patronising aside, the judge wondered out loud if Joy might have been better occupied reuniting these people with their parents. Joy retorted irately that *IT* in fact operated a hotline for runaways and their families, and that, since us boys were too busy with our comic books, she actually handled most of the calls. I looked at the jury. King-Hamilton had taken the superior sneer a tad too far and Joy had them right in the palm of her hand.

Expert witnesses are an almost mandatory interlude in an obscenity trial, but I'm really not sure how much they sway the jury. Lenny Bruce complained about the need for the defence to 'schlep up dozens of expert witnesses' to prove that his work was not obscene. Lenny very rightly contended that it reversed the entire principle of guilty until proven innocent. The onus is placed on the defence to demonstrate clearly that the material in question is innocuous, instead of the prosecution being compelled to show its potential harm. Nevertheless we followed tradition.

We brought in comic-book expert George Perry, who gave the court a concise history lesson on satire and sexuality in comic strips. He was supported by George Melly, ever-affable in his art-critic hat. Professor Bernard Crick, in his capacity as a humanist, vouched for our inner morality. Germaine took the stand, to an audible groan from both judge and prosecution, and became embroiled in a lengthy debate with the prosecuting counsel about Alexander Pope, in the course of which she cut him to shreds. It was highly entertaining, but of questionable benefit to our case.

The closing defence speeches come last, following the prosecution, and I was the final speaker. All in all, we felt that we had made our case very well up to the point when King-Hamilton reached his final summing-up. The judge went straight for the jugular, and our hearts descended to our boots. Ninety per cent of the time a jury will follow the judge's instructions, should he care to be specific, and, if he was anything, King-Hamilton was specific.

'In this country in peacetime there is no press censorship.' The statement was delivered with an expression that seemed to indicate he considered it a very bad idea. 'The body that decides if anything is obscene is not a censor, but a jury armed with common sense and good taste. The only point at issue, to wit, is whether or not this magazine is obscene. If you find any one item in the magazine obscene, it is sufficient to render the whole magazine obscene. Bear in mind the probability that some of the readers are already corrupted, but it's possible for some to be further corrupted . . . There are some items liberally sprinkled with four letters. What is the effect of them on young children? The motive of the author, artist or publisher is irrelevant. You cannot get someone to give evidence that they have been corrupted or depraved. In a civilised society there must be a line of conduct below which what is published is regarded as obscene. The position of that line is not fixed by the "New Morality Brigade", it is fixed by the public at large. Mr Farren contends that the magazine has social merit because it makes jokes about serious problems, drugs, pornography and violence. He says, "I don't have a great deal of faith in the sanctity of marriage." It may have surprised you that anyone could come forward to tell you that anything in this magazine has literary or artistic merit . . . but the world is full of surprises.'

In other words, find the scum guilty as quickly as you can, then we can all go home for tea. The jury retired and, having given our word not to leave the precincts of the Old Bailey, we were not confined to the underground cells of the labyrinth, but discovered the little-known Old Bailey bar that, for reasons we never discovered, was not subject to the prevailing licensing laws. As the long afternoon inched on, the drinking grew progressively heavier. We now had nothing to lose, and if the day was going to end in Wormwood Scrubs, I preferred to know as little as possible about it. When word came that the jury had asked if the judge would be willing to accept a majority verdict, we assumed the worst. One hold-out wanted to let us go and eleven had voted for the chop. The majority verdict was a comparatively new innovation in British law, and a few years earlier we would have walked, at least to a new trial, on a hung jury. King-Hamilton seemed also to have assumed that the majority verdict was a guilty one. He sent the jurors back for one last token try at unanimity, and then, after an hour, announced that he would go with the decision of the majority. I was less than steady as we climbed the stairs to the dock, and I was swaying when the foreman pronounced us not guilty by a majority of eleven to one.

The news took a moment to sink in. We'd done it. We'd won. King-Hamilton's face was a study in fury. The jury – his jury – had betrayed him. One of our barristers was curtly told that the judge saw no reason why we should be awarded costs, and then King-Hamilton stormed from court and all was over. After being in that dock for a subjective eternity, I experienced trouble knowing what to do next; my mind was in a state of exhausted shock. A screw ushered me into the well of the court where Ingrid, who had sat among the lawyers taking notes for the duration, took Edward and me by the arm. Joy was crying. Out in the corridor, wellwishers and the media surrounded us. Felix was shaking me by the hand. People were slapping me on the back and hugging me. Richard Neville congratulated Edward while I talked to reporters. Su Small had organised a car and a party. I was floating. Victory is sweet, oh my droogs. Don't let anyone tell you different. Nothing hollow about this one. Solid! Free at last, free at last!

We'd won, but in the next few days I had to face the fact that I was exhausted. Mercifully, Roger Hutchinson had come down from Yorkshire to replace Paul Lewis as editor. He was a good lad and could keep *IT* going. I was so creatively and emotionally tapped-out that my only viable option was to get as fucked up as possible and see where the tide might wash me.

The Great Nitrous Oxide Heist

The imagination of Philip K. Dick was hardly needed to see the situation as at least a trailer for dystopian collapse. The protracted struggle between government and unions had commenced. The era of riot shields and flying pickets was upon us. The miners had walked out in their first series of strikes, protesting against pit closures and redundancies. As the strike took hold, coal supplies to the power stations dwindled and the demand for electricity in many cities, including London, began to exceed the available supply. Emergency plans went into action. The first was to cut the industrial working week to three days, but as the miners' strike bit deeper and the power stations struggled to remain online, other more drastic measures were seen to be needed.

Rather than impose random blackouts when the capital's drain on the National Grid became more than it could handle, the city was divided into an enormous checkerboard of electric squares, measuring maybe a quarter of a mile on each side. According to a prearranged rota, alternating squares were cut off from all power for periods of around two hours. The only exceptions were hospitals, police stations and other vital services.

An alarmist might have expected angry mobs to run amok in the eerily darkened streets. Resonances of the last days of Tsarist Russia were unmistakable, but instead of rioters being cut down by Cossacks, we went visiting. People hit the streets, but not to loot and burn, only to drop in on friends who had power. Rather than sit round in a silent, candlelit flat, slowly freezing, we made our way to the home of one of the gang who continued to be blessed with TV, music and an electric fire. What did we do there? We got high-high. And, in an economy that looked about to go Weimar, a considerable degree of criminal ingenuity was needed to ensure this. One of the most ingenious schemes was the Great Nitrous Oxide Heist.

Although the statute of limitations is up many times over, I'll still refrain from revealing the names of the malefactors, even though they should have full credit for their acute observation and bold opportunism. Power was never shut off to hospitals, but even they eliminated all unnecessary lights. At St Charles Hospital, at the top of Ladbroke Grove, one of the lights deemed needless was a floodlight over a huge stack of cylinders full of both nitrous oxide and oxygen, piled against an outside wall. The light had been positioned so that the night-security guard could keep an eye on the stack, but in the energy crunch it was decided they could forgo that floodlight, reasoning that no one in their right mind would attempt to make off with these big, heavy, four-foot-long, iron cylinders. The hospital administrators hadn't, unfortunately, allowed for the deviousness or cunning of veteran, battle-hardened drugfiends, and the extremes to which they were willing to go for some novel intoxication.

No one was too interested in the oxygen, but the nitrous oxide was something else. Laughing gas, the same stuff the dentist used, and its potential for abuse had preceded it. Boss Goodman had returned from California to tell of attending a nitrous-oxide party hosted by the Hell's Angels backstage at a Grateful Dead show. This and similar tales, plus recall of post-dental hallucinations, was quite enough to convince our anonymous drugfiends that a raid on the St Charles cylinder dump would be a worthwhile caper. A truck was backed up and as many cylinders as could be manhandled into it – while the perpetrators' nerve held – were removed and driven to a basement in Cambridge Gardens.

According to Boss, the Angels' tank came with a screw-on chrome valve complete with pressure gauge and multiple hoses. Our delivery system was far less sophisticated. We opened the valve with a spanner, and gaffer-taped a length of bicycle-tyre inner tube to the nozzle. Suck on the rubber and see the elephant. When civilisation seemed to be collapsing all around us, what was there to lose? The trick was to sit on a chair or couch – part of the circle – and, when your turn came, the tank would be manoeuvred so that it was gripped between the knees. You leaned forward and twisted the spanner. As the gas flowed, ice would rapidly form on the outside of the tank, sometimes freezing your jeans to the metal as you lost consciousness. When you started to fall forward, the next person in line – who by that time had come down and wanted to go up again – would pull you off the hose, wrestle the tank from between your nerveless extremities and start again.

The joy of nitrous oxide is not only in the full-blown, candy-land hallucinations, but in the accompanying time distortion. The objective few seconds of high – before the gas is taken away by the next greedy bastard – can stretch to subjective hours. In my most vivid memories of the experience, I seemed to fly indefinitely over the bright plains and through the colourful canyons of a Dan Dare/ Flash Gordon, comic-book alien planet. A joyous experience of total escape, and it was probably lucky that our supply was limited, because we could have made incredible fools of ourselves, and maybe even sustained damage, behind the allure of the tank and hose. The aftermath of the Great Nitrous Oxide Heist had a slightly macabre air. When the original raiding party became uncomfortable with the empty tanks lying around, they decided that a second mission was called for to dump them into the Thames off Putney Bridge, a task that one of the volunteers compared to dumping bodies.

We'll Always Have Paris

I love Paris, especially in the springtime. It always reminds me of . . . teargas. It was so essentially French that its rock 'n' rollers should still be acting out the revolutionary pose when glam rock had pretty much taken over the rest of the planet. This cultural time-lag was brought forcibly home when an invitation was extended to me to perform at a Maoist rock festival at the vast Palais des Sports. The teargas in question was liberally used by the *gendarmerie* to break up the riot that ensued, both within and without the stadium. In this instance the disturbance owed absolutely nothing to any rabble-rousing on the part of the performers. As far as I could tell, it was just one more example of overexcited in-fighting on the part of various factions in the ever-volatile French Left. My hosts at this Gallic bunfight, it transpired, were Maoists, and as far as I could piece it together, they had some major beef with a Trot group who'd decided that the festival should be free and had attempted to storm the turnstiles of the big Paris stadium. The riot police had arrived with their sirens playing full third tones, and everyone immediately engaged in a spot of rock-throwing, gas-billowing, blast-from-the-past nostalgia for '68.

The Pink Fairies had also been invited to the Mao-fest, so we combined forces, giving the promoters two acts for the price of one. By this time Larry Wallis was the band's guitarist and the boy from Walworth made it easier for me to play with them, now that the negative vibes of Paul Rudolph were no longer around. The presence of Larry also helped to ensure that we confronted the French with an attitude more recalcitrant than the sum of its parts. The problem with the French is that everything has to be defined by political philosophy. A perfect example occurred on the night we arrived in town. We had been taken by our Maoist hosts to La Coupole. The restaurant had such a tradition of catering to all of bohemian Paris, since who knows when, that it was possible to find punks at the bar rubbing shoulders with left-wing politicians. What looked like a bike gang walked in, and I enquired of my comrade host who they might be. He replied that they were Stalinists, and we shouldn't have anything to do with them. I could only shrug. They looked like a bunch of drunken French bikers to me, but what did I know?

Very little, it would seem. At the end of the meal the hosts declared the idea of the promoters buying dinner for the musicians a bourgeois concept, and we were expected to pay for our own Steak Tartare. Crème Brûlée and the gallons of booze we'd consumed. The Pink Fairies and I were aghast. Maoist they might be, but they looked like *escargot*-fed rich kids, and instantly we registered our displeasure at this sudden attack of inappropriate Red Guard socialism by rising as one from our seats and leaving them stuck with the bill. To add greater injury, H, who was the general English-contingent escort and make-it-nice-and-easy guy, grinned at us. 'I nicked their car keys.'

The Maoists had been driving around in a large, almost new Mercedes, which, led by H, we then proceeded to commandeer. On returning to our hotel in Pigalle sometime around dawn, we were confronted by our decidedly angry hosts.

'You steal our car.'

We shook our heads. 'We borrow your car.'

And H, who spoke perfect French but didn't choose to, explained, 'We decided that we were putting the *people*'s car to the best possible use.'

The next day was even better. We'd been flown into town a couple of days early so that we could do some radio and TV promotion, which involved the consumption of more alcohol, and also left us plenty of time to take the Metro to Clichy to pay homage to Henry Miller and buy illegal flick-knives to smuggle home with us. Since the Maoists no longer wanted to come out to play with us class traitors, we saw them only when they came to collect us for a visit to a radio or TV station, and even these short exposures to our collectively swinish Anglo-behaviour were enough to bring down the disapprobation of what we termed the 'attitude squad'. We avoided them, and they avoided us, and the net result was that Larry,

Sandy, Boss, Russell, Little Ian, Larry's mate Al, H and I were pretty much left to our own devices. To leave a rock & roll band in a romantic foreign city with too much time on their hands is invariably a bad idea, and this occasion proved no exception.

The phone call came at about the point when we were going to do something gauche and stupid, like vanishing into the stripjoints of Pigalle. The only other alternative was to troop out to Père Lachaise cemetery and light a candle on Jim Morrison's grave. John Fenton was on the phone. He was at 'this place in Odeon' where we 'wouldn't believe what was going down'. Fenton was a longtime rock & roll hustler who had come into the business as a very young man, working on Beatlemania merchandising. He won his spurs in the era of the wild and crazy rock & roll managers like Andrew Loog Oldham and Tony Secunda, but had, I think, knocked a few synapses out of whack during the psychedelic finale to the Sixties. He had then decided – Ken Kesey notwithstanding – that electric-shock therapy was the answer and, after a protracted treatment of voltage jolts, he recommended the juice to all and sundry for everything that might mentally ail them. (I'll pass, thank you, John.) In the wake of the ECT, John had embraced the idea of rock & roll revolution, and had taken on the management of a band called Third World War. This was a quartet of pre-punk, semi-skinheads, whose songs like 'Ascension Day', 'Teddy Teeth Goes Sailing' and 'Preaching Violence' advocated an armed, working-class uprising as Britain's only salvation. In many ways they were a near-precursor of the Clash.

At 'this place in Odeon', the excursion decisively shifted gear. I don't know what you call a service flat in Paris. With decor as impersonal as my hotel suite, the moderately large apartment was designed for a more protracted but equally anonymous stay. Although solid background facts were, even then, as blurred as our brains, the place appeared to belong to a character called Marie-France, a pre-operative transsexual who, at the moment we arrived, was testing the homophobic limits of Third World War by parading around stark naked, apart from red high heels, lipstick and mascara. Marie-France had clearly been taking killer hormones, which had made her almost all woman, from her blonde perm to her feminine hips and *Playboy* Playmate breasts that I could only imagine had come courtesy of a fine plastic surgeon. A tiny set of genitals were all that remained of her former masculinity, presumably shrunk by the medication. Third World War seemed uncomfortable, but were trying to act sophisticated. Fenton was enjoying the joke, and H was grinning broadly, taking all at face value, having probably witnessed weirder things in his times with Zappa and Hendrix.

I think Fenton had half-expected us to freak out at the unexpected nude apparition, but we'd really come too far to be shocked by mere sexual oddities. It would surely take plague or mass murder to upset us now. Marie-France also had a friend, whose name I think was René, but I wouldn't bet money on it. He was an equally attractive and feminine young man, but more in a Françoise Hardy mode, a definite counterpoint to Marie-France's Marilyn impersonation, and, for the moment, he was keeping his frock on. I guess the moment of truth came when Marie-France climbed onto Larry's lap, and Larry had to make the decision for all of us. The situation, as I read it, was pretty much thus: Mick Farren and the Pink Fairies, both collectively and singly might have been essentially heterosexual, but had fostered a reputation – a notoriety even – as supposed connoisseurs of the bizarre, and the bizarre was now squirming on the guitarist's lap. He could figuratively and actually drop Marie-France on his bare arse, or enter one more of those portals of excess that we still fondly believed led to the Palace of Wisdom. Larry, God bless him, made the correct choice for any seeker after truth. He started playfully necking with Marie-France, although he hedged his bets by changing her name, right there and then, to 'Murray French', using a broad South London pronunciation.

'Okay, Murray French, so where are we going?'

Marie-France seemed a little mystified, so Larry amplified. 'I mean, we're in Paris. We don't want to sit around here all night, do we?'

It wasn't only a matter of insatiable bi-curiosity. The vanguard theorem of rock 'n' roll had been 'deliberate gender confusion is a body blow to the system' for the previous eighteen months. Indeed, Larry had even written a song, 'I Wish I Was a Girl'. Honour dictated that we must pursue this line of investigation without fear or favour to wherever it might take us. Although he may not always have adhered to its edicts, Larry Wallis has a very well-developed sense of honour. Out on a spree or damned to eternity, we were in for the penny, and the pound was somewhere in front of us. We weren't needed for anything until a two o'clock sound-check the next afternoon. At something around nine in the evening, we had some seventeen hours to quest into the unknown and clearly it was time to get questing.

Out on the streets we were treated to a new and unknown Paris. In this magical time, before HIV was gene-spliced at Fort Detrick, Maryland, Paris had seemingly become the transvestite capital of the planet, and we were getting the grand tour of this very Parisian velvet underground. We club-hopped and took cabs to scarlet streets of shame. The very chicest of the transgender chic had flocked to Paris in their tens of thousands. In addition to the domestic *royales*, crops of Spanish boys flourished, having fled Franco and never gone home. (Let's not forget that the Generalissimo, the last of the classic Euro-fascists, only died in 1975.) Arab and Afro exotics from former French colonies were already on the run from rock-throwing Muslim fundamentalists, while a large contingent of Brazilians flashed and glittered, but I never did find out what their story might be. Social research was all too quickly drowned in a near-overdose of Pernod and glamour. Marie-France was welcomed by sisters every place we went, and I suspect she may well have scored *beaucoup* brownie points for bringing along this hard-drinking, rough-trade rock band, all lace, leather, butch poses and unkempt hair. Maybe these were the new gender-revolt groupies. We did find ourselves arriving at one place as Brian Eno and other members of Roxy Music were leaving.

In an interlude in Les Halles, we stopped for oysters at a market stall, where one was supposed to shuck open the molluscs with a very sharp dagger-like implement. (In Paris, people do things like stop for oysters.) At the oyster stand all I succeeded in achieving was to stab myself in the fleshy part of my left hand and bleed copiously. It hurt, but it certainly got René's attention. (Or maybe it wasn't René, but someone exactly like him. Being drunk in a place you don't speak the language can be exceedingly dislocating.) He bound up my wound and generally comforted me, and somehow we found our way into two cabs, which Marie-France instructed to take us all back to our hotel. The party was being taken off the streets to relocate behind closed doors. The numbers, however, had been whittled down to just Marie-France, René, the Pink Fairies and me. We had mislaid Fenton, Third World War and, unfortunately, H along the way.

Needless to say, we walked into the hotel lobby as if we owned the place, which, to our mind we did. It was our hotel and what we did there was nobody's business but our own. (Unless, of course, the *gendarmerie* came into the picture.) The night clerk didn't exactly see it that way. At the sight of Marie-France and René, he bounded out from behind his desk, arms spread, barring our passage. After a great deal of verbal confusion, Sandy (the only one of us who spoke French) informed the rest of us that we were not allowed to take women to our rooms. It was hard to know where to direct our fury. The night clerk either needed bribing or punching, but the French Maoists were also targets of wrath. What was it with these lame bastards? First they expected us to pay for our own welcome-to-Paris dinner party, and now they'd booked us into a hotel where the night clerk was also the custodian of morality. (And anyway, you bloody fool, they aren't girls at all!) Cursing the Maoists and railing at the night clerk didn't get us anywhere except to set the clerk rumbling something about the aforementioned *gendarmerie*. Marie-France and René had a fast discussion in French, and then Larry and I were pulled out into yet another cab. Russell started to follow us, but the cab driver objected to taking five. Marie-France yelled an address at Russell, but he looked baffled.

A half-hour later Larry and I found ourselves swilling warm and naked gin while our every need was ministered to by these adoring creations of the Paris night, without a qualm or backward glance, and with an almost total lack of conversation. The wisdom was confirmed. Sexual deviance is actually very simple. You just don't think about it. Turn off your mind and your arse will float downstream. Or, as Obi Won Kenobi would put it, 'Put your trust in the Force, Luke.'

We must have slept/passed out for a few hours, because the next thing I knew it was one-fifteen, just forty-five minutes to the sound-check, and I was only starting to face the day and the hangover. The other three looked as bad as I felt; plus Marie-France and René, considerably less adoring now, wanted us the fuck out of there. They were already putting on their make-up, preparing to go about their transvestite day business. Larry and I regarded an inch of gin left in a bottle on the kitchen table. Would we sink that low? Of course we would. We both took a swig and headed out to get a cab to the Palais des Sports, and the sound-check for which we were already unforgivably late. Arriving at the gig, we discovered the stadium was in a state of siege. The anti-Maoists were picketing violently and the riot squad had resorted to gas. Fortunately the pig-headedness and cop-hate of the Parisian cab driver worked for us this time, and ultimately we made it to the artists' entrance and found our way to the stage, looking bleary and tousled, only to discover that we were the lead subject of the day's backstage gossip. The story had already made the rounds that Farren and Wallis had vanished into the night with a gang of hot and heavy drag queens. A writer from *Sounds* had been along for the ride. I think the intention was that he should write nice things about Third World War; instead, he led with the tale of Mick 'n' Larry's cross-gender vanishing act.

The show was uneventful, apart from the odd catch of old teargas in the throat. We weren't great, but we weren't terrible, and we did have a huge stadium stage to ponce around on. When we weren't playing, Daevid Allen and the rest of Gong took us under their wing and introduced us to *Monsieur Le Dealer*, and smoking hash became the order of the rest of the day. Marie-France turned up looking heavily drugged and oddly unkempt. The magic had gone, and Larry and Sandy were now busy trying to pick some real girls. The next morning we found ourselves forced to do a runner from the hotel when it turned out that the Maoists weren't able to pay the bill. We arrived at the airport just as a massive thunderstorm blew up out of nowhere and all planes were grounded. Even when the storm passed and take-offs were resumed, an Air France official brought us the news that our plane wouldn't leave for a few more hours, but drinks and dinner were on the airline. The free stuff failed to mollify us. After all we'd been through, we turned ugly. We demanded to know the nature of the fucking problem, except for Sandy, who had wisely ingested all the drugs on his person so that he'd be clean going through Heathrow Customs and was now hard-pressed to do anything but stand and sway.

'Your plane has unfortunately been struck by lightning.'

'Our plane has been struck by lightning?'

'*Exactement*.'

Our plane had been struck by lightning. Find that in your phrasebook.

Chapter Nine

Settle Down and Write a Book

Have you ever noticed how few directors can make a convincing movie about a novelist at work? Usually the actor playing the novelist hammers away on a manual typewriter until he has a pile of paper about half an inch thick and then declares it a novel. Oddly enough, that's about the thickness of a short movie script. Even a modest novel is at least two inches thick, and the manuscript of a real epic takes both hands to lift. The two movies that, for me, most accurately reflect how it feels to wrestle with the problem of writing fiction are *The Shining* and *Misery*, and both, of course, are based on the work of Stephen King. You see where I'm going with this? The act of writing may contain a definite element of horror.

In *The Shining* Jack Nicholson explains to wife Shelley Duvall how he isn't writing just when she hears his typewriter clacking. He's writing when he isn't typing; he's writing when he's just staring into space; he's even writing when he's stretched out on the couch with his eyes closed. He makes it clear that writing is a continuous and neverending process. Of course, Jack is wrestling with both alcoholism and paranormal demons, but what's new about that in the writing game? *Misery* is far more allegorical. The demented Angel of Death, serial-killer nurse and number-one-fan, played by Kathy Bates, forces the injured James Caan to write one more of the romance novels he's so come to loathe, going all the way to smashing his ankles with a sledgehammer to keep him focused. The Kathy Bates character is, of course, another kind of demon, the muse grown psychotic, the demands of editors and agents, the public who can make or break you. All the combined factors that simply will not allow the writer to halt the process are embodied in one horrendous personality.

The joke about the writer's primary function being to avoid writing is, at best, a very marginal one. In the new life I was constructing for myself after the *Nasty Tales* trial and the gradual collapse of the underground press, I discovered plenty of ways to delay the inevitable. I would get up at around noon, and go down to a pub called the Princess Alexandra where I could expect to find a quorum of a drinking crew that included Edward, Boss, Roger Hutchinson, John Manly, a friend of John's with the impossible name of Andy Colquhoun, Lemmy and Dikmik from Hawkwind, and maybe Russell or Sandy from the Pink Fairies. The Princess Alexandra (the Alex) was diagonally across Portobello Road from Henekey's, the prime freak pub of the time. We had moved across the street, almost in protest, when the carriage trade in Henekey's grew too intrusive and we started feeling like a collective tourist attraction. The Alex had nothing going for it except that no one went there, and it had a pool table in the back. The pub would cover me until after three, but then I had to get down to the dreaded process of writing.

Ingrid and I had moved back into the Grove. After a couple of loud parties, the raid by Special Branch and a low-key feud between Boss and Ingrid over conduct in the kitchen, we had worn out our welcome at Clifton Gardens. But by a unique rental synchronicity. Joy and Jamie moved out of Chesterton Road to share an expensively large flat off the Old Brompton Road with publisher William Bloom, whom Jamie had persuaded to publish his first novel; there they would remain until the end of their relationship. (As, indeed, Ingrid and I would remain at Chesterton Road until the end of ours.) Although the top-floor flat at 56 Chesterton Road was not as spacious as Clifton Gardens, it had the feel of a protective eyrie in which I could hole up and get on with the next phase of my life.

The underground press had gone down with a certain slow dignity. *OZ* had been put to sleep in the wake of the trial, with the mutual consent of Jim, Felix and Richard. *Friends* (later known as *Frendz* after a debt-dodging legal restructure) hung on for as long as it could, but the debts rapidly returned, as formidable as ever. Roger, Caroline and Edward kept *IT* rolling for the longest, but they too were unable to solve the constant financial problems. It wasn't so much that the underground papers had run their course. Corporate publishing now moved in on the more viable areas of the underground press and co-opted them.

The first publications that invaded what had previously been our turf were the four national weekly music papers – *Melody Maker*, *New Musical Express*, *Disc* and *Sounds*. Already engaged in their own war of attrition, they leeched away the advertising and, with their large circulation and real national distribution, got preferential treatment from artists and publicists. In many respects the music papers had no choice. With a rock culture growing freakier by the minute, they were compelled to get freaky themselves. Nick Logan, the bright ex-mod who ran *NME*, seemed best equipped to make the transition and keep up with the speed of change. Where the other editors had neither the courage nor the knowledge to go for it, and constantly hesitated on the brink, fearful that every trend was a just a nine-day wonder, Logan appeared to have a similar bellwether instinct to David Bowie. He was also able to delegate and was the first to make the radical, but wholly obvious, move of actually hiring some writers who had cut their teeth, won their spurs, made their bones – whatever rite-of-passage cliché you might favour – in the underground. The first and, in my opinion, the best were Charles Shaar Murray, an early protégé of Felix and one of the *Schoolkid's OZ* collective, and Nick Kent, who had started to build a rep for himself as a rock correspondent-in-the-field at *Frendz*.

Logan was also keeping a firm eye on a magazine coming out of Detroit called *Creem*. Where *Rolling Stone* had become pious and patronising, and was close to being in the pockets of the big record companies, *Creem* was wild and reckless. Best of all, the formula was working. As the anti-*Rolling Stone* mag, *Creem* was building itself a readership that outstripped that of any underground paper and put it on the way to being a US national magazine. In a strictly rock & roll context, *Creem* was actually achieving the over-under crossover, and publisher Barry Kramer was doing it out of a commune in Walled Lake, Michigan, still with enough of a foot in the counterculture for the FBI to have the magazine under surveillance for a while, as a possible safe-house for the revolutionary bombers of the Weather Underground. *Creem*, however, wasn't looking back at the Sixties, or attempting to gene-slice rock 'n' roll into some James Taylor orthodoxy. *Creem* was a magazine of the raw, urban and teenage. *Creem* liked the dumb. Its logo was an anthropomorphic cartoon beer can that greeted readers with the cheery slogan 'Boy howdy!' It championed the likes of Alice Cooper, Bowie, Roxy Music, the Stooges, Lou Reed, the New York Dolls and the MC5. Kramer also had two powerful writing machines. Dave Marsh may well have been the best-informed rock critic on the planet, and Lester Bangs — poor dead-before-his-time Lester — was the passionate and unrivalled gonzo stylist. Logan was buying reprints of Bangs and Marsh, plus other *Creem* luminaries like Ben Edmunds and Jaan Uhelszki, and running them in *NME*. He was one of the few who knew in his gut that punk was coming.

My own recruitment to *NME* was still a while down the pike. In the meantime, I had to concentrate on my writing, and put it out there to be judged, without the protection of my own publication. With ultimately narcissistic nepotism, I had been my own editor and publisher for what was now running to two or three years. This had to stop. I needed to see if I could survive in the real world, buy groceries and pay the rent on my craft and talent. The material problems could, at least in part, be solved in the scuzzy editorial offices of various T&A girlie magazines, and by the chance to supply mildly raunchy grey text at 10p a word, to go between the colour spreads of naked women.

Maybe some are still under the illusion that writing for the girlie glossies in that libertine era was a died-and-gone-to-heaven, Hugh Hefner fantasy of casting couches, hot tubs and hot running bimbos. The truth was quite depressingly the opposite. The words that spring to mind are, at best, tacky; at worst, wretched. The truth is that all but the most prestigious of skin monthlies were produced out of publishing sweatshops, where the only women were serious secretaries, bookkeepers and picture editors. The girlie sets came from agencies who specialised in that kind of thing, and no vast-breasted models were ever to be seen in the organic flesh. The girlie-mag industry was also chickenshit in the extreme. When we turned in our copy, they worried about lesbianism; and ambiguity frightened them. Don't even mention S&M or bondage; plus, we writers were expected to remain within the strict vocabulary of the near-illiterate.

In the USA, Larry Flynt was pushing the envelope by making *Hustler* increasingly gynaecological. In Europe hard porn was selling on the newsstands, but in London publishers like Paul Raymond agonised over how far they might push an already sagging envelope. *Nasty Tales* had inadvertently given them a gift. After our court victory, it was tacitly assumed that almost anything in print was legal, if it was clearly marked ADULTS ONLY, but the T&A publishers still cringed and worried. Every now and then I might get an honest-to-God short fiction piece published, or be assigned a medium-cool, true-crime story, but most of the time the whole transaction was extremely depressing, except for the moment the cheque fell through the letter box.

With a facility for language, and an extremely well-developed imagination, I clearly deserved more than a life hacking for skin mags. The primary target had to be books – specifically a novel – and I figured I was ready for it. Edward and I had already done a slim piece of non-fiction that William Bloom had published during the brief time he had an imprint at Hutchinson, before he went off to the Sahara and became a Sufi or something. *Watch Out, Kids* was a colourful and graphic-intensive history of youth rebellion, and a fairly wild countercultural political statement. It might well have been called *The IT Annual*, heavy as it was with the best of underground graphics, but the text was all mine, so I got the glory – such as it was. For some reason, though, I've always felt that fiction is the highest form of writing and, with the same recklessness with which I dived into the Deviants, I figured I was ready for the plunge into a novel. I'd been honing my imagination since I was a small child, when I'd spent a lot of time in retreat, passing otherwise unbearable periods in fully formed and highly detailed fantasy worlds. Thus I opted for a form of science fiction. Fantasy, I figured, was a fine way of avoiding the issue of how much of myself I was really prepared to reveal – as though I seriously believed that one could hide anything behind exposed fantasies. I guess if I hadn't had that illusion of detachment, I would never have had the courage to get started.

Arrogant as ever, though, science fiction had to be written according to my own terms. Too many psychedelics had flashed through my neurons for me to write any *Dan Dare: Pilot of the Future*, no matter how many millions George Lucas might be investing to make *Star Wars* the most magnificent Saturday-morning serial of all time. Science fiction had experienced a revolution in the mid-Sixties with the so-called New Wave. Kurt Vonnegut, Brian Aldiss, Harlan Ellison, Samuel R. Delany, Thomas Disch and the mighty, amphetamine-fuelled Philip K. Dick had all banished space opera. They concurred with T. S. Eliot: the way might well be hidden in the mind. Argument continued as to whether William Burroughs could be classified as a science-fiction writer. My vote was a wholehearted yes, but others tended to disagree. Uncle Bill was, of course, the pinnacle to which I aspired, but knowing considerably more about literature than I'd know about music at the start of the Deviants, I was well aware that aspiring was about the outer limit of my capability. I needed to prove I could write a novel before I started deconstructing the form.

When I was a very small boy, I evolved a formula for climbing Mount Everest. Knowing next to nothing about mountaineering, death or the limitations of human endurance, I figured it was just a matter of putting one foot in front of the other, and not stopping until I reached the top. In a later state of innocence, I decided the writing of a novel could be achieved by much the same process, maybe with the addition of the old Daffy Duck admonition never to look down when you're walking off the edge of the cliff into thin air. The novelist started on page one and advanced page by page until eventually he came to the conclusion. In the case of this first novel, I was even ahead of the game. I already had the first fifteen or sixteen pages in the form of a short story. All that remained was for me to create a suitable environment in which to write.

An awful lot of nonsense has been said about the writer and his environment. Some writers can be positively fetishistic about their working conditions. When Jack, in *The Shining*, tells Shelley that he needs absolute peace and quiet, his character is, of course, already insane. I would set far more store by Charlie Bukowski, who figured that 'no writer worth a damn ever wrote in peace and quiet'. The great New York sports writer Red Smith is another source of irrefutable truth for the neophyte. 'There's nothing to writing. All you do is sit down and open a vein.' I quickly discovered that opening the vein is the hard part – that's what hurts – and the bleeding is relatively painless. Thus the old gag about 'avoiding writing' is really an explanation of how starting requires all the effort, but, once you get under way, you're in the fantasy world moving your characters through wondrous places on adventures that are – you hope – much more exciting than the mundane room in which you're doing the work.

Rarefied peace and quiet might have been nice, but I suspect – even had it been possible – it would have produced a prose style equally rarefied and, for me, wholly unacceptable. My instincts were to go with the Bukowski maxim, but I really had little or no choice in the matter. Ladbroke Grove was a turbulent environment of incipient crisis, seductive stimulants, constant distraction and people dropping by. Lemmy, now playing bass for Hawkwind, could be counted on to turn up at all hours of the day or night, as speed challenged him to go for days on end without sleep and he felt the need for company or to borrow money. John Manly, a local entrepreneur, came over pretty regularly, sometimes with guitar player Andy Colquhoun, allowing Andy and I to make the first acquaintance that slowly but ultimately led to friendship, and then to a songwriting and performing partnership that would last into the next millennium. Gwen might stop by from time to time, as did Mark Williams, and Felix when he could be dragged out of the West End. Of course Edward, Boss, Gez and Roger Hutchinson were always in and out, although Gez came less frequently after he shacked up with a woman called Tuppy Owens, a rising mogul in the sex-toy industry.

The traffic was heavy around Chesterton Road, but the fledgling author adapted accordingly. Indeed, the furious energy that some critics claimed was the overwhelming strength of my first efforts may well have been a product of the equally energetic environment. Ingrid and I lived a near-Japanese, floor-based existence. We formed our personal nests. Books, pads, pens, drinks, toys, unanswered mail, the flick-knife from Paris, an antique Navy Colt revolver, a green telephone and a red tray with a picture of a Vargas pin-up girl, which contained the house drugs and paraphernalia, all lay around within easy reach. (Look, Ma, no coffee table.) All was observed by a moth-eaten stuffed ant-eater that Lemmy had christened Mrs Anderson, which he would inherit when I left town. A human skull that Ingrid had given me for Christmas took pride of shelf space, and I still have it to this day.

Phone ringing, TV blaring, I wrote – stoned or straight – a green rollerball pen moving compulsively across yellow legal pads. Despite all the interruptions, even with company, even through adventures with Parisian drag queens, I wrote, and Ingrid organised the flow. She edited, advised and copy typed. I suppose some might find this sexist and exploitative, but at the time I was on an astonishing roll, and she seemed happy to be a part of it. She might not agree after all these years, but I can't say; you'd have to ask her. Sometimes I wrote the novel, at other times I hacked nonsense for the rent. Nonsense and the novel, the novel and nonsense, a continuous cycle, heading into a whole new creative territory.

Kill 'Em and Eat 'Em

In the darkness before the dawn, the acid still hadn't run its course, but a certain resignation had set in and, with it, a demented feeling that we were never to leave the place. We were doomed for ever to this field, like rock & roll Flying Dutchmen. The question that then presented itself was: how would we survive? The conversational carousel went round and round, and the painted ponies – as was still their wont – went up and down and kept telling us that cannibalism was the only answer.

'Kill 'em and eat 'em.'

The sequence of events that had brought us to the very precipital edge of eating our own had started eight hours earlier, in mid-afternoon, when John the Bog, the old-time acid dealer from Middle Earth, who had earned his nickname because his place of business was the men's lavatory, showed up in our camp. He came equipped with a bottle of liquid lysergic acid, of the sinister colour that's now known as *X-Files* green, but back then didn't even have a name. The collective – comprising the Pink Fairies, the former underground press gang and a slew of other Ladbroke Grove reprobates – formed a line and held out their right hands, palms down, fists loosely clenched. John produced an eye dropper and proceeded down the line as though inspecting the platoon. He dropped a roughly measured dose on the back of each of our hands. The idea was that we should consume the psychedelic by licking the stain on our skin, but even before I could do that, I felt a distinct tingle as some of the drug was already being dermally absorbed. The tingle told me the stuff was maybe the strongest I'd ever encountered, and it carried the promise that anything could happen. With the acid on the back of my hand, and obviously too late now to turn back, I licked, along with all the rest, and away we went.

The Wheeley Rock Festival, one of the last of the big Sixties-style events to be held in the Seventies, had proved a mess from start to finish. Fires had started in the dry grass on the camp site and a couple of cars had exploded in flames. An alliance of outlaw motorcycle clubs had gone toe-to-toe in a grudge match with the festival security, but were soundly routed. The Pink Fairies had been effectively too hammered to play, but had gone on anyway. As the hallucinatory night dragged on, we hit the wall of acid boredom and started to convince ourselves that we were living in the most final of the Final Days, condemned to endure the fall of civilisation on this wretched festival site. We knew we'd survive, the only question was by what means. No matter how many times we approached the problem, or from what direction, we kept coming back to the inescapable conclusion. By far the least complicated solution would be to live off the flesh of all these worthless, witless, left-over hippies.

'Kill 'em and eat 'em.'

Finally Boss had enough. He seized an army-surplus machete, which had been brought down as part of our festival equipment. 'I'm going out to get dinner!'

After his dramatic exit, the rest of us looked at each other. In one possible future, Boss would return dragging a dead hippie by the foot and, at that juncture, we would be morally obligated to eat the kill, abandoning all pretence of humanity. As it turned out, Boss didn't return for maybe an hour or more, and when he did he seemed to have forgotten the whole thing, although he did remember to bring the machete back. Mercifully, we'd been spared damnation, but I couldn't help but wonder if that was the kind of incident that had launched the Manson family. I felt this was a serious LSD near-miss, and decided, in the future, that the horror show always lurking beneath the surface must be strictly confined to fiction.

Aid and Comfort to *NME*

The first story I wrote for *NME* was about the Bruce Lee cult. For a while I'd watched the rock weekly move closer and closer to becoming a faux-underground paper (as far as anything could be faux-underground inside the monolithic International Publishing Corporation that, at the time, owned everything from the *Daily Mirror* to *Woman's Own*), but I'd avoided making any moves in that direction. The initial overture had come from Charles Shaar Murray at a party on Portobello Road. He suggested that I should meet Ian McDonald, the deputy editor, I guess as a preliminary to going one-on-one with Nick Logan. I'd heard that I made Logan nervous, and maybe he felt he needed an initial buffer. McDonald – I-Mac as he was universally known – was one of the gentlest and most soul-searching cats I've ever encountered. He made me extremely welcome and comfortable. He knew I viewed working for IPC as somewhere between taking the king's shilling and cutting a deal with Lucifer, and was racked with ambiguity.

At first I'd tried to have my cake and eat it, too, by writing about anything but music. Like I said, Bruce Lee, *Star Trek* and Evel Knievel's jetbike. I thought if I didn't actually get into the rock-crit business, I could stay honest. But who did I think I was kidding? I knew there's no such thing as a demi-virgin or part-time whore, so in the end I figured I might as well get stuck in with the rest. Germaine hadn't called me a wheezing Jeremiah for nothing. With the clout and contacts to ensure my choice of assignments, I commenced mercilessly laying about the fools and philistines of rock-biz like Jesus clearing the temple. Rock & roll had sunk to that slough of pampered foolishness where Yes, Deep Purple and ELP were regarded as truly great musicians, and tours by the Rolling Stones, Led Zeppelin or the Who would be a mobile, multimillion-dollar bacchanalia involving private jets, helicopters, convoys of majestic Kenilworth semi-trucks and limousines driven into hotel swimming pools. Drug abuse wasn't considered fun unless it was a dance with death, groupie culture had reached its orgiastic pinnacle and the nuts were running the fruitcake. Friday afternoons at most major record labels in London, New York and Los Angeles were completely consumed by the business of arranging the weekend's cocaine supply. Nothing was a higher priority.

In the middle of all this major lunacy, Nick Kent and Charlie Murray were gleefully using *NME* to promote themselves as stars in their own right. The critic as celeb. As physical figures, Kent and Murray couldn't have been more dissimilar. Kent was tall and narrow, epicene and wasted, a definite Keith Richards clone in tattered black leather and grubby silk scarves, like Isadora Duncan on methadone. Charlie, on the other hand, was a nervously determined young man with an Hebraic afro, a wardrobe inspired by the E Street Band and a devotee of amphetamine sulphate. The pair's commonality was as kick-arse and opinionated writers, with a devotion to rock 'n' roll like diamonds in their prose.

That I should join them as another bullshit star byline seemed manageable. What *NME* needed to complete the team was a gonzo alcoholic who knew the Bukowski-Thompson opening tactic of starting a story by describing the hangover. If I couldn't lose myself in the role, I could just about lose my self-loathing, provided I dived deep enough. If you're going to behave disgracefully, go the whole hog and be hanged for a goat. As I saw it, a personality cult forming around a writer is actually not a bad thing. It worked for Frank Harris, Damon Runyon, Dorothy Parker, Marge Proops, Jimmy Breslin, Harlan Ellison, Pete Hammill and Hunter S. Thompson. At *Creem*, Lester Bangs was single-handedly raising the circulation and, back home, the punters seemed to love it when Kent feuded with Lou Reed, or Bryan Ferry took umbrage at some comment of Charlie's. The readership could agree or violently object, but at least they were able to rest assured they were getting the straight dope, because they knew exactly where the writer was coming from. While Jann Wenner at *Rolling Stone* reduced his writers to Stepford typists by forbidding them to trash the stars, Logan gave us our head and we built up a readership of comprehensive-school misfits who dug and depended on our shtick.

The free stuff was also a great temptation.

With UK radio still a thing of pathos, the weekly music rags had a massive influence on record sales, and the record labels would do just about anything to get our attention, short of sending over a hooker and an envelope of money. (This had proved just *too* illegal in the

Alan Freed Fifties.) The payola and record-industry perks started out as seductive and, once we were corrupted, exceedingly handy, not to say needed. Stuff came from the record companies all the time. They sent us T-shirts, workshirts, bowling jackets, Levi jackets, cheap watches and junk jewellery, silk scarves and cowboy belt buckles, mechanical toys and other bits of crap and, of course, the inexhaustible supply of duff records that could be traded for a quid or so at the Record Exchange on Golborne Road. One Christmas, Company A sent over a case of Remy Martin, while Company B gave each of us a small mirror bearing a picture of the world's most famous wabbit eating a carrot, and later a publicity hack came round to fill the mirrors for us. Best of all, they'd fly us to exotic and romantic places, limousine-class all the way, to see their rotten bands in the best and most lavish circumstances.

The irony in all this was that the freebies made not the slightest difference to what we wrote. That's the trick of the inveterate renegade. Take the bribe, but never deliver. I don't believe that Kent, Murray, Chris Salewicz, Max Bell or I ever wrote a good piece about a lousy band because we'd been pimp-stroked by a publicist. Indeed, sometimes quite the reverse. If a company steamed in too hard with the gifts and junkets, it created suspicion. Why was the hype so desperate? Was someone up there less than confident?

The further I penetrated *NME*, the more freedom Nick Logan seemed willing to offer me, to the point that he asked if I wanted to edit a new front section of pictures, gossip and fast-punch short items. The name of this short-attention-span section was 'Thrills' – and I went for it. I never could resist playing newspapers, and this gave me a chance to continue the kind of pre-*USA Today* stuff we'd tried at *IT*. I also negotiated a fairly attractive rate for these short items, and very quickly a number of the writers – Max Bell, Chris Salewicz, Angie Errigo, Julie Webb, even Charlie, all rowed in with the kind of stuff I needed. Chrissie Hynde cut her journalistic teeth on 'Thrills', Bob Geldof sent items from Dublin and Lisa Robinson filed a regular report on the latest from Manhattan in general and Max's Kansas City in particular. Photographers Pennie Smith and Joe Stevens, both graduates of *IT* and *Frendz*, knew I'd always run a picture of a superstar looking inane or witless.

The great advantage of the 'Thrills' section was that it gave everyone the chance to write about subjects other than music. In addition to rock-world gossip – like Cher's plastic surgery, Keith Richards' Swiss blood changes, and speculation about what the hell might be wrong with Elvis Presley as he grew visibly fatter and madder – I also ran TV-related stories, bits on movies and comic books, and fashion *in extremis*. Old underground press contacts came up with stories on bizarre media events, weird performance art, animal rights, the environment, recreational drugs and drug enforcement. I was also able to run cartoons on a regular basis, recruit Edward and other former *Nasty Tales* contributors, and include a weekly contribution by Ray Lowry, possibly the greatest rock 'n' roll single-frame cartoonist of all time. Beyond that it came down to anything that took my fancy. Logan might look wearily askance when I added a story about zoo-bound penguins incinerated in a cargo-plane disaster, but he'd let it run. Later in the game, after Logan had recruited a frightened and occasionally frightening young writer by the name of Julie Burchill, the eccentric grew sickly weird.

Julie Burchill claimed that she had tried for the job on *NME* because, as a bi-sexual fan, she wanted to meet Patti Smith. She had apparently swung Nick Logan to her side by a brilliant self-serving instinct to drop names heavy with mod cachet, like the Isley Brothers, Arthur Coney and Eddie Kendricks. She was comprehensively uneducated, but learning at an alarming rate, and she had a facility with words that I, at least, recognised as outstanding. I was certain Burchill would turn out to be a fearsomely self-promoting talent, but after a couple of juvenile indiscretions on her part, Logan bowed to record-company pressure not to let her loose on their artists. She was seconded to 'Thrills' for Lois Lane duty, and every morning she took an expense-account cab to the cosmopolitan newsagents on Old Compton Street to grab all the magazines that took her fancy and then comb them for the peculiar, the bizarre and the fatuous. A waste in that she really needed to write, but at least she could be moderately happy looking through magazines and sharpening her nails, while pulling me the most twisted stories she could find. Hideous death in the Philippines. Virgin Mary frenzy in Guatemala. Frustration builds motivation.

Moving in the 'Thrills' pages away from strict rock coverage was, however, sowing the seeds of a definite identity crisis at the paper. The circulation climbed like a Titan missile. We topped *Melody Maker*, the previous market leader, and strutted round like high roosters on the dung-heap. I might be working for the Man, but at least I had hundreds of thousands of young minds to deprave and corrupt. Winning a circulation war may be the ultimate glory, but it doesn't always make for a happy ship. *NME* editorial was seriously divided. On one side, the underground-press vets, and those who'd come after – Chris Salewicz, Pete Erskine, Max Bell – all considered ourselves the agents of glory. Across the schism, the original staff, from the days when rock criticism was little more than the rewriting of press releases, felt eclipsed and threatened by this flashy clique. Traditionally *NME* was – by very definition – a music paper pure and simple; for music, by music and of music. We radicals argued that the paper must grow to be more than that; establishing a cultural connection with a young and significant audience, now that reader estimates had exceeded one million. Why not have an editorial policy that accepted the readership was united by rock & roll but didn't end there? The related, but non-musical, was also needed. The Seventies were hopping, and we needed to report how high.

Cinema, as one example, was in a golden age. In 1971 Stanley Kubrick showed, if not the shape of youth to come, then at least its attitudes in *A Clockwork Orange*. In 1973 *The Exorcist* triggered incidents of infanticide and baby roasting by religious psychotics across the planet. In 1976 *Taxi Driver* had as much to say about pressure psychosis and moral bankruptcy as Patti Smith's 'Piss Factory', and even gave Joe Strummer the idea for a new haircut. The Curtis Mayfield score for *Superfly*, or the Jimmy Cliff soundtrack for *The Harder They Come*, simply couldn't be divorced from the films (or the coke and the ganja for that matter). Followings formed around actors like Robert De Niro, Al Pacino, Pierre Clementi, Susan Sarandon, Brad Dourif, Michael Moriarty, Harvey Keitel and John Hurt. Directors like Martin Scorsese, Francis Ford Coppola, John Carpenter, Lindsay Anderson and Werner Herzog were in the same firmament as rock stars. The 1976 *Rocky Horror Picture Show*, with its midnight matinées and costumed, participating audience, was a rock phenomenon all by itself. The decade even ended with the 1979 release of *Apocalypse Now*, which, among all its other achievements, provided the Clash with the phrase 'Charlie don't surf'.

The obvious question was how the hell could we ignore all this? Previously films were ignored unless directly rock-related, like *Woodstock, The Song Remains the Same* or *Gimme Shelter*. If we were really pop-comprehensive, what rationale could there be for running a lead story on some mediocre rock band the week that *The Godfather Part II* was released? It wasn't just a question of movies, even though our readers might latch on to anything from *Mean Streets* to *Isla She-Wolf of the SS*. When Charlie Murray coined the term 'trash aesthetic', he was talking in terms of a spectrum of entertainment media – from the writing of Iceberg Slim and the comic books of Howard Chaykin to the comedy of Billy Connolly or Richard Pryor, or the latest in Harley Davidsons. With so much of Seventies rock rooted in flash, style and display, how could the hair, make-up and costumes be ignored? How could one talk to Malcolm McLaren and not Vivienne Westwood?

Rock stars were highly public about subjects other than music. When Pete Towshend embraced Meher Baba, Jimmy Page expressed a fascination with Aleister Crowley, or Bob Marley sang about the 'politics of Trenchtown' might it not be incumbent upon *NME* to provide nutshell synopses of any of the above? As it turned out, reggae would force the paper to run quite a bit on West Indian politics, and the politics of West Indians in the UK, and shortly after Page declared himself a devotee of Crowley, I interviewed filmmaker Kenneth Anger about Crowley and his beliefs. The counter-argument was that Murray, myself and the rest constituted a fifth column subverting a respectable music paper into a post-underground tabloid rag. And of course they were right.

Corporate skirmishing ground the soul. Had I been to the Old Bailey and back just to countenance this volume of blather? The drinking increased. I was over at the pub a lot, and now and then a half-bottle could be found in the desk drawer. I'd hit the record companies for marathon martini-to-cognac, expense-account lunches, and the more I drank, the more I pitied myself. Poor fucking me. The Seventies may have been the sell-out decade, but my mother had raised me at least to try for the ethical high ground, and here I was deep in the salient and all but out of moral ammunition.

When the inevitable counterstrike came, it was swift, without warning and literally hit us where we lived. When I'd first gone to work for Logan, the paper's home had been in an anonymous office on Long Acre in Covent Garden, shared with the *New Scientist*. It was funky, ugly and rarely visited by management, and our *New Scientist* neighbours were as much a thorn in the IPC side as we were. They were always blowing whistles on environmental cover-ups and nasty government-weapons projects, and bringing the wrath of the City and Downing Street down on IPC. At *NME*, on the other hand, we took drugs. In our maze of Kafkaesque corridors, an archaically soundproofed record-review room, like something out of Broadcasting House, was ideal for smoking joints and listening to Tappa Zukie or Big Youth. It was an environment in which you could make believe you were working on a small independent publication. (Yeah, and Bambi's mum was only wounded.)

Then we were evicted. They moved us out. In the name of property rationalisation – whatever that was – we were winkled out of our comfy nook in the near-West End and transported to King's Reach Tower, south of the Thames, hard by Waterloo Bridge, where the IPC board of directors wanted all its magazines stacked like utensils, handy to keep an eye on. King's Reach Tower was – and I presume still is – a hideous example of the Sixties Piece-of-Crap School of corporate architecture and cowboy construction, externally thirty storeys of ugly glass and internally open-plan with cubicle partitions. Weird things happened when the wind rose. King's Reach undulated, smelled of chemicals and an eerie harmonic whistling echoed up the lift shafts whenever the wind gusted off the Thames. A few windows had popped, in the early days, and the helipad was *never* used. Strike action for relocation was mooted, but we couldn't raise a majority vote and the cultural schism turned bitter. Neither IPC nor *NME*, though, realised that the problems of format changes or the move to King's Reach would prove minor compared with what was to come. The early recognition and the fast and wholehearted embrace of punk by the paper proved a nose-ringed Pandora's box that we'd gleefully upend.

Rodney Biggenheimer's English Disco

The tall fourteen-year-old redhead in the blue-velvet hotpants was a mess of streaked mascara, as if she'd recently been crying. Her nose was red, one false eyelash was coming off and she was tottering slightly on her silver platforms. A friend explained, 'She's not in a very good mood, she got raped last night by (*insert name of member of seventies English megaband*).'

Another warm, deceptive, smog and jasmine night in Los Angeles, another *NME* junket, and I'd wandered away from whatever act or artist the record company was trying to promote to check out the tall tales coming back to London about a joint where the very young and very extreme groupies gathered. Shall we really talk Caligula-decadent? Rodney Biggenheimer's English Disco features in the more sanitised histories of rock 'n' roll as the hub of LA Glitter, where scenester and KROQ DJ Rodney promoted Slade, Sweet, Queen, Bowie and Bolan, and where Joan Jett and Lita Ford got their start with the Runaways. But, as far as I could see, it was also an overt meat market where big-name stars from big-name bands, especially big-name *English* stars, could pick up, exploit and humiliate exceedingly and illegally young girls and boys. And forget discreet. This was coke in the lav and blowjobs not even under cover of the tablecloth, because they didn't have any, probably because Rodney wasn't smart enough to have a mob connection for linen.

The stars took tables, and the little ladies and the scattering of young boys clustered in skittish groups for a strong shot of peer pressure before braving the unknown, or even the known. They looked so like underdeveloped, teenybopper-garbed junior versions of the blank-eyed whores on Sunset that it was both sad and alarming. Sequinned hotpants and halters, platform shoes, feather boas and far too much baby make-up, over-nervous, loud as drag queens – they were but children, trying to cultivate the boredom of the utterly jaded and unequivocally pliant. At Rodney's I sensed corruption. Sexual free expression? I don't think so. It was nothing but a whorehouse where the coin of the realm was fame, and like everything else in the mid-Seventies fame was well out of control.

These were days of yore before Michael Jackson, or even Roman Polanski, when everything was legal as long as you didn't get caught, and the maxim of the famous was 'It don't apply to me'. Take what you want but grab it fast. HIV was loose back then, only the incubation period was so damned long that nobody knew about it. And ultimately, early in the Reagan era, even the baby *demi-mondaines* on the Strip would wise up to the concept of material girlhood, and the ethos of Sable Starr, Cyrinda Fox, Miss Pamela and the GTOs would be replaced by that of Vicki Morgan and Heidi Fleiss.

Carnival

Although I missed the big outbreak of violence in 1976, Carnival one year earlier had clearly demonstrated the direction in which the hard wind was blowing. The weight of matters was clear as early as Friday night. Traditionally Carnival started there. As soon as it was dark, the sound systems would crank up in the big echoing bays under the Westway. Scratch, dub and talkover, Red Stripe by the case and chalices fit for the Palace were making the rounds. Pass the kutchie to the *left*-hand side. Of all the nights of Carnival, Friday was my favourite. It was a little tentative, mostly local, mostly natty dread, and comparatively free of tourists from other parts of the city. Maybe a spot of crime, but nothing to concern the self-confident. From the get-go, though, this night had a different vibe. Even at home, when I declared my desire to take a stroll and see what was what, Ingrid declined, and I figured later she'd already sensed something I had yet to discover, on the tube or maybe coming back from the shops. Undaunted, I wandered out and very soon ran into I-Mac, also checking it out. Together we followed the path on the north side of the Westway, heading east from Portobello, infiltrating the barn-sized concrete bays, with a sound system doing business in each of them. State-of-the-art speakers were mixed in with boomers from old radiograms, and equally weird selections of amps were wired in impossible series, but all functioned by the grace of Jah-Electric, and played a selection as eclectic as the gear, from the Melodians and the Skatalites to U-Roy, King Tubby and Max Romeo.

I think the hairs on I-Mac's neck started twitching first, and I put it down to his being a somewhat more timid soul than I; but, in a short while, the bad feeling was on me, too. We were becoming invisible. Writers from James Baldwin to Malcolm X describe the sensation of the 'invisible nigger', when no one looks at you or even acknowledges that you exist. Now it was our turn. The musicians, street dreads and quid-deal boys we knew from around the pubs greeted us cordially enough, but it didn't overcome a general vibe of too many pork-pie-hat-and-raincoat rudies, probably up from Brixton, on the razzle in another manor, and in that early lurking phase of sussing out the lay I was seeing the whites of too many eyes. The guys we knew from the Sixties were now old gangsters. New youth was abroad and feisty; too many five-oh incidents tolerated, too much shit eaten and now too much to prove. They didn't give a rat's arse about recent local history, how (along with the talkover DJs) it was the Pink Fairies and Hawkwind who had first opened up the underside of the Westway to live music, by the simple process of setting up the gear, rocking out and being dragged off to the nick, if push came to shove, which it often did.

You couldn't blame the youth. From our point of view, the coppers working out of Ladbroke Grove and Harrow Road nicks had been behaving like confrontation bastards, without diplomacy or common sense. The most farcical piece of law enforcement came when some rookie cop searched Bob Marley for dope outside Island Studios on Basing Street; an affront to Rastafari on a par with busting the Pope. Such petty harassment was routine in All Saints Road and the nearby streets, where the Mangrove Restaurant had always been the hub of local militancy. Paranoia began to set in: rumours circulated of officers with covert ties to the National Front, who gave the tacit nod to any skinhead moonstomp. More rumours told of an armed heavy mob with 9mms. The police were apparently going to pour on the pressure until a fuse blew. The first white Special Patrol Group Ford Transit vans began appearing on the streets, and the only real question was how high the amperage of the fuse.

Pretty much the same was happening to white freaks as to the dreads and rudies. Lemmy couldn't walk a block without being stopped and frisked. Shirley Divers and I were tossed in the drunk tank on a Saturday night for walking out of the Hammersmith Odeon with champagne glasses in our hands during a party. What the hell did they think they were doing? Nit-picking us to death? Part of the reason we moved from Henekey's to the Princess Alex was that the plods had decided the interior of Henekey's saloon bar was part of their assigned beat. As many white doors were being kicked in at unreasonable times in the morning, afternoon and evening as West Indian ones; the police, intent on enforcing the letter of the law, were stoking the pressure cooker.

Media clowning also exacerbated the tension. David Bowie made what was possibly the dumbest and most overweening error of his entire career when he announced that 'Britain could benefit from a fascist leader', and supposedly indicated he was the boy for the job by posing for pictures at Victoria Station in an open-topped black Mercedes, giving what looked uncomfortably like a Nazi salute. A couple of months later Eric Clapton – the man who learned everything he knew from Elmore James and B. B. King – added his dash of own madness by endorsing Enoch Powell's racism live onstage. Margaret Thatcher locked down the leadership of the Tory party and, with Labour disintegrating like the *Pequod* after the final headbutt from Moby-Dick, it was only a matter of time before she swept to power and that chalk-on-a-blackboard voice would be berating us daily from the TV.

Carnival Saturday started out happily enough, moms and kids and dogs and all manner of good-smelling stuff cooking on the pavements, and the gang was out in force, waving to women we hadn't seen in a while. Everyone was strutting their stuff, intersecting the procession as it zigzagged on its inexplicable route of steel bands, whistles and fat ladies in turbans with whom you would not want to mess. Lot of cops, but that was to be expected, and still the cans of Red Stripe and Carlsberg Special Brew were on sale from a plastic dustbin full of ice on every doorstep.

My first inkling that all was not well came when I noticed I was mitigating my swagger and holding my beer closer to my chest. Straighten up, stiffen the spine and walk a bit more Max Cadey. Rudies were up from Brixton in force; the ska revival had brought back the hats over the eyes and the Thelonious Monk shades. Sad to tell, but the average rudie didn't give shit about Monk, just dug the shades. Early on they'd been tentative, blind-eyed watchful, but as Brew took hold they grew more boisterous. Responding in kind, the Met pushed a number of white SPG vans through the pedestrian-packed, closed-to-traffic streets, forcing their display of inconvenient authority through a crowd who uniformly yelled abuse. A testosterone compact was being made. Gauntlets were going down in the baboon dance of taunt and counter-taunt.

Sunday proved even worse. The rudies escalated to hit-and-run handbag snatching. First they robbed solo or in pairs working together, but then they joined into packs. A lot of helmets and white cop shirts suddenly appeared in the crowd. Each time a rudie was busted it triggered a mass stampede, very close to full-scale wilding. Fifty-strong rushes with hands grabbing at anything that could be ripped from the suddenly confused. I encountered Boss and we decided it was time to load up on beer and repair to Edward's flat, a Portobello top floor from which we could see everything. Having accurately agreed with Ingrid that carnival was 'going to be a fucking drag this year', Edward had sworn he wasn't stirring all weekend. He had, however, invited everyone to a Watch-It-out-of-the-Window Party.

For a while the epicentre of the trouble was down Portobello to the south of us. We could see nothing, but could hear shouts and screams, and an ebb and flow of mass roaring, against a constant background of sirens. Richard Adams stumbled in bleeding, having been punched in the face and robbed of his camera. Boss started waxing exceeding macho, not to say Rudyard Kipling racist, and informed us he wasn't about to stay cooped up indoors, and that it was as much his carnival as anyone else's. He made his *Man Who Would Be King* exit, but returned fairly quickly and freely admitted he'd underestimated the state of the battle. 'It's fucking *stupid* out there.'

As the shadows lengthened and the TV cameras went away, buses rolled up and fresh coppers were deployed – and deployed like a bloody Roman legion. It was the first time I'd seen English police with helmets and riot shields. They threw a line across Portobello Road at Cambridge Gardens, pavement-to-pavement on the north side. They'd taken the high ground, the top of a steepish section of street, that commanded all of Portobello Green and the rest of the open space created by the Westway flyover and the old tube-train bridge beside it. The police had coolly defined the battlefield.

The double ranks of coppers closed up, until they were a Plexiglas-shield wall. The rudies massed under the bridge and flyover, building in numbers and hostility, crowded into a brick-walled bottleneck. Bottle- and beercan-throwing sorties rushed out and then retreated. The cops caught the missiles on their shields, but held their ground, while more and more aspiring rioters gathered in the bottleneck under the bridge, ensuring that sheer weight of numbers must eventually force the rudies into a frontal charge. I suppose, in theory, they could have dispersed, but blood was up beyond any back-down. As if to dispel the most lingering doubt, the cops did something that caused those of those of us hanging out of Edward's window to stare in amazement. Clashing truncheons beat on shields and London bobbies roared non-verbal defiance straight out of *Zulu*. They must have been rehearsing according to the dictates of Shaka and Cetshwayo at Hendon Police College; they'd welded themselves into a West London *impi* of entirely the wrong colour.

Rudies began to emerge from under the bridge, tentatively at first, but in growing numbers. They advanced up the slope towards the shield wall, yelling, throwing stuff, working themselves up to break into a run. Just when the charge of the rudies was about to coalesce, the cops pre-empted them. They charged. The rudies fled, but were trapped by the bottleneck that had previously been their shelter. The cops were out to put the hu on as many of the opposition as they could. Beatings were administered. A lesson was being taught here, sunshine. Some kids tried to escape, but found themselves outflanked, and the round-up wasn't pleasant. Leaving a lot of bleeding rudies, the blue *impi* withdrew in good order and re-formed the shield wall. The rudies gave the coppers best and melted away to pub, bus and tube.

The lesson had been both taught and learned. At the next year's re-match, a mob of more than just rude boys hit hard early and without restraint. The police cars burned on TV across a world that marvelled at British race riots, and banners were ostentatiously unfurled, red flags and black flags, red, gold and green, the Anarchist Circle A and the Broken Cross; flags whipping and snapping against driven Wagnerian clouds. Except that the music wasn't Wagner; it sounded like Sham 69 without the subtlety. The Nazi mosh pit and Stalinist romance. Rock Against Racism v. The Doc Marten Jungen. On to Brixton and Broadwater. Double-plus ungood.

Mo the Roller

Double-plus good for the novelist, though. In fact, I was probably one of luckiest sons-of-bitches on God's green Earth, in that I got a deal on my first novel with no rejections and almost no effort. I'd run into a character called Michael Dempsey. An odd cove, but we seemed to recognise each other as a kind of kin. Dempsey was a highly educated, alcoholic Irishman, puffy like Dylan Thomas and constantly suffering epiphanies. I first met him in the very early Seventies, when he waxed angry and aggressive at post-hippie political meetings, spouting the basic Socialist Workers' Party line, but doing it with a level of abuse and artery-popping vehemence that set him apart from the rest of the Chelsea Reds.

The saving factor in Dempsey's personality was a short, grasshopper attention span. He dropped the SWP and their dour doctrines within a matter of months, which was just as well because if he hadn't, we might never have come to know each other. Later he admitted he had only joined the party to ease his way into bed with some woman he fancied, but after attending a few meetings, his natural anti-establishment fervour had bought the whole ideological package. His Red rabidity while with the SWP was typical of Dempsey's bull-headed and often drunkenly myopic dedication to the cause of the moment. Dempsey saw himself as a *Room at the Top* character: the angry scholarship boy from the northern town who had made it to university and laboriously learned to eat his fish with the correct fork. Unfortunately, like most *Room at the Top* characters, he had bad attacks of class-traitor guilt, which, coupled with a Fenian love of lost causes, would precipitate black-dog whisky drunks and trigger unspeakable incidents at totally the wrong cocktail parties.

I first met Dempsey at the instigation of my then agent, the marvellous Abner Stein. Dempsey and the legendary Sonny Mehta were the two star editors at Granada Publishing. Dempsey had been responsible for bringing both Ed Sanders and Hunter S. Thompson to the house. Stein was a suave, swift-witted, expatriate New Yorker who had seemed to enjoy the tempo and civility of English publishing, but still maintained a Sixth Avenue savoir-faire and Manhattan determination that enabled him to run rings round the coterie of upper-class twits who seemed, at the time, to have been installed in publishing, because, in the opinion of their families, publishing houses were places where idiot second sons could do the least damage.

Dempsey took on the challenge of publishing and marketing books with typical bull-at-a-gate radicalism. He wanted to put out books that upset people and was a natural magnet for trouble. That was, of course, why Abner paired the two of us in the first place. When I arrived on the scene Dempsey was under intense fire from the legal big guns of the Church of Scientology over the chapter in Ed Sanders' book *The Family* that alleged links between Scientology and the Manson family. Dempsey was also an editor who liked to hang out with his authors, if they'd have him, and this helped sculpt his legend. When he raised hell with J. G. Ballard through the painful creation of the novel *Crash*, it triggered another obsession. He bought a huge old Mercedes and, although I don't know if he ever consummated hammer-down, high-speed vehicular sex, he certainly constituted a menace to the public at large. Inevitably he wrecked the Teutonic beast and was banned from driving, although that did little to deter him.

We found an initial kinship in the demon drink, and any vestige of the hippie-hating Marxist-Leninist was swiftly drowned in Jameson's. When I showed him the initial chapters of my first novel *The Texts of Festival*, a fantasy set in a new Dark Age with technology on a par with *The Wild Bunch* and a fractured memory of twentieth-century pop-culture, he went bananas and wanted to publish it. I don't think any author had it so easy. Many may have copped more cash, but in terms of a lack of hassle and grief, the deal was unparalleled. This is not to say that, later in life, I didn't suffer my share of rejection by dyslectic bastards who decided that one or other of my deathless masterpieces 'wasn't for them'. First time round, though, I rode into town in a first-class compartment of outrageous good fortune.

The Texts of Festival was rapidly followed by *The Tale of Willy's Rats*, a sex, drugs and rock 'n' roll minor opus about a fictional rock band. Dempsey didn't think it was the best I could do, but deemed it publishable and put it out in lurid paperback with a T&A cover. Now I was looking at a third novel and I really had to put up or shut up. With athletes it's 'going for the burn'; with writers (at least, this writer) it's 'dipping in the slime'. A matter of sliding a fist and even a forearm into the unholy ooze that collects in the dark depths of the imagination. Into the Parisian-sewers-of-the-mind with you, boy, and see what you can find. And the first thing I stumbled across, among the albino rats and phantom organists, was the very idea I needed.

During the merry days at *IT* I had written and published a story called *Mo the Roller*. In an environment known as the 'Damaged World', even reality itself had achieved a state of terminal entropy, and the inhabitants of this happy nightmare had to generate their own by means of devices known as stasis generators. To create something the size of a city required huge Nikola Tesla devices buried in the foundations, but an individual could be provided with a plausible physical existence by a device about the size of a Walkman, slung on the belt or carried in a handbag. Without a stasis generator, all became the Nothings – ageless and dimensionless, infinite wastes of time and matter, shimmering grey, all colours and none. If you tossed a beer can into the Nothings, it smoked, evaporated and was no more. Entropy even took care of the garbage.

When Ingrid read the first detailed description of the Nothings, lolling in Biba velvet in front of the Magicoal electric fire at Chesterton Road, she informed me they were a classic and accurate, if maybe idiot-savant, description of clinical depression. I then explained the system by which all material goods and artefacts were beamed in from Stuff Central and life was exactly what one made it, either collectively or as an individual. Ingrid leaned forward, and wrapped her arms around her knees protectively and considered this. 'Stuff?'

'Every kind of stuff.'

'From Stuff Central?'

'Anything you desire.'

'I suppose it does have an elegant simplicity.'

'And saves a great deal of time.'

Mo the Roller I'd only written in enough of the metaphysical quasi-technology to support a bizarre game of pool. In the novel, *The Quest of the DNA Cowboys*, I had to expand the concept and blend in the details to support an entire fantasy universe. For the raw materials, I pillaged everything from *Star Trek* and *Kung Fu* to the Marquis de Sade and Sam Peckinpah. I had huge domesticated lizards with twin brains; I had a pre-teen evil dictator of her own private universe; I had living, growing biocomputers, tended by monks who also had their own futuristic martial-arts disciplines. Fanciful weapons, medieval jails, public hangings, Albert Speer architecture, gunfights, some obligatory whips and chains, stiletto heels and femmes fatales in tight and fetishistic clothing, orgies and organisms, and monstrous undefined monsters called Disruptors which sucked up every semblance of life or logic into their all-consuming maws. In a bout of wishfulfilment, I also created a comprehensive pharmacy of fictional narcotics and psychotropics.

The Quest of the DNA Cowboys, and its two sequels, *The Synaptic Manhunt* and *The Neural Atrocity*, were crammed with a fine and chaotic ground-clutter of contemporary pop culture. No effort at distortion went untried to realise more fully those fantasy worlds to which I'd been given tiny tantalising glimpses by Robert Johnson, Jim Morrison or Bob Dylan. I wanted the full picture of what lay beyond the crossroads or inside the Gates of Eden, fleshed out in fully formed (if surreal) geography. By the time I'd completed some 700 printed pages that made up the three volumes, I was pretty damned happy. The plan was for the *DNA Cowboys* trilogy to make me world-famous and rich for life, but like most plans of its kind, it didn't quite pan out that way. (In retrospect I think it was a good thing. Fame would have made me even more insufferable and would have compelled me to die young.) The first snag was defining what I'd done. W.H. Smith and other legitimate booksellers didn't know what to do with these books. A few got racked as science fiction, but many stores reacted with the suspicion that these three tomes might be inexplicable to all but psychedelic drug-users. At times like this an author learns the value of a good editor, and Dempsey wasn't the most diligent of mentors.

Sweating the details wasn't his strong suit, and also he had the memory of a drunk. He could get the Granada sales force good and plastered, but forget that the object of the mission was to hype them on moving the books into the shops. And then, of course, he magnificently self-destructed at the Frankfurt Book Fair, charging rounds of booze and hookers to Granada and wiping out about fourteen months' worth of the Book Division's promo budget. The

[354]

pièce de résistance came when he tossed a recliner chair out of a fifth-floor window.

The three books sold to exactly those for whom they were intended, but, with Dempsey not only fired from Granada, but banned from the building, they simply lay and waited to be picked up by the few in the know. No advertising, no fanfare, no reviews in the *Sunday Times*. In fact, enough were picked up to make the exercise worthwhile and, in short order, the first printing was gone. No one however, was sufficiently involved to order a reprint, and over the years the trilogy became much sought-after rarities. All in all, the project left me feeling a lot like Kilgore Trout, Kurt Vonnegut's archetypal fucked-over novelist.

I was exceedingly pissed-off at Michael Dempsey until I discovered that his flamboyant exit had not been as mindlessly excessive as it might have appeared. He had not only organised his severance from Granada, but had voided his contract with the company. This left him free to start his own publishing company with capital that he'd miraculously raised, despite his track record and predispositions. We went on to do two more books together. *Get On Down* was a beautifully printed collection of rock & roll posters that proved to be a great source of pride and pleasure. It concentrated mainly on the psychedelic era. Obviously this was to my own taste, and a period of intense graphic as well as musical innovation, but this was not the only motivation.

Psychedelic art was disappearing at an alarming rate, and the only comprehensive collections of psychedelia belonged to people as careful as Miles, and of course Felix, who seemed to have collected everything and already had a set of big, brass-bound plan-chests for his hoard of posters, artwork and printed ephemera. The time was right to reproduce the best of the graphic work in book form, before the endangered species vanished entirely. The quest to preserve graphic psychedelia for posterity triggered another of Michael's manic enthusiasms. The finished book was designed by Richard Adams and manufactured by a Dutch fine-art printer who used an incredibly expensive colour process to give a near-perfect reproduction of the metallic golds and silvers, but Dempsey still wanted to keep the cover price low enough for the book to be street-accessible. The numbers never really crunched, and although the book sold well, *Get On*

Down cost Dempsey and his backers a small fortune by the final accounting. No small part of the cost was a monster champagne-and-acid party at a bookstore in Charing Cross Road. Hundreds showed up, including a huge contingent of punks, who stole everything that wasn't nailed down, and Dempsey got about as drunk as was survivably possible.

The presence of a large number of punks at the *Get On Down* party was no accident. Dempsey was early in his recognition of the importance of punk. In the beginning he reacted like a publisher and made a deal with Mark P., the creator of the fanzine *Sniffing Glue*, to publish a collection of his writing in book form, but, as always with Dempsey, it didn't stop there. By a series of coincidences and hustles he wound up managing the band the Adverts, who then proceeded to have a minor hit with the single 'Gary Gilmore's Eyes'. Dempsey's home became filled with speed-rapping punks and others nodding out on heroin, and he himself made the acquaintance of both drugs, in addition to his usual whisky intake. The band's two focal points, TV Smith and Gaye Advert, were, to say the least, a volatile handful, especially in the first flush of their brief success, but while his life seemed to be reduced to a chaos of nose rings, tattoos and bad dope, Dempsey still went ahead and published my sixth novel, *The Feelies*. This book ran closely parallel with the punk ethic in which Dempsey had enmeshed himself. In a stressed-out and overpopulated near-future, a form of virtual reality is being marketed as the next opiate of the people, while massive TV game shows pit near-psychotic greed against the fear of mind-bending humiliation. The packaging of *The Feelies* was, in its own way, just as elaborate as that of *Get On Down*. Instead of a modest paperback, Dempsey – flying on a punk-rock hit single, Glenlivet and amphetamine sulphate – ordered an illustrated de-luxe soft-cover extravaganza.

I have no idea how many the book sold. I had to be content with no money, but a truly fabulous insider reaction. Maximalist guitar virtuoso and cyberpunk critic Glenn Branca hailed *The Feelies* one of the definite forerunners of the hot genre of the Eighties and Nineties. And that was the way of it with Dempsey. The primary objective might not be achieved, but the collateral conquests could be unexpected pleasures. He had the knack of making me feel like the hot young literary star-boy, and I basked shamelessly in the heat.

Ingrid and I went to parties in places we hadn't been to before and, in some cases, places we didn't even know existed. I recall a high-ceilinged gentlemen's club on Piccadilly where Michael Moorcock beamed like a huge affable Viking, while Harlan Ellison, overwarm in leather jeans and hyperactivity, complimented me on my style and called me 'kid', which did great things for my ego considering that I was now in my early thirties.

I met Anthony Burgess, who was drunk and talkative, and Jim Ballard, who never really seemed to have escaped from that Japanese internment camp. I encountered Michael Herr, who had covered the war in Vietnam for *Rolling Stone* and would later write the voiceover parts for *Apocalypse Now*. I went on a whisky-sampling pub crawl with Ralph Steadman and Dempsey, which ended in yet another weird after-hours criminal shebeen in Earls Court. All in all, it's a miracle any of us came out it alive, and of course poor Dempsey didn't. In the early Eighties, after a hard night's drinking, he attempted to change a light bulb at the top of the stairs in his flat and tumbled to his death. God rest him.

Dancehall Style

When I wasn't writing or posing as the literary hepcat, many midnights would find me in Dingwall's Dancehall, a nightclub in what came to be called Camden Lock, but until Dingwall's opened was nothing more than a mysterious opening at the end of the formidable British Rail wall that ran down Chalk Farm Road, east from the Roundhouse. Dingwall's was where I ruined my liver for most of the Seventies, and a lot of my more flamboyant memories are entwined around the long, narrow, live-music and drinking joint. I watched Richard Nixon resign in Dingwall's – raising our glasses and screaming, 'Gotcha, you fucking bastard!' as though his downfall had been part of some huge group effort. I saw Wilko Johnson with Dr Feelgood for the first time there, and Eric Clapton sitting in with Buddy Guy. I saw Bo Diddley. I saw Country Joe McDonald, and Johnny Thunders and the Heartbreakers, Kilburn and the High Roads, Blondie, and Mick Green and the Pirates, and I played there myself once or twice. My face was once slashed with broken glass, but I escaped with only a small scar on my upper lip. Injury was not without compensation, however. I was immediately tended like a fallen hero, for an entire weekend, by a dark-haired Swede called Asa. If you want to get the girl, kid, lose the fight.

The overall impression was not unlike a long, narrow barn or maybe a western saloon with a slick coat of polymer on all the woodwork. In terms of ambience and attitude, H could have designed Dingwall's with me in mind. He'd taken everything he'd learned at the Speakeasy and improved it, refined the assets and eliminated the majority of the drawbacks. The sum total was a long bar, away from the music, with a sufficiency of bar tenders. The noisy end of the club had enough lines of sight to see the bands if you really desired. The DJ booth was manned by Boss on many of the more epic nights. H – and then Boss, when he took over as manager – maintained a booking policy that never quite allowed a mosh pit to form. Although punk was coming in, it wasn't permitted to take over. Punks gobbed, fought, stole, made a mess and didn't spend money. Dingwall's was *our* joint, the freaks who'd made it through and had at least the price of a Jack Daniels, a Red Stripe and maybe a half-gram of coke.

Dingwall's was elitist enough for Frank Zappa to dine in peace, but with no who's-cute-and-who-isn't door policy. Everyone knew and everyone, for the most part, respected how it was. Billy Idol and Mick Jones would drink there, but they never played at Dingwall's. The punks showed up for reggae acts like U-Roy, Burning Spear and Clint Eastwood, but they were expected to behave. I assume that both the Camden Town gangsters and the local scuffers had been paid off to their satisfaction. Certainly the police took a reasonably laissez-faire attitude towards the milling drunks who fumbled from the premises around 2.10 a.m. groping for cabs, and about the only serious underworld incident was when a crazy Greek bouncer – who'd seemingly been hired as a favour to some minor Kentish Town Godfather – went berserk with a machete and almost killed a guitar player. (I think Martin Stone, although I wouldn't swear to it.)

As a regular at Dingwall's, I found myself living the pretensions of the drunken scribe with no quarter. I may not yet have been writing as well as Dylan Thomas, Tennessee Williams or Dorothy Parker, but I was starting to match their drinking. And was I having a good time?

Truthfully? Yes, I think I was. Drunks are always sorry for themselves, and I was definitely no exception – *poor me, poor me, now pour me another.* All aspirations to literature have to come with a full load of communicable torture and angst. On the other hand, life had become pretty comfortable. Friendships felt as solid as I'd ever known them. Some of us had now been in the fray for a full decade and I pretty much knew who I could count on in times of stress.

Amazingly, although much of the outside world appeared to be in a hopeless downhill slide, a number of the other old-timers were doing pretty well for themselves. The biggest surprise in the neighbourhood was the sudden rise to fame of Hawkwind. After labouring long and hard in the raw, solar wind, they had scored a completely unforeseen top-ten hit with the uncharacteristically short and radio-friendly 'Silver Machine'. Mercifully the band appeared little affected, either in lifestyle or attitude, by having their pictures in the papers or being on *Top of the Pops*. Certainly chart success didn't allay Lemmy's constant need to borrow money from all and sundry. (A T-shirt was commissioned that read 'LEMMY A QUID 'TIL FRIDAY'.) The Hawk Lords continued to dine on the grease and flypaper at the Mountain Grill, and their only concession to pop stardom was going to gigs in a Mercedes bus. Manager Douglas Smith looked more stressed-out and Bill-Graham haggard than ever, but began drinking a much better brand of Scotch. The overall outcome of Hawkwind having a hit was that their lightshow, designed and furiously operated by Jonathan Smeaton, the ramrod of Liquid Len and the Lensmen, became truly stunning. Sadly, the Pink Fairies couldn't emulate their old running buddies' sudden jump in record sales, and continued to stumble on, doing some memorable shows to baying yahoo mobs, but all too frequently snatching defeat from the jaws of victory at crucial moments, and sending themselves back to the salt mines without passing Go or collecting their £200. The yahoos loved them well enough, however, for Sandy and Larry to be found propping up the bar at Dingwall's on any given night.

As well as the old lags, Dingwall's served as a catalyst for new faces and new encounters, and, of those new faces, by far the most outwardly psychopathic was that of Wilko Johnson. Like the Who, Dr Feelgood drew a furious energy from the mutual enmity of the two front men, and their best shows always teetered on the edge of violence. Wilko and the late Lee Brilleaux had exactly the same guitarist/singer animosity that had made Townshend and Daltrey so formidable and dangerous. The only real difference was that Townshend and Daltrey evolved some Marquess of Queensberry system that allowed them to continue all the way to infinity, while Wilko and Brilleaux hit critical mass after just three albums. While they lasted, though, the original Feelgoods were something, and I'll never forget them doing 'Riot in Cell Block Number Nine' at the Hammersmith Odeon. Amid whirling, *film noir* spotlights, Brilleaux and Wilko advanced on the footlights with all the menace of an authentic breakout at the Big House, and I continue to rate the album *Stupidity*, recorded on that tour, as one of the greatest all-time live recordings.

I think one of the reasons Wilko and I got along was that he needed someone with whom he could have an intelligent conversation. The other original Feelgoods embraced the thug culture of Canvey Island villains, especially Brilleaux, who, while an outstanding performer and always courteous to me, could be scary in the extremity of his right-wing politics and flares of Ronnie Kray temper. Wilko was educated and highly literate, as obsessed with the writing and performances of Bill Burroughs as I was, but also a fan of the romantic poets and their opium intake. For Wilko, life with the other Feelgoods, aside from when they were playing, was a wasteland arid of intellect.

Wilko was, to say the least, an oddity. In terms of guitarist presentation, he was the total anti-Keith. No mascara and scarves for this boy. With eyes that turned psychotic at will, and the pudding-bowl haircut of a homicidal schoolboy in the movie ... *If*, Wilko, in his shabby black pinstripe suit, black shirt buttoned to the neck, would clutch his black telecaster like an AK-47 and execute full stage-width slides and shuffles not unlike the ones the young Wayne Kramer stole from James Brown. Jagged, staccato and minimal, Wilko was about as antithetical – both in shape and sound – to the self-indulgent shag-haircut breed of guitar heroes as it was possible to be and remain on the same planet. In that, he provided the template for generations of punk guitar stranglers as yet unborn.

Although Wilko was smart and funny as hell, he appeared to like his private life complicated in the extreme, and as we came to know and trust each other, these complications often showed up at the door of Chesterton Road. With a wife and child out in Southend, a stripper mistress in the big bad city, and little truck with either discretion or deception, his options for rock-star soap opera were unlimited, particularly when the ever-popular sulphate served as emotional rocket fuel. The doorbell would ring and there would be a wide-eyed Wilko, often with girlfriend Maria, or now and again with Lemmy. (When it came to the sulphate, Lemmy and Wilk could match each other nostril to nostril, hour by hour and day by day, if need be.) Most times he was simply looking for a convivial place to pass the seemingly eternal night of the men who never sleep. On other occasions, though, epic drama would be in progress, triggered by some skirmish in his endless domestic trench warfare, and he'd be issuing speed-freak ultimatums that pendulumed between murder and suicide – the weapon of fantasy invariably being a serrated bread knife. Mercifully, the deathwish was never realised and everyone remained, if not happy, then at least unsliced. (Or as Ian Dury, who had Wilko as a Blockhead for a while after his departure from Dr Feelgood, commented, 'At times Mr Johnson could be a bit of a ballerina.')

Being a regular at Dingwall's also caused resumptions of contact with characters whom I hadn't seen in a very long time. Guy Stevens, usually drunk, late and abusive, was on his way to produce the Clash's masterpiece 'London Calling' and then drop dead. To see Guy in his last hurrah was, to put it charitably, educational, but another unexpected reunion with Tony Secunda proved far more momentarily beneficial. Since I'd last seen him with the Move, he'd had a hand in the rising fortunes of Marc Bolan. He'd managed the folk ensemble Steeleye Span, and had kept Steve Took alive by going in to bat for a fairly large accrual of royalties that Took had earned on the back of Bolan's success. At Dingwall's, Secunda was in the phase of never meeting a bag of cocaine he didn't like. Frequently Tony would give me a ride back to Chesterton Road, and then come in and start doing up the eight-ball he seemed invariably to have with him as a chemical security blanket. Cokeheads aren't usually Mother Theresa when it comes to altruism, and I could only assume that Tony needed someone with whom he could argue, on and around the paranoid nuances of the Great Global Conspiracy to Control

Everything. I learned early in the game that being up for such discussion could garner a bonanza of free nose-candy. We often went at it until ten or eleven in the morning, when Tony would decide that he should look in at his office, and I'd take a couple of Ingrid's Valium and collapse. One fateful night, however, we didn't make it to Chesterton Road at all, and went through that unique bonding experience of guys who get thrown in the drunk-tank together.

The combination of cocaine and alcohol is a circus unto itself. The booze makes you act stupid, while the coke energises you to continue the stupidity almost indefinitely. On the night in question our condition by closing time was such that Tony shouldn't have been driving, and I'm not sure if I was even truly capable of being a passenger. Ingrid was with us, but I don't know where she positioned herself in this unsteady equation. Even before we'd reached Edgware Road, Tony and I were engaged in a pointless argument about God knows what, and, by the time we made the turn onto the iron railway bridge at the end of Golborne Road, in the shadow of Trellick Tower, the debate had reached such a crescendo that he braked in the middle of the bridge. Leaving the car – doors open, lights on and engine running – Tony grabbed an aerosol paint can and sprang out to consolidate whatever point he was making by writing it in letters three feet high on the grey Victorian iron.

That Tony had a spray can so readily to hand was a product of an obsession with graffiti that he was espousing at the time. If he'd ever fallen in with the painter Jean-Michel Basquiat, who came to fame under the tagger pseudonym 'Samo', they might have formed an unholy alliance. By this time Tony was managing Lemmy's first version of Motorhead and had decided a graffiti campaign was a perfect adjunct to their uncompromising, down-with-the-street image. Every time he spotted a suitable wall, he'd spray the word 'Motorhead' on it, and I believe one or two of his efforts survive to this day.

On the bridge Tony was swaying a little, and instead of inscribing a stunning riposte, he'd only managed a couple of abstract curves when a blue light flashed behind us. A half-dozen coppers poured from the back of a Black Maria, laid their meaty hands on Tony and me and hustled us to the van. We went quietly, taken completely by surprise. One problem had been overlooked, however. In their eagerness to apprehend us, the law had entirely failed to notice Ingrid sitting in Tony's car, engine still idling, lights blazing and doors gaping. They quite literally drove past it without comment as they hauled us off to Ladbroke Grove nick.

Ingrid had never driven in her life and was at something of a loss as she saw us carried off. I don't think Tony or I would have blamed her had she stormed angrily out of the car, left it exactly where it was and walked home, at that point little more than 300 yards away. Ingrid, though, with her Scandinavian sense of civic responsibility, at least felt obligated to move the car over to the curb. As she told it, she was just wondering how to accomplish this when an amiable hippie wandered down the road. She asked him if he knew how to park a car. He not only did, but turned it off, locked it and then walked her to the end of the street.

It was fortunate that Tony and I had gone quietly. We were simply assumed to be drunk. At about eight in the morning we were charged with defacing public property and being drunk and disorderly, and were released to get cleaned up before appearing at Marylebone Magistrates Court an hour and half later. Back at Chesterton Road, Ingrid said nothing to me, just gave Tony his keys, informed him of the whereabouts of his car and went back to bed. In court, feeling like shit, we took the easy way out. We pleaded guilty, apologised to the magistrate for wasting his time and accepted a five-pound fine on each count.

I suppose I really should have felt content in this period. I was still living from project to project, and from pay cheque to pay cheque, but the cheques were sufficiently large to have a little fun. I had a home with a rent pegged to 1969 prices. I had an attractive blonde girlfriend who seemed infinitely tolerant of my antics. I had a growing reputation as a writer, and I was allowed to retreat into my fictional fantasy worlds any time I wanted. I had both a bar and a nightclub where everyone knew my name and the bar tenders would cash my cheques. I had even got thrown into jail for the night just to keep my credibility up to snuff. What more did I need?'

If I dug deep enough I could find something. In this case, it was how the fun didn't come without high levels of self-deception. As we've already seen, the Grove – nay, the whole post-industrial, post-imperial, fucked-up country-in-denial – seemed to be losing its sanity as it slid closer to the abyss of ugliness. Outside the cosy groove I'd ground for myself, much was unwell in Old England. Few were getting much satisfaction, but I'd had my fill of tag-team street politics. I tried to tell myself 'Fuck it'. We had a new generation on the rise to do the street fighting, didn't we? It was their turn to incite the riots and play the rama-lama. I pretended I wanted nothing but the part of a venerable observer. I was chronically burned out on the prophet-of-doom shtick. Hey, guys, I'm too young to be Howard Beale. (Maybe now, but not then.) I've done my tour of duty. I have my Purple Heart for brain trauma, yo. What I didn't have was the knowledge that the rama-lama, like the Corleone family, doesn't let you go that easily.

Chapter Ten

The *Titanic* Sails at Dawn

It's 19 June 1976, and in three months I'll be thirty-two. I'm already old by contemporary standards, but I'm not in the least happy. In another year I'll be thirty-three, the age at which John Reed died and Jesus Christ was nailed on the cross, sucking vinegar. Worse than that, my first love – rock & roll – seems to be going to hell in a hand-basket.

My determination to get out of the prophet-of-doom, rabble-rouser business had lasted about as long as any of my tenuous attempts to quit cigarettes. On this day in June *NME* published a lengthy diatribe of my dissatisfaction under the headline THE TITANIC SAILS AT DAWN, a decade-old quote from Bob Dylan's 'Desolation Row'. The peg on which the 3,000-word piece was conveniently hung was a stuffed bag of mail from disgruntled readers about how the current crop of first-division rock shows sucked the big one. Stadium rock had come to the UK, and no one seemed in the least bit pleased about it. Their immediate targets were recent shows by the Rolling Stones at Earls Court and the Who at Charlton football ground. That Princess Margaret had been spotted hanging around with the Stones seemed to be the last straw for our naturally disgruntled readers.

Responding with an angry diatribe to a fat mailbag is an easy ploy to expand the fan base, but my motives when I sat down to write the piece were not completely self-serving. I've always found it hard to stay mad at the Who for very long. The Stones, on the other hand, along with Rod Stewart, Elton John and visiting Americans like the Eagles, were starting to get right up my nose. I was coming to the conclusion that the current overblown stadium rock was not the music Eddie Cochran had died for. I used the SS *Titanic* as the obvious metaphor for the hubris of superstar rock as it wallowed in a lavish mire of luxury: the iceberg was the growing discontent among an audience that felt itself increasingly exploited. I ended the piece with these words:

> *If rock and roll is not being currently presented in an acceptable manner, and, from the letters we've been getting at the NME, this would seem to be the case, it is time for the Seventies generation to start producing their own ideas and ease out the old farts who are still pushing tired ideas left over from the Sixties.*
>
> *The time seems to be right for original thinking and new inventive concepts, not only in the music but in the way that it is staged and promoted.*
>
> *It may be difficult in the current economic climate, and it may be a question of taking rock back to street level and starting all over again.*
>
> *Putting the Beatles back together isn't going to be the salvation of rock and roll. Four kids playing to their own contemporaries might.*
>
> *And that, gentle reader, is where you come in.*

Some commentators would later claim that the article represented a contributory factor to the inception of punk, but that's nonsense. By the time the rant was published, the Sex Pistols had played as far afield as Manchester Lesser Free Trade Hall and a club called the Crypt in Middlesbrough. Patti Smith's album *Horses* had been a cult hit for six months or more. Indeed, the famous incident at the Hundred Club in Oxford Street, when Sid Vicious put the brute boot in on a fallen Nick Kent – the attack chronicled in just about every history of punk all the way to the Alex Cox movie *Sid and Nancy* – occurred the very day before the issue of *NME* featuring the 'Titanic' piece hit the stands in central London. Punk was already well established among the pogo cognoscenti long before I put pen to paper.

Stepping back from the historical long view that the phenomenon really started with Eddie Cochran, punk as London knew it was spawned in much the same twin epicentres as the hippies. One bunch doing a street thing in the Grove and another, slightly more biased to trash, cash and fashion, doing much the same in Chelsea. The action in the Grove seemed to be among a fluctuating stew of musicians who orbited the bands the London SS and the 101ers, and who had something going in the Elgin – a pub with a bad reputation for low-rent speedfreaks and drooling cases of mandy damage – and would emerge as the Clash and the Damned.

The Chelsea boys and girls were a bit more of a mystery, but that was how it had always been. A certain coterie attended parties at the chic Butler's Wharf studio of glass sculptor Andrew Logan. Logan had been around since the early Seventies, but I never really bothered to figure him out. Chrissie Hynde seemed to be in this same crowd, and I can only imagine Nick Kent too, since they were conducting an angular romance at around that time. I remember being introduced to a set of names. One was a character called Malcolm McLaren, who'd had something to do with the final red-leather phase of the New York Dolls and spouted second-hand situationism. He claimed to be a one-time Sixties activist, although I fail to recall him ever being anwhere I was. Apparently he'd become disillusioned with the failure of his generation to achieve 'genuine or wacky changes', and had opened a shop instead. His partner Vivienne Westwood took care of the commercial end by printing Tom-of-Sweden drawings on T-shirts. Bernie Rhodes, who would later manage the Clash, hung around, seemingly attempting to ape Malcolm. In addition a strange woman called Jordan and a crew of thug-like youth seemed to make up the numbers, but what did I know? My fish were fried elsewhere, and the rise of the Sex Pistols, Siouxsie or the Pretenders is hardly mine to recount.

If the *NME* rant contributed anything, it was to spread the ripples a little wider in the pond. And I was dealing the propaganda from a stacked deck. When I exhorted the youth of England to seek the rama-lama among their own contemporaries, I was sneakily aware that something worth the seeking definitely lurked, waiting to be found. I felt I was bringing punk to the lumpen. (And what better place for it?) But that was as far as it went. I'd always considered it my task to break ground, not follow the plough. Also, I wasn't quite ready to venture too close to out-of-tune fuzz guitars and tuneless vocals.

The Non-Judicial Use of Handcuffs

Julie Burchill has already gone fully, if not scandalously, public with anecdotes about our affair in the Seventies. I guess we all build our histories as we become aware of encroaching time – I'm shamelessly doing so here – and writers get especially good at it when the bloom of youth is fled and the tales and the commentary are all that remain. The most implacable truth can be improved in the telling, and I'm rather honoured to be included in her narrative:

I was stalking Micky; drunken old fool that he was, he didn't get the hint for ages . . . So I poured myself into my Levis . . . shrugged on my leather jacket . . . stole a red, red apple from a greengrocer's in Westbourne Grove and turned up on his doorstep one morning when I knew his girlfriend was away.

It was high noon but when he opened the door I knew he had just woken up. He rubbed his eyes with beautiful fists. 'Julie?'

'Hello, Micky.' I bit into the apple. He gulped and swallowed. I smouldered up his three doorsteps at him. 'Aren't you going to ask me . . . in?'

'Yeah . . . sure.' He stepped back, as he always did for me, and I passed him into the hallway. He pointed up. 'The flat's up there.'

'Right.' I put my hand on the banister and felt him tremble. 'Micky?'

'Yeah?'

'You know this thing sado-masochism?'

'Yeah.'

'Can you show me, please?'

Annie Lennox had it down. To abuse and be abused are the infinitely interchangeable sides of the same coin, but how many of the boys and girls wanted to flip that coin and roll it over on their knuckles? Appealing to fetishistic triggers from the wrong side of midnight is hardly cricket, but I was well and truly stalked and now, with all available nonchalance, I attempted to live up to a few of her teen expectations. I was highly flattered to have this young woman with all this raw talent hanging round me and making me feel like Lee Marvin.

She was well aware that my life was going through a phase during which, if I wasn't sleeping, I was either sober and working or out on the town and drunk. What she seemed to like about me was that I'd been through the wars and was still snarling, 'Fuck 'em if they can't take a joke.' Julie seemed able to tolerate me well, after most had given up and left me to my whisky strangeness. In fact she seemed to be everywhere I went, and even when I was well into the zone of the werewolves she seemed to show up. I would find her in cabs with me and wonder how she got there, but be dimly aware that we were drifting towards an inevitable impropriety probably worth some comment on a slow-gossip day.

When floating through the nets and entanglements of the very young and determined, one can run an all-too-serious risk of overreaching yourself and appearing a total fool for your presumption. There's no more damned fool than a fool revealing a mistaken passion, and I simply waited to see what might happen next. I also had to consider the matter of Tony Parsons. Parsons had been recruited to *NME* at exactly the same time as Julie, part of the same package of new punk blood, and he seemed to have taken a proprietorial interest in her, exuding tribal warnings that if any of us 'old hippies' laid a hand on her, we'd have him to reckon with.

The mating habits of punks seemed alien and a little atavistic, all the way back to mods under the pier at Brighton. If Parsons had some yob bee-in-his-bonnet that there was anything between Julie and me, then a minor outbreak of primate unpleasantness was definitely on the cards and should probably be avoided. On the other hand, I wasn't about to allow his Y-chromosome jitterbugging to disturb me, now that she was so explicitly on my doorstep. Hell, no, even though a colleague had warned me that I should watch out for him.

'Oh yeah?'

'You're the only thing in the way of him being you.'

I wasn't sure that I totally agreed with the theory, but I knew what he meant. As far as I was concerned, Parsons was a half light-year from paying the kind of dues I'd slapped on the counter over the years, but his ambition was palpable.

In the wake of Julie's overt doorstep proposition, the ensuing romance was doomed to have a discretionary short shelf-life. And then, of course, she couldn't resist the teen temptation to flaunt, and the inevitable fist-fight broke out – as it happened, in the empty file room of the *NME* offices at King's Reach Tower. I swear it was a blighted building. I figure if the two of us hadn't been consciously set up for the confrontation, its inevitability had been subliminally promoted, but once a charged distillation of testosterone is bent on throwing punches, the reasons why become a trifle redundant. With Parsons' Roy-of-the-Rovers physique, and eleven years on me, I knew I wasn't liable to do much damage, short of hitting him with a typewriter or something equally industrial. My best, and probably only, strategy was to keep ducking and weaving, covering up until he realised, fit as he was, that he wasn't really going to be able to hurt me.

Meanwhile, Julie was seemingly delighted. In her own words, 'I sat on my desk, dangling my legs like an innocent ten-year-old, and I couldn't help but smirk. My dream had come true; I really and truly was, at the age of seventeen, a fully-fledged femme fatale.' Femme fatale, definite devilment, DNA round the twist, and no easy thing being a principal player in the fantasy of another, but punks demanded violent complexity in all areas.

Nothing But the Haircuts

I was being flash in leather jeans and black wool jacket with a tie belt and a symbolic thunderbird on the back, an amalgam of Geronimo, Robin Hood and a Klingon space pirate. As you might guess, I rather fancied myself. The costume hardly fitted in at the Roxy Club, where the boys seemed uniform in black jeans and motorcycle jackets, or ripped and torn ted drapes and bondage strides, while Siouxie and her cohorts had strategised to startle in a dog-eared, laddered-stocking version of Ilsa She Wolf of the Confidential Leather Catalogues. In theory, in a place like the Roxy, 'do what you will' should once more have been the law – straight back to Aleister Crowley and no messing – but, as I was quickly to learn from John Rotten himself, punk enforced a dress code as draconian as the Flamingo at the height of mod. The punks were far less tolerant of deviance and aberration than the hippies had ever been, unless said deviance and aberration conformed to their own norms of perversity.

The Roxy Club was a made-over transvestite refuge in Covent Garden and qualified as the Big City ground zero for the first punk detonations, the showcase for the first wave bands and the consolidated fashion parade of the new style. Déjà bloody vu. 'The art-school dance goes on for ever,' as old George Melly observed. The hippie counterculture had made its first stand in a borrowed ballroom. In our case, an old Irish dance club, and the punks had a definite advantage in finding themselves a former drag-queen hangout. The immediate neighbourhood was better conditioned to wandering travesties. The styles and attitudes may have been diametrically different, but the fundamental ambience was unmistakable. Crowley's Rites of Eleusis rode again and Nietzschean finality was back in new threads and haircut.

Every youth movement likes to flatter itself that it was born fully formed on the half-shell, and exempt from any cultural genealogy. No punk walking would have admitted that he or she was of a noble dissident tradition going directly back through the freaks of the Sixties, the beat generation, Crowley and the Dadaists to, at the very least, Lord George Byron and the opium-den romantics, if not Ned Ludd and Wat Tyler. I was happy to see a new generation of bohemian urban guerrillas on the move, going up against the status quo, attacking the target from yet another angle, but I'd seen a hell of a lot of it before. The primary difference was that the hippies operated in a period of economic abundance, while punks were scavenging on the leftovers of a post-affluent society. Such was the difference a decade made.

I'd hardly started on my first Roxy beer when Rotten spotted me from across the crowded room and started in my direction with a couple of spiky-haired goombahs in tow. I'd never met Rotten before, although we certainly knew each other from our pictures in the paper. I knew confrontation was on the cards, but I was fairly confident. What kudos would there be in duffing up Mick Farren, for fuck's sake? I was hardly Nick Kent. Punks seemed to respect this, with the possible exception of Tony Parsons.

Now Rotten was in front of me, but he didn't say a word. Instead, he leaned forward and extended a hand to the cuff of my jeans. The leathers had a slight flare to them. No loon-pants nonsense, oh dear me, no; just enough to make them slide over the tops of my pale-blue cowboy boots. Rotten measured the flare with his thumb and forefinger like a disapproving East End tailor. His expression said it all. So, grandad, not so hip as we thought we were, are we?

Rotten had adopted the old mod's ruthless sense of fashion, but I wasn't prepared to give ground. My cowboy boots might be just too boring and American, but I liked them, and I cringed for no punk. A shrug of: who gives a fuck, what do I know? I'm not even in the game, Boy John. As I'd long ago told the mods in Brighton, 'I'm a beatnik like Bob Dy-lan.' That seemed to do the trick. I believed that my status had just been defined for all to see. I was an old fart with far too much track record to fuck with. I was the real deal, when rising punk mini-stars didn't know shit from their elbows. And, my Lord, did I milk *that* for all it was worth. If you can't have your youth back, be the veteran with the 1,000-yard stare.

Beneath my jaded bluff, though, I was generally impressed with young Rotten. He was a presence to be very strongly reckoned with. The achievement I most admired, beyond the artfully contrived persona, was the way he'd pulled off the very difficult trick of singing rock & roll in his native London accent, when all but a few of us had striven to sound American, sometimes at the risk of sounding as dumb as Mick Jagger on 'The Girl with the Faraway Eyes'. John Lennon might have concocted himself a mid-Atlantic, post-Beatle drawl, somewhere between the Mersey and the Hudson, but the last geezer really to sing with a cockney accent had been Joe Brown of Joe Brown and the Bruvvers. To rock in cockney always seemed to conjure a perky gorblimey factor, the musical equivalent of Barbara Windsor, and hardly the sneering and snarling of our early American role models. To drop one's 'h's on a Howlin' Wolf tune is just too bizarre. Rotten, however, had taken the cute and turned it as feral as a Limehouse wharf rat – though I suspect he had watched a lot of Ian Dury before anyone noticed. He'd also managed to introduce an element of the Victorian music-hall drunk into the standard Gene Vincent/Jim Morrison microphone clutch, and folded in our most treasured English influences – Tony Hancock, Arthur English, even Wilfred Bramble. (In fact, a lot of Wilfred Bramble.)

Rotten, unlike so many of his more gothic cohorts, was also colourful. He shied away from funereal S&M black, and was bright, primary, even garish. Brooding like Byron was boring. Onstage he was a put-on merchant, a ruffian joker, with a scathing humour and disdainful body language. He incited, but then turned round and scorned what he'd achieved. He'd whip a crowd into the expected adoration, and then castigate them for their masochism. I recall at (I think) the Hundred Club – but not on the night Kent was stomped – Rotten standing and regarding the bouncing crowd and slowly shaking his head, as if dismayed at how easily the sheep were led. Apt that Rotten's most well-recalled words, over and above the lyrics of the Pistols' three legendary singles, should be the terminal comment at the end of their final show at Winterland in San Francisco. 'Ever feel you've been had?'

A con-artist to the last, Lydon could play the post-modern Artful Dodger because, in the Sex Pistols, he had his very own cartoon dark-half. I can only assume that was why Glenn Matlock was eased out of the band and Sid Vicious eased in. Sid could be John's suicidal second banana, eliminating the need for Johnny to carve his own flesh; a Frankenstein creation who, considering the general quality control of the era, inevitably had to fall apart, all seams ripping. He was seemingly without function, except first to mutilate himself and then die as an encore, providing an early and much needed martyr. Dumb as a bull in a bullring, he lurched down Satan's shortcut. Couldn't sing, couldn't play, but an idiot savant who, stoned and in the dark, could find the trail left by Jones, Jimi and Jim. Like Iggy before him, he was punk's stuntman, who refused to fake the falls. When Sid fell, he was obliged to hurt himself. The only permitted airbag was a degenerate consumption of powdered drugs. Although I tended to look at Sid as little more than a degenerate surly thug, I couldn't fail to recognise his comatose charisma, the lacerated, lights-on-but-no-one-home beauty. Rotten might have been the Dodger, but Sid was the Face of '78.

When they were together, Rotten seemed to be able to exert a mad-scientist control over Sid. 'Back, Igor! Boring, Sidney!' The ringmaster lash kept Sid in check during the early days, but later, when Nancy wielded her whip, control was out and black-vinyl death seemed inevitable. I saw no redeeming qualities in Nancy Spungen; a chipped nails-on-a-blackboard horror show with an accent to chill the blood; an overripe USDA peach, doing its best to fall as far as possible from the Middle American tree. With Rotten on the one hand pulling Sid to notoriety and confrontation, Nancy followed a needle dream of junkie domesticity in which she would have all of his attention.

'Boring, Sidney.'

The word boring became one of the most overworked in the punk vocabulary, and it rubbed me up the wrong way. It may have had its place as the warning to the babbling speedfreak when the noise grew too irritating – 'You're boring, man. Fuck off.' Aside from that, I always considered it the cry of attention deficit, the symptom of the challenged attention span, and punk boredom was universal. They were bored by *everything*. Sex was boring. Emotions were boring. Compassion and concern were doubly boring. Jaded and pretending to drown in ennui, they adopted the terminally nihilist pose of being so desensitised that no stimuli could work, except maybe hard drugs and high-velocity, electric-razor music. Just to complicate matters, any movement that latches on to self-mutilation attracts the dysfunctionally self-mutilating. The hippies quickly learned how the psychotic, the dregs and the predators were attracted like a magnet to any sub-culture, but unfortunately the punks had to discover it all over again for themselves, and pay the freight of discovery.

Unfocused, short-span, television babies faced a primary dilemma. I can only paraphrase Nietzsche one more tedious time. 'How long can one be bored with monsters without becoming a monster oneself?' Does one tell jokes about Dachau to shock, or because they're funny? Does a nihilist revolution have, by definition, to be treated like an all-too-tedious chore? In the same way, if no future exists, what point in exploration or adventure? And without a future, what use history? Obviously the total denial of historical research was pure bullshit. John Rotten knew enough to do the old Monkees' tune 'Stepping Stone', and even Sid would resort to the Eddie Cochran catalogue when backed into the corner at Max's. Although to state it openly at the time might have been inadvisable, I saw much of punk as a critique of the Sixties counterculture, in the same way that Marxism is frequently accused of being nothing more than a critique of capitalism. The sad part was that, with their stance of 'we don't need no stinking education', punks remained clueless as to what my generation had actually been about. I recall a totally pointless conversation when I tried to set some sociopathic punk luminary

straight on recent history. I think it may have been the acne-cursed
poetess and critic Jane Suck. She started the dialogue with a sweeping
statement it was hard to let pass.

'There's nothing left but mindless fucking violence.'

Now where had I heard that before? 'You think so?'

'Peace and love failed, man, and that's why you hippies are such
fucking useless wankers.'

Ms Suck hadn't seen me in 1969. 'It wasn't all peace and love, kid.'

'Yes, it was. Fucking beads and granny glasses. What a fucking
joke.'

I wasn't aware at the time that part of her vehemence may have
been because she saw me as a challenge to her unrequited crush on
Julie Burchill. 'Vietnam?'

(Sniff.) 'Not the same thing, man.'

'The Weather Underground?'

'What?'

'How about the Manson family?'

'Not the same thing, man.'

The Clash, on the other hand, being from the Grove, manifested
considerably less boredom. In spite of the song 'I'm So Bored with
the USA', they looked more like an entity I recognised; a pragmatic
political rock band with all that entailed, both good and bad –
especially in contrast to the Pistols' uncertainty as to whether they
were a band or a Malcolm McLaren conceptual art event. The Clash
had an appreciation of both rock history and the immediate
surrounding culture, and were ready and willing to embrace both.
They had the professed interest in ganja and reggae of a band who cut
Junior Murvin's 'Police and Thieves', and they also knew their rockabilly well enough to dig up Vince Taylor's 'Long Black Cadillac'.
They shamelessly relished all the overgrown schoolboy stuff like war
movies, westerns, Mafia folklore and the SAS. They were hip to
Vietnam, Fidel, the Spanish Civil War and Chairman Mao's Long
March, the same stuff that turned me on when I was starting out.

They also kept things simple. I figured this was because they were
preaching revolution to some really dumb bastards. The Clash
worked with a highly threatening Fifth Column pogoing and
gobbing right in front of them. While Souixsie found anti-Semitism
shockingly chic, a sector of the crowd went further, allowing

themselves to be incited by grim background figures with lines to the National Front, and a message that fascism was the cure for boredom. I know Nazi regalia – all the way back to the Hell's Angels – has been displayed to scare the squares, but if the foul ideology comes out of the box right along with daggers and armbands, we have big potential trouble. When their song 'White Riot' began to be co-opted by the baby-Blackshirts as a battle hymn for burning Brixton, something drastic had to be done, and Joe Strummer went to some lengths – including a massive espousal of the newly formed Rock Against Racism – to make it clear that 'a riot of our own' meant a white uprising against the ruling class, not a fucking race war. He was confronted with the unenviable burden of quickly educating a crowd to whom education – and, in some cases, rational thought – was a major anathema, and I greatly admired the way he went about it.

Country, Blue Grass & Blues

Never was a nightspot less aptly named, but it wasn't Hilly Kristal's fault. All he'd really wanted was a quiet little club, under a wino flophouse called the Palace, with Bill Monroe and Willy Dixon on the jukebox, and a clientele drawn from the more discerning of the Bowery drunks and the New York chapter of the Hell's Angels, who had their club house over on 3rd Street. The full but rarely used name was CBGB&OMFUG, the acronym for Country, Blue Grass, Blues, and Other Music For Uplifting Gormandisers. The destruction of Hilly's original vision began when the band Television – Tom Verlaine, Richard Hell, Richard Lloyd and Billy Ficca – walked in one day looking for a place to play, and conned Hilly into giving them the joint one night a week. Television was short-lived but seminal, and would put out the single 'Little Johnny Jewel', a watershed for New York punk. Television was followed into CBGB by Patti Smith and Deborah Harry, in the Stilettos and then in Blondie. Talking Heads talked their way in, and finally the Ramones became long-haired, torn-Levis, resident Neanderthals and hey-ho, away it went. Television's one night expanded to seven, plus Sunday afternoons, and Hilly found himself presiding over an all-time cultural legend.

In essence, CBGB was the logical extension of Max's Kansas City. I had not visited New York early enough to have witnessed Max's in its prime, with David and Angela Bowie sticking Alice Cooper with the bill at the end of the night. I didn't see Deborah Harry as a waitress or Jackie Cooper giving head in the phone booth. By the time I first went there, it was already down to Johnny Thunders trying to borrow twenty bucks. It was Willy De Ville and Genya Raven onstage, but even they were rapidly heading downtown. The spare-change route from Union Square to the Bowery is a tradition older than rock & roll, older than Huntz Hall and the original Bowery Boys, almost as old as New York itself, and all downhill.

It probably also didn't help that Hilly had Club 82 just around the corner. Like London's Roxy, it was a time-honoured drag club, but with a longer and far more raunchy track record going back to the Fifties, or even earlier. It had been annexed like the Roxy, not by punks but by the androgynous glitter kids of Bowie's Aladdin Sâne period, when the Dolls had played a landmark show there in full drag. Whoever took me there had filled me in on the legend. In days of yore, Club 82 had seemingly been the screaming end. Errol Flynn would attempt to play the piano with his penis, and human faeces had been served as an entrée. When I visited, though, hardly a scream was being raised. Some disgruntled old queens sat at the bar, bitter and reflecting archly how the wannabe young with their Revlon ignorance had killed the Golden Age of Tallulah Bankhead. As Club 82 sank into its Weimar twilight, the Dolls' followers had only to step across the street.

CBGB can be hard on the recall. I drank there through most of the Eighties and even played the joint when Henry Beck, John Collins, Victoria Rose and I had swamp-surfed in the acoustic, post-art, anti-folk combo called Tijuana Bible. However, I clearly remember that, back in the mid-Seventies, when I was still a visitor from London, I saw the Ramones enough times to be left in no doubt that, within the minimalist tracks of their avowed pinhead simplicity, they were the tightest and most streamlined punk band, bar none.

I also recall watching the Dead Boys but, needless to say, not the night Stiv Bators got his dick sucked onstage by one of the waitresses. I always seem to miss the significant stuff. Instead of copping the oral and then hanging himself with his belt, his self-destructive shtick of the night was to hurl himself from the stage and smash into a full table of drinks, spilling booze, breaking glass and cutting himself. The damage was fairly impressive, but I figured Stiv had been paying rather too close attention to the combined moves of Rotten and Vicious. I was also grateful he didn't choose my table to fall into, otherwise I suppose I would have felt morally obliged to smack him. Spilled cognac is spilled cognac.

I know I saw Richard Hell, because when the English touring party that consisted of me, Boss Goodman and *NME* photographer Chalkie Davies checked into the George Washington Hotel on one particular visit, a package was waiting for us. (I usually stayed at the Washington. Enough cheap Mickey-Spillane, 23rd-Street grime for romance, but not such a free fire zone as the Chelsea. No Viva shrieking.) Hell was on Sire at the time, just as the Deviants had been some eight or nine years earlier, and Seymour Stein had seen to it that one of his publicity people had sent over a bunch of albums, pictures, press releases. I was grateful for the present, but still had a few reservations about Hell. No argument that he was, and still is, a poet of stature among his contemporaries, but I couldn't resist an uncharitable thought that part of his rock 'n' roll mystique was down to the rumour that he was hung like a horse. I mean, Hell didn't sing no better than I did, and I was out of the business.

Where Richard Hell went, also went Legs McNeil, who along with John Holstrom had founded *Punk* magazine, which had caused a great deal of interest around *NME*. I think Legs was well aware of that fact because, from the moment we were introduced, he seemed intent on demonstrating how much of a skinny, smart-mouthed, beer-swilling, gadfly irritant he could be – as in actually licking the net stockings of the Bettie Page print on my T-shirt. I decided, with Legs, I only had two options. To swat him or to make friends with this joker-provocateur, and we've been firm friends on and off ever since.

I also first met Lester Bangs in the sagging and pasty flesh at CBGB. After the formalities of mutual admiration were over, and we knew each other well enough for me to take him to task, I began to berate him for clinging to rock crit like an accursed security blanket. So much talent being feloniously wasted on silly records and even sillier musicians; get the fuck outta here, Bangs, and write a detective novel, or at the very least some destructured Bukowski short stories. (Don't forget I was full of my own adventures in science fiction at the time.) The man would snarl and suck on his bottle of Rolling Rock, and I'd wax furious at the waste. Lester was also very taken with the idea of performing. My only advice there was to lose some weight and shave the moustache, but it also caused me to reflect that my own swearing off playing rock 'n' roll was maybe a little drastic. Tragically, none of the Lester Bangs might-have-beens ever were. The man, failing to heed all advice, was struck down by a fatuous overdose of Valium and over-the-counter flu remedies.

Even before Lester's demise, or Johnny Thunders determinedly marking himself for death, I wasn't so innocent as to believe that New York didn't exact its share of victims. On the other hand, it had a contradictory sense of permanence. In contrast to London, people there seemed in for the long haul. The town was also remarkably free of ageism. In London I had constantly to remind snotty arseholes that I wasn't any boring old fart from the Sixties. In New York I felt like a gunfighter in my prime with the chops to survive. I found the density of bohemianism in New York guaranteed a lot more people like myself who had bridged the Sixties/Seventies gap – Lou Reed, Sam Shepard, Patti Smith, Deborah Harry, Viva and others of the gang from the Warhol Factory, Jim Fourrat of the Pink Panthers, and street characters like David Peel, the psychotic Yippie Dana Beale, Ugly George. Moondog was always on Sixth Avenue outside Black Rock keeping people honest. In New York I discovered fewer dictates of fashion and a far greater diversity. New York had no unilateral punk style. Willy De Ville in pimp-bebop sharkskin and a pencil moustache, through the Cramps' proto-gothic, to Dee Dee Ramone, the self-confessed, leather-jacket rent hustler from 53rd and 3rd. Photographer Joe Stevens flourished there with a history all the way back to the days of acoustic Bob Dylan, but was in CBGB every night, lord of the lens. Thus it really shouldn't have come as any surprise when a short, somewhat strange figure came up to me and asked if I was Mick Farren and, if I was, did I want to make a record?

Terry Ork resembled nothing more than a short, gay, amiable werewolf, and, as I understood the gist of the conversation, he wanted me to cut some tracks. I figured it was just some New York, ripped-in-the-small-hours flattery by a guy who'd been scared by a

Deviants record when he was a kid. Cutting cynically to the chase, I demanded to know when this mythic session – which would be my first time in a studio in seven years – might go down. I expected some vague maybe-baby, I'll-get-back-to-you, but to my surprise Terry replied, 'Wednesday.'

'Wednesday?'

Wednesday was just forty-eight hours away. Maybe less; the night was already late. Boss was with me on this particular trip, so I looked at him for some kind of reinforcement. 'Think I should do this?'

'What have you got to lose?'

On that count I wasn't sure, but offering me time in a studio is like offering a narcissist a room full of mirrors. 'Going to come along with me?'

'Wouldn't miss it.'

Maybe I should have had a bit more initial trust in Terry Ork. He had, after all, been the manager of Television, shot dope with Jim Carroll and had a history going all the way back to the Sixties Warhol Factory. The project in hand was the creation of two albums, one consisting of weird and unlikely people singing songs by or associated with the Rolling Stones, and another of equally weird people singing the Phil Spector catalogue. Both were forerunners of the tribute CDs that have grown so tedious in recent years, although we didn't know it at the time. What better vehicle could there be with which to sneak out of retirement? Besides, I was in New York; if I fucked up too badly, who in London was going to hear about it? As it turned out, I couldn't have been more in error. I did fuck up (depending on how you looked at it) – and not only did everyone hear about it, but they actually heard it.

The studio where Terry had recording time was a couple of hours out of the city in White Plains, and the plan was that we would take a train from Grand Central. This was sounding better and better; not only a recording studio, but a train ride.

'So who's the band going to be?'

It seemed that the whole deal was being produced by a guy called John Tiven, now a well-placed face in the modern music business. He would play guitar and keyboards, if we needed them. To this day I do not recall the name of the bass player, but I won't forget the drums were played by Marc Bell. Marc had been the drummer with

Wayne/Jayne County and Richard Hell's Voidoids, and would very shortly join the Ramones, changing his name to Marky Ramone. I still claim that Marc was the instigator of all the trouble. The arrangement was that Boss and I would meet Marc at Grand Central, I think at around ten in the morning, and travel up to White Plains together. All went according to plan. The only change was that I'd invited along a back-up singer called Janis Cafasso, an ex-girlfriend of Johnny Thunders (there seemed to be a lot of his ex-girlfriends) to help me out with the vocals. I think a sub-text motivation was that working together in the studio might be the prelude to an out-of-town romance, but I never found out if this was to be, as whisky became my only preoccupation, aside from the music.

As we settled into our seats Marc produced a pint of Jack Daniels from inside his coat, like a gambler pulling out a marked deck. Boss glanced in my direction as Marc took a swig and passed me the bottle. Boss knew how I could be after a breakfast of straight bourbon, but I was heedless of the look. I was nervous, and embarking on an adventure, goddamn it. At the studio, more Jack was waiting. I've never found it an effective production technique to get the performers blind drunk, but, on the other hand, I wasn't the one producing the sessions, and in those days I was rarely able to resist a bottle in front of me. Better than a frontal lobotomy, as the old joke goes, but in this instance, not by very much.

As requested, I had selected two songs – one by the Rolling Stones and one by Phil Spector. The Stones song was 'Play with Fire', the Spector tune was the Teddy Bears' hit 'To Know Him Is to Love Him'. Terry also wanted me to cut a version of 'Lost Johnny', a song I'd written with Lemmy. If all went well, in addition to the cuts on the two projected albums, he might also put out a single. Okay, cool, and the band went to work putting down the tracks. I managed the guide vocals with only a couple of shots from the second bottle of Jack, then began on the finished vocal of 'Lost Johnny'. So far, so good.

We moved on to 'Play with Fire', but the vocals did not go well, and as I sweated them I drank, hitting the bottle so hard that I was in a state of intermittent blackout when we finally got to 'To Know Him Is to Love Him'. Our arrangement accelerated the Spector rock-a-ballad to a breakneck Ramones thrash, and I launched into it without harness or safety net. All I can recall is going into some stream-of-horror consciousness, 'I'm here/All alone/Just me/And the microphone'. And, with that, the task was complete. The rest of the night was, at best, a confusion of fragmented images. Seemingly I wasn't the only one fucking up. I can remember sitting in a shady pizza joint with large pictures of Frank Sinatra and the Pope on the walls; feeling like shit, but unable to leave because one of the company apparently needed to cop some smack, and we were waiting for the fucking man.

Amid the next day's hangover, I mercilessly beat up on myself. I'd had one more shot in the studio, and all I'd done was hit the booze and fuck up. Then Terry Ork came by with a couple of cassette copies and seemed overjoyed with the result.

Huh?

I listened to the intro to 'Lost Johnny', sick with trepidation. Did I really have to go through the whole thing twice? The vocal came in and I discovered, to my amazement, that by the intervention of some benign demon hand, it had worked. By the time we got to 'To Know Him Is to Love Him', I was laughing fit to fall off my chair. This wasn't a fuck-up, I hadn't blown it. The end result was *psychotically funny*. The tapes contained a magnificent dementia, wholly unobtainable except by methods as twisted as those employed.

When I arrived back in England, I discovered that this Manhattan/White Plains adventure had been but a first step.

Vampires Stole My Lunch Money

I was back, proud, and I was loving every tactile moment of it. Live at Dingwall's with the de-luxe treatment. *One-two-three-four*, and away we go! Let Alan Powell pound, let the guitars of Larry and Andy schlang and grind. Hail, hail, rock 'n' roll. I was gracing a London stage in my own right for the very first time. Not with the Deviants. (*No-no!*) It was me, with a backing band that, for want of a better idea, I'd called the Good Guys. (*Yeh-yeh!*) Larry Wallis and Andy Colquhoun on guitar, Alan Powell on drums, Gary Tibbs playing bass, but I was the star of my own fucking show, ultimately responsible, but also the ultimate recipient of the accolades. Not bad, huh? (*Shooby-do bop do-wah!*)

Everyone was being so amazingly nice. I felt welcomed home like the prodigal. Elvis Costello had complimented me on the quality of my lyrics. Everyone from Lemmy and Wilko to Chrissie Hynde and Judy Nylon, from the Hell's Angels to the Pink Fuzzy Bunnies Against Racism, had shown up to wish me well. Abner Stein and Dempsey were there to lend their support, and a bunch of punks came, curious to see what the old boys might be up to. The Dingwall's management had not only supplied us with a bucket of Red Stripe on ice, but also a large bottle of Jack Daniels and five shot-glasses. On first observing this charitable gift, I realised it could well be my – and Larry's – downfall, and I resolved to pace myself, even though pacing has never been my strong suit. Perhaps the best gift of all came from Jonathan Smeaton, still with Hawkwind, but readying himself to go into the bigtime and light everyone from Billy Idol to the Stones. During the afternoon soundcheck, Smeaton had shown up, unasked and entirely of his own volition, with a couple of his crew and a whole mess of lights, to augment the regular Dingwall's rig.

'We figured you might like a bit of extra drama.'

I could have hugged him. The band had played a number of shows before Dingwall's; some good, some indifferent, and one at Sussex University in Brighton at which everything – from our memories to the technology – broke down. Now we were finally on home turf, and not fucking up was a matter of regimental honour. Boss capped the general generosity by acting as DJ that night, even though he now managed the club, and played a straight twenty minutes of Eddie Cochran, Little Richard and the like before we hit the stage, ensuring that the crowd was warm, rowdy and receptive. A recently unearthed tape demonstrates that I was drunk, aggressive and affecting a somewhat more gorblimey accent than usual. I fluffed the opening to 'I Want a Drink', but, on the other hand, I went into an extended Beefheart-like coda to 'Half Price Drinks', during which (if the tape is to be believed) the band stood back and listened in disbelief. Can't sing, huh? I'll fucking show you. I don't think I went down on my knees to testify, but it was close. I'd had six years to ponder the moves and tricks, and I was putting them all through their paces.

Smeaton's lights, even with my eyes closed in concentration, bored through my eyelids, the colour of blood with contrasting yellow floaters, and electric inspiration streamed from on high. I was bathed in the radiant breath of whatever god looks out for rock & rollers. Being lavishly illuminated can do wonders for the performing ego. I was having my night and – for this audience – I could do no wrong. Of course, the tape proves that technically I did dozens of things wrong, and the scrappy moments were as frequent as the inspired ones, but we were the Dogs of War, not Madame Fifi's Precision Dancing Poodles, and we could afford scrappy. The suspension of disbelief was in place and the Reichian orgone circuit was never more complete. I poured all the whisky-sweat and energy I could summon into the crowd, and they returned it multifold. The upward spiral built into an increasingly vibrant and vindicating arc. As we encored with Gene Vincent's 'Say Mama', they may not have been lending their ears to bel canto, but the punters had been well and truly entertained.

The trip from White Plains to headlining at Dingwall's was a long one: not in time, but in its creative stages. Terry Ork was as good as his word and put out a single. The album of Phil Spector material – eventually entitled *Bionic Gold* – came out a little later, and that might have been that, except that one day Jake Riviera accosted me and, with a definite air of challenge, demanded to know if I wanted to record for Stiff. By this point, Stiff was the hot and pre-eminent independent label. Larry was already in there on a retainer, having made a single called 'Between the Lines' with the Pink Fairies, and then having been hired as full-time number two house-producer after Nick Lowe. At that moment he was producing Wreckless Eric – a weird and wild talent, who fell too much under the shadow of Elvis Costello and never really obtained the recognition he deserved. Stiff was by no means either an exclusive punk or pub rock label. It had the Damned and Elvis Costello, Ian Dury and Nick Lowe, and for a while Richard Hell and Television for the UK.

The offer almost certainly came in the pub on Alexander Street next door to the Stiff offices. I had probably gone down there to meet up with Larry. When Jake put the question to me, I know I answered carefully. Jake could be a terrible wind-up merchant and master deflator of egos. I didn't want to come over all eager and then find myself the butt of some cruel and unusual joke. 'I suppose I could do that.'

'Say an EP, four tracks?'

'Sounds manageable.'

'And Larry would produce?'

'Of course.'

'So let's do it.'

I nodded. Let's do it. I waited for the laugh, but no laugh came, and a couple of weeks later we went into Pathway Studios, which everyone claimed had the best sound this side of Sun Studios in Memphis, and where most of the Stiff masterpieces were recorded. Learning from my mistakes in New York, whisky was banned from the studio and, about four hours into the first session, cocaine was also banned. We'd had a toot at the very start to get us rolling, and then spent three hours attempting to eliminate weird noises from the drums that may not actually have existed, and all those involved become very edgy and irritated with each other. With the twin downfalls banished, however, everything progressed as smooth as a rhapsody. Larry was producing, as agreed, and he also played one of the guitars. A reunion was engineered with Paul Rudolph, who provided an extra guitar. Andy Colquhoun on bass, and Alan Powell, over from Hawkwind on drums, completed the conspiracy.

I don't think it took more than three days, and Jake drove over a couple of times in his Buick Riviera (what else would he drive?) and took us down the pub. All in all, such a good time was had by all that I bought everyone a pair of red plastic goggles in a discount toy store and they became the sessions' Order of Merit. Of the four tracks cut, I particularly liked the EP's title song, 'Screwed Up', and the archly punk 'Let's Loot the Supermarket Again Like We Did Last Summer'. The greatest pleasure of the whole episode was being produced by Larry Wallis. He did the diametric reverse of everyone else I'd ever worked with, and treated my weird singing as absolutely acceptable. He didn't try to force me into some familiar, but – for me – highly contorted, rock & roll mould. It was something that should have happened years before, but I guess that an idea before its time has to learn to wait.

Waiting, however, turned out not to be on the cards in this

halcyon time. Shortly after completing the Stiff EP, I received a phone call from an outfit called Logo Records.

'We've just acquired the Transatlantic catalogue, and we're re-releasing two of your old records.'

'You're kidding me.'

'We wondered if you'd be willing to help promote them.'

'I'd rather make a new one.'

Pause.

'Really?'

'Really.'

'Listen, Mick, can we get back to you?'

I assumed I'd heard the last of that, but forty-eight hours later the phone rang again. 'We'd very much like to make an album with you, if we can work out a budget.'

The budget wasn't great, but in a matter of weeks we were back in Pathway. The interval between completing the work for Stiff and commencing the Logo album – eventually endowed with the cryptic title *Vampires Stole My Lunch Money* – was so short that it almost seemed to be two phases of the same project, with only a protracted coffee-break in between. The line-up was essentially the same, except that Paul Rudolph was out of the picture – I think he had gone back to Canada – and Larry and Andy were now sharing the bass and guitar chores, while Al Powell again played drums.

With the initial tracks down, some guests came in to add a little icing to the cake. Most significantly, Wilko on guitar and Sonja Kristina and Chrissie Hynde to do back-up vocals. Since we'd last seen her, Sonja had enjoyed a moderate degree of success with a progressive pop band called Curved Air. Later she would marry Stewart Copeland, the drummer with the Police, only to lose him to an African safari fling with model Lauren Hutton. Chrissie, on the other hand, was still a star who'd yet to crest the horizon. After hanging out with the Chelsea punks for a while, she'd graduated to the Grove, where she wound up crashing at the basement home of my estranged (but still undivorced) wife Joy in Ledbury Road. As previously mentioned, Chrissie had done some writing for *NME*, but her heart was far from being in journalism. She wanted to create her own music, and with the energy and determination of an American in a strange land, she beat her head against the boys' club bastions that still largely surrounded even punk rock. Along the way, she engaged in just about any project that would place her on a stage or in a recording studio, from an hilariously offensive single under the *nom de guerre* the Moors Murders, to strange and girlish Brill Building parodies with Judy Nylon and Patti Paladin, before she formed the Pretenders and carved her own influential niche in rock history.

My contact with Chrissie and her ambitions mainly involved listening to her play guitar and sing each time I visited Joy's – relations between the two of us being at least reasonably cordial now that she had dropped Jamie Mandelkau and become the tea-making, drug-dispensing den-mother to a whole coterie of local rockers. Sometimes Chrissie and I would goof around singing Johnny Cash songs in dubious harmony, but at others she'd play her own compositions. At the time, they struck me as strange and compelling, and her devil-may-care disregard for the accepted conventions of rhyme patterns and standard verse structures was stunning. Although they sounded nothing like her, the only people I could think of who worked in this way were Syd Barrett, Took and, now and then, Neil Young. Nick Lowe, on the other hand, had dismissed the same songs as formless and unworkable, but since, within a year, they would constitute the string of hits like 'Brass in Pocket' that would follow her first chart success with Ray Davies' 'Stop Your Sobbing', I guess the master's instincts for pure pop failed him in her case.

Except for those fortunate bands with massive corporate bucks behind them, every record becomes a race against time and the money running out, and this was doubly if not trebly so with *Vampires*. Working on a low budget can produce crippling frustrations, but, at the same time, introduce all kinds of entertaining factors. Primarily it forces all concerned to focus on the mission, rather than wasting time shooting pool, playing pinball or attempting to write entirely new songs from the ground up, right there in the studio. We went back into Pathway prepped and ready to burn like Joan of Arc. I admit we went down the pub on a fairly regular basis – to do otherwise would have caused mutiny in the ranks – but cocaine and whisky were still *verboten*.

Having negotiated a dusk-to-dawn fiscal sweetheart of a deal with engineer Chas Heatherington, we'd gone back to long all-night sessions. As producer, Larry had decided that we would abandon the cut-ups, blackouts and all the Mothers of Invention tricks of yesteryear, and would create an album of properly crafted, well-produced songs, and I bowed to his decision even though I missed the Zappa tricks. That's why you recruit a producer in the first place. You trust his judgement. Again we rented electronic outboard boxes from an obliging Pink Floyd sound guy to obtain the maximum magic for our money. We even had some cheap and sneaky laughs when we discovered that, when not in use, the echo plates clearly picked up all conversation in the TV room and relayed it to the control booth. Hilarity knew no bounds the night we eavesdropped on drugged girlfriends talking about the boys, although keyholing doesn't come without a few unwanted insights.

The negative side of a low budget is that you can only do so much, and the moment comes when you have to stop and turn in your efforts as product. I was very aware that we'd spent most of our money on five or six of our favourite tracks, while the remainder had been banged down as little more than jamming, art-school R&B, with only a thin coat of metalflake. Despite this perceived defect, critic Ira A. Robbins wrote:

Released at the height of the punk wave but springing from a much deeper creative well, Vampires Stole My Lunch Money *is Farren's solo masterpiece . . . he dishes out a harrowingly honest collection of songs about drinking, dissolution, depression and desperation. About as powerful as rock gets, this nakedly painful LP is not recommended to sissies, born-again Christians and prohibitionists.*

After the completion of the record, I didn't exactly feel this way. I fretted about the cheaply finished filler. Larry also had a bad bout of pre-release jitters, and Lemmy further undermined my confidence in the work by pointing out – well after the fact – that not only could I have used Motorhead as a backing band, but I was a fool not to have done so. I know a wind-up when I meet one, and this was a wind-up, but I didn't have time to get depressed. I had to transform the recording ensemble into a live band – the one-time-only Good Guys – and hit the trail of gigs that would lead to the already described night of fabulousness at Dingwall's. In the middle of these endeavours, to add an historic and quite surreal element from the far external, Elvis Presley breathed his last on the toilet at Graceland.

The Night Elvis Died

Larry Wallis had temporarily moved out on his girlfriend Shirley and was living in a place called the Church, which was exactly that. An old church, or, at the very least, a chapel; Methodist, I think, abandoned and deconsecrated, and then taken over – either officially or unofficially – by a bunch of long-haired marginals and turned into a kind of bickering squatter commune. To this day, I've never been sure exactly where the Church was located. Innate snobbery has always prevented me from truly understanding the geography of South London. Larry occupied what had previously been the Church's church hall, a structure of institutional wooden walls and a tin roof, which had once housed whist drives, jumble sales, Sunday-school classes, and had doubtless reverberated regularly to the sound of 'All Things Bright and Beautiful' to the accompaniment of a wheezing pedal-harmonium. A small stage that had borne its share of nativity plays and harvest-festival pageants added, in the new Wallis incarnation, a touch of split-level theatrical exotica, while the crossbeams supporting the roof offered a certain suspension potential, had ropes and pulleys ever been introduced.

The place must have been a monster to heat in the winter, and if memory serves, heating was one of the major causes of the constant bickering. At this moment in the narration, however, it was benign August, so no thermal worries, although inclemency would play a crucial part in what was to come. After visiting the off-licence, we went to work with a couple of six-packs and a half-bottle of Scotch, in addition to the ever-present bong to see us through. The task at hand was the preparation of demos for *Vampires Stole My Lunch Money*. When Larry decamped to the Church, he took his Sony quarter-inch four-track, his mixing board, his drum machine and the Auratone mini-speakers that were then all the rage, and of which he was inordinately proud. After spending a couple of weeks wiring together the set-up, he was living in his own home studio. Although common enough today, back then home studios were unknown, except among big-arse wealthy rock stars, but Larry had a way with technology.

As always, at any home of Larry's, the TV was on, but as the avowed aim was to write a handful of great pop songs, the sound was down. I think the tune we were working on was 'Half Price Drinks', yet another lament of the bar-room floozie. Thematically a happy-hour close-relative of the country standard 'Honky Tonk Angels', but a relentless mid-tempo four-four shlang instead of a country twang made it pure rock 'n' roll. We'd hoped to sell it to Marianne Faithfull, but since she didn't want it, we cut it ourselves. Partway through tracking the demo, the skies opened in a spectacular summer thunderstorm, complete with blue-black anvil clouds and forked lightning against a night sky.

Although absorbed by the task at hand, our eyes went instinctively to the screen when a break-in newsflash came up on the TV. This was back in the days when breaking in on the show in progress was reserved for really serious stuff, like the outbreak of war, the fall of governments and the death of kings. The image on the eighteen-inch Trinitron was suddenly of a grinning, lip-curled, short-haired Elvis Presley from one of the later and most execrable beach movies, but I knew in an instant. No hesitation. Someone in the newsroom had grabbed the very first colour still that came to hand. That the flashing lightning and rolling thunder might be a little too operatic and implausible never entered my mind.

'Fucking hell, he's dead!'

Larry lunged for the volume and we just caught the final recap. '. . . singer Elvis Presley dies at forty-three in his home in Memphis, Tennessee.'

My first instinct was to phone Ingrid. Perhaps I should head home. Ingrid was the ultimate true fan and Elvis-believer, and maybe I should be with her. Or maybe I shouldn't. Maybe she'd want to cope with her Elvis-grief in Nordic privacy. The speculation turned out to be irrelevant. All I heard was an engaged signal. I wondered idly who'd beat me to the dial. Lemmy was too self-absorbed, even though he was having an affair with her at around this time. Perhaps she and I were in that weird limbo of attempting to call each other simultaneously. I hung up and dialled again, but the line remained busy. It then occurred to me that Ingrid might not have the TV on at all, and that the ongoing call was totally unElvis-related. She still laughed, because she had yet to hear.

The next few newsflashes were vague. Paramedics had been called to Graceland, but attempts at resuscitation had failed. A heart attack was suspected, but no information was being released, pending an autopsy. We might have bought the heart-attack story – Elvis had, after all, become a fat, self-indulgent bastard over the preceding couple of years – but *Elvis: What Happened?* (a book about Elvis' last years by three of his bodyguards, Red West, Sonny West and Dave Hibbler, all members of the inner circle of the Memphis Mafia) had already come out, revealing, among other obsessive-compulsive transgressions and side-effects of global adoration, Elvis' truly imperial pill habit.

'Think he ODed?'

'Has to be on the cards.'

'So what do you think he ODed on?'

'Being Elvis.'

'Seriously.'

'Probably a whole combination of stuff. Qualuudes, Demerol, Percodan, you name it.'

My suspicions surrounding Elvis and his drug intake actually went as far back as 1970 and the release of the movie *Elvis: That's the Way It Is.* Ingrid, Edward, Boss, John Manly, I and maybe one or two others had made a mass outing to the Westbourne Grove Odeon to see the feature-length documentary on Elvis' return to the live stage. During a rehearsal sequence when Elvis was goofing with the band and all but fell off his stool, I turned to Boss and whispered, 'The guy's as high as a kite.'

Boss looked at me as though I was nuts, but afterwards, in the pub, the subject came up again. 'You really believe Elvis was fucked-up?'

I was now on the defensive. 'High as a kite. What the fuck do you think? Why should he be any different to everyone else?'

Boss and Edward continued to look at me as though I was

projecting. Ingrid, as ever, kept her own counsel, although I think she'd suspected Elvis' drug intake all along. It took seven years for my perception to be vindicated, and Boss was big enough to be the first to admit it.

The thunderstorm had started to abate a little when I finally got Ingrid on the phone. 'Did you hear?'

'Yes.'

Her tone gave no clue as to how she was feeling, but Ingrid could have remained enigmatically neutral through an outbreak of thermo-nuclear global war. Showing emotion had been a Class-A felony among the von Essens for many generations.

'I'll be home as soon as I can.'

'I thought you had stuff to do?'

'Elvis' death has rather put a damper on things.'

After the rain, no mini-cab was to be swiftly had, but as I was finally leaving, Larry made a remark. 'You know, Micky, it was really something to be with you when you heard that Elvis died. It's one of those things that you don't ever forget.'

The deaths of kings are not static occurrences. They are a time of movement and change, speed and activity. When they shot John Kennedy, we had a conspiracy to build. With Elvis, it proved more paranormal than paranoid. The world was gearing up for twenty years of trailer-park grief, which verged perilously close to a religion. By morning 'Memories' would be all over the TV and radio. After a respectable interval I called Felix. I didn't even have to explain why I was calling.

'Are we going to?'

'I don't see how we can't.'

'Lots of pink and black'

'Plenty of black and some funeral purple.'

We were not only going to put out the top-class and most reverent Elvis Presley Memorial Poster Magazine on the stands, but accomplish it in record time. The crew assembled in the pub first thing (which for us meant about one-thirty in the afternoon) and went to work until the job was finished. I think I was the nominal editor, but Felix was the hands-on publisher, bolstering the troops when they flagged by any means necessary; arguing about the exact tone of the pictures and the hastily written copy. He, too, was paying his respects to Elvis by showing the publishing industry that he could turn out a quality product at near the speed of light. The one shot went on sale four days later, beating everyone except the actual daily papers with their four-page insert supplements. Thirty-two pages of full colour, primarily the young Elvis, gorgeous and beautiful, as everyone really wanted him. In the same time space I also managed the lengthy *NME* cover story/obituary. Despite being semi-retired from the weekly, I brooked no argument that the assignment wasn't mine by right.

Yes, we made a buck on the poster mag, but, along with the *NME* obituary, it was also my tribute, my personal wreath on the freshly turned grave. An indication that my honourable intentions had glimmered through – and of the universal impact of Elvis Presley – was provided by the young, Cliff Richard-hip Indian couple who ran the newsagents on the corner of Chesterton Road and Ladbroke Grove. Most days, before either hailing a cab or getting on the number fifteen or fifty-two bus to wherever the day demanded, I would pick up my twenty Rothman's, maybe a *Daily Mirror* or the *2000AD* comic I had reserved for me. We'd generally exchange pleasantries, but that was the limit of our relationship. It came completely out of the blue when they thanked me for my piece in *NME*, and said how they'd found it respectful and very reflective of the way they felt. Up to that moment I hadn't been aware they had any idea who I was, or that – although they sold *NME* and were carrying Felix's poster mag – they even so much as looked at them. Apparently Elvis, *in extremis*, cut through all barriers of race, class and religion. I remembered, of course, how huge Elvis had been in India, where his worst beach movies fitted almost perfectly with the garish and inexplicable Technicolor excesses of the sub-continent's all-singing, all-dancing pop cinema, and where he found his last mass audience for those aesthetic atrocities.

I was perfectly serious when I said that Elvis had ODed on being Elvis. One individual could never be the primary player in so many insecure teen dreams, and the object of such planetary hysterias, and survive. The Rastafarians had made some dire predictions for 1977, when the 'two sevens clashed'. Was the Dead Elvis our white-boy rocker slice of the karma?

Sixteen Coaches Long

In 1977 the two sevens may have clashed, but at least 1978 commenced with one positive event. Wayne Kramer was released from federal prison, after serving twenty-one months of a five-year sentence for cocaine possession with intent to distribute; better than that, he was able to come to England to cut a single and have his own triumphal night at Dingwall's.

In the time since the MC5 had played Phun City, Wayne and I had evolved a friendship just about as tight as it could be, with him in Detroit and me in London. Whenever possible, as I traversed the USA, I'd made it a habit to stop over. Not that Detroit has too much to offer the casual tourist, unless he's curiously obsessed with the study of heinous smoke-stack industry and inner-city decay. If the object of my mission hadn't been to visit Wayne and his girlfriend Sam – short for Samantha – Miller, I'd never have gone there at all. The early Seventies, OPEC and the energy crisis had not been economically kind to the Motor City. The Big Three US car makers – Ford, Chrysler and General Motors – had taken the ostrich point of view towards the short-term energy crisis, long-term fossil-fuel depletion, atmospheric pollution and the need, as demonstrated by the Germans and the Japanese, generally to downsize the car and introduce it to higher levels of fuel efficiency.

Sales of gas guzzlers had plummeted, plants posted lay-offs and the United Auto Workers who did keep their jobs were mainly on short time. Detroit became one version of a not-too-pleasant shape of things to come. After dark, the sidewalks emptied. Corner shops kept their doors locked and buzzed in customers, liquor stores had armed guards behind one-way glass. Along with the rest of the city, Wayne had hardly been prospering since the demise of the MC5. Even though he was a hometown celeb, he was down to playing bars on a Friday night for unemployment-cheque drunks, and explaining to the bentnoses from the local musicians' union how come he was eight months behind with his dues. What the fuck? It's the life of the vast majority of musicians, if they're lucky enough to work at all.

Boss and I had been in Los Angeles, using my *NME* credentials to do the town. The plan had been to fly to LA and continue having fun for as long as it seemed feasible. When we'd exhausted the

Hollywood potential – but, we hoped, not our money – we would take the train from there to Detroit, to stay a few days and get drunk with Wayne Kramer and brighten his miserable Motown-bound life. The idea of riding Amtrak could be filed under schoolboy adventure, and when we talked to Wayne on the phone, we discovered that his life was actually far from miserable. In fact, he sounded in fine fettle; he told me he had a brand-new car and obliquely indicated – as one would on a public telephone – that the white powder was blowing in the wind as thick as in Alaska in February. Easily calculating that such a lifestyle could not be maintained on bar-band wages, we deduced he had entered the cocaine trade on some modest semi-pro, retail level, and that gave us all the more incentive to ride the rails.

The journey to Detroit commenced in the early evening with a bottle of tequila. Back in those days, Boss and I had yet to learn the finer points of tequila and we'd opted for the cheaper, clear variety, instead of the more expensive but more merciful gold. As the train moved out through the eastern sprawl of the Los Angeles basin, we worked on the bottle like drunken *charros*. Amtrak trains move exceedingly slowly by European standards. The tracks are so poorly maintained that they scarcely ever exceed fifty miles an hour. At this snail's pace, the train hadn't reached anywhere significant before the two us fell into a stupor and it didn't matter anyway.

We woke a little after dawn somewhere in the desert with sunlight streaming in the train window, searing a bad cheap-tequila hangover. A hangover on a transcontinental train is not something I recommend. Aside from the light, the sway of the carriage and the clack of the wheels are connected to both the brain and the stomach, and constitute a cruel form of mechanised torture. Fortunately the restaurant car started serving breakfast early, so we were able to stuff our queasy stomachs with pancakes and sausage, and then, after a decent interval, move on to the bar car for Bloody Marys. The bar car became our second home for the duration, where we indulged those transitory buddyships between strangers on a train.

The LA Limited took us only as far as Chicago, where we switched to a less lavish provincial commuter train, with no restaurant or bar car. Now all we had to do was look forward to the good times a-coming when we hooked up with Wayne, an anticipation that made what actually came to pass even more of a shock. By the time we reached Detroit it must have been around eleven in the evening. Not too many folks seemed to use trains in the Motor City. We were the only passengers alighting, and, if that wasn't sufficiently *Twilight Zone*, no one was waiting for us. Where was Wayne, the cocaine, the fancy car – all that we'd been promised and led to expect?

Finally a car pulled into the forecourt of the station. Nothing fancy, though, a decrepit Mercury with a smashed-in door held together with gaffer tape and coat hangers. Sam got out. 'Hi, guys.'

'Hi, Sam.'

Pretty, but hardly intellectual, Sam was direct and down-to-earth, and not afraid to ask for what she wanted when she wanted it. Right now, she was absolutely direct. 'Wayne's been busted.'

'You're kidding? How bad is it?'

'It's bad, Mick. Wayne only just made bail. He's sleeping.'

The drive to where Wayne and Sam were living took about as long as Sam needed to deliver the condensed version of what had transpired while we'd been riding the rails. Some months earlier Wayne had been approached at a gig by a couple of wiseguy-looking individuals who wanted him to hook them up with some coke. Figuring he could make a bit for himself, Wayne had gone along. Over the course of the next few months the guys had come back, not once, but on a regular basis, looking each time for larger and larger quantities. Truth was only revealed when the amounts had grown to such a size that, in the event of a bust, they represented serious jailtime. At that point, the buyers – with a full *Kojak/Barretta* sense of drama – produced guns and badges and identified themselves as Federal Drug Enforcement Agents. For Wayne and his partners in crime, the rock and the hard place had come together like the crack of doom. This nasty dénouement had transpired while Boss and I had been carousing on Amtrak.

We learned of further complications. The cocaine seized by the Feds had been fronted to Wayne's gullible cartel by a bunch of *genuine* wiseguys. Not only were Boss and I visiting a shell-shocked crew in full bust-aftermath, but ones who feared the possibility of death execution-style by local mafiosi seeking to make examples. Already Timmy, Wayne's bass player, had been handcuffed to a wooden piling on one of the less attractive margins of Lake Michigan, while the owners of the coke ascertained that a bust had actually happened and wasn't just a cover story for an inept rip-off. Timmy was now carrying a gun at all times. Another co-conspirator, known only as the Bug, was contemplating jumping bail and going on the run, while Wayne realised that if he was going to have any future in rock & roll, he would have to stand still for trial and sentencing.

'Chuck Berry went to jail, right?'

'Right, Wayne.'

'But who needs it?'

'Right, Wayne.'

I suppose some individuals might simply have turned tail and caught the next train out, but a gentleman has to stand by his friends in their time of tribulation, even if a bullet in the back of the head for being in the wrong place at the wrong time is an eventuality – maybe an outside eventuality, but an eventuality all the same. In Wayne's shoes, I would have been scared shitless, and I expect he was, but outwardly he was handling the situation with an amazing and fatalistic, if-you-can't-do-the-time-don't-do-the-crime aplomb. Handling it, in fact, better that I did one particular evening, when we went to see the band play at some cheesy Detroit roadhouse that featured a special on cheap tequila between sets.

Somewhere down the row of shots, one of those guys who isn't quite a roadie but hangs out with the band anyway put out a line of white powder. Whether I cared what it was or not by that time is debatable, but I snorted like a hog, and then discovered it was some kind of foul animal tranquilliser that precipitated me into a pink-bubblegum, undulating plastic nightmare. Not Pepperland at all, man. People definitely turned uglier and I had no sense of time whatsoever. According to Boss, I remained fairly together while still at the nightclub – albeit by the standards of the excessively bombed – but began to panic badly on the ride home on the high-speed, white neon, concrete labyrinth that is the Detroit urban highway system by night. I had somehow managed to convince myself that Wayne, who was driving, was as fucked up as I was, and that vehicular destruction was but a twist of the wheel away. Back at Wayne's house, I went from bad to worse, managing to lock myself in the spare room, break the door knob and then punch out a mirror, I suppose in emulation of *Tommy*.

Needless to say, in the morning I wasn't the most popular guest at the party, and it wasn't until some months later that Boss and I finally admitted to each other that we had both been hearing imagined gangsters in the night. The climate did nothing to alleviate the general misery. It was humid high-summer in the city, and temperatures in the nineties turned the air toxic green with car-plant emissions. Too hot to cook in the house, we attempted a back-yard barbecue one night, only to have a police helicopter hover overhead, like it was Da Nang, lighting up the back yard with its blinding searchlight. We feared a second, follow-up drug raid, but it turned out to be nothing more than a routine airborne patrol.

Subsequently, despite all kind of personal letters and intercessions, like the entire staff of *NME* writing to the judge regarding Wayne's value to the community as a musician, the judge gave him five years. After Wayne was sent down, Jake Riviera revealed a whole other side of himself, by suggesting that Stiff should release a charity single of two of Wayne's songs, both to keep his name alive and to ensure that he had a bit of money when he was released. Fortunately I had some tapes – songs we'd written, plus other stuff recorded by the current band – and I was able to turn these over to Jake. Wayne got out just in time to see punk in full cry and to be hailed as one of its founding fathers. This took him completely by surprise. Seemingly the new cultural revolution hadn't penetrated as far as the Federal Correction Institution at Lexington, Kentucky, and, as Wayne put it, 'I still thought a punk was a guy who took it up the arse from other prisoners.' Bemusedly at first, but rapidly adjusting, he found himself bracketed with Lou Reed and Iggy, and even with your humble servant, now being referred to in the music press as the Godfathers of Punk. Unfortunately the emergent movement appeared to be falling apart so rapidly that we wondered how long there'd be any punk for us to Godfather over.

Lost in the Supermarket

Interviewed by Legs McNeil for his 1996 book *Please Kill Me – The Uncensored Oral History of Punk*, I find myself quoted in a mood of high judgemental dudgeon, but, of course, we'd been sitting on the patio of a pub called the Cat & Fiddle on Sunset Boulevard and he'd been feeding me Bud and Jack Daniels while I talked into the microphone.

'Well, it broke up, didn't it? It was the Eighties. And there was cocaine. Shovels full of cocaine. And ingesting drugs doesn't require a lot of talent, and that's why I think we brought ourselves down to Sid, who, it could be said, was the ultimate product of the entire punk movement. I mean Sid was completely worthless, ha, ha, ha.

'So drugs brought money back and Ronald Reagan was elected president, and, you know, shit went on. In fact, that's the sad part; hippies survived Nixon, but punk caved in to Ronald Reagan, know what I'm saying? Punk couldn't actually take a good challenge.'

Legs and I have grown old playing snotty punk v. grizzled old hippie routine since he first licked my Bettie Page T-shirt in CBGBs and, two decades later, the exchange was being continued for publication. This was not to say that punk wasn't, or isn't, a fascinating phenomenon. If punk died almost as soon as it was born, it was only on one specific level. On another, it so totally perpetuated itself that it continues to this day, and shows no sign of departing. It took twenty years for rock & roll to advance from Little Richard to the Damned, but another twenty years to move from the Ramones to Green Day. For a movement that rejected the future as a concept, it has proved itself uncommonly resilient. In the year 2001 we even find it cross-fertilising with rap in the form of Kid Rock.

The major resentment I had towards punks was that it was bloody easy when everyone was doing it. Ten years earlier I'd been on my own, with only Iggy and the MC5 3,000 miles away. The punks even had the supporting players and extras in place, but still they didn't seem to be capable of making the potency last. We'd kept the hippie counterculture viable for five, if not six, years and punk wilted after scarcely three. The front on which they attacked society was narrowly limited and I believe that was one cause of their relatively fast neutralisation. They used rock 'n' roll as a spearhead, just as we had ten years earlier, but they skimped on the peripherals. Like Ney at Waterloo, throwing in his cavalry without infantry support, punk went for the single, impossible *coup de grâce*, and when that achieved only a brief and chimerical shock, they had no fallback.

Punk created its magazines, its comic books, its clothing designers, a graphic style, filmmakers, mass events and an absurd theatre of drugged outrage, but with nothing like the creator-to-punter ratio of the Sixties counterculture. Punk also had its wheeler-dealers – although McLaren and Bernie Rhodes did turn out to be little more than short-order scam artists, ultimately outmogulled by the likes of Seymour Stein and his discovery of Madonna. Punk's main oversight was an anti-romantic acceptance of all reality at its most negative. I'll go to my grave believing that all revolutionary aspirations inevitably come with a high degree of unreality and seductive self-deception. A golden dream of perfection, no matter how immediately unworkable, must be the moonlight in the murk. To paraphrase Oscar Wilde, if you're lying in the gutter, you might as well be looking at the stars, rather than a lighted second-floor window. Trite but true, the hippies had too many dreams and the punks too few. Ugliness as a shock tactic, and that widespread promotion of mindless anger as a weapon of agitprop had their uses, but they hardly led to either the Palaces of Wisdom or even the gates of Eden. The other question that remained determinedly unanswered was: if mindlessness becomes all-consumingly chic, who the hell is going to do the thinking?

Through no fault of their own, the punks also found themselves punching shadows. For protest to run amok, it requires an *ancien régime* with the heft of true danger. The overt madness of Nixon, Kissinger, LBJ and Wilson bore little resemblance to the contemptibly limited lunacy of Reagan and Thatcher, or even the mendacious Jeane Kirkpatrick. Thank God Wilson was hammerlocked by the Labour Left to keep us out of Vietnam, but the grunts, the gunships and the B52s were there on TV. In the new era the B52s were a band. To hit the streets in opposition to something as tangible as a brutal and immoral war was far easier than to pit your energy against the nebulous smoke and mirrors behind which the New Right would attempt to obliterate the last vestiges of socialism, and the voodoo economics that would enable the super-rich to inherit what was left of the Earth. With the experience of the wild upheavals of the Sixties behind them, those in authority were also far more skilled at dissipating the energy of the mob by pitting street crews one against the other – punks against skinheads, blacks against the SPG. (Yes, I still think of the police as a street gang, the biggest gang in town.)

The centres of power have traditionally protected themselves by sparking pointless buffer conflicts, and having the young and disaffected square off against each, rather than identifying the true tyrant.

Hindsight has made me a little kinder to the original punks. Like the hippies, they were just another uprising. The second I'd experienced, and I still hope for more to come. In our naivety we'd thought we were fighting the class war to end class wars and the Age of Aquarius was only a day away. Typical zealot error. All we had going was a major skirmish. Youth revolts may have little sense of history, but that doesn't mean they are devoid of it. They have a noble, if disgruntled, pedigree of churls and malcontents, a continuous guerrilla Bohemia, an endless Children's Crusade, Peasants' Revolt and Beggar's Opera winding down the centuries on a trail of chaos and disorder, through Nihilists and Anarchists, Pre-Raphaelites and Romantics, all the way back to twelfth- and thirteenth-century troublemakers like the Cathars and Adamites, Robin Hood and Merlin, the interdicted Dionysians and the persecuted Bacchae. The historical linkage goes by no single name, just a charged mission to resist for ever any and all means by which an authoritarian elite seeks the eradication of free will, free thought and individualism. If I believe in anything, besides a shared sense of absurdity, it has to be this thread of creative resistance, and both the trick and the moral responsibility are to make sure it extends ever into the future, and generations yet to come are made well aware that you have to keep a close eye on the bastards.

We tend to think of mass mind control and mass manipulation as something new, but it's quite as old as the first leader's will to power. The enemy is any regime that keeps its peasantry in the grip of perpetual superstitious fear, strives for the lockstep proletariat of *Metropolis* or an underclass reduced to belligerent stupidity. The tools of control and manipulation are simple to spot – the Roman spectacle of bread and circuses; the desensitisation in a culture collapsing under the maintenance of an imperial war machine; Christian cathedrals that awed the peons and instilled in them the fear of God and his appointed clergy; the soulless diversion of bad television; military hysteria, Inquisitions, witch hunts and Cold Wars; some future culture of mindless happy-face obedience, and a daily dose of some fifth-generation Prozac; or a population dumbed down by a constant hosing with brain-frequency microwaves.

The fight between freedom and control, between conformity and dissent, swings backwards and forwards, in all manner of guises and forms and under cover of a hundred deceptions. Sometimes the hero is Jimi Hendrix, sometimes George Jacques Danton, Vincent Van Gogh or Lenny Bruce, a self-immolating Buddhist monk or the Mahatma. In communist Albania, one needed a licence to own a typewriter. In the post-industrial data age, would-be censors attempt to deny large sections of the internet to children who understand the technology better than they do. Yes, my friends, they really do need to be watched constantly.

Redemption? I Don't Think So

We were circling Parliament Square, past Big Ben, the statues of Winston Churchill and Richard I – the famous homicidal gay psychopath king – and drummer Al Powell announced that he was going to vote for Thatcher. 'Someone's gotta be in charge here.'

'Are you kidding me?' Was he winding me up? Apparently not. I think that was actually the moment I decided I wanted out, that it was time metaphorically to take ship and seek adventures elsewhere. If Al from Hawkwind could make such a statement, Britain as a nation had surely become so demoralised and collectively depressed that it would run, lemming-like, to any self-proclaimed authoritarian who promised an illusion of strength, order and a return to some greetings-card past that had never really existed. England wanted its nanny. It wanted to delegate adult thought and will to an implausible matriarch, whom they believed would soundly spank and send to bed with no supper all those perceived as troublemakers, and this list plainly included the unions, the young, minorities and probably dissidents like myself.

I'd already been spending so much time in the USA that it was the obvious alternative. Except that America also wanted its daddy and a return to the days of Eisenhower, before Elvis Presley, drugs, protest and sexual revolution, when all was right with the world, they knew the enemy and it was definitely not them. In the run-up to Reagan's bid for the presidency, I watched in awe as a woman in her fifties, a clerk or maybe a secretary, was asked why she was intending to vote for Reagan. 'He'll make it like I was young . . .' She swiftly corrected the Freudian give-away. 'He'll make it like *when* I was young.'

A mess? Certainly. As bad as it was in the UK? Probably not, but I was by no means sure. Nixon had dubbed them the Silent Majority, but, by the end of the Seventies, they were far from silent and rapidly forming ranks behind the ageing actor with Alzheimer's, who had already made his bones as the ultra-conservative Governor of California during the protest years. The Reagan faithful – an unholy coalition of arch-conservatism, the Christian Right, big money and the military industrial complex – had been mobilising since 1976, when they'd failed to unseat Gerald Ford at that year's Republican convention. That Reagan intended to play high-stakes, shit-or-bust poker with the USSR, while Thatcher dismantled the British Revolution of 1945 and showed him the way to privatise the New Deal, was no secret. Indeed, it was central to both their election platforms.

I guess I knew in my heart I'd opt for America in the end. How in the name of all that was holy could I remain in a country where the Prime Minister could command such heights of bourgeois ignorance that she felt able to refer to Francis Bacon as 'that awful artist who paints those horrible pictures'. That hideous voice was like chalk on a blackboard, enough on its own to make me flee. Some wag had coined the nickname Attila the Hen, but I wanted no part of the woman, even as an adversary. I figured that after a few months of TV exposure to the blue suits, the impossible platinum coif and the stench-under-the-nose expression, I might be forced to strap dynamite all over my body and walk into Parliament with the Zen-violent intention of 'taking some of the bastards with me'.

I'd be misstating the case if I left you with the idea that my sole motivation was to flee what I considered would be, for me, a highly inclement political climate. The course of the Seventies – although not without its share of alarms and adventures – demonstrated a visible narrowing of creative options. Money was tight. Music seemed to be increasingly defined by costume and haircut, and publishers were hinting that I should give up the Burroughsian aspirations I had reconnoitred in *The DNA Cowboys* trilogy and consolidate my position. *Star Wars* had managed to set the science-fiction genre back a good twenty years and, until the coming of cyberpunk, the demand was, if not for actual Dan Dare spaceships and rayguns, then something very close. Conservatism wasn't concentrated in Westminster. My growing inclination was to turn my face to the west wind and embark for the Americas without further ado. Not to re-create myself like Bowie, and not to knock the Merrie UK, either. I felt enough like a rat leaving the ship of fools. I was going to the big American playground to test my strength.

Of course, when I say the Americas, I actually mean New York City, and, as any New Yorker will tell you, 'New York ain't America.' New York is a city from Victorian science fiction where zeppelins should have moored at the needle of the Chrysler Building. Fortunately it all went horribly and humanly wrong, so the Bowery became strewn with bums scrabbling for a pint of Night Train as the thorazine wore off, drag-queen whores defended their turf with stiletto heels, and a documented species of Mole People lived in the abandoned tunnels under Grand Central Station. I could find bars with Hank Williams and Louis Jordan on the jukebox that served booze till four in the morning.

I also estimated that New York would be the ideal place to weather out the Eighties. Ron didn't share Maggie's narrow, shopkeeper's-daughter concept of how things should be in a well-regulated nation state. He might borrow the awful woman's rhetoric, but he was only there to let the greed rip. Tom Wolfe's Masters of the Universe were just waiting for Reagan to let slip their leashes, to light the Bonfire of the Vanities. The military industrial complex, with an Evil Empire to huff and puff about, was poised for a convulsion of gluttony equal to a Stephen King pie-eating contest. It would be an era of robber barons in the USA, and New York was a city built by robber barons, but instantly subverted by the poor, into a wild and exotic melting pot of ethnicity that refused to melt. What better place to observe the new face of fascism, that which would soon be known as yuppie? In my estimation, New York was also well defended on a cultural level. Reagan might let the Moral Majority have its way in middle America, gutting school libraries, teaching creationism as science and attacking everything from abortion rights to topless donut shops. But they'd keep it in Ohio. What the hell were the Christian Right going to do when confronted with Holly Woodlawn or Karen Findlay? Throw them into camps? Even to go near that idea would be to court a bloody city-wide Stonewall II. This was the city that had been home to Lucky Luciano and *Mad* magazine. The Gotham of *Batman*. Its sin looked impregnable.

Besides, I was in love again, as much as two drunks can be in love until one sobers up and starts smelling that metaphorical coffee. I had met Betsy when she was a Director of Publicity at Arista Records, working for the unpredictable Clive Davis, with responsibility for the notarisation of Lou Reed, Iggy and Patti Smith. I had admired her Veronica Lake hair, sunglasses and fast verbals on an earlier visit and, when she, I and Lester Bangs had lunch together, it extended into an epic drinking bout that concluded with the two of us losing Lester somewhere along the way and repairing to the George Washington Hotel, where we had amazing sex that was primarily amazing in that it happened at all, considering the quantities of Dewars-on-the-rocks and Jack-with-a-beer that we'd put away respectively. After a few days, infatuation set in, to the point that it seemed out of the question simply to return to London and think no more about it.

Do other women sense, even if you don't tell them, when all is not well back at hearth and home? In London I had found myself walking round in a complete state of self-denial, telling myself: okay, so things with Ingrid were a bit rocky, we'll get over it. Meanwhile, the other side of my brain was kicking down the barn door, writing graphic fictional suicides in *The Feelies* and lyric lines like 'living in a phone booth with a vampire bat' and 'maybe you really wanted to be used', and pretending that it was just my imagination. It probably also didn't help that I managed to burn down the apartment at Chesterton Road. The last thing I wanted to do was to cause Ingrid pain, but I had decided that my future lay in New York rather than London. To stack the deck a little more, Betsy and I were in the magical getting-to-know-you, wonder-of-us phase, and how could a nine-year-old rocky relationship compete with that?

As always, as soon as I'd privately made the decision to leave London, everything began happening. A new fiction deal came down the pike. It would turn out to be *The Song of Phaid the Gambler*, but the parameters of the deal made clear that it was definitely a setback in the direction of rayguns. At the same time I found myself becoming involved in a sudden influx of music projects. Although we had completed *Vampires Stole My Lunch Money*, that was far from the end of it. I was no longer writing songs with Lemmy, but had started working regularly with Andy Colquhoun on material for his new band Warsaw Pakt. In the process I commenced a solid friendship and creative partnership with Andy – and Helga, his feisty Bavarian girlfriend, soon to be his wife – that has functioned until this day and produced a canon of songs that must now number close to fifty. In addition to the Warsaw Pakt work, Andy and I finished up mixing the single 'Broken Statue' that followed *Vampires Stole My Lunch Money* when Larry, the designated producer, lost his mind, broke his phone and barricaded himself in his apartment with multiple bottles of Johnny Walker Red, some grams of cocaine and a young woman called Vashta.

The ties that bind are hard to sever, and to wrench yourself away from the place where you were, at least figuratively, born and raised is never easy, but equally difficult is to halt a process once it's in motion. I'd filled out all the forms, I'd disposed of my extraneous stuff. I'd turned in my British Relay TV set and started the process of giving up my flat. The final hurdle was surmounted when John Dean at the US Embassy – the individual we met all the way back in the prologue – could find no legal grounds to exclude me from becoming a Resident Alien. All that remained was to endure being X-rayed, checked for literacy and blood-tested, just to see if I was sufficiently fit and smart to take my life in my hands on Avenue D. I had become the traditional folk figure, the immigrant headed for the new world, only I wasn't travelling steerage in some disgusting Victorian steamship, I was flying in one of Freddie Laker's DC10s. (Remember Laker? A fifty-quid fare from Heathrow to JFK until Mrs Thatcher put a stop to it.) I was not fleeing poverty, religious persecution or seeking redemption. I was no huddled mass. I was merely on the brink of a new and limitless terrain of adventure, and I was pledged to embrace it as fully as I'd embraced the last one.

Epilogue

The Piaf Summation

'Don't you regret any of the things you did back then. I mean, all the drugs and stuff.'

Every so often some idiot feels the need to ask. I usually snarl. I don't like the question, since it seems to imply that I should assume some unwarranted responsibility. At a minimum it's like we had a bloody great party and never bothered to clean up afterwards. My answer is unequivocal. 'Not a fucking thing.'

If I really feel irritated, I elaborate and inform the questioner how it would not surprise me, if I were a kid today – with access to the dot.com and automatic weapons – if I slipped into my black Rommel overcoat and went off to machine-gun the high school. (Remember, us English lads had . . . *If* long before the Trenchcoat Mafia watched *Matrix* and *The Crow*.) In my youth such was the level of my rage, but, fortunately for the rest of you, I didn't have the technology or firepower. The world is still in need of considerable improvement. Indeed, if the human race doesn't evolve a whole new set of protocols for taking care of business, it will be lucky to survive extinction. Question is: do we deserve to survive extinction?

'I am an angry youth who never managed to grow up, so get the fuck out of my way.'

'Don't you think rather a lot of yourself? The hero of your own epic?'

'Sometimes you have to think like a hero just to behave like a decent human being.'

'But how do you justify the drugs . . .?'

'Justify? Do me a favour? Here in 2001 the entire developed world is out of its tree on everything from endorphins to Gincoba. Cell phones are frying its brains, as it chokes on the rapidly warming atmosphere.'

'But you don't regret the drugs you took yourself?'

'I was an idiot clown with an emotionally dangerous job. It went with the territory of the apprentice Holy Fool. Days have come and gone when the only way to stay sane was to see the humorous side of nuclear annihilation. In a word, no, I don't.'

'You said you had a "dangerous job"?'

'I was questing into the unknown. Danger lies within the territory.'

'Danger for whom?'

'That's a moot point.'

'You didn't ever weigh the consequences?'

'St Brendan hardly weighed the consequences when he set out to discover America in a leather boat, and you can hardly blame him for Shiloh, Wounded Knee or *Charlie's Angels*. The adventurer doesn't tabulate all the possible negative options. He or she just goes. Imagine how it felt to be the very first guy to eat an oyster. What trust that slime-in-a-rock was food.'

'No hints of doubt?'

During the writing of this book, strange dreams struggled up from the subconscious that proved both disturbing and, now and again, problem-solving. 'The human soul does not come with a built-in firewall.'

'Huh?'

Bibliography and Discography

FICTION

The Texts of Festival
The Quest of the DNA Cowboys
The Neutral Atrocity
The Synaptic Manhunt
Protectorate
Phaid the Gambler
Citizen Phaid
Their Masters' War
The Long Orbit
The Armageddon Crazy
The Last Stand of the DNA Cowboys
Mars — The Red Planet
The Feelies
Necrom
The Time of Feasting
Darklost
Jim Morrison's Adventures in the Afterlife

NON-FICTION

Watch Out Kids
Get on Down
The Black Leather Jacket
Elvis and the Colonel
The Hitchhiker's Guide to Elvis
The CIA Files
Conspiracies, Lies, and Hidden Agendas

POETRY

The Lonesome Death of Gene Vincent
The Road to Armageddon is Best Travelled by Cadillac

PLAYS

The Last Words of Dutch Schultz
A Criminal Sorority
South of the Border

RECORDINGS

Ptooff! (The Deviants)
Disposable (The Deviants)
Deviants #3 (The Deviants)
Mona (Mick Farren)
Play with Fire (Mick Farren)
Screwed Up (Mick Farren and The Deviants)
Vampires Stole My Lunch Money (Mick Farren)
Human Garbage (The Deviants)
Who Shot You Dutch? (with Wayne Kramer and Don Was)
Partial Recall (Mick Farren and The Deviants)
Fragments of Broken Probes (Mick Farren and The Deviants)
Death Tongue (with Wayne Kramer and John Collins)
Gringo Madness (Tijuana Bible)
The Death Ray Tapes (with Jack Lancaster)
Eating Jello with a Heated Fork (Deviants ixvi)
The Deviants Have Left the Planet (Mick Farren and The Deviants)
Barbarian Princes – Live in Japan (The Deviants)
This CD is Condemned (Mick Farren and The Deviants)

A more detailed listing of these works can be found at the Funtopia
website: http://www.thanatosoft.freeserve.co.uk/index.htm

Index